Rising Suns, Rising Daughters

Gender, Class and Power in Japan

Joanna Liddle

and Sachiko Nakajima

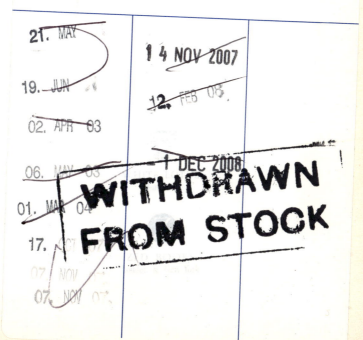

Rising Suns, Rising Daughters was first published in 2000 by
Zed Books Ltd, 7 Cynthia Street, London N1 9JF, UK,
and Room 400, 175 Fifth Avenue, New York, NY 10010, USA

Published in Thailand by White Lotus Company Ltd,
GPO Box 1141, Bangkok, 100501

Distributed in the USA exclusively by Palgrave, a division of St Martin's Press,
LLC, 175 Fifth Avenue, New York, NY 10010, USA

Designed and typeset in Monotype Joanna by Illuminati, Grosmont
Cover designed by Andrew Corbett
Printed and bound in the United Kingdom by Biddles Ltd,
Guildford and King's Lynn

ISBN 1 85649 878 6 (Hb)
ISBN 1 85649 879 4 (Pb)

Contents

Preface   ix

Introduction   1
The Idea   1
The Women   2
The Fieldwork   3
The Objectives   4
The Book   4

PART I   **Women and the Global Political Economy**   **5**

Chapter 1   The Women's Movement   7
Gender Politics in the New Heisei Era   7
The 'Second Wave' Women's Movement   9
The 'First Wave' Women's Movement   12

Chapter 2   Japan Enters Global Politics   17
Japan's Resistance to Western Imperialism   17
Maintaining Class Power at Home   18
Resisting Subordination Abroad   20
Japanese Imperialism: Joining the Elite   23
Competing with the West   25

Chapter 3   Women and the Subordination of Japan   28
Gender, Class and the Struggle for Global Power   28

Japan's Weakness and the Woman Question   32
Motives of the Male Reformers   36

Chapter 4   Creating a New Japanese Womanhood   40
Extending Control over Women in the Family   41
Education for Women   45
Excluding Women from Politics   47

Chapter 5   Building a New Japan: Good Wives,
Wise Mothers   50
Women's Contribution to National Wealth   51
Women's Contribution to Military Strength   54

Chapter 6   Building a New Japan: Working Women   59
Going Out to Work: Factory Girls   59
Going Out to Work: Prostitutes   65
Gender and Global Distinction   70

PART II   Women, Class and Power before
the Western Intrusions   73

Chapter 7   The Bases of Power   75

Chapter 8   Women and Class   77
Gender, Class and Feudalism   77
Women's Disinheritance   81

Chapter 9   The Rise of the Military Class   85
The Struggle for Power   85
Family Forms   89
Land Inheritance   91

Chapter 10   Civil War   96
Formation of the Social Classes after the
Fourteenth Century   96

Chapter 11   Women's Position and Social Class   100
Consolidating Women's Subordination in the Military
Class   100

Women of the Lower Classes: Peasant Women 104
Women of the Lower Classes: Merchant Women 107
Gender, Class and Power before the Western Intrusions 109

PART III   Yearning for the Sky and the Stars   111

Chapter 12   The New Woman   113
              Movements for Change, Spaces for Resistance 113
              Middle-Class Women 'Going Out to Work' 116
              'A Field of Struggles' 119

Chapter 13   Militarist Expansionism   123
              The Colonies: 'Civilisation and Enlightenment' 124
              War: Repression and Opportunity 126
              Contradictory Gendering 131

Chapter 14   Defeat of the Militarist Project   134
              Material Loss and Social Absence 135
              Progressive Discourse 137
              Erosion of Authority Systems 142
              Taking Advantage of Change 145

Chapter 15   The US Occupation   149
              The Occupation Reforms 149
              The US Occupation's Approach to Women 153
              Women and the Reforms 156
              Constant Quiet Struggles 159

PART IV   Gender, Class and Power in Employment,
           Education and the Family   161

Chapter 16   Class and the Reproduction of Power   163
              The Significance of Class in Japan 163
              Analysing Power 167

Chapter 17   Employment as a Field of Power   172
              Women's Positioning in the Employment Field 173

Women's Participation in the Employment Field   174
Power Distribution in the Employment Field   181
Employment Position and Social Class   182
Gender and Class Origin   185
Class Origins and Women's Access to Power in the
    Employment Field   192

Chapter 18   Education as a Field of Power   193
The Development of Education   193
Women's Positioning in the Educational Field   196
Power Distribution in the Educational Field   198
Education and Social Origin   199
Elite Education and Class Reproduction   203
Gender, Cultural Capital and Class Reproduction   206
Professional Women's Education   209
Class Origins and Women's Access to Power in the
    Educational Field   212

Chapter 19   The Family as a Field of Power   215
Women's Positioning in the Field of the Family   216
Biological and Class Reproduction   217
Power Distribution in the Family and the Connections
    between the Fields   222

PART V   Becoming a Professional Woman:
    The Struggle for Change   225

Chapter 20   Gendered Class Identities   227

Chapter 21   Discourses of Gendered Class Identity   232
Competing Discourses of Femininity   233
Competing Discourses of Masculinity   239

Chapter 22   Regulatory Social Practices   245
Social Practices in Education   245
Social Practices in Employment   250
Social Practices in the Family   255
Reproducing Family and Class Distinction   259

Chapter 23   Contradictions of Middle-Class Femininity   261
              Contradictions in Education   261
              Contradictions in Employment   264
              Contradictions in the Family   269
              The Struggle for Change   275

PART VI   Becoming a Professional Woman:
             Achieving the Right to Compete   277

Chapter 24   Transforming Gendered Class Identities   279

Chapter 25   Changing Social Practice   282
              Establishing a Professional Career   282
              Negotiating New Family Lifestyles   288

Chapter 26   Changing Subjectivities   298
              Supporting the Family   298
              Developing a Mature Self   299
              Contributing to Society   301
              Being, and Failing to Be, the Professional Housewife 304
              Being a Working Woman   306
              Different Worlds   309

Chapter 27   Women in the New Heisei Era   311
              Continuity and Change   311
              Representing Women's Subjectivities   317
              Achieving the Right to Compete   323

Conclusion   Rising Daughters   325

              Bibliography   329

              Index   337

This book is dedicated to
Hirano Takako,
colleague and friend,
who died in 1991.

Preface

Many stories are hidden in our research material which have not been told. Inevitably a process of selection has taken place, and we have chosen to tell this story, of women struggling to change their conditions in the context of wider struggles over class and nation. We hope that we have nevertheless portrayed their lives in a way which they would recognise, neither distancing ourselves from their pains and pleasures, nor glorifying their struggles and achievements. We would like to thank them most sincerely for allowing us access into their changing lives. Without their warmth and openness, we could never have embarked on this project.

In many ways this book has been a collective enterprise, beginning with the first study when colleagues in Japan took up the idea on which two of us had worked in India. Our gratitude to Kanda Michiko and Kobayashi Koichiro constitutes a debt which cannot be repaid, since they introduced Hirano Takako as co-researcher and provided a base for the study. Tragically, Hirano Takako died two years after the second study. Nakajima Sachiko nobly stepped into the breach.

Both authors are grateful to the University of Warwick for funding Joanna Liddle's travel to Japan and Nakajima Sachiko's journey to the UK. We would like to thank our families, friends and colleagues who have waited so patiently and refused to cross us off their list during the long gestation of this book. Particular thanks are due to colleagues and friends who have read drafts, discussed issues and given valuable comments, especially Terry Lovell, Shima Satomi, Jim Beckford and Jill Hardman. We are deeply grateful to the 'production team' of John Banks, Jill Hardman, Jake Bharier and Jenny Peacock, who spent much of their Easter reading, commenting, correcting, restructuring and proofreading

ix

the final manuscript. John in particular requires special acknowledgement, since he has acted not only as research assistant, editor, statistics advisor, IT expert, literary stylist and general manager, but also as cook, cleaner, shopper, washer, emotional support and general 'wife' throughout the process. As feminists, we believe that the support women give to men goes unrecognised and unvalued. We will not contribute to the invisibility of caring work by giving token thanks when the relationship is reversed. Shima Satomi acknowledged her husband's support during her research by paying tribute to his 'immense suffering'. This is a much more fitting recognition of devotion, and we pay it to John.

Introduction

The Idea

This book examines the changing position of women and gender relations in Japan in the context of the global political economy, and argues that gender is crucial to struggles over class power and global dominance. It includes both historical and contemporary material, tracing the transformation of gendered class identities at different historical moments, and interweaving the stories of individual women with social and historical analysis. It identifies the emergence of middle-class women from the domestic sphere and into public life with the rise of feminist politics and the women's liberation movement in Japan. It demonstrates that gender divisions are crucially linked to the construction of class, and shows how gendered class identities are used as a resource in the struggle for power between nations. Japan is a valuable location in which to study gender in the context of global change because, although it is now a developed capitalist country, Japan has been subordinated to the western powers in differing ways and to different extents over the last hundred years or more, has struggled successfully and unsuccessfully at different times to compete with global imperialism, and has also been a colonial power itself.

We trace the complex history of women's power in Japan by focusing on four key periods. At the Meiji Restoration of the late nineteenth century we locate women's organised struggles to change gender relations in the context of the state's attempt to construct new gender identities under the influence of global power relations, and the West's use of women's subordination to position Japan as a backward and inferior country. In the centuries before the western intrusions, we will argue, the decline of female power was closely tied to the development of the class structure based on rights to land. In the wartime period of the twentieth century, we examine the dramatic changes to women's position which form the backdrop to the experiences of the women in our study. And we look at how the expansion of the economy in the second half of that century enabled middle-class women to emerge from domesticity, enter positions of influence in public life, and achieve radical changes in social practices and subjectivities.

Our empirical study focuses on women employed on a long-term basis in a professional career: women who have attempted to compete in the labour market on an equal basis with men. Although they constitute a minority group, these women are important partly because they have broken their way into positions of responsibility and power normally reserved for men, and partly because they challenge the dichotomised gendered identities signifying class position in Japan, and the orientalist ideas and preconceptions of the Japanese woman in the West. The study presents evidence on the importance of class background in women's access to positions of influence in public life. It examines both the social forces arising from gender, class and international relations, and the agency of women themselves in dealing with these forces to initiate change and construct new identities. And it challenges the unitary image of Japanese women that is prevalent in different forms in the West and in Japan, and attempts to explain the construction of such images in terms of the contest for global distinction.

The Women

The women in this study were educated to college level, and employed in medium to large organisations in jobs where their education was a necessary qualification. In this respect they can be classed as professional workers. We talked to 120 women, equally divided between four professions. Two of the professions, education and medicine, were open to women before the Second World War, albeit at a lower level than for men. The other two professions, government service and corporate management, are occupations which women began to enter only after the Second World War. The respondents were equally divided between university teachers in four-year coeducational universities, doctors working in university hospitals or large city hospitals, administrative officers in government ministries qualified as top-grade civil servants, and managers or highly qualified professionals in private companies.[1] The respondents covered a wide spread of ages from the early twenties to the late sixties, the youngest being 23 and the oldest 67.[2] The women were born between 1910 and 1954, and constitute a cohort of two generations who were the first to embark on professional careers, whose combined life-cycles covered most of the twentieth century, and whose careers took place during the expansion of the economy after the war.

The Fieldwork

The empirical chapters examine evidence from a questionnaire and interview study of 120 Japanese women working in professional or managerial positions.[3] Most interviews lasted at least an hour, some a great deal longer. The first fieldwork study was carried out in 1977. A total of 50 respondents were interviewed in English and 70 in Japanese, depending on the choice of the respondent. With few exceptions, the interviews were attended by both the British researcher, Joanna Liddle,

---

1. The academics were selected randomly from those women employed in Tokyo in the List of Women University Faculty Members, extracted from the *List of University Employees in Japan*, published by the Women's Problems Section of the Prime Minister's Office. The doctors were selected randomly from those women employed in Tokyo hospitals in the *Survey of Doctors, Dentists and Pharmacists* compiled by the Health Statistics Section, Ministry of Health and Welfare, and published by the Ministry's Secretariat Statistics and Information Department. The government officials were selected randomly from those women working in Tokyo from the *List of Akebono Kai* (the list of top-grade female civil servants) published by the Women's First Division Association. The managerial workers were selected from the *List of Qualified Workers* compiled and published by the Women's Problems Section of the Prime Minister's Office. Of the four categories, only the women managers were rather few in number, and it was therefore difficult to find enough respondents from which to make a random selection. As a result, two of the managers were unqualified, having risen through the hierarchy rather than entered as graduates, and some had vocational rather than academic qualifications. Although the managers do not constitute a random sample, they do constitute a population, albeit with missing cases, and we may therefore draw statistical conclusions with some confidence.

2. The sample included 15 women in their twenties, 38 in their thirties, 42 in their forties, 23 in their fifties, and 2 in their sixties. The age profile of each profession was different, with few younger academics or managers, and few older doctors or government servants.

3. Information was collected in three ways. First, a structured questionnaire containing questions on factual background information with respect to family, education, friends and employment, as well as relevant personal data. The questionnaires were handed directly to the respondents at interview with the request to return them by mail. Second, a semi-structured interview containing questions on the respondent's experiences and the attitudes of others, under the same four headings. These areas could be opened up for wider discussion if appropriate. Third, an unstructured interview with six topic areas and suggested questions under each topic, designed to explore women's consciousness and attitudes to work. The aim of this part was to explore how a woman saw the social world and her place in it, following her leads rather than a series of pre-set and limiting questions.

and the Japanese researcher, Hirano Takako, regardless of the language in which the interview was conducted. The second study was undertaken in 1989, when we were able to trace 66 (55 per cent) of the original 120 respondents. This study consisted of a questionnaire survey. All the respondents' names have been changed in the text. Except for the co-author's name on the cover, Japanese names are always given in the Japanese form, in which family names come before personal names.

The Objectives

• We focus on a group of Japanese women who challenge many of the dichotomised categories of class-based and nation-based gender identities attributed to women in Japan; for example, between the 'corporate warrior' and the 'professional housewife'; between the 'middle-class housewife' and the 'lower-class working mother'; and between the 'oppressed Japanese woman' and the 'liberated western woman'.

• We examine the fusion of gender and class, and argue that class is crucial to understanding the production of gender relations in Japan, both historically and today.

• We locate gendered class relations in the context of changes in the global political economy, showing how women and gender are used in the struggle for power between nation-states, and highlighting the significance of gender for international relations.

• We focus on Japan as a country which has experienced both sides of the colonial divide, facilitating the analysis of the changing experience and position of women within the context of changes to the global political economy.

• We develop a new conceptual framework for understanding gender in the context of global change, which may be applied more widely than the specific location in which it has been developed.

The Book

The book is divided into six parts. Parts I to III constitute a historical analysis of the changing relationship between gender and class before and after Japan's entry into the global contest for power. Parts IV to VI constitute an empirical analysis of the relationship between gender and class in the twentieth century looking at the category of professional women. Each part begins with a 'gateway' which briefly and clearly signposts the reader through the following chapters.

PART I

Women and the
Global Political Economy

Part I begins with two short histories which provide an essential context to the chapters that follow. The first introduces the women's movement, the second outlines Japan's entry into global politics.

In Chapter 3 we set out a new framework for understanding the relationships between gender, class and power in a global context. We then use this perspective to examine the changing position of women in Japan within the context of imperialism, and to explore the state's construction and reconstruction of Japanese womanhood in a class-divided society.

Chapter 1

The Women's Movement

Gender Politics in the New Heisei Era

The year 1989 marked the start of a new era in Japan's history. The long Showa period which presided over much of the turbulent twentieth century, from Hirohito's accession to the throne in 1926 to his death in January 1989, came to a close. Akihito took his place as the new Heisei sovereign, giving his name to the era of 'Achieving Peace' (Beasley 1990: 262). In July, Doi Takako became the first woman to lead a political party to victory, winning the Upper House general election for the Japan Socialist Party. The landslide victory doubled the proportion of women MPs in the Upper House to 13 per cent, largely on the basis of women's protest votes (Nuita 1989: 2).

The discontent of women voters centred around three main issues, all of which were constructed as 'women's issues'. First was the cost of consumer goods and the ruling Liberal Democratic Party's (LDP) forcing of a 3 per cent consumption tax through the Diet against fierce public and parliamentary opposition (Nuita 1989: 3). Second was corruption in politics, an issue which had been raised by the suffragist Independent MP Ichikawa Fusae (Nuita 1981: 4), and which Doi Takako explicitly constructed as a problem of masculine politics, with the argument that 'Japanese politics are so corrupt that women can't keep quiet any more' (Hara 1989: 6–7). The third issue was prostitution (Hara 1989: 7). Uno Sosuke was Prime Minister for only two months before resigning over the election defeat and rumours that he kept prostitutes. Kaifu Toshiki, the new LDP Prime Minister appointed to replace Uno, declared that his priority was to appoint women to the Cabinet in an effort to restore women's support for his party. He made the female political analyst

Takahara Sumiko head of the Economic Planning Agency, and chose as Minister of the Environment Moriyama Mayumi, a female former Labour Ministry civil servant who had been head of the Women's Bureau. A mere sixteen days after Uno's resignation, Yamashita Tokuo, the Chief Cabinet Secretary, became the first Cabinet Minister ever to resign directly over a sex scandal, after acknowledging a three-year relationship with a prostitute. With only two weeks' experience as a Minister, Mrs Moriyama was promoted to replace Yamashita in a post regarded as second in command to the Prime Minister, one which no woman had filled before (Hara 1989: 7).

The Prime Minister's promotion of Moriyama was clearly intended to regain women voters' confidence and undermine the wave of criticism directed at the ruling males of the LDP over their political, financial and sexual dishonesty. Kaifu's statement said that he had picked Moriyama because of his administration's desire to listen carefully to the people in carrying out political and tax reforms: 'Mrs Moriyama has experience as a housewife as well as a bureaucrat and can see things from a consumer's viewpoint. She will be able to include the people's perspective in policy decisions' (Hong Kong Standard 1989: 1). The Prime Minister's statement was notable in that it categorised the female perspective as a 'people's perspective' rather than a specific sectional interest. Women as housewives and consumers had come to represent 'the people' in prime-ministerial discourse.

These events are significant for an understanding of the changing relationship between gender and power. First, the appointment of a woman with little ministerial experience to the top Cabinet post would have been unthinkable before the 1989 election. Second, for a top Cabinet Minister to resign over a sex scandal suggests that the private arena of sexual relations was coming to be seen as a public issue for men. Although Kanai Yoshiko argues that the election result did not represent a radical change in women's consciousness, she nevertheless categorises the result as 'epoch-making' (Kanai 1994: 225–37). None of these changes in discourse and practice could have happened without the consistent campaigning of feminists in Japan.

In the next section we argue that contemporary Japanese feminism is diverse and able to contain many perspectives, but that a major division exists within the movement. Although feminism has developed a broad social base, among the mass of women a more conservative form is dominant, based on a traditional set of perspectives on gender relations and women's power. The minority section of the movement, in contrast, has its roots in radical ideas and political currents which recognise the connections between gender, class and imperialism within the global political economy.

The 'Second Wave' Women's Movement

As Kanai Yoshiko argues, the women's vote in the 1989 election was largely a conservative expression of what is known in Japan as 'house-wife feminism'; this explains why the efforts to win women voters back to the LDP were successful, and why the power of the female vote failed to develop into a sustained critique of gender relations. Kanai's critique refers not to criticism of housewives but to an ethnocentric, class-based perspective which gives priority to improving the lives of middle-class housewives while ignoring wider issues of difference, inequality and poverty within the global political economy (Kanai 1996: 7–10; Matsui 1990: 443–4).

Women's activism after the Second World War, while it was not necessarily feminist in content, nevertheless demonstrated a concern with social and political issues. Women campaigned against food and water pollution and against price rises, and handled consumer com-plaints (Matsui 1975: 32–9). They campaigned for peace, and against nuclear bombs and nuclear power. In 1960, women from more than forty women's groups joined trade unionists, students and leftist organ-isations to oppose US bases in Japan and the revival of Japanese militar-ism (Mackie 1988: 60–61).

The progressive movement

The 'second wave' of the feminist movement emerged in the early 1970s among women who had been active in the student movement of the late 1960s. The radical student movement arose out of opposition to the US–Japan Security Treaty and US military bases, the Vietnam War, the pollution of industrial capitalism, and minority groups' struggle for civil rights. The student movement had trained women in political activism but had also discriminated against them, treating them as 'housekeepers and sex objects' (Matsui 1990: 437–8). In reaction, the women's liberation movement emerged, campaigning on issues such as rape and sexuality, and in 1972 defeating the government's attempt to erode abortion rights (Mackie 1988: 62–3; Japanese Women Speak Out 1975: 85).

The movement's radical roots meant that its concern with feminist issues was informed by a critical perspective on class, militarism, indus-trialisation and the Third World. The document produced in 1975 for the UN's International Women's Year, entitled *Japanese Women Speak Out*, raised issues not only of gender but also of class, race, ethnicity, nationalism and the imperialism of Japan's economic intrusion in Asia (1975: 5). In response to these issues, there was a rapid expansion of feminist activity though journals such as *Asian Women's Liberation* (*Ajia to josei kaiho*) and *Feminist*. The late 1970s also saw the foundation of organisations like the All Japan Feminist Association (Mackie 1988: 67) and the Asian Women's Liberation Group, which acknowledged Japanese women's own part in Japanese imperialism and stated that '[Japan's] high economic growth rate was achieved at the cost of the lives of countless Koreans and Vietnamese' (Asian Women's Liberation Committee 1977: 2).

In the 1980s, feminist activism expanded its social base. This expansion was fuelled by a proposed revision to the abortion law supported by Shinto fundamentalists. Over seventy women's groups formed the League Against the Revision of the Eugenic Protection Law (*Yusei-hogo-ho kaiaku soshi renmei*). A series of meetings was organised in major cities which mobilised thousands of women, and the bill was stopped in 1983. This issue significantly broadened the base of the women's movement (Matsui 1990: 441). In the same year, as women took action against nuclear weapons in Europe, feminist rallies in Japan against military co-operation with the USA were organised by Women Who Refuse to Follow the Road to War (*Senso e no michi o yurusanai onnatachi no kai*) (Mackie 1988: 73–4).

Housewife feminism

The feminism developed by the mass of women, however, while it addressed the issue of sexuality and reproduction in relation to abortion, also reflected the main concerns of most Japanese women in their role as housewives, and developed into a specifically Japanese form of feminism which Shiota Sakiko identified as housewife feminism (Kanai 1996: 13). Rapid economic growth, a burgeoning middle class, and a government determined to keep women in the home meant that for many people the ideal of the full-time housewife was possible for the first time. Throughout these post-war decades, middle-class housewives have been the mainstay of voluntary community activities, consumer and peace movements (Matsui 1975: 32–9). As Matsui Machiko points out, these issues emerged from women's traditional caring role in the family, reproducing their positions as wives and mothers, while preserving gendered power relations (Matsui 1990: 443–4).

This form of housewife feminism is explicable because married women's work is mostly part-time and temporary, reproducing women's financial dependence on the family. Many women become full-time housewives after having children because of the lack of and hostility to childcare, the employers' creation of a gendered two-track career system (see Part IV), and a tax system which means that there is little choice other than a part-time wage and consequent exemption from tax, unless a woman can command a professional salary (AMPO 1996: 96, 188). These factors, together with the exhausting hours of those pursuing the full-time managerial career track, all contribute to the M-shaped work-participation curve of women in Japan, and mean that women pity rather than envy men with such jobs (Kanai 1996: 9–10; Hendry 1993: 224–40).

The problem with housewife feminism is that it is about improving middle-class women's lifestyles, without any recognition of gendered power relations, or the significance of class in creating gendered power, or any attempt to change traditional roles. As Kanai says, the split between the 'professional housewife' and the 'corporate warrior' is made to seem natural, but actually it is this structure which subordinates women and is neither made visible nor challenged. Critiques of housewife feminism by Matsui Machiko (Matsui 1990: 445) and Kanai Yoshiko (Kanai 1996: 7–15) argue that the failure to challenge traditional gender roles can be understood in terms of the attempt to establish a specifically Japanese feminine identity based on traditional Japanese culture. This has resulted in, first, the adoption of a community approach as opposed to the individualism of western feminism; and, second an essentialist maternalism based on the glorification of motherhood, which looks back both to the state's mobilisation of women's reproductive power during the war, and to earlier 'matriarchal' times when women's fertility was celebrated.

Doi's 'third way'

It is this perspective on gender which was challenged by Doi Takako when she led the Socialist Party to victory in 1989. Johnson argues that since the nineteenth century women activists have legitimated political reforms for women in terms of the well-being of their communities using essentialist discourse: that women are more moral, nurturing and peaceful than men. In the twentieth century, other feminists have prioritised the personal fulfilment of individuals. Individualism is seen as western, while maternalism is both biologically essentialist and seen as essentially and specifically Japanese; this leads to nationalist perspectives and the idea of Japanese superiority, a discourse known as

'Japanism'. Doi, however, adopted a third way, which was to appeal to the Constitution using the discourse of democracy rather than motherhood and morality, or individual self-fulfilment (Johnson 1992: 393). Certainly, as Mackie points out, this approach accepts capitalism and works within the Constitution, yet that Constitution is one of the most liberal in the world (Mackie 1988: 59). What Doi's discourse did was to enable her to oppose gendered power relations and the social hierarchies of the emperor system without resorting to either nationalistic ideas of Japanese ethnic superiority or western concepts of individualism (Johnson 1992: 393).

What is unclear from Johnson's analysis of Doi's challenge to gendered power is how far gender relations can be understood within a framework of constitutional capitalist democracy without an explicit consideration of class divisions. Class differences, though they are recognised by both Doi and Johnson, remain largely unquestioned, while the predominantly middle-class character of the women's movement is acknowledged and then forgotten, despite the historical link between the development of housewife feminism and the expansion of the middle class in postwar Japan. It is this link between gender, class and power that we wish to examine. We will argue that gender relations cannot be understood separately from class divisions in the context of a capitalist economy.

We now look at the 'first wave' of the women's liberation movement, showing how women's organised struggles to change gender relations must be understood in the context of the attempt by the state to construct new gender identities with which to engage in the global contest for power.

The 'First Wave' Women's Movement

In 1878, Kusunose Kita, who had assumed responsibility as household head for the property and tax liability of her husband after his death in 1872, complained that unlike male household heads, she had no right as a woman to vote for district assembly representatives, nor to act as legal guarantor for property: 'the only equality I share with men who are the heads of their households is the onerous duty of paying taxes' (Sievers 1983: 29). The first women activists emerged from the People's Rights Movement (Jiyu minken undo), a right-wing movement formed in 1874 to demand an elected assembly. At first this was far from being a movement for popular democracy (Halliday 1975: 30), nor were the early leaders interested in the woman question. As Sievers states, 'most leaders were openly hostile to women's rights arguments within the framework of popular rights' (Sievers 1983: 28). By 1878, however, the movement was being taken over by farmers and merchants, and the need to mobilise women was recognised (Jayawardena 1986: 238). The issue of votes for women was raised with limited success in some local assemblies, and women in Kochi were allowed to vote between 1880 and 1888 (Jayawardena 1986: 230; Sievers 1983: 29; Nolte 1986: 702). The case of Kusunose Kita had a great impact on Ueki Emori, a member of the People's Rights Movement (PRM), who from 1879 was one of the few who stood unambiguously for equal rights (Sievers 1983: 30), publishing articles arguing for women's equality, female suffrage and the abolition of the family system (Tanaka 1977: 3–4).

'Daughters Confined in Boxes'

In 1882, Kishida Toshiko was the first woman to speak for women's rights on a popular-rights platform. From then until after the start of Japan's war with China in 1931, the women's movement in Japan was a growing and developing presence, despite heavy state repression. Kishida was a learned and intelligent woman from a wealthy merchant family, who had acted as tutor to the empress. She spoke on Liberal Party platforms (the successor to the PRM) until its dissolution because of government repression in 1884 (Jayawardena 1986: 238–40), and she was arrested and jailed for a week in 1883 for her famous speech 'Daughters Confined in Boxes' (*Hako iri musume*), which attacked the family system, and middle- and upper-class women's seclusion in the home. She was to develop a sophisticated analysis of women's position which recognised the links with class and state power, although her audience was largely limited to the literate middle classes. During this time women's political activity increased rapidly. Kishida inspired the feminism of Fukuda Hideko, who was arrested and jailed for ten months for the 1885 Osaka Incident, a plan to challenge the government (Sievers 1983: 37, 42, 47–8).

The working-class women's movement

The industrial action of women textile workers at the Amamiya Silk Mill in Kofu, striking against worsening conditions of employment, wage reductions and abuse by male employers and supervisors, was the genesis of a working-class women's movement which was to develop fully some decades later (Sievers 1983: 50–51). Women were first organised into the labour movement twenty years after it began in 1897.

The socialist Commoners' Society (*Heiminsha*) attracted women like Fukuda Hideko and Kanno Suga, who were dissatisfied with the middle-class social reform groups (Tanaka 1977: 25–7). From 1905, the Society campaigned with limited success on education and economic independence, and the right of women to attend political meetings (Nolte 1986: 696). In 1907, Fukuda started the first political women's journal, called *Women of the World* (*Sekai fujin*), subsequently closed down by the government in 1909. Kanno, an anarchist-socialist, wrote about prostitution, female chastity, male hypocrisy and the class system (Jayawardena 1986: 241, 243). She was later arrested for the plot to assassinate the emperor, and executed in 1911 (Sievers 1983: 158–62). Socialist women's organisations such as Yamakawa Kikue's Red Wave Society (*Sekiran kai*) continued to struggle for better conditions for women, including the abolition of paternal dominance in the family, equal opportunities in education and employment, and the abolition of licensed prostitution. The government responded to their demands with hostility, including the immediate dissolution in 1925 of the first political party to articulate these demands, the Peasant Labour Party (*Rodo nomin to*) (Tanaka 1977: 25–6, 30–31).

The Bluestockings

In the meantime, the rapid development of capitalism, the rise of the middle class and the expansion of education for women had all contributed to the emergence in 1911 of the *Seito* group, the Bluestockings, who launched a women's literary journal of the same name, and whose famous members included Hiratsuka Raicho and Yosano Akiko. *Seito* represented the first direct attempt by women to put the critique of the family system into practice. Ideas of free love and marriage brought into question the 'feudalistic' family system, and *Seito* members went beyond theory by conducting sexual relationships and having children, yet refusing to marry, even though this meant they had no recognised place in Japanese society (Tanaka 1977: 16–18). In 1915, Ito Noe took over as editor. The government banned several issues on the grounds that the articles were corrupting the traditional values of Japanese women, and *Seito* stopped publishing in 1916, partly as a result of government censorship and harassment. Ito Noe and her partner Osugi Sakae were persistently harassed by the police until 1923 when, in the turmoil of the great earthquake, they were arrested and murdered in police cells as enemies of the state (Jayawardena 1986: 246–7). But the impact of *Seito* was enormous, moving the feminist debate on to questioning the entire gendered basis of society. As Tanaka argues, *Seito* began without social analysis, focusing on personal liberation through literary activity. This in itself was threatening to the government, because the old order inhibited self-development in order to tie women into the family. But state oppression and the reactions to the ideas and lifestyles of the *Seito* group forced them to become more political, and to combine personal liberation with a broader political understanding of women's position in society (Tanaka 1977: 17–18).

Female suffrage

Although government repression associated with the great treason trial of Kanno Suga in 1911 had stifled political action, and the demise of *Seito* in 1916 was a further reverse, this did not mean the end of feminism. In 1919, Hiratsuka Raicho and Ichikawa Fusae formed the New Women's Society (*Shin fujin kyokai*). Over the next decade, many new and existing women's organisations, appealing to a new constituency of educated women, adopted the struggle for suffrage. As Nolte points out, these organisations were overwhelmingly middle class; nevertheless, the mass support which they gave to women's suffrage resulted in the right of women to attend political meetings being passed by both Houses of the Diet in 1922. In 1925, the Lower House passed a resolution in favour of female suffrage, and by 1928 support came from leftist and centrist political parties. In 1930 and 1931 women's suffrage bills received majorities in the Lower House, but were defeated in the Upper House. Women continued to campaign, until the start of the war with China in 1931 effectively silenced the issue of the extension of political rights until 1945 (Nolte 1986: 690, 697–9, 702–13).

Divided women

Nolte argues that the two strands of the women's movement had a complex relationship. Yamakawa, leader of the working-class movement, 'treated bourgeois feminism with contempt in theory and cooperation in practice' (Nolte 1986: 701). In 1921 she left the New Women's Society and the campaign for suffrage, castigating Hiratsuka for self-serving individualism and an incoherent theoretical analysis. Hiratsuka's response was to declare that there were now 'two women's movements, bourgeois and proletarian'; while Yosano Akiko emphasised the non-class character of the movement, and others, including Ichikawa Fusae, worked in both its labour and its suffrage wings. Yamakawa later returned to support votes for women, and as Nolte points out, although the movement was separated organisationally along class lines, the two branches often co-operated on campaigns and had many common aims, including revision of the civil code, equal pay and opportunity, maternity provision, and the abolition of prostitution (Nolte 1986: 701).

Although the outbreak of war in 1931 temporarily put an end to debates on political rights, the critique of women's position was connected from the start with the issue of Japan's subordination to the western powers. We will argue that the links between the position of women and the status of the country were variously constructed in the different stages of Japan's changing relationship to the world imperialist system. At first, during Japan's subordination under free-trade imperialism, the position of women was seen by both the imperial powers and the Japanese reformers as a crucial part of the explanation for Japan's economic and military weakness. During the second phase, in the process of resisting subordinate status, Japan used the construction of a new womanhood to demonstrate its position as a civilised nation and its equality with the West. During the third stage, in the process of becoming an imperialist power itself, Japan used women to help construct the nation-state and create an empire. In the process of reconstructing womanhood in the context of the global political economy, however, Japan also produced new social divisions which created distinctions between the classes, upheld the power of the ruling elite, and reproduced deep cleavages between women. Before engaging in this analysis, it is necessary to outline the events from Japan's forcible entry into global politics in 1853 to its defeat in the Pacific War in 1945.

Chapter 2

Japan Enters Global Politics

Japan's Resistance to Western Imperialism

Any analysis of the approach to women in Japan must be looked at in the context of the global political economy and the competition between the western powers for hegemony in East Asia and the Pacific; in particular, the US challenge to the European colonisers, using the non-military imperialist strategy of the 'open-door' policy on trade known as 'free-trade imperialism' (Beasley 1990: 27). The perspective we adopt is that while Japan was fully responsible for the suppression and exploitation of its own colonies, Japanese expansionism was driven by the western powers' attempt to subordinate Japan into global imperialism. The goal of US policy was to secure China as its main market. This required the establishment of travel and refuelling stations across the Pacific, by military force if necessary – for example in Hawaii, Guam, the Philippines and Japan. Indeed, Japan was first seen by the USA in the 1850s as a coaling station on the route to Shanghai (Halliday 1975: 87–8).

Japan was forced out of its policy of national seclusion in 1853, when the US fleet arrived to demand trade and shipping facilities, backed up by the threat of warships, returning the following year for a reply. The Japanese government stalled but recognised in 1856 that it would either have to sign a trade agreement or be attacked by a navy which was more technologically advanced than any military force it could offer in resistance. In 1858, the US consul used fear of Britain, the dominant imperialist power in the area, to bludgeon Japan into agreeing to what became known as the 'unequal treaties', despite much opposition and deep divisions within the Japanese ruling group. Japan then agreed similar terms with Britain, France, Russia and the

Netherlands. Thus by 1859 Japan had become subordinated into free-trade imperialism with the establishment of the treaty port system, which was a parallel to the one imposed by the West on China. The important provisions of this system were that foreigners could set up commercial and residential premises in designated foreign settlements in the treaty ports, that foreigners could live under their own laws, and that they could trade at the ports free of official interference at low fixed rates of customs duty. The humiliation of the unequal treaties was followed by military defeats at Kagoshima Bay in 1863 and Shimonoseki Straits in 1864 (Beasley 1990: 27–34, 44–7).

Internally, Japan's subordination resulted in 1867 in the resignation of the military government (the *bakufu*) and its head (the *shogun*), followed by armed conflict between the shogunate and the monarchists, and a *coup d'état* which restored the emperor Meiji to the throne in 1868. This event, known as the Meiji Restoration, is often portrayed as the signal for a process of reform, modernisation and democratisation, releasing Japan from 'feudal'[1] relations, and liberating the people from military government. It is true that the discontents of the *samurai* (warriors), the peasants and the merchants, as well as those of the feudal lords who were not part of the shogun's inner circle, erupted because of the external crisis. But it is important to recognise that although there was a change in the composition of the ruling class and the relations of production, the upheaval which took place did not constitute a radical change in the social classes, and although feudalism was undermined, it was not completely destroyed. What is represented by domestic events after 1868 is Japan's attempt to resist subordination abroad by developing a strong state and proving itself a civilised country, while maintaining the power of the ruling class at home.

Maintaining Class Power at Home

The change of political regime was brought about by a coalition of middle-ranking samurai, rich farmers from the rural areas, and successful urban and rural merchants, brought together by their opposition to the foreign interventions and the shogun's capitulation to the unequal treaties. These groups struggled to break the stranglehold of the unequal treaties at the same time as holding down the discontents of the mass of the population in order to retain power for themselves.

---

1. It should be noted, however, that despite certain parallels, feudalism in Japan does not refer to the same social formation as in Europe (Beasley 1990: 3; Tsurumi 1970: 93).

After the fall of the military government, middle-ranking samurai from the outer provinces ousted the feudal lords and nobles from the government, and most of the top posts in the new bureaucracy were filled by people from wealthy families, the sons of wealthy former samurai, merchants and landlords (Beasley 1990: 57, 66–7). The revolution brought about a change to a capitalist society, but it was carried out largely by the dissatisfied lower and middle ranks of the former ruling military class (Crump 1983: 3). The success of these leaders is explained not by the rise of the middle class – since the merchant middle class, having been cut off from foreign trade since the seventeenth century, was neither autonomous nor strong enough to assume power – but by the fact that the revolution to abolish feudalism was incomplete. Feudal domains were abolished in 1871, but feudalism was not completely destroyed (Beasley 1990: 61–2). The feudal lords were given significant amounts of capital as compensation for their lands, and many of them established capitalist industries in the rural areas. As Halliday puts it, there was 'a change in the relations of production, but not of power' (Halliday 1975: 43–6). There was certainly discontent among the commoners, and this led to unrest and peasant uprisings, but not to revolution (Beasley 1990: 70).

In the 1870s, the demand for a constitution and an elected legislature was led by expansionist samurai who, when they were defeated over the proposal to invade Korea, petitioned for an elected Diet to rally disaffected samurai, richer farmers and prosperous merchants. Although the People's Rights Movement subsequently demanded freedom and political rights, it came to represent widely different perspectives: from the search for social justice to a xenophobic right-wing nationalism. The Constitution and the Diet were instituted in 1889. The example of the Constitution shows clearly the multiple agenda that was being pursued. In the first place, the government sent an envoy to Berlin and Vienna to find authoritarian models so that the new Constitution would be recognised as based on that of a 'civilised country', but would also provide for a strong state. But the first draft was rejected by the Executive Council as too progressive, since it transferred too much power from the emperor to the elected assembly. As the statesman Ito Hirobumi said, the aim was to 'disarm the critics, not to cede real power' (Beasley 1990: 72–7).

Liberalisation and repression

The Diet, too, especially in the early days, was designed to gain respectability abroad while maintaining a high degree of centralised political control by the landed class. The Diet was to consist of an elected Lower House (the House of Representatives) and an appointed or hereditary Upper House (the House of Peers). There was to be equal authority between the two Houses, with the Peers naturally favouring the government (Beasley 1990: 77–8), but in any case the Upper House was dominated by the big landlords and the Lower House by the middle and smaller landlords, especially in the early Diets (Halliday 1975: 46). The Cabinet was accountable not to the Diet but to the emperor, who retained financial powers and the right to adjourn the Diet. In the first election for the Lower House in 1890, the property criterion allowed only 1 per cent of the population to vote. By 1912 this had risen to 3 per cent. In 1898 the new Civil Code was introduced, again based on a German model, marking an important stage in Japan's acceptance by the West as a 'civilised' state, since it was on the basis of the Code that Britain agreed to release Japan from the terms of the extraterritoriality clause in the unequal treaties. It was not until 1925 that universal male suffrage was introduced, raising the electorate from 3 million to 13 million (Beasley 1990: 78, 133–7, 143).

Each of these changes, however, was accompanied by some form of repression. Throughout the early Meiji period – in 1875, 1877 and 1880 – laws to control the press were established. In 1887, two years before the introduction of the Constitution and the Diet, the Peace Preservation law was instituted controlling the advocacy of parliamentary rights. In 1900, two years after the Civil Code was promulgated, the Security Police law was introduced, making strikes and collective bargaining illegal. And in 1925, only a week after the Male Suffrage law, a new Peace Preservation law made it illegal to attempt to overthrow the Japanese government or the institution of private property (Beasley 1990: 75, 126, 137, 184). These initiatives were clearly aimed at strengthening the power of the state and the position of the ruling class, and limiting popular participation in national decision-making. They were intended both as a counterbalance to Japan's need to demonstrate 'civilised' democratic values and as a way of refusing the western powers' attempts to subdue the country.

Resisting Subordination Abroad

Japan's determination to extricate itself from its subordinate status and compete on equal terms with the West was effected by developing industrial capitalism, modernising the military forces, and acquiring a colonial empire of its own in East Asia, to be known as the Greater East Asia Co-Prosperity Sphere (*Dai toa kyoei ken*). This strategy was embodied in the slogan 'national wealth, military strength' (*fukoku kyohei*). The policy was modelled on that of the western powers, but it was unique because Japan first had to break out of its subordinated position. With this goal, Japan had only two alternatives: to succeed by becoming an imperial power itself, or to fail and remain subordinate. Halliday argues that military force and a strong state constituted the only ways of achieving this from within a position of subordination to the West, because the decision to submit or compete was forced on Japan at too early a stage of its capitalist development, when it had no finance capital, few raw materials and no heavy industry. Despite rapid industrialisation, Japan's weakness in finance capital meant that it was unable to compete with the new imperialism in the form of the open-door approach to trade. Nationalist military expansion was a way of resolving the crisis of capital at home and abroad: at home, it prevented both class and gender struggle as the war destroyed popular support for the democratic rights movement; abroad, it allowed Japan to compete with the West militarily where it could not compete economically (Halliday 1975: 130–33). This is not to exonerate Japan from its responsibility for suppressing its East Asian colonies, but it is to include the West in the scope of culpability, since the origin of the suppression may be identified as the contest by the West for global dominance.

Economic disasters

Despite the fact that before the arrival of the western powers Japan had already achieved the first stages of capitalist development through private enterprise in farming and commerce (Beasley 1990: 10,114), the unequal treaties had a damaging effect on the Japanese economy.

With only coal and copper as raw materials, Japan was largely an agricultural country exporting silk and tea (Halliday 1975: 52–3). But changes in the land laws to bring Japan into line with a capitalist economy had a damaging effect on agriculture. In 1872, land was transformed into private property, and in 1873 the land tax was revised, changing from a tax based on the size of the harvest, and payable to the feudal lord, into a cash tax based on the value of the land and payable to the government at a fixed annual rate regardless of the harvest. Many tenant farmers fell into debt during poor harvests and were evicted by the owners of the land, while small independent cultivators were forced to sell their land and become tenants because they could not pay the taxes. In the ten years after 1868 there were 200 agrarian uprisings as well as samurai rebellions. A study of Osaka in 1885 showed that the new tax system left many poor farmers without enough food to survive between harvests. Between 1884 and 1886, one-eighth of the entire area of arable land was given over to creditors. The collapse of agriculture led to high levels of poverty, unemployment and destitution, as peasants escaped to the cities to work in the factories, to beg or to steal, took up arms and were crushed by the army, or starved to death (Tsurumi 1990: 20–23, 104).

As imports increased, the balance of payments was seriously undermined. Imports rose from 34 per cent of total trade in 1863 to 71 per cent in 1870. Imports were 34 million yen in 1870, compared with exports of only 14 million yen. In common with other countries, 'cheap English textiles flooded in, destroying domestic industry, narrowing the tax base as cottage industry declined, and creating monetary chaos' (Halliday 1975: 47). The treaties resulted in foreign merchants controlling exports and imports, and because of low customs duties there was no protection against cheap foreign imports (Beasley 1990: 108). Many handicraft industries were destroyed as cheap machine-made foreign goods such as textiles made in India came flooding in (Tsurumi 1990: 20).

Breaking free

The flood of imports increased the trade imbalance at a time when the government was trying to build a modern army and an industrial structure to compete with the West. The government was seriously short of foreign exchange, foreign loans were not easily obtained, and in any case foreign debt would undermine national autonomy even more. In 1880, Iwakura Tomomi declared that he would rather sell the islands of Kyushu and Shikoku to a foreign country than borrow 50 million yen from London (Tsurumi 1990: 22–3). Japan managed to fight off a takeover by foreign capital – partly because investment was not seen as attractive, due to high inflation, and the fact that Japan was not on the gold standard, and partly because of state policy which, on Bismarck's advice, discouraged foreign investment, repaid foreign loans as quickly as possible, and bought back foreign-owned capital equipment (Halliday 1975: 55). The results of this policy were evident towards the end of the century. The proportion of foreign control of Japan's foreign trade amounted to 80 per cent in 1890, 60 per cent in 1900 and less than 50 per cent in 1920. Not until late in the nineteenth century was Japan able to start to break free of the unequal treaties. In 1894 it signed a treaty with Britain which agreed that extraterritoriality would end with the new Civil Code (promulgated in 1898) in return for foreign merchants being allowed access to all Japan. But, following the signing of this treaty with the dominant western power, it was the military victories over China and Russia, and the acquisition of colonies of its own, which enabled Japan to join the elite (Beasley 1990: 111, 143).

Japanese Imperialism: Joining the Elite

Japan began to consider expansion as early as 1873, when a proposal was made to invade Korea. Although this was rejected for fear of antagonising the West, it was later agreed to pursue economic links with Korea through a version of the West's treaty port system, and in 1876 a Japanese naval expedition forced Korea to open its ports to trade. But this antagonised China, which saw Korea as one of its vassal states, and over the next twenty years China manoeuvred to ease Japan out of trade with Korea, until in 1894 China declared war on Japan. Japan emerged victorious in 1895, having taken control of Korea and advanced on China (Beasley 1990: 72, 144–6). The peace treaty gave to Japan the Liaotung Peninsula, Taiwan, and a huge indemnity from China of 360 million yen, which brought a profit of 160 million yen to Japan after paying for the war and helped the country to upgrade from the silver to the gold standard. Five days after the Sino-Japanese treaty, however, Russia, Germany and France signed the Triple Intervention, which forced Japan to abandon the Liaotung Peninsula, its most important strategic gain, in return for a larger indemnity (Halliday 1975: 85–6). While Japanese merchants now got privileged access to Chinese and Korean markets, producing export-led growth (Beasley 1990: 110), and Taiwan became Japan's colonial training ground, Japan was forced to recognise that the western powers could still strip it of its military gains (Halliday 1975: 86).

In 1899 and 1900, anti-foreign rebellions in China gave Russia the excuse to seize Manchuria on the grounds that the rebels threatened the railways. But Japan and Britain wanted to stop further Russian advances into China, and signed the Anglo-Japanese Alliance treaty in 1902 (Beasley 1990: 149). This treaty also reflected Japan's strategy of getting support from the strongest of the western powers in order to keep any territorial gains it might achieve. Although Russia agreed to withdraw from Manchuria, it prevaricated, and Japan declared war on Russia in 1904. Japan's victory over Russia 'electrified the world', because this was the first time in several centuries that a non-western country had defeated a Caucasian imperialist power, a defeat that contributed to the first Russian Revolution in 1905 (Halliday 1975: 86, 91).

Japan got Russian recognition of her rights in Korea, and Russia conceded rights to Japan over mining, railway, fishing, timber and land. Japan also took over Russian rights in the Liaotung Peninsula and South Manchuria, including the South Manchurian Railway (the equivalent of the East India Company in India) (Beasley 1990: 149–53). Japan then signed a new trade agreement with Russia to consolidate Japan's and Russia's holdings in China against US pressure, and renewed the Anglo-Japanese Alliance, thereby accepting UK rule over India, and the Franco-Japanese trade agreement respecting French control of Indochina. By so doing, Japan consolidated its links with the West at the expense of the people of Asia (Halliday 1975: 92). These moves undermined Japan's later claims that the intention was to liberate Asia from western domination and create a community of equals. As the reformer Fukuzawa Yukichi said as early as 1885, 'We cannot treat [China and Korea] with special consideration just because they are our neighbours, we must treat them just as Westerners do' (Hicks 1995: 11).

Direct control

As the Koreans turned to violence in 1909, Japan decided that indirect control was not enough, and annexed Korea in 1910 (Beasley 1990: 153–4). Japan then decided that it needed a more bilateral relationship with China than the treaty port system, and took advantage of the diplomatic turmoil associated with the First World War to gain dominance in China through the imposition of the 21 Demands, while Britain and the USA looked on (Halliday 1975: 95). Japan's aim was to dominate the development of China's limitless natural resources; it gained support from the dominant western powers for its special position in Asia, but attracted much hostility from the nationalist Chinese (Beasley 1990: 153–4, 157).

At the Versailles conference, thanks to the secret treaties signed in 1917 with Britain, France, Russia and Italy, the West confirmed Japan's gains in China. The Bolshevik Revolution of 1917 had stimulated imperialist unity, and meant that Russia was no longer a threat in Manchuria. The Chinese, however, like the Koreans before them, assumed that US support for every country's right to independence would apply to China, too, and asked the conference not to recognise Japanese gains in China. The powers refused – an action which later contributed to the Chinese revolution (Halliday 1975: 95–8).

The Washington Conference of 1921–22 was called by the USA after the USA and Britain had agreed that they needed to reduce Japan's wartime gains in China, and to improve the treaty port system in China to their own advantage in view of the growth of Chinese nationalism (Beasley 1990: 162). The First World War probably benefited Japan more than anyone, for it had increased military sales, especially to Russia. After the war, Japan expanded its markets still further – for example, into India. Over a twenty-year period (1913/14–1935) Britain's share of India's cotton cloth market fell from 97 per cent to 47 per cent, whilst Japan's share rose from 0.3 per cent to 51 per cent, accounting for the entire UK loss. The Washington Conference enhanced the western nations' ability to continue their plunder of China, and consolidated the open-door policy of the USA. Japan was required to return former territories to China, while the powers promised to allow China more autonomy in trade and government. These clauses were standard open-door provisions and were meant to restrain Japan from seeking exclusive rights (Halliday 1975: 94–5, 99, 128–9; Beasley 1990: 163).

Competing with the West

The period leading up to the Pacific War may be divided according to the priority given to the economic as opposed to the military strategy of competition with the West. Until 1931, Japan continued to follow a policy of co-operation and compromise with the West, despite conflicting interests (Halliday 1975: 126). In 1927, power struggles in China began to affect Manchuria (Beasley 1990: 169–70). After the nationalist coup against the communists in 1927, the West supported the nationalists, but a more threatened Japan decided to fight the nationalists, alienating Japan from the Washington group. Only Japan had possessions in Korea, and semi-colonial rights in South Manchuria, and was not Caucasian. Only Japan was singled out as a threat to the economic interests of the other powers in China (Halliday 1975: 117).

In 1929 the US stock market collapsed, and the depression in world trade devastated businesses and farms (Beasley 1990: 171). British and US barriers against Japanese exports after the crash were seen as a refusal to allow Japan to solve its own economic problems by peaceful economic expansion when the dominance of the western powers was under threat (Halliday 1975: xxvi). Japan feared losing Manchuria at a time when it needed markets, capital and raw materials from abroad. So it was that in 1931 the Japanese army planned an event, known as the Manchurian Incident, to justify occupation. A bomb exploded on the railway near Mukden, and Japanese troops immediately moved in. In 1932 the conflict spread to China itself when the fighting moved to Shanghai and Nanking (Beasley 1990: 173). The year 1931 marked Japan's move to the military strategy for becoming an imperialist power, and the Pacific War was a continuation of the war which Japan fought in China from 1931 to 1945, known in Japan as the 'Fifteen Years War' (Halliday 1975: 130–33).

Japan goes to war

Japan's aim was to industrialise Manchuria and northern China further for the war machine, exploiting raw materials to produce arms, aircraft, automobiles and trains in Manchuria and Japan. In 1936 the nationalists joined forces with the communists to oppose Japan, and although Japan added some territories, the nationalists refused to surrender. In 1937 another 'incident' near Beijing justified Japan's move into northern China, and in 1938 and 1939 there were unsuccessful clashes with Russia. The outbreak of World War II in 1939 meant that Japan could escalate the fighting in China to the whole country, without challenge from the West. In 1940 Japan signed a Tripartite Pact with Italy and Germany, and a Neutrality Agreement with Russia in 1941. Japan believed that Germany would win in Europe, leaving the colonies of Britain, France and the Netherlands defenceless (Beasley 1990: 176, 195–200).

In 1941 Japan sent troops to Indochina, worsening the already difficult relationship with the USA. The USA responded by freezing Japanese assets in the USA and stopping oil exports. Japan faced a crisis. The Cabinet tried to negotiate with the USA, but when the USA refused, Japan broke off relations, bombed Pearl Harbor, and then attacked the colonial powers in South-East Asia, taking over Hong Kong, the Philippines, Malaya, the Dutch East Indies and Burma (Beasley 1990: 176, 202–4). As Halliday says, Japan fought a brilliant war, destroying both the colonial armies and the British, French and Dutch empires (Halliday 1975: 145).

By 1943, however, Japan was on the defensive. The needs of the war blocked economic development as oil supplies and other materials were diverted from the colonies to Japan, and commodities like tea, coffee and sugar were cut off from their western markets. Inflation, unemployment, war damage and enemy attacks led to economic destabilisation, popular discontent, the rise of nationalist movements and guerrilla warfare (Beasley 1990: 205–8). US bombers attacked industry and transport, and firebombed major cities. By 1945 Japan's war machine had largely been destroyed, and there was a shortage of steel and military manpower, between two and three million Japanese having died between 1937 and 1945 (Tsurumi 1970: 80). Air resistance was reduced to *kamikaze* bombers flying antiquated planes. In July 1945 the Potsdam Declaration demanded unconditional surrender, and the USA dropped atomic bombs on 6 and 9 August. Japan's surrender was publicly announced by the emperor on 15 August (Beasley 1990: 208–11).

Chapter 3

Women and the
Subordination of Japan

Gender, Class and the Struggle for Global Power

In this chapter we first set out a way of understanding the relationship between gender and class divisions and the struggle for global power. We then develop an analysis of gender relations in the 'first' modernisation period. In order to understand the connection between gender, class and power in a global context, we will draw on Terry Lovell's (2000) appropriation of Pierre Bourdieu's (1984) 'fields of power', and extend it to the contest for power between nations.

Bourdieu understands society as fields of power which are organised by the distribution of different forms of capital. Economic capital includes income, wealth, property and inheritances. Social capital is based on social networks and who you know, group memberships and connections generated through networks of relationships. Cultural capital in terms of education, knowledge and taste is expressed in three forms: the embodied, referring to long-lasting dispositions of the mind and body; the objectified, referring to goods and commodities; and the institutionalised, referring mainly to educational credentials which ratify cultural capital. Symbolic capital is the form which different types of capital take when they are recognised as legitimate. Thus, the value of these various capitals in the social field is assessed by the extent to which they can be converted into symbolic capital, and therefore be recognised as legitimate within the social field. Bourdieu defines symbolic capital as 'the acquisition of an image or reputation for competence, respectability and honourability that are easily converted into political positions as a local or national notable' (Bourdieu 1984: 291).

Women as objects

As Lovell points out, however, the subjects of Bourdieu's social spaces are men. It is men who inherit, invest and accumulate capitals of various kinds, and convert them into symbolic capital to acquire respect, honour and power; or, conversely, who trade in 'non-convertible currencies' in 'protected markets' which produce power deficits, because in the struggle for recognition of different social truths, the capitals of those who are less well armed with the resources to impose their truths are not valued or acknowledged as legitimate. According to Bourdieu, however, women figure not as subjects of the struggle, but as objects of it. Bourdieu (1990a) identifies a division of labour in marriage and the family in which women, rather than accumulating capital for themselves, are exchanged between and have value for men as repositories of family capital (Lovell 2000: 16–17).

As social objects, women bring economic capital to marriage in the form of marriage settlements or dowries; they bring social capital in the form of new kinship networks and political alliances; and they bring cultural capital such as physical beauty, aesthetic or moral sense, artistic accomplishments or intelligence. Women are responsible for embodying, displaying and transmitting cultural capital on the family's behalf. As mothers and teachers they are crucial in transmitting 'culture, class and social belonging' across generations; this provides families with a stake in women's acquisition of cultural capital. Women's responsibilities for maintaining kinship relations are central to the accumulation of social capital within family networks and sustaining links between men (di Leonardo 1987), while in 'classes with sufficient distance from necessity' to be able to engage in the struggle over symbolic capital, women's role is to convert family capital into symbolic capital by displaying cultural taste (Lovell 2000: 26–30).

Women as subjects

But, as Lovell points out, while women may indeed be positioned as objects, it is doubtful that women always position themselves in this way. Women cannot 'be seen only as social objects whose value lies in their functions in relation to the economy of symbolic goods.... Women exist as actual social subjects in social space and not only as objects' (Lovell 2000: 19–20). Recognising women as subjects as well as objects enables Lovell to move beyond the positioning of them as mere embodiments and repositories of male capital and to identify the ways in which women also take up positions that enable them to make innovative investments in new markets. For in order to display and

transmit family capitals, women too must acquire cultural capital, and
for those women who are distanced from necessity, the cultural capital
they embody could sometimes be deployed in an industrialised society
– not on, or not solely on, the marriage market, but on the labour
market, to acquire an occupation in their own right together with the
various forms of capital that go with it (Lovell 2000: 26).

The 'women's movement' represents women's collective struggle for
power, the struggle for 'gender mobility', the attempt to move out of
an object positioning to a subject positioning. We understand women's
struggle for power as a move from a position as social objects and the
repositories of value for men in the family to a position as social subjects and accumulators of capital in their own right. Mobility means an
escape from historical positioning and constraints, but as Skeggs (1997:
12) points out, mobility requires capitals, and this goes not only for
gender movement but also for class movement. We would suggest that
it also goes for global mobility. We will argue that women's power in
Japan has always been connected with their class position, although the
ways in which this connection has been manifested varies in different
social contexts and historical periods. We also argue that the specificities
of gender and class cannot be separated from movements in international relations and the global political economy.

Significant changes in gender relations occurred during the 'first'
modernisation period from 1868 to 1945, and again in the 'second'
modernisation period after the Second World War, in the context of the
struggle with the western imperial powers and the rapid development
of capitalism. These changes enabled small numbers of women to free
themselves from their position as the repositories of social, economic
and cultural capital for their male family members. Notwithstanding
the dramatic abolition of class divisions in their earlier forms during
both periods of modernisation, we will argue that for women class is
a central component of this process of moving from object to subject
positions. We will concur with Pierre Bourdieu that 'Sexual properties
are as inseparable from class properties as the yellowness of a lemon
is from its acidity', and will demonstrate that in Japan, as in other
industrialised countries, 'a class is defined in an essential respect by the
place and value it gives to the two sexes' (Bourdieu 1984: 107). We will
argue that Japan is not an exception to this, although the particular way
in which sexual and class properties are combined is unique to Japan,
since it is both culturally and historically specific. We will demonstrate
this through a historical analysis of the changing position of women
before and after Japan's entry into the global 'field' (Parts I–II), and

through the empirical analysis of a category of women who challenge the dichotomised gendered identities signifying class position in the contemporary period (Parts IV–VI).

State symbolic power

In Part II we will argue that before the Meiji Restoration women had become the repositories of symbolic power for the dominant class. After Meiji, important changes occurred in the position of women, as the state attempted to construct new gender identities in the face of changing global power relations. In Part I we argue that the state continued to construct women as repositories of class power, but that the changes in women's position also reflected the production of women as repositories of symbolic power for the *state*.

Nira Yuval-Davis and Floya Anthias (1989: 7) conceptualise women as signifiers of national differences, and we agree with Yuval-Davis (1997: 41–2) that difference is always connected to power. While Bourdieu (in Wacquant 1993: 39) understands the state as a *source* of symbolic capital – through, for example, the recognition given by the state to cultural capital in the form of educational qualifications – we argue that states also *seek* symbolic capital; that states compete for respectability and distinction on the global stage; and that they draw upon particular articulations of gender and class as forms of symbolic capital to compete for global power.

Bourdieu argues that in the competition for power and distinction there are two forms of struggle: over the material basis for power – that is, the form of capital which provides the resource base in the field of power; and over the legitimacy of the material basis for power – that is, the process of convincing others that the dominant form of capital is legitimate (Wacquant 1993: 25). The key mechanism in converting forms of capital into power is the process of legitimation. Legitimating the power of the dominant nation is as important as the struggle for military and economic dominance. Our argument is that one of the key mechanisms by which states claim recognition for their power is through the symbolic capital of gendered class identities. Thus not only are genders and classes socially mobile, but also states seek to move up the hierarchy of global 'respectability' as measured on the scale of 'civilisation'.

The actions of the Japanese state in relation to women have to be understood in the context of Japan's dual positioning in the world imperialist system and the changing class relations taking place within the country after 1868, as the holders of feudal power fought to maintain their dominance in the face of capitalist development. The state's approach to women was largely repressive, but the forces for changing women's position came from the western powers' attempt to classify Japan as backward and uncivilised, from the male social reformers trying to forge a new Japanese identity which would be globally respectable, and from women themselves, who were seeking a greater measure of control over their lives. In Part III we look at how women themselves took up the challenge.

In the rest of this chapter, however, we examine the connection between the position of women in Japan and the status of the country in the hierarchy of nations, showing the different ways in which the links were constructed at various stages of Japan's relationship with the world imperialist system. We will argue that, in the first stage, during Japan's subordination under free-trade imperialism, the position of women was seen by both the imperial powers and the Japanese reformers as a crucial part of the explanation for Japan's economic and military weakness.

Japan's Weakness and the Woman Question

Several years before the first women activists began to campaign for women's rights, and at about the same time as the start of the People's Rights Movement, the position of women had been discussed by male social reformers in Japan concerned about their country's standing in the wider world. The problem of Japan's relationship with the West was one of the dominant themes after the country had been forced to open its doors to trade, and the woman question formed one of the central issues in the debates on the extent to which Japan was a civilised country.

The most influential forum in which men discussed the woman question was the Meiji Six Society (*Meirokusha*), which was founded in 1873 with the aim of promoting 'civilisation and enlightenment' (Braisted 1976: xviii). The members were mostly intellectuals and government officials who attempted to integrate western ideas with Japanese culture and society, without presenting any consistent view on how this might be achieved or the appropriate balance between them. The issues debated in their *Meiji Six Journal* (*Meiroku zasshi*) were focused on trying to explain the West's power, and how Japan could compete with it (Sievers 1983: 16–17).

Two of the most famous members were Mori Arinori and Fukuzawa Yukichi, who were also among the most liberal in their approach to women. Mori was from a wealthy former samurai family, had lived in the West, and served as a diplomat and later as Education Minister. He was the first to attack the institution of concubinage in *Meiroku zasshi*, arguing for monogamy and equality in marriage. Fukuzawa was from a lowly samurai family, and founded the school which later became the famous Keio University. He was never a member of the government, and published his own *People's Journal* (*Minkan zasshi*) in which he discussed prostitution, concubinage, women's property rights, monogamy and divorce amongst other topics, and often disagreed with the other members of the Meiji Six Society. Both the journals closed down when new press censorship laws were introduced in 1875 (Braisted 1976: xxiii–xxv), although Fukuzawa continued to write articles on women and gender relations in newspapers and magazines, such as his essay *On Japanese Women* in 1885, and his critique of the seventeenth-century Confucian text *Greater Learning for Women* (*Onna daigaku*) in 1899 (Kiyooka 1988).

An examination of Fukuzawa's and Mori's writings on the woman question reveals two important aspects of the approach of the most liberal of the early social reformers. First, they saw the position of women as intricately tied up with the question of Japan's weakness in the global political economy; second, their primary concern in arguing for an improvement in women's position was the subjugation of the Japanese nation, not the subordination of women.

'Uncivilised ways'

Only five years before *Meirokusha* started, in 1868, Japan had been forced to open its doors to the rest of the world. Japan's position as an economically and industrially undeveloped country, and its inability to defend itself against the encroachment of the western powers in the East Asian region, led to its construction by the West as a backward and inferior culture. One of the crucial elements in this construction of Japan as uncivilised, as in many other countries which had fallen under the power of the western imperialists (see Liddle and Joshi 1986; and Sinha 1995 on India), was the nature of gender relations, and how these differed from those of the West.

The association between Japanese forms of male power and the lowly position of the country in the hierarchy of civilisation was not only constructed by the West but also adopted by Japanese reformers concerned about, and seeking explanations for, Japan's global weakness. The power of this association, and the difficulty of conceptualising the position of women outside its framework, are evident in a book written in 1891 by Alice Bacon, an American who lived in Japan and was a friend of Tsuda Umeko and Yamakawa Sutematsu, two of the first group of five girls and young women sent to the USA in 1871 to study US home life (Bacon 1891: viii; Kawahara 1962: 45). *Japanese Girls and Women* was written to rectify the fact that 'one half of the population has been ... altogether misunderstood' (Bacon 1891: v). In an otherwise positive and sympathetic account, Bacon nevertheless makes the same connection between Japan's backwardness in comparison with the West and the position of women:

> until the position of the wife and mother in Japan is improved and made secure, little permanence can be expected in the progress of the nation toward what is best and highest in the Western civilisation ... that Japan is infinitely ahead of other Oriental countries ... is greatly to her credit; but that she is far behind the civilised nations of Europe and America, ... [is] a fact that, unless changed, must sooner or later be a stumbling-block in the path of her progress. (Bacon 1891: 115–16)

This perspective was adopted by many of the male reformers of the 'enlightenment period', and although it acted as a powerful motive for change, the myth of female equality in the West, and the assumption of western cultural superiority associated with it, had a profound effect on these men. As Fujiwara Keiko says:

> Newspaper editorials and magazine articles from the mid-1880s reveal how concerned people were with the ... [fact] that foreigners, who had hitherto been allowed to live only in the foreign concessions in the treaty ports, would be permitted to live unrestricted among the Japanese. What would Westerners think of Japan's social customs? Its uncivilised social customs and oppression of women would be in the full view of Westerners.... Fukuzawa ... was ashamed of the uncivilised ways of his people and feared that Japan would not be able to join the ranks of the civilised nations of the world. (Fujiwara 1988: viii–ix)

As Fukuzawa himself wrote in 1899: 'the freedom for foreigners to live amongst the Japanese is to come within a few months' time. Are our people going to leave things as they are and still expect to preserve the dignity of a nation?' (Fukuzawa 1899: 200).

Weakening the race

In the first place, the inferiority of Japanese culture, as manifested in Japanese gender relations, was accepted by many Japanese reformers, as well as western observers, as a factor which helped to explain the backward position of Japan on the world stage in both biological and social terms. For example, in a statement reminiscent of the discourses on Indian biological inferiority (Liddle and Rai 1998: 503), Fukuzawa claimed:

> Women, having grown weak both in body and mind, are then worthless in the support of the family or the country. When they bring forth children, too few of the infants grow up healthy, and the hereditary physique of the Japanese is becoming weak. Soon it will be said that there is no race in the world with a worse physique than the Japanese. We deserve this for the ill-treatment we have given women through past history. (Kiyooka 1988: 54)

Women's weakness affected not only the biological strength of the Japanese race, but also the size of the labour force available to make the country strong:

> in the civilised countries of the West, much of the social intercourse is managed by women, and even though they do not run society, they work in harmony among men and help smooth the situation.... in carrying out the business of the nation, in the West both men and women divide the burden between them, while ... [in Japan only half of them, the men only, carry the burden ... the labour force that performs the national business in Japan is only half that of the West. (Kiyooka 1988: 117)

But the superiority of the West on the grounds of the strength and freedom of its women, in contrast to the women of Japan, was not seen just as a factor explaining Japan's weakness, but also as a cause of Japan's shame and social ostracism from the global community. In his essay *On Morality*, which argues against polygamy, concubinage and prostitution, Fukuzawa writes: 'the whole world is dominated by Western civilisation today, and anyone who opposes it will be ostracised from the human society; a nation, too, will find itself outside the circle of nations' (Kiyooka 1988: 79).

There were two serious flaws in Fukuzawa's argument, the first of which was identified by Kishida Toshiko, whom we first met in Chapter 1. She recognised as false the claims of western countries that European and American women already possessed equality. Kishida declared that sexual equality was indeed an index of civilisation, but that no country in the world gave women equal rights, so Japan's backwardness was no disadvantage; rather, Japan had the opportunity to be the first to achieve civilisation (Sievers 1983: 37). Equally, Fukuzawa's view that women in Japan were excluded from the work necessary to make the country strong was incorrect, based as it was on a particular class perspective in which women of the ruling samurai class were confined to the home and not permitted to work outside it. This did not, however, apply to women of the peasant, artisan and merchant classes, who took an active part in agriculture, fishing, mining, manufacturing, selling, running family businesses, and providing domestic services to the wealthy and landed classes (see Hunter 1993).

Motives of the Male Reformers

In 1885, the same year that Fukuzawa published On Japanese Women, Mori Arinori was appointed Minister of Education in the face of considerable opposition from more conservative members of the government (Stephens 1991: 34). Mori attacked traditional marriage and family practices, and double standards of morality, in his essay On Wives and Concubines, and supported women's education, egalitarian contractual marriage and monogamy (Braisted 1976: 143–5, 190, 252, 331–3). For example: 'Looking at marriage customs in our country today, the husband treats the wife as he pleases, and there is still no national legislation against arbitrary divorce by the husband simply because she does not please him' (Braisted 1976: 104–5); and:

> It is common practice, however, for men to use women as playthings, to gain pleasure from indulging licentiously and inconsiderately in sake, lewdness, music, and songs, and to refrain from mingling with women unless they share in these pleasures. It is not idle slander that in the eyes of the foreigners ours is the most immoral country in the world. (Braisted 1976: 253)

Mori himself undertook a contractual marriage of the kind he proposed in 1875, but the couple were divorced in 1886 (Braisted 1976: 331–3, 340).

Although his critics accused him of favouring equal rights, Mori denied that his attempts to improve women's position had anything to do with the question of women's rights. He proclaimed:

> I appear in the essays of Kato and others to be the pioneer in advocating equal rights for men and women. In my earlier essays on wives and concubines, I indeed said that husbands and wives should be honoured without distinction as they are on the same level. I absolutely did not touch on equal rights, however. (Braisted 1976: 399)

Mori's primary aim was to raise the position of Japan in the global community, whether through changes to women's position in the family or through female education. As Stephens points out, Mori was a nationalist who said publicly that education was for the benefit of the state, not the individual, and this approach is reflected in the fact that as Education Minister he imbued the compulsory education system with nationalistic moral exhortation and the teacher training sector with military discipline and character training, and allowed academic freedom only to the elite university sector (Stephens 1991: 34–6). His approach is also revealed in his comment in 1872 on women textile workers in Lowell, USA, during his time as chargé d'affaires in Washington: 'the factory girls might be counted by the acre; ... the motto over the factory should be Work or Die.... If something like this enterprise can be transported to Japan, what may we not expect, in the future, from that empire?' (Sievers 1983: 207).

Race not rights

Reformers like Mori and Fukuzawa, while they argued for sexual equality and took a stand against the slavery involved in men's relationship to women (Sievers 1983: 217), were not concerned primarily with the position of women, but with the position of Japan in relation to the western imperialists. In On Japanese Women, Fukuzawa, too, denied that his aim was to promote equal rights, despite his statement: 'What I aim at is simply equality between the sexes' (Sievers 1983: 35). But in the same essay he takes this statement further to reveal his real concern: 'The basic purpose of my argument is not to side with women to contest their rights. My purpose is the improvement of the Japanese race' (Sievers 1983: 36).

It may be thought that this is merely a strategic argument adopted by Fukuzawa because it would be easier to argue for women's rights through the alignment with Japanese nationalism rather than on its own terms. But other evidence tends to suggest that while he supported the notion of women's equality, any costs in the process of bringing it about had to continue to be paid by women, not men. That Fukuzawa was not primarily concerned with women's welfare may be seen from the fact that his opposition to polygamy and concubinage is ambivalent: on the one hand he argues that it is a matter of morality, fairness and human rights; on the other hand he says that since it is impossible to make the majority of men conform to monogamy and fidelity, it is better in the meantime simply to conceal polygamous relationships. Again, it might be thought that this is simply a pragmatic approach, taking the first step towards elimination by making concubinage shameful. But Fukuzawa's method of making concubinage and prostitution shameful is to shame concubines and prostitutes rather than shaming the men who demand the right to sexual services. He recommends 'First, the exclusion of all concubines from the society of ordinary women', including wives who were formerly concubines. 'Such women must ... not be accorded the respect due to legitimate wives' (Sievers 1983: 79–80, 100). 'Second, whether a geisha or a prostitute, anyone who ... commits illicit acts for money must be ostracised from human society.... What will the results be? ... prostitutes, geisha and concubines ... will no longer be considered human beings' (Sievers 1983: 100–101), and:

> I am hoping for the degradation of prostitutes in Japan to the level of those in the West. The official practice of protecting prostitutes from syphilis may appear to be a social service, but from another point of view, it serves to assure men of loose morality of their physical safety. It would be much better to eliminate medical check-ups and let the danger of syphilic infection be a deterrent. (Sievers 1983: 102)

This approach, which Fukuzawa himself terms 'ruthless', would sacrifice prostitutes' health, as well as that of the men's wives and children, for the sake of the dignity of the nation, despite his recognition of women's economic powerlessness and inequality, amounting to slavery, and of prostitutes as 'great benefactors who, at great pains to themselves, are serving the whole society' (Sievers 1983: 89). Fukuzawa's approach is reminiscent of the arguments which arose in Britain at the time of the Contagious Diseases Acts 1864 and 1886, when the moral panic over national vigour was stimulated by the high incidence of venereal disease amongst the troops in the Crimea (Walkowitz 1980). The approach of the male reformers may be contrasted with the feminist approach of Kishida Toshiko, who wanted to shame polygamous men and exclude them from political office (Sievers 1983: 97). So it is clear that the position of women was strongly connected in the minds of the male reformers with Japan's uncivilised status in the hierarchy of nations, a discourse which emanated from the West; and the reformers' primary concern with improving the status of the nation, rather than with the condition of women *per se*, itself reflected the approach of the majority of western critics.

We will now show how, in the process of refusing subordinate status, Japan constructed a new womanhood as a demonstration of its equality with the West and as a means of proving its civilised status. The Japanese state did open up to women in some areas – for example, in education – but there was also repression in the reforms. We will show that the changes to women's position were designed to create a new Japanese womanhood which would gain international respectability abroad while retaining male control at home. In this process, class was a crucial consideration.

Chapter 4

Creating a New Japanese Womanhood

The construction by the Meiji state of the new Japanese woman was heavily influenced by two important factors: one was the western critique of Japanese gender relations, on the basis of which the discourse of Japan's inferiority as a nation was built. This factor led the state, encouraged by the male social reformers, to seek a form of womanhood which would gain the approval of the West – by, for example, introducing a modern education system. The second factor was the breakdown of male control over women as a result of the abolition of the feudal system of control through the class structure. Thus the aim was to create a new form of womanhood, and new forms of male control, which would be acceptable to the western powers. This was done by replacing the feudal system (see Part II) with the 'family–state' system, whereby the male heads of household were given authority over the women and younger men of the family, and were in turn subordinated to the emperor as head of state. The new form of womanhood constructed within this system comprised both progressive and regressive aspects.

The new Japanese womanhood is reflected through crucial issues on which legislation was passed by the Meiji state. These were changes to women's position which were applied universally to all Japanese women after the Restoration, in contrast to the strongly class-divided construction of women in the pre-Meiji era. The first was the position of women in the family; second was the introduction of women's education; and third was women's formal exclusion from political rights. The first two were considered important by both male reformers and western critics. Only the women activists were concerned about all three.

Extending Control over Women in the Family

The organisation of the family was one of the greatest issues of concern to almost all the feminists who were active during the period, from Kishida's 'Daughters Confined in Boxes' critique in 1883 to the Tokyo Women's Reform Society's (TWRS) campaigns against concubinage in the late nineteenth and early twentieth centuries, and *Seito* members' opposition to the institution of marriage from 1911 to 1916.

In 1871 the people were formally released from feudal social relations as the feudal domains were abolished and formed into prefectures under the emperor as the new head of state (Beasley 1990: 61). The abolition of the domains meant the eradication of the feudal system of social regulation (though not the erasure of the political power of various feudal elements), through which women had been under the control of the male head of the family, who was himself accountable by law and custom through the class structure to his feudal lord or *daimyo*, the lords being in turn responsible to the shogun. This system of social regulation had been upheld by the military power of the sword-bearing samurai class, supported by the Confucian principles of loyalty and filial piety and the hierarchical relationships of master and servant, father and son, husband and wife. In 1871, too, the Family Registration Law was introduced; this enabled families to transfer their community member-ship, previously based on class categories, from the *daimyo*'s domain to the state in the form of the prefecture, based on place of residence.

During the Meiji period a form of samurisation took place which reconstructed the gendered identities of the Japanese population as a means of establishing new forms of social regulation based on the models of the former ruling military class. For men, *bushido* or the way of the warrior, which promoted the 'will to die', was transformed from a samurai ethic in obligation to the feudal lord into a universal ethic for the whole of the male population in obligation to the emperor as representative and head of the nation-state. Following on from the abolition of the four-class feudal structure, the Conscription Ordinance of 1872 stressed the equality of the classes. This equality referred to the duty of every man to become a soldier, where previously this had been the privilege of the military class. The 1878 Admonition to Soldiers stated that the modern army must be founded on the traditional way of the warrior, and the Meiji government demanded that all men show the loyalty and courage of the warrior, as the samurai had done before them. Yanagita shows that initially, at least, commoners were anxious to adopt samurai norms of behaviour: 'As soon as the rumour got round that "there is no more distinction between samurai and peasants" people rushed to imitate the lifestyle of the samurai' (Tsurumi 1970: 82–6).

The 'equality of the four classes', which was a slogan of the modernisation process, actually referred to the samurisation of the former non-samurai classes. It did not mean that there were no class divisions, but that old divisions were abolished and new ones were created. The new Meiji class hierarchy consisted of the imperial household (*kozoku*), peers (*kazoku*), former samurai (*shizoku*), commoners (*heimin*), and 'outcastes' (*buraku-min*). The peers included former shoguns, feudal barons, court nobles and those samurai responsible for the Meiji Restoration (Tsurumi 1970: 82, 86).

Samurisation for all women

A similar process of samurisation occurred for women, but whereas men were constructed as potential soldiers 'willing to die' for the state, women were constructed on the samurai model as wives and mothers confined to the family sphere. In 1898 the new conservative Civil Code was passed, drawing upon the model of the family that was prevalent in the former military class, and applying it to women of all classes. As Sievers says, this model was one of the most repressive in Japanese history, requiring of married women a chaste and secluded lifestyle and the surrender of rights in property or progeny to the husband's family. The Code increased women's subordination across the whole population, where previously the most severe strictures had been largely confined to the ruling class. As Takamure Itsue said: 'the Meiji Civil Code was an attempt to convert all Japan into a single samurai model of the family' (Sievers 1983: 111).

The Civil Code laid down the rules for the family system, based on an authoritarian German model which was designed to sustain rather than undermine traditional aspects of society, and gave patriarchal rights to the head of household. An earlier, more liberal draft of the Code based on a French model was rejected because it was too influenced by the French natural rights approach (Hunter 1989: 72). The rejected draft had allowed adultery as a cause of divorce for both men and women, and a more liberal system of inheritance (Igeta 1982: 41–76). The Code was also based on the Japanese model of the family system, or *ie*. As Hendry says, 'the whole notion of a "family system" was a concept created in the face of outside influences to explain Japanese behaviour in a comparative context' (Hendry 1987: 22). The *ie* means more than the 'family'; it contains a sense of 'lineage', 'house', or 'household', and signifies both a building and a sense of continuity, including as it does deceased ancestors and imagined descendants (Hendry 1987: 23). Thus Japan used both European and Japanese models to re-establish women's subordination in the family.

As Hunter says, the new family law embodied a 'codification of the patriarchal family system, which rested on the existence of the *ie* as the basic unit of operation' (Hunter 1989: 72). The Code laid down that property held in common by the *ie* must be registered as belonging to the household head, which meant that any property a woman brought with her at marriage became legally owned by the household head. Male primogeniture was institutionalised. Permission of the household head (and parents if different) was required for marriage of men under 30 and women under 25. Divorce was allowed by mutual consent, but women could be divorced for adultery, whereas men could not. A woman's adultery was a civil and criminal offence, liable to two years' imprisonment, whereas a man's was neither (Hendry 1981: 15–22). The Code gave authority to the household head, and control over the members' property and place of residence (Nolte 1986: 693). The Confucian family ideology was also re-established as official doctrine (Miyake 1991: 276), and the Code readopted the classes of family relationship in which wives were second-class relatives but husbands were first-class relatives (Hendry 1981: 21).

The 'stain' of polygamy

The issue of male polygamy was particularly focused upon by western critics and male reformers as an index of Japan's backwardness. The 1871 family law code had classed wives and concubines equally in a second-class relationship to the husband (Hicks 1995: 208). As a result, polygamy came under sustained attack from both the reformers and the women activists. Fukuzawa wrote about how ashamed he felt when a woman from the USA first observed the system of concubinage: 'I felt that one grave stain on our new Japan had been exposed and my shame was similar to that of being subjected to a public whipping in the open market'; 'the shame incurred when the Western people observe the custom [of polygamy] with scorn is enough to make us reconsider' (Kiyooka 1988: 200, 149). And in 1885 he wrote: 'When the civilisation advances, men's private behaviour will contribute to the realisation of a morally upright society where all people will follow the law of one husband to one wife' (Kiyooka 1988: 79). In 1886 the TWRS began to campaign against concubinage, and in 1889 *Women's Education Magazine* (*Jogaku zasshi*) reported on the petition for monogamy being circulated by women throughout the country (Igeta 1982: 41–76). As a result of these campaigns, the principle of monogamy was accepted in the 1898 Civil Code (Hicks 1995: 209). Indirectly, however, the revised family law continued to permit men to act under the same double standards as before because of its provision that adultery was an offence only for women (Sievers 1983: 111).

Thus while Japan claimed a civilised status equal to that of the West by formally instituting monogamy and basing its revised family law code on a European model, it also reasserted men's control over women in the family by institutionalising the sexual double standard, and conferring both authority and the ownership of property on the patri-archal head of the family, in ways which were acceptable to the West, subsuming all families into this legal framework in the name of 'beautiful tradition' (Junpu bizoku) (Igeta 1982: 41–76). This 'tradition' was precisely that of the former ruling class, now applied to the whole population, in which there had previously been (and continued to be) considerable diversity in family forms and codes of behaviour. For example, despite the attempt to samurise family morality, from the 1890s to the 1920s 40 per cent of marriages in Tokyo were common-law relationships, and lower-class urban women took their children with them when the relationship ended rather than having to leave them behind as the father's property, in marked contrast to samurised middle-class norms (Uno 1993: 50, 57). In rural areas as late as 1935, middle-class morality was hardly practised, as men and women had affairs before and after marriage, children were born out of wedlock, and open discussion of sex scandalised the town-bred teachers and other outsiders (Smith and Wiswell 1982: 61, 67, 117).

Part of the reason for the reproduction of former ruling-class mod-els of masculinity and femininity for the whole of the population was that although there had been significant diversification in the creation of the middle class through the entry of the merchant class, the feudal system of social relations based on landownership had not been fully eradicated – even though the four classes of the feudal system had in theory been abolished. Many members of the former ruling class re-mained in the new elite which governed the country. Thus the dis-course of equality and the process of samurisation did not mean that class differences disappeared after Meiji; nor did it mean that all people were upgraded to ruling-class status. The samurisation process that was introduced for all the people without class distinction occurred selec-tively in ways which could be used for social regulation, as old class differences were reconstructed in new forms. As Tsurumi says, the Meiji elite imposed the disciplines of militarism on all men and the strictures of the patriarchal family–state system on all women, as a way of exerting strong state control over the population in the struggle to compete with the western powers (Tsurumi 1970: 99).

Education for Women

According to Alice Bacon, 'broader education for the women ... and the study ... of the homes of Europe and America' were required to make Japan a civilised country (Bacon 1891: 115). Many social reformers and women's organisations like the TWRS and *Seito* were interested in women's education. This was probably the issue with the most potential for progressive change, which helped to produce – albeit unintentionally – the feminist activists of the early twentieth century.

In 1869 the Meiji state removed class restrictions on college entrance, and in 1871 the government sent the Iwakura mission to Europe and North America to study western institutions, including education systems. The instructions to the envoys were that 'Japan had lost her rights and been made subject to the insults of others', and it was now time to restore equality by changing laws and institutions towards constitutional reform, industrialisation and westernisation (Beasley 1990: 86–7). In 1872 a system of universal education was introduced. The desire to gain international acceptance can be seen by the extent of western influence, as the new system drew on the French model of centralised bureaucratic control, North American models for primary and teacher training schools and curriculum development, and a German model for the universities (Stephens 1991: 23, 31, 38).

The introduction of universal education and the inclusion of all social groups, including women, was made explicit in the 1872 Education Ordinance: 'Learning is no longer to be considered as belonging to the upper classes, but is to be equally the inheritance of nobles and gentry, farmers and artisans, males and females' (Stephens 1991: 23); and 'farmers, craftsmen, merchants, women and children – there shall henceforward be no uneducated members in a community, no uneducated members in a family' (Jayawardena 1986: 234). The universal education system was designed to produce a population that was as literate and informed as the populations of the West.

The purpose of women's education was to produce women as 'good wives, wise mothers' (*ryosai kenbo*). This notion was introduced by the reformer Nakamura Masanao to represent the concept of the new woman as envisaged by the progressives and modernisers (Sievers 1983: 22–3). As Masanao wrote in 1875:

we must invariably have fine mothers if we want effectively to advance the area of enlightenment ... envying the enlightenment of Europe and America[,] I have a deep, irrepressible desire that later generations shall be reared by fine mothers ... to develop fine mothers, there is nothing better than to educate daughters. (Braisted 1976: 401–2)

The good wife, wise mother model was, as Sievers points out, 'a classic model from the nineteenth century west' (Sievers 1983: 23), and it was quite different from the traditional Confucian view which saw young wives and mothers as too inexperienced and ignorant to bring up their children without the help of the parents-in-law (Sievers 1981: 604). Masanao believed that the content of education should be the same for both men and women: 'the training of men and women should be equal and not of two types' (Braisted 1976: 402), although it was for different purposes.

Learning subservience

But in 1890 the Ministry of Education introduced the reactionary Education Rescript, which promoted the emperor system through the elementary schools and prescribed militarism, nationalism, the family–state system and the organismic theory of society based on Herbert Spencer's model of society as a single organism. The Rescript aimed to unite the people and prepare them for war, and contained moral exhortation to young males to be willing to die for the emperor and the state. This message was reinforced through the compulsory period of conscription into the army for men (Tsurumi 1970: 100–102).

For women, the meaning of good wife, wise mother changed when Confucian family ideology became re-established as official doctrine in the Civil Code, and came to mean confinement in the family and subservience to men. The more progressive educators then worked to raise women's status within the family rather than challenge the family system (Miyake 1991: 276). This new form of subordination of women subsequently became one of the central pillars on which Japan's position in the world was built, as taught in the schools. This is demonstrated in Hibino Yutaka's book On the Way of the Subject in Japan (Nippon shindo ron), a commentary for teachers published in 1904, which said:

> the vigorous and unimpeded advance of our culture, the constant increment of our wealth and power, our supremacy in the east, our equality with the other great powers, our imposing part upon the stage of human affairs, all depend on the establishment of a healthy home life, wherein husband determines and wife acquiesces. (Beasley 1990: 83)

By instituting universal literacy in a very short time, basing the education system on western models, and introducing female education designed to produce women who were informed about their place in the family and able to bring enlightenment to their children, Japan gained acknowledgement by the West as a country with a modern education system and a literate population. At the same time, the education system was used, as in the West, to train women for their roles in the family, and later to imbue them with ideas of their subjection to men. The system of universal education spread women's subordination more widely, enabling men to expand their control over women into geographical regions and amongst social classes where gender relations had been much more egalitarian.

Excluding Women from Politics

Votes for women was one issue which remained unresolved until the end of the Second World War, despite intense debate, campaigning by women's organisations, and changing views within the government. The question of women's suffrage was first raised in 1876, was subsequently taken up by women activists in the Progressive Reform Movement (PRM), and was campaigned for consistently until the 1931 war with China, supported by women's organisations, socialist groups, local assemblies and political parties.

The post-Restoration era excluded all women from politics regardless of their wealth, property, power or status. In 1889, women were written out of the new Constitution (Sievers 1983: 51), and this exclusion extended to the highest level of society: although no female sovereigns had reigned for a long time, there had been no prohibition until the Meiji Constitution imposed a formal ban (Igeta 1982: 41–76), presumably to avoid the anomaly of an all-male Diet and Cabinet being responsible to a female sovereign.

In 1890, in response to agitation for democratic participation and votes for women, the last unelected Cabinet amended Article 5 of the Police Security Regulations to exclude all women from all forms of political activity. This meant that despite the adoption of a Constitution in 1889 and an elected Diet, women were excluded not only from political parties but even from sponsoring or attending political meetings; this made it illegal for them even to campaign against their political exclusion. The organisers of the new Diet, who had previously been anti-government opponents, then attempted to exclude women from observing and listening to Diet debates, though this move was successfully challenged by Yajima Kajiko's protest campaign (Sievers 1983: 52–3).

The right for women to attend political meetings was finally passed by both Houses of the Diet in 1922, but the right to join political parties and to vote was consistently blocked by the House of Peers, even though women's suffrage bills were passed by the Lower House in 1930 and 1931, the latter being proposed by no less a person than the Prime Minister (Nolte 1986: 690, 704–5, 712–13). This demonstrates the extent to which feudal interests in the Diet blocked women's participation in politics.

Shifting arguments

There were many arguments for and against votes for women, but perhaps the most interesting aspect is the way ideas about what constituted civilised practice changed over time, and the way references to the West were used on different sides of the debate. In the early days, one of the most powerful arguments for excluding women from political activity was the fact that women in the West did not have the vote. In 1874, when men from the PRM demanded an elected assembly, Tsuda Mamichi, one of the Meiji Six reformers, had argued in his article 'On Government':

> In [Europe and America's] election laws, the common practice is generally to deny this political right [to elect representatives] to women, children and incompetents as well as the ignorant, the illiterate and others who are deficient in understanding.... Of course, we shall also exclude women, children and incompetents. (Braisted 1976: 158)

Indeed, Herbert Spencer, in a letter to Kaneko Kentaro, had advised him to 'make full use of the patriarchal family system in the parliamentary organisation in Japan' (Tsurumi 1970: 107).

In 1925, however, supporters of women's suffrage argued that votes for women were part of the enlightenment heritage, and that Japan's denial of political representation to women was backward in comparison with the West and the Soviet Union. Supporters drew heavily on arguments used in the USA's suffrage campaigns which claimed that women's domesticity would introduce integrity and morality into political life, and referred to the success of women who had achieved elected posts in the USA. On the other hand, Tsuchiya Oki, an opponent of women's rights, argued that women's political activities would lead to social unrest, as in the communist revolution in Russia; while conservative supporters suggested that women's suffrage would prevent radical social change. In 1929, for example, Shimizu Tomesaburo argued that giving women the vote would prevent the unseemly riots witnessed in Britain at the instigation of the Pankhursts and the suffragettes (Nolte 1986: 707–9).

By the late 1920s, most of the opposition had accepted the principle, if not the practice, of female suffrage. In 1930 the Home Ministry established its own women's organisation to support the Prime Minister's suffrage bill, and started citizenship classes in girls' schools in the expectation that local female suffrage would become law in the near future. At this point, Takahashi Takuya criticised the House of Peers for persistently denying women the vote, called upon the heritage of the Meiji Restoration, and insisted that women in Japan ought to be given more rights than women in the USA (Nolte 1986: 708, 711–12).

The debate on women's suffrage shows how fickle the constitution of civilised behaviour was in relation to the treatment of women, since the arguments both changed over time, and were used in different ways on both sides to construct Japan's civilised status. In any case, resistance to women's political rights in the 'civilised' West made it easy to exclude women in Japan, too, without attracting accusations of uncivilised behaviour.

Thus the new womanhood in Japan constructed women as educationally literate for their role in the home, but as legal and political incompetents. This construction enabled Japan to bring its treatment of women into line with that of the western powers while simultaneously retaining men's control over women, by adopting modernised or renovated forms of patriarchal regulation based on former ruling-class practices that were acceptable to and recognised as legitimate by the West. Of course, Japanese women also had their own idea of the constitution of the new womanhood, as can be seen in their debates on the new woman (*atarashii onna*) and on the modern girl (*modan gaaru*), discussed below in Part III. But the new womanhood promoted by the state clearly helped to bring about international respectability for Japan while maintaining men's control over women, by extending to the whole population forms of regulation based on renovated traditions of the patriarchal ruling-class family.

Chapter 5

Building a New Japan:
Good Wives, Wise Mothers

The new Japanese womanhood which the state attempted to impose was, however, more complicated than the production of a unitary form of ideal femininity. The Japanese state's approach to women changed over time, and there were significant differences of opinion on what approach should be taken at any one time (see Havens 1975, Miyake 1991). The continuities were that the state's actions and attitudes towards women were determined largely by the overarching national policy of achieving economic wealth and military power, in order to attain parity with the West. Women's contribution to building the nation was consciously developed and strategically implemented. But the particular forms of that contribution were radically differentiated, and variably acknowledged and valued, according to the class position in which the women were placed. We will argue that the women's issues raised by social reformers, western critics and women activists were dealt with by the state in ways which developed the nation along class lines.

The struggle within Japan between traditionalists and reformers was concerned with the most effective way of challenging the West, not with the kind of Japan they wished to create. But different strategies for achieving nationalist goals were given pre-eminence at different times as the conditions for the struggle against national subordination altered. The reformers were in the ascendant at the start of the Restoration period, as the defeat of the old order destabilised tradition and opened up opportunities for new ways of thinking. But the traditionalists fought back – as reflected in the 1879 and 1890 Rescripts on Education, which condemned indiscriminate westernisation (Beasley 1990: 82, 96), and in the 1898 Civil Code.

Japan began to gain recognition as an equal with the West: first in 1894, with the Anglo-Japanese Treaty, then with successful wars against China and Russia, the annexation of Korea, and release from the unequal treaties in 1911. This heralded the dawn of a new era. It coincided with the reign of the new Taisho emperor from 1912 to 1926, and introduced a less defensive and more liberal period in domestic affairs known as 'Taisho democracy'. The reformers were again in the ascendant, producing responsible party cabinets accountable to the Diet rather than the emperor in 1924, and universal male suffrage in 1925 (Beasley 1990: 137). During this time Japan gained colonies in China by siding with Britain and the USA in World War I, and Japan's economic and military power progressed steadily. But, as we have seen, this buoyancy ended in the world economic crash, producing a reassertion of traditional ideas and the aggressive militarism of the 1930s and 1940s.

In the following sections, we will show how the reconstruction of the Japanese woman enabled Japan to build the state for the struggle against the western powers, simultaneously preserving class divisions and male power. Women were called upon by the state to fulfil the goals of national wealth and military strength in different ways: they were encouraged to create wealth for the country through their position as household managers, their role as carers in the family, and their duty of saving for the national debt; in terms of creating military strength, women were exhorted to produce more sons for the army, as well as to participate in patriotic activities for the military forces at the front and for the population at home.

Women's Contribution to National Wealth

The Meiji state constructed the *ie*, or family, as the building block of the national structure known as the family–state system (*kazoku kokkakan*). Women were subordinated to the patriarchal head of the household, who in turn was subordinated to the head of state in the form of the emperor. This structure, known as the emperor system (*tenno sei*), tied each family into the state, and designated the emperor as the great father of the people. It is enshrined in the Constitution of 1889, which defined the people as subjects of the emperor; in the Imperial Rescript on Education in 1890, which taught loyalty to the head of state and filial piety to the parents; and in the Civil Code of 1898, giving legal authority to the father as household head (Miyake 1991: 270).

Nolte and Hastings show how the patriarchal family was seen as a form of public institution for the maintenance of the nation-state, and women were construed as public officials of the home, through which the family–state system was put into the service of the developing nation. This is expressed in the *Meiji Greater Learning for Women* (*Meiji Onna Daigaku*) sponsored in 1887 by the Education Ministry, which stated: 'the home is a public place where private feelings should be forgotten' (Nolte and Hastings 1991: 156). The state essentially constructed women's household management as a form of public service. Indeed, Nolte and Hastings suggest that the ban on women's political activity was a result of this construction of women as the civil servants of the household, comparable to teachers, priests, police and military officials who were also excluded from political activity (Nolte and Hastings 1991: 156–7).

In the pre-industrial context before the Restoration, women of the lower classes had contributed to craft and agricultural production in the family, and this work was valued at least as much as their reproductive and nurturing roles. Women had contributed as members of a productive household unit before 'work' was separated from 'home' (Caplan 1991: 317). It was around the turn of the century that the Meiji state began to campaign on the 'good wife, wise mother' (*ryosai kenbo*) idea. As Nolte and Hastings point out, until 1910 the state was more concerned with women's responsibilities as wives than as mothers. The Education Ministry promoted the good wife, wise mother idea and encouraged women to contribute to the nation through hard work and efficient household management, the responsible upbringing of children, and care for the old and the sick (Nolte and Hastings 1991: 152, 174).

In speeches in 1887 and 1888, Mori Arinori recognised the value of female education to the state: 'We must not forget that the flourishing of women's education is crucial to the well-being of our country' (Sievers 1983: 108). Mori believed in increased power for women in the home, but the conservatives disagreed, and after 1888 they introduced single-sex schooling and sex-specific curricula which included domestic science for girls (Sievers 1983: 108).

Education and class

In 1899, secondary schools for girls were introduced; the aim was to provide at least one in each prefecture. It was made explicit that, like education for boys, the system of female education was divided along class lines. All girls should receive primary education but, as Minister of Education Kabayama Sukenori argued, secondary schooling should be given to middle-class girls, because the household was the foundation of the nation, and required women to be educated as good wives, wise mothers (Nolte and Hastings 1991: 158). This quotation from the Education Ministry shows how gender, nation and class were brought together:

> Girls marry and become wives and mothers.... Since the family is the root of the nation, it is the vocation of women who become house-wives to be good wives and wise mothers, and girls' High Schools are necessary to provide appropriate education enabling girls from middle- and upper-middle-class families to carry out this vocation. (Sievers 1983: 112)

So clearly the further education of women for family duties in the service of the nation was reserved for women of the middle class. The high schools taught middle-class girls the 'latest scientific methods' of cleaning, dressmaking, nutrition and childrearing, to give the best possible upbringing and environment to the nation's future leaders (Uno 1991: 62). The high schools were also to develop in 'women of leisure' a 'refined taste and gentle and modest character' for their 'duties within the home' (Nolte and Hastings 1991: 158).

This approach was reinforced in 1907, when the former Education Minister Baron Kikuchi declared, in a speech on female education:

> Our female education, then, is based upon the assumption that women marry, and that its object is to fit girls to become good wives and wise mothers.... The house was, and still is, ... the unit of society, not the individual ... the object ... of female education – in a word, to fit girls to be good wives and mothers, proper helpmates and worthy compan-ions of the men of the Meiji, and noble mothers to bring up future generations of Japanese. (Stephens 1991: 66)

Save to build the nation

Women were also urged to help build the nation by budgeting and economising, and to save money or buy war bonds (Miyake 1991: 275). Millions responded, and the government used the money to develop heavy industry and the military at the turn of the century, when the capital markets and private banks were too small-scale to provide sufficient finance. Individual women were singled out for praise and reward by the prefectural government. Taniguchi Kiku, for example, saved money as a schoolgirl by not going home from the dormitory and depositing her travel money in a postal savings system; she then married, and while her husband was fighting in the war with Russia in 1904–05, she managed to economise even more, and donated 10 yen to war relief (Nolte and Hastings 1991: 163, 167).

In the 1920s the government again ran campaigns directed specifically at women to encourage saving, as a means of assisting both employers and the state to accumulate finance capital. In 1923 the Campaign to Improve Livelihood (*Seikatsu Kaizen Undo*) aimed to make home management more efficient by training housewives to run their households in more economical ways. Training included techniques of effective budgeting and economic selection of consumer items, and housewives were exhorted to take decisions on household management for the good of the country, not just the benefit of the family. In 1926 the Home Ministry set up the Standing Committee on Women's Associations to Encourage Thrift (*Kinben shorei fujin dantai jonin iinkai*), recruiting the leaders of middle-class women's organisations, with the aim of studying methods of household economising, promotion of savings and reduction of imports (Nagy 1991: 214–15). The target was to repay the national debt of 150 million yen in six years, through women members committing themselves to saving a hundredth of a yen per day (Nolte 1986: 711). In this way women were encouraged to 'husband' the financial resources of the family for the benefit of the state.

Women's Contribution to Military Strength

As Japan moved from a defensive form of nationalism designed to gain acceptance by the West to an aggressive imperialism in an attempt to compete with the West economically and militarily, the contribution which women could make to building the nation and acquiring colonies for the empire also changed. Women's role as mothers now became more important than their position as wives, and women were exhorted to engage in patriotic activities to support colonial wars. In the 1920s the family was being seriously undermined by the development of capitalism and the migration of labour from the rural areas to work in the factories, and in the 1930s and 1940s this process intensified with the conscription of men for war. The absence of men meant that it was women who were targeted by the state to invigorate the family system (Miyake 1991: 270).

The meaning of good wife, wise mother, therefore, changed its emphasis from the role of household manager under the authority of the husband or father-in-law to that of reproducer of military manpower and mother of the nation. As Miyake shows, women's role as reproducers and nurturers in the preservation of the family system became as important as men's role as soldiers in fighting for the Japanese state (Miyake 1991: 271). Indeed, this approach had begun as early as the war with Russia. In 1905, a senior naval officer had told the elite pupils of the Tokyo Girls' Higher School that their studying to become good wives, wise mothers was as important to the nation as sailors fighting on the sea (Nolte and Hastings 1991: 159). In the 1930s the state proclaimed that women could contribute to military success by having many children and engaging in patriotic activities (Miyake 1991: 272). To this end, in 1937 the state provided welfare and medicine for poor lone mothers with young children under the Mother and Child Protection Law (*Boshi hogo ho*), as a response to feminist demands for maternity protection (Miyake 1991: 272–3; Molony 1993: 131).

Motherhood as national destiny

In 1941, women's youth groups operated government-supported marriage centres, known as the marriage improvement movement, 'to cause women to move from an individualistic view of marriage to a national one and to make young women recognise motherhood as the national destiny' (Havens 1975: 927), although the birth rate failed to respond to this initiative (Havens 1973: 28). The state also pursued its pro-natalist policy through the National Eugenics Law (*Kokumin yosei ho*) of 1940 and the Population Growth Policy Outline (*Jinko seisaku kakuritsu yoko*) of 1941. The former was designed to improve the quality of the population by sterilising those with hereditary diseases while banning contraception for the healthy. The latter focused on the need to increase the population for the sake of the imperial mission to create the Greater East Asian Co-Prosperity Sphere, proposing eleven policies to achieve a total of five children per family over the next ten years, and giving awards for distinguished service to those producing a large family (Miyake 1991: 272, 278–80). The slogan used was 'Reproduce, multiply' (*Umeyo, fuyaseyo*) (Yamazaki 1985: 22). Miyake argues that Japan largely resisted mobilising women for war work not only to restrict them to reproduction, and produce more children for soldiers, but also to revitalise the family–state system on which Japanese nationalism was based, and to associate ideas of fertility and productivity with the power of the state (Miyake 1991: 268).

The emphasis on the subordination of the individual to the state and the empire increased in 1941, when the war with China expanded into the Pacific War. In 1941, the *Way of the Imperial Subject* was published and used as a school textbook:

What we call private life is nothing but the practice of the way of the imperial subject who supports the heavenly throne of the Emperor.... it is not permissible to regard one's private life as subject to one's will and to be indifferent to the nation, and thereby to lead a selfish life. Not even a bowl of food nor a suit of clothes can be regarded as private possessions. Nor is there any private self who is not subject to the nation in play or in sleep. Every one of them is closely related to the nation. Serve the government, attend closely to your trade, parents nurture your children, and children follow your studies; in our nation, all these represent the duties of the people through which they serve the nation. (Stephens 1991: 59–60)

In the same year, new education regulations were introduced. The Principles of Imperial Benevolent Rule were designed to ensure that women were good wives, wise mothers, and that men were enthusiastic nationalists. Article 3 stated:

the national or civic course is aimed at clarifying the national polity, fostering the national spirit and making pupils conscious of their duties for the Empire.... The pupils must be induced to appreciate the happiness of being born in the Empire ... and to understand that the national spirit is based on the aspiration of the Empire, which is to go on developing forever.... The general situation of East Asia in particular and the world in general must be laid before the pupils in an effort to qualify them as future members of a great nation. (Stephens 1991: 67–8)

This was clearly meant to produce a subjectivity which saw Japanese national identity as a source of privilege and pleasure.

Women were also organised into state-sponsored patriotic activities such as supporting widowed families at home, and sending parcels and letters to soldiers at the front (Miyake 1991: 272). As early as the war with Russia, women in patriotic associations like the half-million-strong Patriotic Women's Society (*Aikoku fujinkai*) (Nolte 1986: 695) had cared for wounded soldiers and bereaved families, worked as nurses, made bandages, prepared comfort bags, knitted socks and sewn clothes to be sent to the front. Even earlier, in 1890, the elite Ladies' Volunteer Nursing Association of the Japan Red Cross was established to train nurses who were sent to military hospitals in the wars with China and Russia (Nolte and Hastings 1991: 162). In 1930, as Japan prepared for war with China, the local women's associations were linked into the Greater Japan Associated Women's Societies (*Dai nihon rengo fujinkai*), whose aim was to promote 'the spiritual education which prevailed in our samurai homes before the Restoration', illustrating that the women's societies were led by the former ruling class, and that it was their 'traditions' which were used as the model. In 1932, the Greater Japan National Defence Women's Organisation (*Dai nihon kokubo fujinkai*) was established (Nolte 1986: 710–11). The National Mobilisation Law (*Kokka sodoin ho*) of 1938 organised neighbourhood associations of five households, which relied on women for basic wartime activities such as food rationing and fire drills for air raids. The government appointed leading women to the committees involved in the war effort, and in 1942 all women's organisations were unified into the Greater Japan Women's Association (*Dai nihon fujinkai*) (Jayawardena 1986: 252), which had nine million members in 1943 (Miyake 1991: 272).

Organising women's patriotism

Miyake argues that the state's first recognition of women's value in helping the war effort through mothering, and the acknowledgement of a role outside the home through patriotic activities, explain why feminists such as Ichikawa Fusae and Takamure Itsue co-operated in the government's mobilisation of women for war (Miyake 1991: 273–4). Despite exceptions, such as Yosano Akiko's anti-militarist politics and anti-war poetry, which resulted in her being branded a traitor (Jayawardena 1986: 247), feminists had no systematic critique of imperialism. Rather in the way that British feminists had used the colonies to achieve their own liberation (Chaudhuri and Strobel 1992), feminists in Japan demonstrated women's abilities by organising women's patriotism (Miyake 1991: 274–5). Within the women's movement itself, the third national women's suffrage conference in 1932 had condemned the rise of 'fascism' in Japan, but in 1937 the conference changed its name to the Provisional Women's Conference and came out in support of the war. This is in stark contrast to the approach of village women in Suye, reported by Smith and Wiswell's 1935 study, where the Women's Patriotic Association was formed and promoted by men on nationalistic lines. But the village women did not take it seriously, had no say in its running, and refused to assume the leadership. The head of the Association was the male village teacher, while the women considered the 'uniforms of white aprons to be a foolish extravagance', but nevertheless bought and wore them for inspection by local government officials (Smith and Wiswell 1982: 30).

Thus the Japanese state constructed the nation through its exhortation to and regulation of women in a number of different ways. The family was created as the essential building block of the national structure, within which women, as good wives and wise mothers, became

the public officials of the home. Women were essential to the family–
state system in their role as household managers, educators of children,
and economically efficient consumers saving the family's housekeeping
money to pay off the national debt – all of which activities were crucial
to building the nation and creating national wealth. During times of
war, women were constructed as mothers of the nation and encouraged
to produce more children for the army, as well as keeping the family
going in the absence of men and engaging in voluntary patriotic activities as a form of national service. These activities were central to
establishing colonial rule in East Asia and strengthening the country's
military forces.

Chapter 6

Building a New Japan: Working Women

All the ways outlined in Chapter 5 in which women contributed to the construction of the nation and the empire were consistent with the ideal form of womanhood constructed by the state in terms of modesty and chasteness, and being centred on the home. As we shall argue below, these qualities were restricted to the middle and upper classes. There were other crucially important ways in which women contributed to the wealth and strength of the nation, which are invisible in and inconsistent with the good wife, wise mother model. For it was women, predominantly but not exclusively young unmarried women from poor rural backgrounds, who built up the textile industry and produced the profits on which Japan's industrialisation itself was based; and it was this same class of women who filled the brothels of the licensed prostitution system in the cities of Japan, and who were shipped abroad during the expansionist period to become so-called 'comfort women' for the troops fighting to make Japan a world-class power.

Going Out to Work: Factory Girls

Despite the fact that it was daughters of samurai families who first worked in the new textile mills as an encouragement to others, after the initial period being a factory girl was not an acceptable role for daughters of the middle or upper classes, 'confined' in the 'boxes' of Kishida's critique. The first cotton-spinning mill started at Kagoshima in 1868, when British engineers taught the skills to sons and daughters of samurai families (Kidd 1978: 3). From 1868 to 1872, cheap cotton thread and cloth made up 35 per cent of all imports, and were ruining indigenous industries. The government decided to promote domestic

machine-made production of cotton and silk. In 1872 the large silk mill
at Tomioka was built. In 1878 more drastic measures were adopted, and
by 1886 government efforts and subsidies had helped to create the
beginnings of a modern spinning industry. Textiles began as largely
government enterprises, then from 1882 they were sold cheaply to
private companies and received government support. Textiles accounted
for half of all private factories, and employed three-quarters of all factory
workers. Their workforces were heavily female, and formed a large
proportion of the total labour force during the first period of industrialisation (Tsurumi 1990: 23–6, 35–9). Women also worked in coal
and metal mines, and match factories (Jayawardena 1986: 236).

By 1890, women had become the backbone of the industrial
economy. Although agriculture was the greatest single employer of
female labour, women outnumbered male workers in light industry,
especially textiles, with more than one million women workers (Iwai
1993: 182). Textiles produced 40 per cent of GNP and 60 per cent of
foreign exchange in the late nineteenth and early twentieth centuries
(Nolte and Hastings 1991: 153) As late as 1935, cotton textile production was Japan's most important industry, still accounting for 27 per
cent of Japan's exports (Molony 1993: 219–20). Between 1870 and 1930,
women averaged 60 per cent of the industrial workforce, a proportion
unparalleled in any other country (Sievers 1983: 84). From 1902 to
1919, women constituted between 77 per cent and 81 per cent of the
cotton-spinning workforce, and between 93 per cent and 95 per cent
of the silk reeling workforce. In 1900 there were also 371,780 small
and medium-sized weaving firms, with 773,412 looms and 40,137 male
and 828,407 female workers. Weaving employed four times as many
women as cotton spinning and silk reeling combined (Tsurumi 1990:
10, 174).

Tears of blood

After the first decade women workers in silk and cotton plants were
from poor peasant families. As Kidd says, 'Crucial to the successful
growth of the industry was a plentiful supply of cheap labour, found
primarily amongst young, unmarried women from the countryside'
(Kidd 1978: 59–60). Their reasons for working in the factories are
evident in this workers' song:

> Because I am poor, at age twelve
> I was sold to this factory.
> When my parents told me 'Now it is time to go'

My very heart wept tears of blood....
Mother! I hate the season in the silk plant;
It's from 4 p.m. to 4 a.m....
Their letter says they're waiting for the year's end.
Are they waiting more for the money than for me?
                                        (Tsurumi 1990: 101–2)

In 1925, Hosoi Wakizo wrote the 'Pitiful History of Women Workers'
(*Joko aishi*), documenting the conditions of the factory workers, which
matched those of any other country in the early stages of capitalism
(Molony 1991: 223). In order to compete with the western textile
industry from a position of inequality, first a domestic and then an
international textile war took place, as Japan strove in the 1880s to
produce textiles at a lower price than the West. The domestic textile
war resulted in a series of strikes in 1886, the first of which was at the
Amamiya silk mill in Kofu against longer hours, lower wages and
arbitrary fines. The hours were already dawn to dusk, which meant
4.30 a.m. to 7.30 p.m. in the summer with an hour's break (Tsurumi
1990: 40, 45, 53–4). The women were bound by payments in advance
to their parents (Tanaka 1977: 23) and subject to forced saving, termed
'held-back wages' and often forfeited on various pretexts. At the same
time, loans to workers who could not make ends meet were charged
with heavy interest payments. Women were subject to sexual harassment and intimidation by the male overseers, and were physically beaten
as well as fined for minor misdemeanours. They were often confined
to the dormitories in out-of-work hours, and the food provided by the
company, but paid for by the workers themselves, was often insuffi-
cient. Loss of menstruation was a common complaint, especially for
night-shift workers, because of overwork and physical stress. Many
women ran away, for which they were severely punished if caught, and
fined by default through the held-back wages system if not, since they
were legally bound by the contracts which their fathers had agreed
with their employers. As Patricia Tsurumi says, 'Company officials freely
admitted that routinely thrashing female operatives was part of lower
management's job.' Out of 5,824 female 'leavers' in a cotton-spinning
mill in Hyogo in 1900, 4,846 were runaways (Tsurumi 1990: 118–55,
187–8).

Sickness and death

The way this use of lower-class women in highly exploitative and brutal
conditions of work was reconciled with the state's image of the Japanese woman as the good wife, wise mother was to suggest that women

who went to work in the factories were young, unmarried, and without caring responsibilities for husband, children or parents-in-law, who
would be there on a short-term basis until they got married (Tsurumi
1990: 172). The reality was very different, as demonstrated by the high
suicide rate, the sickness and mortality rates, and the proportion of
married women in the factory labour force. Although the average labour
turnover in the mills was 50 per cent, this did not mean that young
women returned to their homes and continued their lives as if nothing
had changed. No figures are available for suicides, but Sievers points
out that it was common enough for workers from Suwa silk-reeling
mills to claim that the water level of Lake Suwa had changed because
of the frequency of suicides (Sievers 1983: 65, 78). Sickness, particularly tuberculosis, also took a severe toll on workers' lives. One esti-
mate is that one-sixth of women workers died of TB while working in
the industry. The average death rate for mill workers was 19 per thousand compared with 7 per thousand for the population as a whole
(Kidd 1978: 44–5). Tsurumi quotes from Ishihara Osamu's study:

> There are many who run away home because they cannot endure the
> severe illnesses caused by their work.... those who went to the factories
> come home with tuberculosis and die.... companies go to new districts
> where recruiting has not occurred before and – hiding the facts – open
> up these districts as recruiting grounds. (Tsurumi 1990: 91)

In 1909–10, Ishihara, a doctor of medicine, studied 200,000 women
factory workers in 28 prefectures. In one year, 80,000 of these returned
home, of whom 13,000 were seriously ill. Among those who died
from their illnesses, 70 per cent died of TB and TB-related causes (Sievers
1983: 85; Tsurumi 1990: 169; Hunter 1993: 77–8). Of the 120,000 who
remained in the urban areas, some married, but most changed jobs or
became unemployed until they were forced by poverty into prostitution (Sievers 1983: 85). Hosoi said that official statistics in the 1920s
had reported that 11 per cent of licensed prostitutes were former cotton-spinning workers, but he estimated the figure as nearer to 30 per
cent (Tsurumi 1990: 145). In the 1930s, only 22 per cent of women
mill workers returned home to their farms; only a quarter of them
entered registered marriages within a year of their return. Some 40–50
per cent of women workers in industry were married, widowed or
divorced (Molony 1991: 220, 224), demonstrating that factory work
was not only for young single women without children or family
responsibilities.

Exhorting the workers

The benefits to the companies and to the nation of this exploitative work is clear both from the way Japan was able to improve its competitive position in the global market, and from the exhortations given to the workers. The company version of one of the workers' songs went:

> We don't cross the Nomugi Pass for nothing;
> We do it for ourselves and for our parents.
> Boys to the army,
> Girls to the factory.
> Reeling thread is for the country too.
> (Tsurumi 1990: 92)

And another company song linked the workers' output with the building not just of the nation but of the colonies:

> Raw silk,
> Reel, reel the thread.
> Thread is the treasure of the empire!
> More than a hundred million yen worth of exports,
> What can be better than silk thread?
> (Tsurumi 1990: 93)

Workers were lectured on how their patriotic labour would enable Japan to take its rightful place among the nations of the world. *Factory Girls' Lessons*, a book published in 1910, claims that the war with Russia left the country with a debt of over 6 yen per person, so there was an urgent need to make silk to sell: 'Many soldiers died in the Sino-Japanese war and much money was spent in order that Japan could become a first-class country. So let's work hard, make good thread, sell it abroad, and take those high foreign noses down a peg' (Tsurumi 1990: 95).

The first lesson in *The Factory Girls' Reader* of 1911 reads: 'Work with all your might for the country's sake, enabling Japan to become the greatest country in the world' (Tsurumi 1990: 94). But workers knew that the contempt to which they were subjected disguised the profits of their labour, which financed Japan's capitalist development, as their own songs made clear:

> Don't sneer at us
> Calling us 'Factory girls, factory girls'!
> Factory girls are
> Treasure chests for the company.
> (Tsurumi 1990: 97)

From the 1880s onwards, the main weapon of Japanese silk and cotton manufacturers in the international economic war was low wages, a fact acknowledged by the general manager of the leading cotton-spinning firm from 1894 to 1930. Japanese wages in the cotton industry were lower than those of other countries including India. The average monthly wages in cotton spinning in India and Japan in 1890 were as follows:

	Female wages	Male wages
India	¥2.7–4.5	¥4.5–9.0
Japan	¥2.3	¥4.8

This shows that while male workers in Japan earned towards the lower end of the range of Indian male wages, female workers in Japan earned significantly below the lowest wage of the Indian female worker. The relative cost to Japanese employers was even lower than this, because in 1890 almost 70 per cent of Indian cotton spinners were male, whereas just over 70 per cent of Japanese cotton spinners were female (Tsurumi 1990: 153, 193). Much of Japan's military equipment and heavy industrial machinery was imported with the foreign currency earned from the textile industry. As Kidd says, 'In the case of the cotton spinning mill industry, it was the workers who bore the brunt of this race [to compete with the industrialised nations] while reaping none of the reward' (Kidd 1978: 23, 62).

Thus, through the labour of women who 'went out to work' (*dekasegi*), Japan became the world's leading silk exporter in 1912 and the leading cotton manufacturer by 1914. This enabled Japan to buy the modern armaments needed for pursuing its military strategy in the colonies and beyond, and to develop the heavy industry needed to compete financially with the western powers (Sievers 1983: 56). This crucial role in building national wealth and military strength was clearly not reconcilable with the image of the Japanese woman as good wife, wise mother, yet it was a fundamental and accepted part of the experience and identity of a large section of Japanese womanhood. As an old woman interviewed in 1975 said, 'For poor people, going out to work [*dekasegi*] was the thing to do. You were happy if you thought you were able to help your family' (Tsurumi 1990: 100).

This lived experience can only be reconciled with the notion of the ideal Japanese woman as promoted by the state by acknowledging that the two models were fundamentally divided by class. The good wife, wise mother ideal was economically dependent on the family, restricted to the middle class, and used to position Japan as a 'civilised' nation. The factory girl who 'went out to work' came from the lower class, contributed to the support of the family, and created the wealth that helped to transform Japan into a major imperial power.

Going Out to Work: Prostitutes

In contrast to the modesty, chastity and fidelity of the good wife, wise mother stood the state-regulated system of licensed prostitution, in which girls and young women from poverty-stricken families were sold by their parents to become officially registered as public sexual commodities. Although prostitution existed in Japan before the Restoration, it was not institutionalised in all the castle towns because some feudal lords banned the setting up of brothels on their lands. But after 1868, when Japan came under the authority of a central government, prostitution spread to the whole country as land for licensed brothels was specifically set aside for the purpose. The majority of prostitutes were unmarried daughters of poor peasants, forced into the flesh trade because of their parents' destitution, illness or death. Women were recruited by force or deception, or openly as maids and waitresses (Tsurumi 1990: 181−2).

In 1869, the reformer Tsuda Mamichi proposed that the government ban the traffic in human beings, and this proposal was acted upon in 1872 after an internationally embarrassing incident. A Peruvian slave ship, the *Maria Luz*, carrying 232 kidnapped Chinese labourers to South America, berthed at Yokohama for repairs. Some of the Chinese managed to escape, and asked the Japanese for help. Japan agreed, returned the labourers to China and condemned the Peruvians for running a slave trade. The Peruvians defended themselves by arguing that women and girls sold into prostitution in Japan and sent abroad to Shanghai and Seattle were also part of the slave trade. The government prohibited the traffic in persons, and declared slaves and prostitutes free. However, it was still legal to enter prostitution on a voluntary basis, and the trade continued. Between 1897 and 1919, apart from a reduction in numbers to 40,000 around 1901 caused by a short-lived reform campaign which was undermined by the courts, there were between 49,000 and 52,000 women in officially licensed brothels paying tax to the government. These figures excluded unlicensed prostitutes, women in bars and cafés who worked the sex trades, and women who were shipped to overseas brothels in East and South-East Asia (known as *Karayuki-san*) and North

America (known as *Ameyuki-san*), who were often procured by kid-napping or deception (Braisted 1976: 519; Tsurumi 1990: 181–2, 186).

Daughters for sale

Many women were recruited as maids and waitresses by employment agencies, and everyone in the towns knew what this meant. According to Tsurumi, agents would put up signs saying 'People wishing to sell their daughters, please inquire within'. But in the rural areas, girls and young women were lured by agents with the promise of good food, clothing and living accommodation, and parents were told that their daughters would only have to pour drinks. In return, the agents would give the parents a loan against the young woman's future earnings. The woman was not allowed to leave the job before the end of the contract and repayment of the loan. But the loans were extremely difficult to repay because of agents' fees, and the brothel owners' charges for accommodation, food, clothing, cosmetics, bedding, furnishings, heat-ing, medical fees and interest payments on the advance loans. In this way the prostitutes were kept in debt, and many had to continue working beyond their contracted terms. Patricia Tsurumi quotes an example of a woman recruited to work in the Yoshiwara red-light dis-trict in Tokyo whose parents received a 100-yen loan, out of which 65 yen were deducted as fees and travel expenses. The Central Employment Bureau's survey in 1926 showed that more than half of 1,602 women contracted to become licensed prostitutes were staying on after the expiry of their contracts to pay off advance-loan debts (Tsurumi 1990: 182–3).

This prostitute's song tells what it was like:

> I parted from my beloved man
> For the sake of my parents
> I was sold to another province
> Whether north, south, east or west I do not know.
> I have these painful duties to perform
> But it's for my parents and it can't be helped.
> Though I don't begrudge my duty
> I may be hurt having private parts
> Examined by cold-hearted doctors
> A treasure box that I wouldn't even show my parents
> I hate to have examined.   (Tsurumi 1990: 186)

Yamada Waka was shipped to America to become a prostitute; she was later rescued, and married Yamada Kakichi. When they returned to Japan, they joined a group of intellectuals; Yamada Waka became involved in the feminist movement, and wrote for *Seito* (Yamazaki 1985: 7, 115). In 1914 she wrote:

> When I emerged from the underground, I was burning with hatred for people, especially for men. I kept wondering what I could do to get revenge on those devils who had taken advantage of a poor woman and had sucked her blood. I thought of pouring gasoline on their heads and setting them afire. Fighting those men to avenge the poor suffering women – it was a fantasy that filled me with courage. Later, whenever I met a woman who cried because she was being abused by a man, I felt like fighting for her. (Yamazaki 1985: 76)

In Japan, escape from the red-light districts was extremely difficult because the areas were enclosed by barriers, and the gate was controlled by guards who would not allow any prostitute to escape without permission from her master. And although the TWRS campaigned against licensed prostitution, their success in obtaining women's release from their contracts was limited, because the courts would not allow women to leave if they had debts. Those who did escape found it difficult to earn a living in any other way, and if they were caught they were severely punished with beatings and other tortures. A 1910 study of love suicides – people who committed suicide because they could not marry the partner they loved – showed that 99.6 per cent of the women were prostitutes. A letter from a prostitute with TB in Kyoto to the local prefecture pleaded for release:

> Recently I went to the police to get permission to leave the brothel. For some reason the police did not allow me to leave. The reason I want to leave is my poor health.... I do not have any parents or brothers. I am all alone, so my master treats me brutally. Recently one of my co-workers, Yuki, was kicked downstairs from the second floor. She died as a result of that fall. Because of this I have come to fear my master even more than before. So please, please allow me to quit the brothel. You can verify the truth about my master's cruelty by asking around. (Tsurumi 1990: 185)

The TWRS campaigned consistently against the system of state-regulated prostitution, and made clear the link between women's economic dependence on the patriarchal family and their lives in the mills and brothels (Sievers 1983: 103). As heads of household, fathers had the right to sell their daughters after 1872, although daughters were supposed to give their consent (Tsurumi 1990: 182). TWRS also recognised the link between public prostitution and the sexual requirements of trade and empire – in other words, the link with capitalism and imperialism. Women in Japan served as prostitutes for the military forces at home, and women were both sent abroad from Japan and forcibly recruited from the colonies to service Japanese troops and traders there. In 1887, TWRS sent a petition to the government to protest against overseas prostitution, which they saw as a 'national shame' (Sievers 1983: 95). But in 1896, when the distinguished statesman Ito Hirobumi was asked what he thought of the system of public prostitution, he described it as 'splendid', because it enabled filial daughters to help their poverty-stricken parents (Tsurumi 1990: 182).

'Comfort women'

The system of military prostitution in the Japanese war zones operated under the name of 'comfort stations' where the women were known as 'comfort women' (ianfu) (Ahn 1996; Howard 1995). According to Hicks, the number and size of comfort stations were linked to the strength of the Japanese military units in an area. Korea had few, even though it was the main source of recruitment of women, because it was not an active war zone. Japanese women were preferred for the officers, but Koreans, followed by Chinese and South-East Asians, were abducted for the regular troops (Hicks 1995: 22).

The women were seized in slave raids under the strengthened National Mobilisation Law. Women's patriotic organisations were deeply implicated in the military 'comfort women' system. The Women's Voluntary Service Corps (WVSC) directed women to labour in essential war industries, but some were diverted into prostitution, and the WVSC became so identified with prostitution that women who worked in the factories were reluctant to admit belonging to it. Korean 'comfort women' in Wu Tai Shan, a front-line force in Shansi province in China, reported that when units of soldiers arrived or left, they had to welcome them or see them off wearing shoulder bands of the Greater Japan Defence Women's Association. Out of 200,000 women drafted in Korea, 40 per cent were forced to become 'comfort women' (Hicks 1995: 23–6, 132, 227).

The comfort stations system was seen by the military as a way of controlling, rewarding and maintaining the morale of the Japanese forces. The Defence Studies Library documentation defines the purpose of the stations as 'regulating military discipline by devising means of relaxation and comfort'. Troops on Rabaul Island were instructed to use the comfort stations as a duty rather than a recreation, since sex was thought to stop the listlessness and mental imbalance brought on in the tropical climate, and the Air Force believed that sexual deprivation made the pilots accident-prone. In Japan itself, the owner of a silkworm workshop was told that a recreation room was needed to avoid the local women being molested by Korean labourers working on a government bunker. In fact it was used as a 'comfort station' – not by the drafted Korean labourers, but by Japanese army officers supervising the construction (Hicks 1995: 69–71, 82).

Private property; public property

Thus while chastity, modesty and a strict regime of monogamy and sexual fidelity within marriage were required of middle- and upper-class women, prostitution was a necessity for many working-class and poor rural women, as destitute farmers sold their daughters to the mill or the brothel (Tsurumi 1990: 187). The ideal image of the sexually controlled good wife and mother, protected within the family from the sexual desires of men other than her husband, was reserved for those who could afford a secluded lifestyle. The sexuality of poor women, however, was potentially public property, and was acknowledged by elite men as a resource upon which destitute families could subsist. Thus industrialisation and the empire were built not only on the manual labour of women textile workers but also on the sexual labour of the women prostitutes.

In contrast to the ideal woman constructed by the ruling class, then, the reality of life for poor peasant and working-class women during the social dislocations of industrialisation was often a direct challenge to this ideal. Women's role was strongly divided by class, as middle- and upper-class women were confined and protected in the family, while lower-class women were sent out to work by force, deception or economic necessity both before and after marriage. Working-class women created the wealth of Japan's industrial revolution through the lower wages they received in comparison with women in other countries, their greater representation in textiles, and their enforced high productivity. Before the Restoration, only women of the military and landlord class had been confined in the home, while peasant women had taken part in agricultural work and urban merchant women helped in family businesses. After the Restoration it was middle- and upper-class women from wealthy families who embodied the ideal of the good wife, wise mother, while women from the poor rural and urban areas went into employment in factories or brothels to provide for their families.

The new middle class of the Meiji period reconstructed the respectability of the middle-class woman as an important means of signifying its dominant status. This model of the respectable middle-class woman reproduced the renovated image of the former ruling-class woman and, assisted by the state, undermined the movement for the reform of women's position by tying the whole of the female population into the restrictions of the new family–state system, where previously only the ruling-class woman had been so constrained. The new middle-class woman was constructed as the good wife, wise mother as a result of the attempt by the Japanese ruling class to maintain its class dominance as well as to demonstrate its civilised status to the western powers. Thus, the new middle-class woman was created in a form of subordination which, in significant ways, matched the subordination of the middle-class woman in the West.

Gender and Global Distinction

In conclusion, Part I has shown how ideas about Japanese womanhood constructed by the state changed along with Japan's developing relationship to global imperialism. In the initial stage, when Japan was subjugated through the unequal treaties, both the western powers and the Japanese reformers saw the subordination of Japanese women as an explanation of Japan's national weakness. In challenging its inferior status, and as a means of demonstrating its equality, Japan constructed a new form of womanhood which renovated aspects of femininity of the former ruling military class that were consistent with forms of male control in the West. Then, as Japan acquired an empire of its own, specific kinds of gendered identity were used to build the nation and strengthen the empire. However, the changes to women's position were implemented by the state in ways which created new class divisions among the population, reproduced the power of the ruling elite, and drew sharp distinctions between different categories of women.

The new ideal Japanese woman, economically dependent on and sexually controlled and protected within the family, was produced as the norm, but confined to the upper and middle classes; while poor peasant and urban working-class women were forced to go out to work in the factories, or be sexually available as prostitutes, to support their families. This shows both how the middle-class woman, despite being in a minority, was made to stand for the nation, and how her protected respectability was a way of signifying social distance from and superiority to the mass of the urban and rural lower-class population. Class was a crucial means of resolving the contradictions between the demands of the political economy for women's paid productive and sexual labour in the factory and the brothel, as against the demands of the family–state system for the ideal chaste and sexually faithful wife under-taking unpaid domestic, reproductive and sexual labour in the patri-archal family. Thus, these various constructions of womanhood enabled Japan to build the state and create the empire in the struggle against the imperial powers, while simultaneously reproducing new forms of class division and preserving male power.

In Lovell's terms, the idea of education for the production of good wives and wise mothers represented the means for women to acquire the skills, knowledge and cultural capital to display and transmit culture, class and social belonging for the enlightenment of the family (Lovell 2000: 28). We would argue that it was also for the production of symbolic capital for the Japanese nation.

The education of girls, as well as the policies and campaigns di-rected at women, made it clear that the state's model of womanhood required women of all classes to take responsibility for husbanding the economic capital of the family in the interests of the state in their role as 'national housekeepers', no matter how scarce their financial re-sources might be; and to give priority to reproducing and caring for the social capital not only of the family but also of the state in terms of the patriotic activities of reproducing and caring for the military forces. But women of the middle class were clearly distinguished from the rest, and this distinction was signalled and enacted through the introduction of an exclusive kind of secondary education for middle-class girls, which provided for the accumulation of cultural capital in the form of 'scientific' domestic knowledge and skills for the manage-ment of the middle-class household, and the knowledge required for the display and transmission of taste, refinement and gentility for the future leaders of the state.

We argue that the state's investment in an educated womanhood conscious of her position in the family as the repository of economic, social and cultural capital, whether in the reformist mode of Nakamura Masanao or the conservative model of Hibino Yutaka, enabled Japan to convert these forms of capital into symbolic capital *for the nation*, thus acquiring a national 'reputation for competence, respect and honour' (Bourdieu 1984: 291) that could readily be transformed into a position of power on the global stage. This national symbolic capital, derived from the education and domestic occupations of the model Japanese woman, enabled Japan to claim the right to recognition as a civilised state, to demand acceptance as an equal with the West, and to stake a claim to a place among the elite nations. Thus we may say that as social objects, women were the repositories and transmitters of capital for the family, the class and the nation, as the state deployed the capital it had invested in women in the contest with the western powers.

This norm of Japanese womanhood, however, was clearly class-specific, for the teaching of 'advanced' domestic science was not available to lower-class women; nor were they 'sufficiently distanced from necessity' to engage in the display of taste, refinement and gentility. Other female activities also contributed directly to the economic and social capital of the nation, but did not receive recognition as currencies convertible into symbolic capital – such as female manual labour in the textile factories used in the development of Japan's industrialisation, and women's sexual labour in the sustenance of the military forces during Japan's imperialist wars. In a postwar context, Kondo has argued that the inconsistency between the middle-class domestic ideal of womanhood and the working-class necessity for women to take paid work outside the home is resolved through working-class women's construction of their employment as a means of contributing to the survival of the family and a demonstration of their commitment to it. In this way, part-time women workers 'expand the definition of women's proper place' (Kondo 1990: 285).

While this is certainly true, it must be acknowledged that these two different class-based definitions of femininity do not receive equal recognition. On the contrary, women's paid manual and sexual labour produces symbolic deficits in the form of shame, whereas women's contribution to the family as full-time wives and mothers can be converted into respectability and honour for the nation. Differential class values are crucial to understanding how some forms of capital investment by women are denied recognition and cannot be traded for positions of power, while other forms of female capital investment are imbued and constructed with sufficient value to be convertible into positions of power by the men of the family, the class or the nation. Thus, another reason why the middle-class woman constituted Japanese womanhood is that only this model could bring recognition from the West, and confer global respectability.

PART II

Women, Class and Power
before the Western Intrusions

In Part II we first set out the principles underpinning our analysis of power. We then examine the context and impact of women's loss of power in the military class, particularly in relation to their rights to land, in the centuries of 'feudalism'.

We explore how this was facilitated by changes in the form of the family, and also how this process underpinned changes in class relations.

We argue that the process of women's subordination enabled the rise and consolidation of the military class during the civil war period.

Chapter 7

The Bases of Power

In Part II we argue that during the long period of internal warfare and subsequent pacification under a military government, in the centuries preceding the Meiji Restoration, women of the dominant military class had become repositories of symbolic power for the men of that class. The reduction of ruling-class women to the status of social objects represented a gradual erosion of their former position in terms of their right to inherit the material basis of power, and a gradual devaluation of their position in the family. Bourdieu identifies two forms of struggle: over the material basis for power, which in the historical context of feudalism means land; and over the legitimacy of the material basis for power, meaning the recognition of the right to own the land (Wacquant 1993: 25).

We will examine the decline of women's power in the military class, and show first that the material basis for women's deteriorating position and dependence on men rested on men's increasing appropriation of women's landholding rights through changing practices of family inheritance; and second, that after the civil war, when the idea of women as inferior in military skills no longer provided the justification, the legitimation of men's appropriation of women's land rested on the construction of women as mentally and morally inferior to men.

The major struggle over the material basis for military and political power took place between men in the civil war period, as the great landowners fought for supremacy over the land. In this sense – and in accord with Bourdieu (1990b) – the subjects of the social space were men of the military class struggling for dominance in the battlefield. But by the time of full-scale war, women had already been largely dispossessed of their right to inherit land – not through military means, nor by formal changes in the legal codes, but through the practices of their male relatives. Increasingly, men with landholdings began to bequeath less and less to daughters and widows, and more and more to sons, especially sole male heirs. We will show that the decline in women's power occurred at the top of the social hierarchy, where women were increasingly controlled by men within the family, and that the reason for this was crucially connected to the development of the class structure. The appropriation of women's right to land represented an important step in the accumulation of family property by men, and formed one of the material bases for the development and dominance of the military class.

Although it is clear that women of the military class lost power in relation to men during the feudal period, we will argue – with Lovell (2000) and against Bourdieu (1990b) – that women were not reduced to the status of mere social objects. The process of change in gendered power relations should also be seen as a process of struggle, in which women did not uniformly become subordinated to men, but took up positions as social subjects within conditions of constraint, which themselves varied in different circumstances, periods of time and geographical areas. We will argue that the contradictions in the theory of men's relationship to women in the military class, the discrepancies between theory and practice, and the continuity of more egalitarian gender relations in other social classes, demonstrate that women sustained a position as social subjects despite restrictions which attempted to reduce them to the status of social objects.

To examine these arguments on the developing relationship between gender and class hierarchies, we will first consider the arguments of two authors who adopt different perspectives on the importance of the feudal period for women's position, and then put forward our own argument on the connection between gender, class and power before Japan's entry into global politics, through an examination of the rise of the military class and the impact of the civil war.

Chapter 8

Women and Class

Gender, Class and Feudalism

Joyce Ackroyd was one of the first western writers on Japan to recognise the relationship between women's position and the class structure. Her article 'Women in Feudal Japan' (Ackroyd 1959) is considered a germinal work, and is consistently referred to by western authors in debates about gender relations during the centuries of military dominance in Japan (see, for example, Pharr 1977: 224; Robins-Mowry 1983: 23; Uno 1991: 19). Before outlining our own argument, we focus our critique on this article, and on a paper by Nagahara, a Japanese author who takes an alternative position (Nagahara 1982). Ackroyd's thesis is that the deterioration of women's position corresponds directly with the development of feudalism: 'not only did women's plight grow worse as the feudal age progressed, but in every period an exact correspondence may be perceived between the level to which women had sunk and the point of development feudal institutions had reached' (Ackroyd 1959: 67).

The influence of Chinese culture

The nature of the theoretical connection between gender and feudalism is not always easy to identify in Ackroyd's work, although she puts forward several factors to help us understand it. One of these refers to Confucianism and the influence of Chinese culture and social structure. Ackroyd argues that the Taiho legal code (see Chapter 9 below) used by the military class in the twelfth and thirteenth centuries was based on Chinese models, including the 'Confucian idea of the necessary subjection of women' (Ackroyd 1959: 31–2), although she does not explain why or for what purpose women's subjection was 'necessary' other than the part it played in the maintenance of the social order. The Joei code (see Chapter 9) introduced later by the Minamoto military class preserved some of women's rights under traditional Japanese practices but also contained 'arbitrary treatment of women', explained by the fact that as the military class strove to increase its control over the country, it drew on the Confucian theory of subordination which formed the basis of Chinese feudalism – that is, the hierarchies be- tween lord and retainer, parent and child, and husband and wife (Ackroyd 1959: 34).

While it is true that Confucianist ideas from the mainland about a social order based on gender, age and class were influential among the Japanese ruling classes, it must be pointed out that the Japanese took what they wanted from these foreign ideas, and incorporated them into their own very different social conditions. For example, although in China the bureaucracy was dominant, in Japan from the twelfth century onwards the military was the dominant class, and the Japanese never adopted foot-binding, perhaps because of the social requirement for military-class women to train in military skills. Nor was it the case – despite China's power at the time – that Japan was subordinated to China in a colonial relationship, and was therefore compelled to adopt aspects of Chinese culture and social structure. On the contrary, although the influence of Chinese civilisation was great, this influence was both selectively incorporated and underwent a process of indigenisation by the ruling aristocrats during Japan's own period of classical civilisation from the ninth to the eleventh century. Thus the attribution of the development of a gender hierarchy in Japan to Chinese influence in- forms us of a possible historical origin for such ideas, but does not explain its social significance in the context of Japan.

The effect of feudalism

Ackroyd also explains gender hierarchy as a by-product of the feudal hierarchy. Ackroyd identifies three forms of control over a woman which marked her deteriorating position: 'her reduction to economic depend- ence, her subordination in the feudal hierarchy, and her submergence in the husband's family' (Ackroyd 1959: 48). The first of these three indices of their subordination refers to the erosion of women's eco- nomic independence through their exclusion from inheritance, par- ticularly the ownership of land, on the grounds that women could pass land on to other families by bequeathing it to their children:

Obviously the important thing for a clan which depended on its material strength for survival was to keep its holdings intact. As women could will their property to their children, however, much land changed hands through marriage and therefore ... the principle of restricting women's inheritances to life interests only was finally established. (Ackroyd 1959: 44)

The loss of land to other families through women, however, is a problem only in the patrilocal form of family, where women move out of their natal family and bring their children up as part of the husband's family. In the matrilocal form, it is through men that land may be lost to other families, since the children of such men are brought up as part of the mother's family; therefore land bequeathed by fathers to children is transferred to the mother's family. In families where inheritance occurred through both lines, both men and women could 'lose' land to the 'other' side of the family. As Ryang points out, a 'hybridised matrimonial system' operated in the form of a dual system of 'matrilineage in the local clan system and patrilineage in central genealogy', together with a combination of matrilocal and patrilocal residence patterns (Ryang 1998: 20). Why is the potential loss of family property through men in the matrilocal family not posed as a problem?

Ackroyd's second index of control over women is their subordination in the feudal hierarchy through the social order based on gender, age and class:

The strengthening of the feudal bond strengthened the power of the head of the household, for in order to perform his all-important feudal obligations satisfactorily, he in his turn had to exact complete obedience from all the members of his household. Women, already entirely dependent on the head of the household economically, now more than ever came at one remove under a stringent feudal authority which showed an increasing tendency to interfere in the internal affairs of the households coming within its scope. (Ackroyd 1959: 46–7)

But women were not 'already entirely dependent' until after their right to economic support in the natal family had been removed, and their right to family land had been largely abolished. Ackroyd's account suggests that the erosion of women's power happened by default, an unfortunate but fortuitous effect of the feudal system which had to place the entire population under a hierarchical system of control in order to preserve the social order.

Ackroyd's third index of control is women's submergence in the husband's family as a result of changes from a matrilocal to a patrilocal form of family organisation:

> the transition of the military classes from *muko-iri-kon* [taking a husband or matrilocal marriage] to the most advanced form of *yome-iri-kon* [taking a wife or patrilocal marriage] would be earlier than in other sections of society ... because the latter form of marriage was more suited to the maintenance of the military strength of a clan having the father as its focal point and relying on the support of his sons. (Ackroyd 1959: 48)

Here Ackroyd recognises the importance of the change in family residence patterns to the erosion of women's power, but suggests that this is essentially a rational military strategy based on the logic of collective male muscle power. However, collective male muscle power on behalf of the family or the clan could as easily be focused around the mother's brother relying on the support of his nephews in the matrilocal family. We would argue that the significance of the change in family form has as much to do with men's appropriation of women's share of natal family lands as it does with the organisation of male muscle power on behalf of the group. It was only by removing women from their natal families and appropriating their land for male relatives that women were reduced to being 'entirely dependent' and their power was actively, if gradually, taken from them.

In examining the changes in the fourteenth century, Ackroyd claims that whilst the idea of both male and female power coexisted, women's rights were undermined by the 'unstable peace' and the lack of strong central authority to protect women's right to property; and that the reason the patriarchal[1] family was adopted by the military class was that property rights could be upheld only by 'physical strength and military force', which women were unable to carry through (Ackroyd 1959: 43). But again, this fails to explain why the men in a matrilocal family could not equally well organise to defend their property. Ackroyd uses this development to argue that women's subordination was increased – partly because the head of the household's economic control was strengthened not just over the women but over all the family, and partly because feudalism increased its control over society as a whole through the obedience of retainers to feudal lord, children to parents,

---

1. We use the term 'patriarchy' only to refer to the particular family system in which the oldest male has authority over women and younger men, property is inherited from father to son, and sons and daughters-in-law reside in the father's house.

and wives to husbands (Ackroyd 1959: 46–7). Such arguments imply that the radical change in women's position in society, in both family form and land inheritance, is merely an incidental effect of more general increases in control over the population as a whole, and provides no explanation of why men had to own property or women had to be subordinated to men.

Women's Disinheritance

Nagahara takes a very different view of the trajectory of female power during this period (Nagahara 1982). He challenges the view that the fourteenth century was a watershed in women's history – as held by, for example, Fujiki on the changes in punishment for female adultery from confiscation of property to the death penalty, and Amino on the loss of freedom of both men and women as a result of the rise of feudal power (cited in Nagahara 1982). Nagahara disagrees with this view on the grounds that before the fourteenth century, although there were regional differences, the main form of agricultural management was landownership by a large patriarchal clan, which also restricted women's freedom; whereas from the fourteenth century onwards, greater opportunities for women arose both from small-scale farming and from the growth of trade. Economic development and improvements to cultivation enabled small tenant farmers from the headman's class to become small-scale agricultural producers. The dependence of small-scale family farming on women's labour opened up opportunities for them in agricultural family work. Women also laboured in a range of manufacturing processes, although the manufacturers themselves were usually male. There were also opportunities for trade in manufactured goods. Paintings of the period show women selling a wide variety of products. Thus, while he recognises that patriarchal gender relations began to spread at this time, Nagahara argues that agricultural and economic growth, the development of the market and the circulation of currency in the fourteenth century opened up more opportunities for women (Nagahara 1982: 161–71).

Nagahara further argues that although there was a change in the form of land inheritance among the military class from inheritance by all the children to inheritance by one son, the main purpose of this was not to exclude women from inheritance, nor to reduce their status in society, but to abolish the practice of divided inheritance. As the existing system of land rights dissolved, the military class of local landowners had to defend their own estates from aggression by force of arms. In this women were inferior, and in addition there was the danger of lands inherited by women passing into another family through marriage. The change to one-son inheritance occurred only in order to protect and strengthen the system of landownership. Some land could be owned and inherited by women, even after the fourteenth century. These lands were important for providing produce but inferior in status and not fundamental to the maintenance of the landholder's power (Nagahara 1982: 152).

Class and gender

Nagahara's contribution to this debate is extremely important, because he shows that the position of women from the fourteenth century is not as consistently and exclusively negative as Ackroyd's account suggests. There are, however, several problems with Nagahara's argument, for he conflates the classes and again represents the deterioration of women's power as a by-product of other social forces rather than as a central constituent in the hierarchical organisation of society, the development of classes, and the accumulation of property.

First, although it is true that opportunities for women in farm labour and trade opened up, opportunities for them to work in manufacturing and selling were confined to the lower classes, and the fact that women were needed to perform family labour in the fields for the new small-scale family farming enterprises does not automatically mean that they were any more or less free within the family than before. Nagahara fails to recognise the significance of the differences between women of the landowning military class, who had rights to land as proprietors, managers or patrons, and those of the lower classes, who either had no rights to land or whose rights were confined to those of cultivators.

Second, it is not the case that the main point of the change to one-son inheritance was the abolition of divided inheritance rather than the abolition of women's inheritance, since if this were so the inheritance could equally have been passed to one daughter. But the sole-heir principle was gendered, and the property was passed not to any child depending on who was most capable, but to a male child. Nagahara's argument portrays the erosion of women's property rights as an incidental by-product of the need to accumulate land in the military class, rather than as a crucially significant step in the development of the class system based on landownership.

Third, the reasons given by Nagahara and others for the selection of male inheritors are that women were inferior in military ability, and that there was a danger that women's inherited lands would be passed on to a different family through marriage. The explanation that women's rights to land were eroded because of the danger of losing the property to other families either through marriage or through military action is important, but fails to give adequate recognition to the key role of gender relations in either civilian or military struggles for power. This also, as in Ackroyd (1959), conceptualises the decline of female power as an unfortunate but incidental effect of the organisation of the family and the increase in military conflict. Rather than military action, civil war and the feudal system being a cause of women's disinheritance, however, we suggest that women's disinheritance made an important contribution to the rise of the military class, the accumulation of an economic power base from which to prosecute civil war, and the development of the feudal system. Far from being an incidental result, the erosion of women's power constituted not a cause, but a contributory condition for the rise of military class power.

Subordination as a precondition

While we acknowledge the valuable contribution of both Ackroyd and Nagahara to this debate, we will argue that the significance of the change in women's position lies in the fact that women's subordination to men in the military class was a crucial precondition *before* the class system based on the ownership of land could become firmly established; that two of the forms of control over women identified by Ackroyd – submergence in the husband's family and economic dependence – were central prerequisites, not an incidental consequence of feudal class relations. They formed the material basis for the third form of control: women's subordination in the feudal hierarchy. We suggest that these developments in gender relations were vital before the military landholders could consolidate their estates, thereby making way for the civil war period, when the great barons rose up and fought to expand their landholdings. Thus the class system based upon landownership was built upon the gender division. We therefore suggest that women's subordination was not a by-product or an effect, incidental or otherwise, of class relations, but a crucial building block; that military force provides the mechanism, but not the explanation, for women's subordination; and that the development of the patriarchal family facilitated the disinheritance of women from their birthright in the natal family.

Nevertheless, the erosion of women's inheritance is to be characterised not as a uniform or unilinear process, representing a consistent decline of women's power, but as a struggle between the ideas of male and female power in which the notion of male power became ascendant in the dominant class precisely because the erosion of female power contributed to the rise of that class. The complexity of the process through which women's right to property and female power were eroded in the military class can be seen in the fact that the idea of female power retained its strength in other classes and in different regions, in the gap between the theory and the practice of women's subordination in the ruling class, and in the contradictions within the theory itself. To look at these questions, we will examine the period leading up to the fourteenth century, the significance of the changes which occurred in that century, and the reorganisation of classes which followed.

Chapter 9

The Rise of the Military Class

The Struggle for Power

The aristocrats' attempts to centralise power in the eighth century were partially successful in that they facilitated the rise of a classical age between the ninth and eleventh centuries (the Heian era), during which the leisured literary class at the imperial court produced a specifically Japanese culture and civilisation. The struggle between the two ideas of male and female power can clearly be seen in the contradictions within the aristocracy, which was the dominant class in this period. This is represented on the one hand by the exclusion of women from political power and from education in the Chinese classics, their seclusion from men, subjection to Confucian ideas, and the inequalities of the new codes. On the other hand, there is the economic independence of propertied women, their relative freedom of sexual expression (see, for example, the tenth-century novel *Ochikubo Monogatari*), the lack of any form of patrilocal family structure, continued female influence at court, and the ability of talented aristocratic women to create a specifically native Japanese literature (exemplified by the genius of Lady Murasaki's *Tale of Genji* and Sei Shonagon's *Pillow Book*) (Sansom 1978a: 179, 193).

Amongst the peasants, too, although women's formal status declined during this period because, for tax purposes, the head of the household had to be male, women still had property rights in land and housing and were entitled to inherit land, fields, property and positions (Nishimura 1982: 207–47). Peasant women also worked independently in a range of productive activities. Sometimes they held privileged jobs independently of their husbands, such as performing services at the shrine while the husband worked as a carpenter or other artisan. Women were also members of the artisan and merchant guilds on the same basis as men, and sometimes became leaders of the guild (Kuroda 1993: 62–5).

During this time the dominant Fujiwara family consolidated more and more power over the imperial family at the centre, based on its own tax-free estates and its intermarriage with the ruling family. But the attempt to centralise the state was challenged by the regional land-owners, especially the autonomous clans in the east and west, who increased their landholdings until their power was sufficient to chal-lenge the centre. Buddhist priests also began to defend and expand their tax-free lands by force, forming temple armies which raided even the lands and property of the Fujiwara and the emperor. The resulting struggles produced a new military class by the early twelfth century, and Japan was ravaged by civil war, famine and disease as the great families of the Taira and the Minamoto struggled for power with each other and the Fujiwara. Military supremacy was eventually achieved in 1185 by Minamoto Yoritomo, who established a system of military government (*bakufu*) which was sustained for 700 years, though not without considerable conflict (Sansom 1962: 263–70).

The Taiho and Joei codes

Two opposing trends affecting women's position are evident in this period, in the different legal systems for the aristocracy and the military class. Aristocratic law as represented by the Taiho code prescribed joint possession of property for husband and wife, while the new Joei Shikimoku ethical code, adopted in 1232 to regulate the military class, allowed individual possession of property by husband and wife.

The Joei code was the house law of the Minamoto family, and gradu-ally replaced the Taiho code to become the common law of Japan as the military class increased its power. Under the Joei code, the main heir – usually, but not always, the eldest son – inherited the largest portion of the property. Although the other sons and daughters inherited less, sons and daughters had equal rights of inheritance under article 18, reversing the unequal rights in the Taiho code. In addition, article 26 granted equal rights to bequeath and dispose of property, and power to control the peasants attached to the land, and to revoke wills even after they had been approved by the shogunate. The widow had the right to divide up the husband's property and keep part of it herself unless she was considered inferior in martial arts skills, in which case her inheritance would be for her lifetime only. The same stipulation applied to children who were not the chief heir. Under this system, all the successors lived on inherited lands, and were strongly united to form a military force capable of defending the estate's lands (Gomi 1982: 29–59). Single women and widows had the right to adopt sons to inherit their property, although this was not allowed for the aristocracy under the Taiho code (Ackroyd 1959: 38). The transfer of property from husband to wife was recognised in article 21 (Gomi 1982: 29–59). Women inherited estates and the peasants attached to them, bequeathed lands and stewardships to their daughters, performed manorial duties and obligations, managed their own estates through proxies and successfully took lawsuits over land. Husbands left their estates to their widows or left the division of property to them, and some women revoked their husband's wills. Even when a widow was not the heir, she often took over the headship of the household (Ackroyd 1959: 39–41).

The three obediences

The countervailing trend favouring the subordination of women, however, is clear from the Joei's basis in the Confucian theory of social hierarchy, which is a set of moral values and precepts justifying a social order based on class, age and gender: 'if retainers are only loyal to their lords, children filial to their parents, wives obedient to their husbands … the tranquility of society will be assured.' The doctrine of the three obediences (*sanju kun*) appeared at this time in the *Gempei sei suiki*, the great war romance documenting the rise and fall of the Minamoto and Taira families. These strictures came originally from the Chinese writer Lieh Tzu: 'A woman has no way of independence through life. When she is young she obeys her father, when she is married she obeys her husband, when she is widowed she obeys her son' (Robins-Mowry 1983: 20). In contradiction to the last injunction, however, article 18 of the Joei code prescribed filial conduct to mothers as well as to fathers (Ackroyd 1959: 41).

The Buddhist morality tales also adopted an inconsistent approach by promoting the subordination of women while simultaneously overlooking adultery among wives (Ackroyd 1959: 33). Article 24 of the Joei code stated that widow remarriage is really immoral, but that if a widow does remarry, any property inherited from her husband must be returned to his descendants (Ackroyd 1959: 34). Women had certain rights of divorce in the Joei code (Robins-Mowry 1983: 27), but men could divorce their wives at will, and it was usually men who initiated divorce (particularly in the aristocracy, whose members used marriage, divorce and remarriage to further their careers). Women protected themselves by demanding an oath at marriage that they could not be divorced, together with economic compensation for breaking the oath (Ackroyd 1959: 34–7). Article 21 of the Joei code said that a guilty wife would lose property given to her by her husband, but a wife who was the injured party could keep it. Nevertheless, some judges gave property to women who were the guilty party (Ackroyd 1959: 37), revealing the gap between theory and practice.

Women were important in the military class in this period, and did not hesitate to use their power, despite the obstacles they encountered. Hojo Masako is the most famous among them, but not an exceptional example. She was a member of the defeated Taira family, but eloped to marry Minamoto Yoritomo. After Yoritomo's death at the end of the twelfth century she became a nun, and her father became regent, but she later forced her father to resign and exercised power over the new puppet regent herself, becoming known as the 'nun shogun' (Sansom 1962: 304).

Nanbokucho

The Minamoto victory, however, was unstable, and led to the localised fourteenth-century civil war known as nanbokucho. The name given to the period refers to the dispute over sovereignty between two lines of the imperial family, the 'northern' and 'southern' courts, but its significance relates not to the issue of imperial legitimacy but to the struggle for dominance between two military groupings (Sansom 1978b: 59). The significance of this period for an analysis of gender relations is that major changes occurred in land inheritance which profoundly affected the position of women in the military class.

We will argue that these changes, which substantially reduced women's power, were vital to produce the conditions in which the baronies could extend their landholdings, and which in turn brought about the radical reorganisation of the classes in the succeeding two centuries of full-scale civil war. Therefore the development of a social hierarchy based on the ownership of land was centrally dependent on the subordination of women. Although there were various forms of resistance to these changes, including peasant revolts, rice riots, the emergence of subversive religious sects and a rise in democratic feelings, none of these was strong enough to resist the military force of the great landholding barons fighting for supremacy. The fifteenth and sixteenth centuries were characterised by the failure of central authority, civil war, changing alliances and the expansion of the great baronies, until Tokugawa Ieyasu succeeded in pacifying the country at the beginning of the seventeenth century.

In order to examine the change in the material basis for women's power, we will first look at evidence on the historical changes in family forms, then discuss details of the changes in land inheritance in one particularly important area of Japan, published in 1929 by Asakawa Kanichi.

Family Forms

Takamure Itsue (1966) wrote the four-volume *History of Women* as well as *A Study of Maternal Lineage* and *A Study of Visiting Marriage*, in which she documented what she believed to be the transformation of Japan from a matriarchal to a patriarchal society. Takamure came to this work because of her own experience of growing up in a remote village on the southern island of Kyushu, where many of the customs of everyday life were at odds with the policy promoted by the national government. These customs included the position of the eldest daughter as guardian to her younger brothers and sisters and protector of the family, and the separate communities of young men and young women who shared work and leisure, and looked to their peers rather than their parents for permission to marry (Chabot 1985: 287). Takamure suggested that a change of great significance occurred in the military class which moved the organisation of the family from a 'matriarchal' to a 'patriarchal' structure. More recently, Sekiguchi Hiroko and Yoshie Akiko have challenged this view, arguing that before feudalism the family was 'neither a patriarchal family nor a matrilineal system', and that 'descent was either bilineal or bilateral' (Hayakawa 1991: 174). In any case, we will argue that the establishment of a patriarchal family form in the military class, to replace a matrilineal, bilineal or bilateral structure, was connected to the rise of the class and changes in land inheritance.

In *A Study of Visiting Marriage*, Takamure examined the available historical sources, and found evidence that matrilineal and matrilocal marriage existed in the Jomon (ending around 250 BC) and Yayoi (250 BC to 300 AD) periods, that men, women and children lived in their maternal families, and children were raised by the mother's family. In a manner reminiscent of the Nayars of Kerala in India (Ryang 1998: 26), men visited their female partners only in the evening, and either partner could break the relationship by ceasing to visit or receive the other. Property was held in common, and men, women and children were dependent on the maternal family for support. Takamure argued that this was the case up to the tenth century, and that later, property was inherited from mothers to daughters, with sons inheriting only for their lifetime, any property returning to the maternal family at death. Although patrilineal descent in terms of family name was introduced in the fifth and sixth centuries, people still lived with their mother's family. In the seventh and eighth centuries, men began to move in with their wives in the woman's family rather than visiting, and during the 11th century, men and women of the highest class began to live with their children in a separate house given by the woman's family, while the economic responsibility remained with the maternal family. From the ninth century, marriage was called *muko-tori-shiki* or 'taking a bride-groom into the wife's family'. On divorce, a husband would simply leave the house (Chabot 1985: 289; Tsurumi 1977: 3; Ackroyd 1959: 35–6).

Changes in the military-class family

Over a period of time, a change of great significance occurred in the organisation of the military-class family, in that the man's family instead of the woman's began to provide the house for a husband and wife, and later the man and woman began to live with the husband's family after they had children. Subsequently, the wife began to live with the husband's family from the start of marriage; this happened only in the military class (Chabot 1985: 289). At this point, the form of marriage in the military class whereby the wife was taken into the husband's family became known as *yome-tori-shiki* or 'taking a bride into the bridegroom's family' (Tsurumi 1977: 3). Takamure claimed that these changes occurred in the fourteenth century, but more recent authors place the development of the patriarchal form of family structure in the military class in the eleventh century (Hayakawa 1991: 174).

In the lower classes and the rural areas, changes in the marriage patterns did not occur on the same scale or at the same pace. Takamure argued that patriarchal marriage forms were restricted to the military class right up to the nineteenth century, and in some cases, especially in remote areas and in propertyless families, the patriarchal family form had not arrived even in the twentieth century. It was only in the modernisation period after 1868 that the patriarchal form of marriage practised in the dominant military class became specified in law as the sole legitimate form of marriage for the entire society (Chabot 1985: 289).

Takamure shows that matrilineal, matrilocal marriage and *ane-katoku*, or 'inheritance of family property by the eldest daughter', were still widespread in rural communities, especially in north-east Japan, right up to the start of the modernisation period (Tsurumi 1977: 3). Up to this time the marriage customs of the peasants, who constituted 80 per cent of the population, were based on free choice. In the villages young men and women joined the young men's group (wakamono-gumi) and the young women's group (musume-gumi) and met in their yado or 'group house', usually in the home of some trusted adults (Tsurumi 1975: 231). Young men visited the young women's yado as a group in the evening to talk and sing, while the men made ropes or sandals and the women wove or sewed kimono. As they got to know one another, relationships would develop and matches considered suitable by the peer group were recommended to the couple's parents by the young men's group, which pressurised the parents if they resisted by, for example, refusing to help them with jobs needing collective labour. People were expected to marry for love, and the approval of the peer group was more important than that of the parents. Only in the military class, which constituted less than 10 per cent of the population, was the method of arranged marriage (miai) used, and it was not until the modernisation period that the 1898 Civil Code made arranged marriage the only legal form, requiring parental approval for men under 30 and women under 25 (Tsurumi 1977: 3).

We again conclude that in terms of the struggle for land among the military class, the removal of women from their source of economic support in the natal family, and their absorption into and increasing physical control within the marital family, facilitated the subsequent appropriation and accumulation of women's land by men.

Land Inheritance

When Minamoto established the first military administration, the nature of landholding consisted not of direct private ownership but of a diverse set of rights in the land. Each piece of land had numerous rights (shiki) attached, starting with the cultivator's rights to live on and work the land and consume the residue of the produce after tax, and sometimes rights to water, wood, fish and game; then rights to a percentage of the produce might be held by the manager, the proprietor (for administration and defence) and the patron to whom the land was commended for the purpose of tax exemption. These shiki could be divided and transferred, and ownership changed without disturbing the productivity of the land or the tenure of the cultivators. The shiki could be split up among the children; both sons and daughters could inherit them, and they could be passed on to the spouse's family. In an attempt to exercise control over his land rights, Minamoto Yoritomo introduced constables and stewards as provincial military governors. The stewards' rights were specific and local, and they became the lesser local gentry. The constables' rights were more general, and they became the great landholding barons. Stewards' rights could also be inherited by women, who therefore played a part in local government and joined the lesser local gentry in their own right (Sansom 1962: 278–85).

During the fourteenth century, the shiki system, with its diverse sets of rights in land, began to disintegrate and became transformed into a more direct form of ownership. There were still scattered and intermingled landholdings and split shiki, but several changes occurred. First, the focus moved from the shiki rights in land to the actual land itself. Second, the house and land as a unit became more important, and arable land gravitated towards it and became attached to the unit. Third, different shiki land rights belonging to the same place became united into one holding. Fourth, contiguous tracts of land became preferable to scattered and intermingled ones. Fifth, inheritance began to be by male primogeniture (Asakawa 1929: 42–3).

The control of land

The struggles for power within and between the centre and the regions were based on the control of land, since land was the basis of wealth. The fourteenth century was critical in creating the conditions necessary for the radical realignment of social forces and the subsequent consolidation of landed property in the hands of a relatively small number of landowners, which happened in the civil wars of the fifteenth and sixteenth centuries. There were several obstacles to this consolidation before the fourteenth century, including the diverse sets of rights to the produce of the land, the division of rights in the land between a landowner's children, and the tendency for land to pass to another family through marriage. Each of these customary forms of inheritance prevented large-scale concentration of landholding in a single person, and was dealt with by, first, changing the diverse rights of shiki into a form of direct ownership; second, moving from division of the shiki to the nomination of a sole heir; and third, excluding women from inheritance and introducing a system of male primogeniture. As Asakawa writes: 'The common custom of dividing one's estate among children had weakened more than one historic family among the great vassals' (Asakawa 1929: 18). But with the introduction of the patriarchal family, it was not children in general who caused the problem of fragmented landholding:

The complexity of the situation tended continually to increase through the prevailing custom of dividing and devising one's shiki among his children.... Add to this condition another historic custom in Japan, namely, of the woman inheriting shiki ... and, after marriage, transmitting them to her children. The result was an ever changing division and combination, multiplying causes for complication and friction. As the families steadily ramified, and their shiki were correspondingly split, the tendency toward division naturally prevailed greatly over that toward combination. It was not until later ages that the impact of a continual civil war gradually tended to produce in Japan the *universalis successor* of the feudal warrior. (Asakawa 1929: 21–2)

By extracting details of bequests from Asakawa's source-book of wills, we can see what happened in one region of western Japan during the fourteenth-century civil war, when the manor of Shimadzu was destroyed as an integral domain, and the land which had been controlled by a steward under a civilian noble became transformed into the autonomous property of a military baron, notionally entrusted to him by the shogun (Asakawa 1929: 11):

from the custom of dividing domains and shiki among children ... were gradually evolved elements of primogeniture, and out of the parcelled rights and interests of land slowly arose a trend toward a unitary control by a baron built upon a hierarchical organisation of vassalage and infeudation. (Asakawa 1929: 28)

The manor of Shimadzu

Using the example of the manor of Shimadzu, we can see the trends through the documents and wills of one important landed family. First, there were changes in the way the land was divided between the children and the proportions that were given to the chief heir. In 1245, Shibuya Jo-Shin willed his lands to be shared between his four sons and three daughters, the chief heir receiving about half (Asakawa 1929: 122–4, 143). In 1322, Okamoto Shidzushige's will shows a transitional arrangement whereby the estate was divided equally among the children of both sexes – sons Shigetomo and Shigebumi, and the daughter, Otodo-me – but new land was passed down to the two sons with the eldest son receiving two-thirds (Asakawa 1929: 208). In 1349, Shibuya Shigekatsu divided the vast majority of his land between his sons, but insisted that the estates they inherited should subsequently be inherited by one successor only, and that the shares of the others should be for life only (Asakawa 1929: 252–4). By 1371, Shibuya Shigekado writes in his will:

though there are several brothers ... all the domains without a single exception shall be devised to the [heir-general] alone. If there be any who, contrary to this sense, divided the domains among his sons, he should not be regarded as Shigekado's descendant. Since it is ruled thus, if perchance the domains were devised [willed] in parts, the heir-general should, in accordance with the tenor of this letter, seize and hold them in sole control. (Asakawa 1929: 272)

Second, the privilege of land inheritance was increasingly given to sons and grandsons, and withheld from daughters and granddaughters. In 1253, Shibuya Jo-Shin willed to his three daughters lands which were in the domain of one of his sons. This son was instructed to apportion military duty (undertaken by proxies) between the daughters according to their capacity (Asakawa 1929: 143). In 1277, Terao Shigetsune left lands to his granddaughter Taketsuru for all time (that is, not for her lifetime only, which means that she could bequeath them to whomsoever she wanted rather than having to give them back to the paternal side of the family) (Asakawa 1929: 158–9). In 1344, Taki Shigemune left considerable areas of land in different places to his daughter So-Nyo, much of which was inherited for all time (Asakawa 1929: 244). By 1349, Shibuya Shigekatsu laid down that his daughters should have only one portion of one cho (hectare) for life only, and that his sons' daughters should inherit the same amount (Asakawa 1929: 254). In 1371, Shibuya Shigekado willed some token lands to his daughters, but only for life (Asakawa 1929: 273).

As for widows, their inheritance was reduced from the provision of an independent livelihood to dependence on a son or another male partner. In 1277, Terao Shigetsune willed domains and rice-lands to his widow for life. In 1329, Shibuya Koreshige left his widow lands and houses, giving her the same amount as two younger sons (Asakawa 1929: 157, 223). But in 1367, restrictions were placed on a widow's inheritance if she remarried: Shibuya Shigekado, writing about the inheritance of his vassals, says:

As regards one who dies in battle, if he leaves a son, [lands] will be assigned to him in addition to his original holding, when it is practicable to do so. If the child be a daughter, she certainly shall hold for life one half of the original holding. The widow shall be treated in the same manner as a daughter. However, if she otherwise has a male companion, [she] shall not have a holding. (Asakawa 1929: 269–70)

By 1371, Shibuya Shigekado gave no land to his own widow, but instructed that she be cared for by the inheriting son (Asakawa 1929: 272).

Other authors show evidence of parallel changes over the course of the fourteenth century among military-class families, with almost no transfers of land from husband to wife, or parents to daughter, after that century (Ooi 1977; Ootake 1979), although again the change was not universal, and counter-examples are also offered (Tabata 1987).

Thus it can be seen that following the creation of the patrilocal, patrilineal family among the military class, a trend developed by which successive male heads of a powerful and successful military family gradually but increasingly stripped women of their right to family property and appropriated it for the men, and that these changes took place *before* the two hundred years of full-scale civil war in the fifteenth and sixteenth centuries, in which the great barons fought to extend their landholdings and the social classes were reorganised.

For this reason, we argue that the control of women in the patriarchal family and the appropriation of women's property rights by men among the ruling class were two of the most important developments in the creation of the social hierarchy built upon class and property relations. These developments reduced women of the ruling class to the status of social objects, dependent for their sustenance on their relationship to their husbands, and stripped of the entitlement to own landed property in their own right.

Chapter 10

Civil War

Formation of the Social Classes
after the Fourteenth Century

The two centuries of civil war that followed the fourteenth century brought about an expansion in the landholdings of the great military barons (*daimyo*) and clear divisions between the social classes. It was for the sake of consolidating their hold on the land that the *daimyo*, in alliance with the less powerful landowning families, came to control the family affairs of their vassals, including marriage, adoption, family headship, inheritance and division of property. To maintain and expand his power over other barons, the overlord controlled the lives not only of his own family but also of his military retainers, and even his better-off farmers and craftsworkers (Sansom 1962: 352, 366–7).

Classes of people and rights in land became distinctly differentiated between warriors and peasants. The peasants became identified by their rights of use over the land, while the warriors claimed rights of revenue and political control. At first the minor warrior and the more prosperous peasant led similar lives, except that the soldier occasionally gave military service, but the class division gradually widened, and the warriors became nobles while the peasants remained as commoners. This division of classes evolved from the divided consolidation of the two kinds of rights, in use and in revenue, and was further widened by the rulers for the purpose of social control. It did not result from the artificial closure of one class for self-protection against the other. In the civil war periods the division was more easily surmounted, because commoners could engage in warfare and assert their personal ability (Asakawa 1929: 50–51, 73, 80).

A second significant change in class relations resulted from the increase in trade between Japan and China. The great barons became important merchant venturers, and the improvements in roads, transport, seaports and strategic towns carried out to prosecute the civil war also benefited trade. As domestic trade grew, so army contractors and a moneylender class developed, as did trade guilds to safeguard merchants' interests. The military administration and the old aristocracy borrowed from the merchant moneylenders as they lost power, office and lands in the civil war, and a privileged urban mercantile class arose. Anyone with power imposed excessive charges, and the peasants were the only class unable to pass these on; this led to agrarian revolts, which the peasants sometimes won against the military, the merchants, the priests and the government, as well as obtaining debt amnesties (Sansom 1962: 356–64).

The rise and fall of the great houses deprived many warriors of their landholdings, leading to the creation of a class of landless soldiers known as ronin, who were often unruly and aggressive, and sometimes joined in the riots. The constables had the most power; the shogunate was powerless, and the imperial family and the old aristocracy were impoverished. The Buddhist priests militantly defended their lands, and there was a growth in populist Buddhist sects, including the egalitarian Jodo sect, which attracted the lower classes, and the militant Lotus sect, which attracted the warriors. Interestingly, both sects regarded women as capable of enlightenment. There was also a rising democratic feeling in the country, but both this and the religious resistance against the power of the overlords were forcibly repressed (Sansom 1962: 368–9, 378, 409).

In the latter half of the sixteenth century, the warriors were mostly detached from the land which supported them and segregated in castle towns, with the main social division between the soldier and the peasant, followed by the artisans and merchants (Asakawa 1929: 44). As Samson says, this was an age of ferment, when the social order disintegrated and a violent reorganisation of the classes took place (Sansom 1962: 364).

Male primogeniture

Male primogeniture became strongly established in the military class during this period (Asakawa 1929: 43). Women of the military class were trained in martial arts, archery and fencing, and a wife became known as kanai or okusan, meaning the person in the innermost recesses of the house (Robins-Mowry 1983: 20–21). There are few recorded examples of widows inheriting their husband's property at this time, although daughters sometimes inherited equally with the male heir even in powerful warriors' families, and widows often wielded significant power as head of the household (Kurushima 1993: 103–12). But fathers without sons began to adopt a son-in-law, and the pattern of inheritance changed from the property being divided between all the children, with the most suitable son receiving the major share, to giving the whole estate to one son. This meant that the whole family was economically dependent on the sole heir. Other sons often left the estate and acquired land of their own, or formed alliances with unrelated households, while daughters left the estate on marriage.

In the fifteenth and sixteenth centuries the daughter's inheritance was reduced to a dowry rather than a means of livelihood, for which one-thousandth of the estate was considered appropriate, given only to the eldest daughter for her lifetime, although there were still examples of eternal and life inheritance amongst women (Tabata 1982). By the sixteenth century, women's property rights had become almost non-existent, as their inheritance was eroded in practice rather than through formal exclusions. Unmarried women became economically dependent on their brothers; the only way they could leave the family estate was through marriage, which was controlled by the landlord, and since they had no property of their own, married women became dependent on their husbands. The overlord also controlled women through their husbands (Ackroyd 1959: 46–7). Among ordinary people, the daimyo's rules laid down that men, women and children had to be returned respectively to their lords, husbands and parents, while kidnapping and selling other men's wives and children was treated as robbery, showing that they were seen as men's property (Tabata 1982: 209).

Daimyo house laws

The new social institutions were reflected in the house laws of the daimyo and were designed to safeguard their domains under the influence of a military regime, including oppressive restrictions and extreme punishments such as torture for the lower classes, and decapitation or permission to commit suicide for the samurai. As the civil war began to draw to a close towards the end of the sixteenth century, with Oda Nobunaga, then Hideyoshi Toyotomi and finally Tokugawa Ieyasu establishing supremacy, the classes were further differentiated. This was reflected in the differentiation between the women of different classes, but especially between women of the ruling military class and those of the lower classes. Three of the rules set out by Hideyoshi in 1585, 1586 and 1587 reflect the new social structure: first, no one in service, from the soldier to the peasant, could leave employment without the over-lord's permission; second, there was a rigid division of classes, whereby a warrior could not become a townsman, a peasant could not leave the land and do paid work, and a landowner could not give protection to vagrants who had abandoned the land; third, a clear class distinction was made between peasants and warriors, as peasants had to hand in their weapons, while for the warrior the sword became a symbol of his rank (Sansom 1962: 431–3).

Hideyoshi gave rewards of land to men of the warrior class for their military services, or confirmed the great barons in their ownership of their estates. Rewards were also given to women servants and court women, but in the form of money not land. This system represented the formal establishment of land-ruling by the state known as *kokudaka*. In practice the land was owned and controlled by the *daimyo*, but in formal terms the *daimyo* lost ownership of their estates and were en-trusted with the land by the shogun as head of state (Wakita 1982: 1–30). This system of landownership, which formed the basis of feudal social relations, was preserved through the creation of a rigid class structure in which the ruling class was armed and the lower classes were disarmed (Oufuji 1989: 126–8), and also ruling-class women were disinherited, confined within the patriarchal family, and subject to increasingly strict ideological controls. In Chapter 11 we examine the process by which women's exclusion from the material basis of power was legitimated, the distinction between women of different classes, and the sites in which women's power remained strong.

Chapter 11

Women's Position
and Social Class

Consolidating Women's Subordination
in the Military Class

By 1600, when the Tokugawa family finally established dominance over Japan, only a dozen of the 250 great barons or *daimyo* of the previous century remained. The rest had been replaced by other families emerging from the ranks of the lower vassals, an origin shared by Tokugawa Ieyasu himself (Sansom 1962: 405, 408). Tokugawa established his capital at Edo, was made shogun in 1603, and defeated his final rivals in 1615 at the siege of Osaka (Sansom 1962: 416). The Tokugawa family managed to hold the centre and rule over a unified Japan for the next 250 years (the Edo period) by imposing a military dictatorship and martial law, closing the country to foreign intervention, holding down social change, and tightening the divisions between the classes.

Bakuhan law is the legal system prescribed by the military government (*bakufu*) and the *daimyo*. The *bakufu* laid down laws, and the *daimyo* legislated for their own territories in conformity with *bakufu* law. These were mainly for the soldiers, with a few restrictions for ordinary people. *Bakuhan* family laws were designed to maintain permanent rule, and different laws were applied to different classes. For the military class were prescribed literature, arms, frugality, and a ban on debauchery. A warrior could kill a member of the lower classes for verbal abuse or rude behaviour, and be let off an offence which would be criminal if committed by a commoner, but he might have to commit suicide for an offence pardonable in a commoner (Sansom 1962: 448, 461, 465).

There were also different rules of marriage and succession for warriors and commoners, different status symbols and codes for each class, rules for maintaining order in the *daimyo*'s domains and relations between the *daimyo*, and regulations for alliances between *daimyo* and other dangerous activities such as marriage, since marriage had implications for political alliances. The restrictions on marriage by the *bakufu* indicate the extent to which women had become objects of exchange between men for the purpose of political alliances.

The principles of law were loyalty and duty between master and retainer in the military class, extended as an ideal for all the classes (Sansom 1962: 464–5, 561–2). The warrior's code was loyalty to the lord, truthfulness to one's word, faith between friends, plus a sense of propriety, filial piety, support for the old, and a sense of personal honour and shame (Asakawa 1929: 53–4). For the samurai, inheritance was by the eldest son; women of the ruling class were excluded from ownership of the lands, and became dependent on the head of the household. If there were no sons, a son-in-law would be adopted as heir. Any marriage required the consent of the master (Nagano 1982: 163–91).

Bakufu laws in practice

During the seventeenth century, men of the military class became dominant, and were made responsible for the behaviour of the family within the feudal hierarchy. Marriage was controlled not just by the family but by the feudal superior. Only men could initiate divorce, which they effected by what became known as the three-and-a-half-line letter – that is, a simple statement of intention. It was at this period that the seven reasons for divorcing a wife, first listed in the eighth century, were put into practice (Robins-Mowry 1983: 26–7), although among the warriors there were no grounds for a wife to divorce her husband. There were, however, circumstances under which she could not be divorced. Women's adultery was punishable by death, and the husband's right to kill an adulterous wife and her partner became not only permissible but obligatory; the soldier was forced to repress his natural feelings of affection. A married man could not be guilty of adultery with an unmarried woman, whilst concubinage was regarded as a necessity for the production of a male heir. Education for a samurai woman consisted of sewing, hairdressing and simple writing. She was married at the age of 13 to 16, and her place was in the kitchen (Ackroyd 1959: 56–61).

Despite the fact that in criminal law a master could kill a servant as disciplinary action and parents could sell their children, nevertheless a husband could not kill his wife or force her into prostitution or concubinage, on pain of death (unless she had committed adultery). A female heir could divorce her husband despite the fact that this was impossible in law. If there was no son in a warrior family, the daughter would marry by 'taking-a-bridegroom', and although the son-in-law would be the formal successor, in practice the daughter would be the real head of the household. If she did not get on with her husband, it was possible for her to divorce him even though in strictly legal terms it was impossible for a woman of the warrior class to initiate a divorce. But informally her parents and relatives could make the necessary arrangements and apply to the *daimyo* for a divorce. If it was granted, the husband would have to leave the household and his children (Wakita 1982: 1–30).

It was a principle of the *bakufu* that *oku* – meaning 'inside', 'personal' or 'private' – must be separated from *omote* – meaning 'outside', 'government' or 'public' (Kubo 1993: 146–55). Men and women were divided along these lines in the warrior class: public, outside work was for men; private, inside work was done by women. The idea that women's work was 'inside the house' produced a tendency to regard the free movement of women outside the house alone as damaging to the men's honour. In this respect the warrior class was different from the other classes. Among the more lowly warrior families, wives and daughters had to help support the family by weaving or other work which could be done in the house, but they could not work outside (Oufuji 1989: 56–9). Women's mobility was controlled through the *onna tegata* or 'women's note' system. Because of the fear of uprisings, the hostage system was instituted, and constant searches were made at the boundaries of the towns for 'inward guns and outward women', since women leaving the towns could signify a plot to overthrow the government. Women who wanted to move around, therefore, had to carry a note recognised by the *bakufu*. This restriction was extended to other regional areas, and eventually became a general requirement for women (Nagano 1982: 163–91).

Gentle obedience...

In 1672, Kaibara Ekken wrote 'Greater Learning for Women' (the *Onna Daigaku*), a neo-Confucian text which became a classic moral text for young brides of the military class (Robins-Mowry 1983: 26). Whilst the moral code of the warrior, the *bushido*, teaches 'submission to authority, utter devotion to one's overlord, and self-sacrifice of all private interest' (Shingoro 1905: 21), the parallel code for women became the *Onna Daigaku*. The *Onna Daigaku* outlines gentle obedience, chastity, mercy and quietness as the ideal qualities in a woman, and insists on the segregation of the sexes. It indicates the seven reasons for divorcing a woman: disobedience, infertility, lewdness, jealousy, disease, gossiping and stealing, as well as the two which protect a barren wife from divorce – if the man has children by a concubine, or if the wife's 'heart be virtuous and her conduct correct and free from jealousy, in which case a child of the same blood must be adopted' (Kaibara 1905: 36–7). It sets out the wife's duties, which are to her husband (as the husband's is to his lord), to her parents-in-law and brothers-in-law, and the maintenance of family harmony and a well-ordered house. It deals with the treatment of servants, advising her to serve her parents-in-law in person, and to ignore the gossip of low-born servants who will only make trouble and disturb the harmony of the house. She must correct their worst faults, and help them when needed, but pay no attention to their minor faults. Finally, the book identifies women's five failings: disobedience, anger, slander, jealousy, and stupidity (the worst, and parent to the others). A woman's passivity means that she is unable to recognise her duties, and should therefore always follow her husband rather than trust herself. Her affection for her children is a mistake (Kaibara 1905: 38–46).

As Shingoro Takaishi says in his introduction to the 1905 publication of the *Onna Daigaku*, self-sacrifice of private interests to the common good is the basic principle of the moral code for women: 'humility in place of ostentation, reserve in place of *réclame*, self-sacrifice in place of selfishness, forbearance in place of impetuosity, and complete submission to authority' (Shingoro 1905: 11). Despite Kaibara's claim in the introduction that the book was found even on the shelves of the poorest merchants (Kaibara 1905: 12), it is clear that women of the ruling rather than the lower classes are its intended audience. One section is devoted to the treatment of servants, and Kaibara expresses his contempt for such people in the statement 'in her dealings with these low people, a woman will find many things to disapprove of' (Kaibara 1905: 44). Indeed, Kaibara acknowledged that lower-class women did not follow these rules: 'the women of lower classes, ignoring all rules of this nature [sex segregation], behave themselves disorderly; they contaminate their reputations, bring down reproach upon the head of their parents and brothers, and spend their whole lives in an unprofitable manner' (Kaibara 1905: 35).

...or *Amazonian women?*

Nitobe Inazo – writing after the Meiji Restoration, but speaking of his own experience of the military moral code of *bushido* – gives a different view of the code for women. He identifies two aspects of the ideal woman: the domestic and the martial, which he terms Amazonian. The *bushido* moral code developed mainly for men, and its view of female virtue was 'far from feminine' (Nitobe 1905: 139). Women were expected to be as heroic as men, and were trained to repress their feelings and to fence with the long-handled sword for the purpose of protecting their own honour and to train their sons. Just as the samurai was taught how to commit suicide for the purpose of saving his honour, and to place his robes under his knees to ensure that he fell forward in dignity after committing suicide, so the samurai woman was taught how to kill herself with a cut to the throat, and to tie her legs together to preserve the modesty of her body in death. Chastity was valued more than life itself, and was vigorously defended; women of the warrior class were given a small sword to carry to use against either their attacker or themselves. A woman was *naijo*, the inner help. She sacrificed herself for her husband, home and family, just as her husband sacrificed himself for his lord and his country. Nitobe confirms that 'in no class did [woman] experience less freedom than amongst the samurai ... the lower the social class – as, for instance, amongst small artisans – the more equal was the position of husband and wife' (Nitobe 1905: 140–42, 145–7, 150). This consolidation of women's subordination in the period of pacification may be understood as part of the process of legitimating their exclusion from the material basis of class power when the argument about their inferior military abilities no longer had purchase.

Women of the Lower Classes: Peasant Women

The lives of women of the ruling class were in marked contrast to those of the lower classes, of whom farmers or peasants were next in the status hierarchy. Walthall shows that peasant women engaged in many activities that were forbidden to women of the military class. They travelled, attended school, undertook paid work, chose their own marriage partners, engaged in matrilocal marriages, committed adultery and divorced without too much shame, remarried and served as household heads (Walthall 1991: 42–70). As Bernstein says, 'promiscuous girls, barren wives, wilful daughters-in-law, and divorcees all managed to survive relatively unstigmatised by village social sanctions' (Bernstein 1991: 4). Although women's formal status in the villages was low, they maintained the right to possess fields and to cultivate them (Tabata 1982: 246) In the sixteenth century there were many female artisans, and women of the lower classes could become head of the merchants' guild at the market, perform ceremonies equally with men in the village, and come and go as they wished without their husbands' permission (Kuroda 1993: 81–92).

Sugano shows that women worked extensively in farm labour. In Aizu, Fukushima, women did the transplanting, cutting and threshing, while men organised the planting. Men threshed twelve and women nine bundles of rice per day. Men's paid work consisted mainly of straw manufactures, whereas women's was weaving hemp, cotton and silk. A large amount of concentrated labour-power was required for rice production at times of planting and harvesting, so women's labour was vital. Women's labour was also valued because the process of rice transplanting or *taue* was connected with the idea of their fertility, and women were thought of as skilled with their fingers. Smallholding farmers were independent, so they formed *yui*, a special organisation of five to ten people to organise planting and harvesting, and sometimes paid labour. Up to the mid-seventeenth century, women's paid work was mainly restricted to weaving, but by organising their own *yui* they were able to co-operate in agricultural work and the exchange of information, which enabled them to vary the amount of work they did, and to raise its value (Sugano 1982: 63–94).

Different lives

There were also differences within the peasant class. Among better-off peasants, the main role of the farmer's wife was household management, and the preparation of food and clothing. Such women did not engage in agriculture except for *taue* or rice transplanting. The wife held the purse and managed the household economy, as well as being responsible for the care of old people and the education of children. Among poorer peasants the wife had to engage in farming as well as housework. Women also sold produce, and later in the period many peasant wives introduced new techniques from Kyoto, and hired female artisans to do silk spinning and textile manufacture. As women took on more economic roles, many of the husbands took on housework and childcare (Oufuji 1989: 174–86). Miyashita shows that there was a class differentiation within the peasant class, whereby the richer peasants with more land had a better economic basis for controlling female members of the family, while in poorer families the economic power of the head of the household was weaker; he was therefore less able to exert control over the women (Miyashita 1982: 35–40).

Miyashita also provides evidence which challenges the view that primogeniture spread downwards from the military class to the peasants, leading to a more patriarchal family form in the rural areas. In Komayaga, in the Osaka area, various forms of inheritance operated, and when he compared the two periods 1694–1720 and 1722–49, he found that in the later period there were fewer instances of primogeniture, but more cases of inheritance by 'adopted son' (signifying inheritance by daughters married to the adopted son); inheritance by widows remained the same. Also in the later period there was a higher proportion of primogeniture among the richer peasants than among poorer peasants (Miyashita 1982: 41–2).

Despite these differences within the peasant class, however, the *daimyo* strove to maintain equality among the peasants. The village was made even more self-governing and more responsible than before. At the same time, high taxes, resulting in little if any agricultural surplus, made accumulation of land unprofitable for the peasants, and meant that peasant holdings remained relatively equal, whilst division and alienation of the peasant estate was deliberately restricted (Asakawa 1929: 73–4). As Beasley points out, although there was equality in the peasant class, it was an equality of misery because of the burden of taxation (Beasley 1990: 8); but this equality did mean that there were significantly fewer gendered restrictions on women than in the military class.

Amongst farmers' wives, according to folklore, women had the 'right of housewife', which was as strong as that of the household head. It was possessed by the mother-in-law until it was transferred to the daughter-in-law, in a ritual known as the transfer of the rice spatula, signifying management of the household. Until then, the daughter-in-law was required to practice unilateral self-sacrifice and obedience. Women were heavily involved in agricultural labour, and did 40 per cent of the work (Nagashima 1993: 122–31).

Women became established as labourers in the mid-eighteenth century as they took up paid work spinning and weaving. In that century there were hundreds of female weaving artisans aged between 12 and 18 in the local weaving towns, and they earned the same as male peasants. In the nineteenth century, women left the farms and began to work in the textile industry (Nagashima 1993: 122–31).

Women also took part in resistance against the conditions of life in the villages, and in peasant uprisings. There were more than 3,000 uprisings in the Edo period, and women played an important role in the rice riots in the towns and cities – for example, in the famous Tenmei famines of 1783–87, in Ida town, Ogawa and Kubo. In 1856, women initiated the *nyobo ikki* or wife uprisings in Kaga, Etchu and Noto, in which 2,000 women and children demonstrated and protested in front of the landlord's castle; and in 1882 women fought armed battles along with men in several villages (Katakura 1993: 157–67).

Mutual aid

Yanagita Kunio's work on folklore and the common people of Japan attempts to rebalance the heavy emphasis on political elites. Yanagita argues that although the ruling class has received greater attention, it was actually the majority peasant class which led major social changes, based on a system of values and traditions which were distinct from those of the military rulers, as shown by his folk studies of the village of Tono. The elite and common traditions coexist, just as older forms of social organisation coexist with newer forms. For example: 'forms of marriage as well as clan organisations, in some places, are entirely changed, whereas in other places they exist just as they were in previous days' (Tsurumi 1975: 228). Equally, while the ruling class promoted filial piety, loyalty to the feudal lord, or, after the breakdown of the feudal system, to the emperor as the divine representative, and obedience of the wife to the husband, the folk tales spoke of the continuity of the family at the expense of the elderly, presented the rivers and mountains as the village gods, and acknowledged the wisdom and leadership of the village women (Tsurumi 1975: 225–6, 234).

The ruling class emphasised – and itself conformed to – obedience to the hierarchy, but the peasants put stress on mutual aid groups of many different kinds for the purposes of survival and social solidarity. These groups occurred within both vertical and horizontal relationships, and operated according to the principles of self-rule. Yanagita cites *ko* groups as an example of indigenous democracy in which adults gathered for various occupational, leisure and religious interests, and the important affairs of the village were discussed. There were also children's groups, *kodomo gumi*, and the young men's and young women's groups, the *wakamono gumi* and *musume gumi*. These groups constituted a traditional form of participatory democracy which had more to do with self-government than the 'autonomous systems' of local government imposed later in the nineteenth century by the undemocratic and unaccountable Meiji ruling elite (Tsurumi 1975: 229–33).

Women of the Lower Classes: Merchant Women

In contrast to both the peasant class in the rural areas and the ruling elite, the merchant class also displayed its own specific characteristics.

The merchants inhabited the towns, and were on the lowest rung of the social hierarchy, but the position of women varied by strata here too. In rich merchants' houses women could own property and land, unlike the majority of samurai women, although it might not be of the first grade, or in the best area. The justification for female heirs was that the merchant had to have a successor with commercial ability, although there was an attempt to ban female heirs in 1730 precisely because there were so many. Women were not allowed to take part in the administration of the towns, but there were many examples of women from the merchant class acting as guarantors for debts and contributing to the maintenance of the emperor's palace (Kubo 1993: 146–55). Lebra shows that significant numbers of matrilineal, matrilocal marriages took place in the merchant class, and if there was no son, or if the son was less competent than the daughter, the daughter could inherit the business and the family headship by 'taking a husband' (Lebra 1991: 131–48).

Hayashi gives examples of the relative freedom and power of women in the merchant class compared with women in the military class. In Ise, the wife of a wealthy merchant, whose name was Shuho, became known as the founder of Mitsui, because while her husband absorbed himself in poetry and music, she ran the family sake and pawnshop business. Shuho's daughter-in-law managed the servants, and maintained social networks with relatives and other merchants, while her son worked in the business. On his death, the husband bequeathed silver to his wife and daughters. In Kiryu, a weaving area, documents show that the wife of a middle-level merchant helped in the business at peak times and engaged in social networking to assist trade. The daughters in this family were well educated, and while the mother went on jaunts to the temple with family and friends, the children were looked after by a nurse. There are few written documents to give us an insight into the lives of lower-level merchants, except where someone was commended by the bakufu for loyalty to the husband or the landlord. Most women in these documents, including housemaids and shopworkers, had been commended for their work in cleaning, sewing or small-scale handicraft manufacture. Lower-class women such as these, with their own occupations, could marry and divorce freely (Hayashi 1982: 95–126).

Thus, the period of pacification under a military government saw the consolidation of women's subordination in the samurai family under the feudal class system, through the legitimation of male dominance and women's exclusion from the material basis for class power. Women were constructed as social objects and male property for the reproduction of the ruling-class family. At the same time, the restraints on samurai women became a mark of respectability and a source of family honour, distinguishing them from lower-class women and signalling the symbolic power of the ruling class.

Gender, Class and Power before the Western Intrusions

In conclusion, we argue in Part II that the decline of women's power in the military class was crucially connected with the rise of that class. The establishment of the patriarchal family and the gradual erosion of women's rights to land were effective in excluding military-class women from the material basis for power, and transforming them into economic and social dependants of men. Women's lands were appropriated not by military aggressors, but at the hands of their male relatives through changing practices of inheritance, in the interests of consolidating the class position of the men. Women's disinheritance occurred at a crucial period: in the century *before* the outbreak of full-scale civil war.

We argue that these developments in gender relations which reduced women's power were vital to produce the conditions in which the military barons could consolidate and expand their estates, and which brought about the reorganisation of classes in the following two centuries of civil war. We therefore suggest that the subordination of women was not a by-product or an effect of feudal class relations, but that the gender division was a vital pillar on which the class system based on the control of land was constructed. Women's exclusion from power, and the appropriation of their land by their fathers and brothers, were facilitated and legitimated by the establishment of the patriarchal family, which constructed women as belonging to their marital rather than their natal families, and were justified in later centuries by the ideologies purveyed in exhortatory moral codes like the *Onna Daigaku*.

Even this process by which women's position as social subjects within the military class was eroded, however, should not be seen as representing a unilinear decline of female power in Japanese society, as evidenced by the fact that women maintained their position as social subjects in relation to men of their own class at lower levels of the social hierarchy, and in different parts of the country; by the fact that the practice of women's subordination in the military class was not fully implemented; and by the contradictions within the theory itself. Although samurai women were subject to increasing constraints, it is not the case that women were universally reduced to the status of social objects, within or outside the dominant class.

The evidence reveals aspects both of women's power and of their powerlessness, suggesting that they were neither fully social subjects at all times and in all places, nor completely reduced to the status of social objects at all levels and in all periods. The trajectory of women's power does not reflect a simple linear decline, nor can men's power be characterised as a consistent progression. Instead, we have tried to show that the question of the existence and persistence of women's power is better understood as a complex struggle between male and female power, in which men's power became dominant in particular sections of society at different historical periods. The evidence reveals aspects of women's power, as well as its regulation, containment and disciplining. Female power was sustained more strongly among the ordinary people concerned with the struggle to produce enough food for the survival of the community than among the dominant class engaged in the political struggle for control of the land and those who cultivated it. For the elite groups, women became part of the struggle for power, deployed as capital for men. Long *before* the western intrusions and external critiques of gender relations in Japan, samurai women were used as objects of value for men, and represented symbolic capital for the ruling class. After the Meiji Restoration, Japanese women were used by not only their own state but also the western powers to make claims about 'competence', 'respectability' and 'honourability' (Bourdieu 1984: 291) in relation to structures of class hierarchy and global power.

PART III

Yearning for the Sky
and the Stars

In Part III, using the experiences of the women in our study, we look at how, after the Second World War, women at the top of the class hierarchy broke out of the forms and systems of social regulation which had previously been developed.

We set out our approach to analysing the women's struggles for change, drawing on Bourdieu's concepts of 'social spaces', 'social positions' and 'fields of power'. We look at how spaces were created for resistance to social regulation.

We examine the transitions which occurred prior to, during and after the war in China and the Second World War, showing how changes in social institutions and systems of authority enabled middle-class women to emerge from domesticity and move into education and employment. This transition will be understood in terms of the move from middle-class women's position as social objects and repositories of family capital, to a position as social subjects and accumulators of capitals in their own right.

We identify the processes in the social field which opened up spaces for women in the context of Japan's struggle with the western powers, focusing on the impact of militarist expansionism, the defeat of the militarist project, and the reforms of the occupation period. We look at the ways in which Japanese women took advantage of the new social spaces that opened up, creating new roles and activities for themselves.

We will look at the changing conditions which made this process possible, and examine how women achieved the changes, by discussing the meaning of the debates on the 'new woman' and the 'modern girl' in the prewar period, as a context for understanding the changes in female employment over the course of the war.

We will question the idea that women's emergence can be attributed primarily to the reforms of the US administration, and examine how women took advantage of those reforms to move into new positions.

Chapter 12

The New Woman

Having argued that the class structure prior to the Meiji period was built upon gender divisions, that women's power was retained at different levels of society and at different historical periods before the intrusion of the West, and that gendered class divisions were reasserted in renovated forms after the early period of Meiji liberalisation, we now look at how women broke out of these renovated forms of social regulation at the top of the class hierarchy, using the experiences of the professional women who contributed to our study. In this chapter, we set out both the context and our approach to understanding these struggles for change.

Movements for Change, Spaces for Resistance

The rise of the middle class prior to the Meiji period (Tsurumi 1970: 209), the forced opening of Japan to global capitalism, and Japan's struggle with the world imperialist system, created diverse movements for social change. As we showed in Part I, after the initial period of liberalisation the state attempted to reassert control over the population, and a conservative reaction set in as Japan fought to establish equality with the West. Japan's release from the unequal treaties and her own colonial gains from the First World War, however, made it increasingly difficult to hold down change amongst those sections of the population who were excluded from the benefits of Japan's rise in the global hierarchy, and this period between the wars became known as Taisho 'democracy'. The 1918 Rice Riots were sparked off by women dockers refusing to load rice on to ships in Uotsu in the face of huge price rises, and discontent spread to Kyoto, Kobe and Osaka. The state

responded with violence, causing the uprising to become more gener-
alised and involving particularly *burakumin* outcaste groups, slum-dwellers,
peasants, miners and students. The revolts were eventually suppressed
with military force. Hundreds of thousands of people were involved in
636 locations, mainly in the rice-producing areas. The 8,000 arrests
which followed finally toppled the government. The riots had a profound effect on the students who set up student–worker organisations
at Tokyo, Kyoto and Waseda Universities and whose leadership provided
many of the future leftist activists (Halliday 1975: 70–72).

While the rural areas saw a big increase in tenancy disputes, in 1920,
20,000 iron workers went on strike and in 1921, 35,000 dockworkers
took over and ran the dockyards in Kobe, again suppressed by the army.
Both the *burakumin* groups and the women's organisations gained support and encouragement from these revolts. Hara Kei, the Prime Minister, was assassinated, and it seemed for a moment that revolution was
possible, especially since the Washington conference was making Japan
feel vulnerable abroad. The destruction in the great earthquake of 1923
provided the excuse for right-wing nationalists to exploit the chaos and
massacre thousands of Koreans, Chinese, outcastes and political opponents, and it was during this time that the feminist Ito Noe and her
husband, the socialist Osugi Sakae, were murdered in police cells
(Halliday 1975: 72–3). In 1925 the Peace Preservation Law (*Chian Iji Ho*)
criminalised liberal and communist thought, stipulating life imprisonment or capital punishment as sanctions, and providing for preventive
custody of leftists (Miyake 1991: 279). As Halliday says, 1912–26 should
be seen not as Taisho 'democracy' but as a period of class struggle
(Halliday 1975: 73). We will argue that this was also a period of gender
struggle, a conflict which centred on class definitions of gender.

In looking at the position of women in this context, it is important
to make distinctions between, first, actions taken by the state in an
attempt to regulate women's behaviour; second, women's own agency;
and third, actions stemming from the fears of men aroused by women's
active resistance to state regulation and male power. As Pettman argues
in another context: 'Colonial authorities, nationalists and traditionalists
frequently ignored women's resistance and agency, using "women" to
pursue other objectives and agendas' (Pettman 1996: 194). In the middle
class, women's resistance and agency emerged in the Taisho period as
a challenge to the boundaries confining them to the family as repositories of value for men, and separating them from the institutions of
cultural and economic capital in the form of education and employment. This challenge was suppressed in the war with China that began

in 1931, as left-wing and feminist activity was forced underground (Mackie 1988: 58), but the contradictions of the state's need for women's paid labour in both the factory and the home intensified. After the end of the Second World War, middle-class women's resistance to their position as social objects broke out with renewed energy in the move into higher education and professional work, and in the development of various kinds of protest movements.

The 'new woman' and the 'modern girl'

Thus, although the Meiji state did use women to pursue other objectives, women's attempts to break down gender divisions, which had been initiated in the Meiji period, became a possibility in the Taisho period. The fears which this created both for men and for the ruling class may be understood within the terms of our analysis. The 'new woman' (*atarashii onna*) who had emerged in the 1920s comprised many different things, including Yosano Akiko's equal rights feminism, Hiratsuka Raicho's maternalist essentialism, Yamakawa Kikue's socialist feminism and Yamada Waka's liberation through the good wife, wise mother of the traditional family (Rodd 1991: 176). But the debate produced by the media on the 'modern girl' (*modan gaaru*) in the 1920s reflected both the confusion and the fear occasioned by women's transcending of the renovated forms of gendered class identity. As Silverberg makes clear, the *modan gaaru* was a construction of the media in which the non-traditional woman was portrayed as militantly autonomous, economically independent, sexually promiscuous, and above all apolitical (Silverberg 1991: 240–43). This portrayal as apolitical was a means of distancing her from any kind of feminist analysis or critique of male power.

Yet there was a paradox over her class status, and we argue that this reflects precisely the confusion caused by the idea of a middle-class woman who was economically independent and sexually autonomous. This confusion also reveals the importance of the model of the middle-class woman in fixing the identities of both middle-class men and working-class women. In other words, the model drew the boundaries between different class and gender positions. For the economically and sexually active woman was identified as a lower-class position, whereas for the middle class, sexual promiscuity and economic independence were what defined men. A sexually autonomous, economically in-dependent, middle-class woman was simply a contradiction.

As examples of the confusion over the *modan gaaru*'s class status, Nii Itaru, the journalist normally credited with coining the term, asked in a women's magazine article whether the *modan gaaru* represented a symbol of proletarian revolution or an expression of middle-class decadence. The right-wing press answered the question by identifying her as part of the communist conspiracy to weaken the children of the wealthy through dissipated living; from the opposite perspective, but in much the same way, the working-class feminist Yamakawa Kikue saw her as passive, indolent and immodest, signifying the dissolution of the declining ruling class. The middle-class feminist Hiratsuka Raicho saw her as the daughter of the 'new woman', interested in western fashions and with time and money on her hands, but not interested in having children and not free of objectification by male desire. The male novelist Tanizaki Junichiro portrayed her as a café waitress who crosses gender boundaries by dressing as a man and adopting male language, until finally she subordinates and infantilises the husband who rescued her from her lower-class profession (Silverberg 1991: 241–9). His novel illustrates men's fear of women's transgression of both class and gender boundaries, and of losing control over the new self-directing middle-class woman.

Silverberg argues that the *modan gaaru* was a symbol of the woman whose productive abilities and sexual activities were no longer confined to the home. This is partly true, but in fact lower-class women's production and sexuality had long been public activities, while it was the middle-class woman who was supposed to act as the model of morality for the lower classes. We argue that it was precisely because it was *middle-class* women who were refusing sexual and economic subordination, thus sundering the recognised connection between gender and class, that the image of the *modan gaaru* captured the middle-class imagination and expressed the fears of the 1920s generation that not only the gender order but also the class structure would be swept away. Thus, the reason for the opacity of the *modan gaaru*'s class identity was her rejection of the class-specific definitions of middle-class Japanese womanhood, which prescribed chastity, fidelity, modesty, dependence, home and family. This rejection both reflected and itself produced the breaking down of class-based gender definitions, and was deeply threatening to the male middle-class view of itself, its identity and its authority.

Middle-Class Women 'Going Out to Work'

In the Taisho period the middle class increased significantly, especially in the cities. 'Middle class' here refers to urban salaried workers with an education which is required for their job. The Tokyo middle class increased from 6 per cent of the workforce in 1908 to 22 per cent by 1920. Middle-class occupations meant white-collar or professional jobs, and for women this was mainly teaching, nursing, midwifery, clerical work in offices and banks, and shop work (Nagy 1991: 201).

The major reasons for middle-class women going out to work in the period between the wars were employer demand, economic necessity and the desire for financial independence. A 1922 survey showed that a majority of middle-class working women were single, widowed or divorced, and a significant proportion of these were heads of household or sole breadwinners, for whom white-collar jobs provided more respectable employment and better salaries than the textile mills. The development of the colonies and the growth of Japanese capitalism created clerical and professional jobs in the expanding bureaucracies of the public and private sectors, and employers discovered that they could replace male by female labour at half the cost – for example, in teaching or transport – as young educated women began to emerge from the expanded girls' higher schools (Nagy 1991: 204–9).

During the wartime period, the civilian male labour force fluctuated in actual numbers from 18.7 million in 1930, up to 19.7 million in 1940, and down to 18.4 million in 1944, while the female labour force increased dramatically, both in actual numbers and as a percentage of the total workforce. There were 10 million women workers in 1930, 12 million in 1940 and 13 million in 1944. Over this period women increased their share of the workforce from 36 per cent to 42 per cent. Employment in the category 'government and the professions', which may be termed middle-class work, increased from 6 per cent to 9 per cent of total employment over the same period. Whilst the actual numbers of both male and female employees in this category rose steadily, the proportion of female to male employees increased significantly, as men's share dropped from 77 per cent to 65 per cent, and women's rose from 23 per cent to 35 per cent (Miyake 1991: 282). Thus women accounted for the entire increase in the size of the total labour force during the wartime period, whilst women's share of middle-class work in government and the professions increased significantly at men's expense.

'Women of questionable virtue'

Nagy argues that there was a negative – or at least an ambivalent – public response to female employment in this period. But in fact this ambivalence was directed not at women's employment in general, which had been accepted since before the Restoration, but at the employment of women of the middle class. Nagy implies this when she says, 'employed women represented a deviation from women's basic calling as wife and mother and must therefore be women of either low class or questionable virtue' (Nagy 1991: 210–11). This formulation, however, accepts the idea of the middle-class woman as the representative of Japanese womanhood as a whole, constructing the low-class wage-earning or sexually active woman as other, and normalising her opposite in the form of the virtuous, dependent, middle-class woman. This demonstrates both the ways in which gender was structured by class, and the way that the middle-class concept of womanhood was constructed as the norm, reflecting its power as the ideal Japanese woman, and the inferiority of other formulations associated with different class positions. Middle-class femininity constituted domesticity, seclusion in the home, economic dependence on the family and the control of women's sexuality. Nagy proposes that this was a model for the lower classes to aspire to (Nagy 1991: 214), but it was also a way of differentiating between the classes and signalling the inadequacy of the lower-class model of womanhood.

The state response to the phenomenon of the middle-class working woman was to try to make it unnecessary by providing employment exchanges for middle-class men, and offering household management courses to women to help housewives to get by more effectively on their husbands' diminishing salaries in a time of high inflation (Nagy 1991: 214). In the wartime period from 1931 to 1945, however, two contradictory processes occurred as the state attempted to re-establish class-based gender identities and to repress new ideas of Japanese womanhood, in the interests of maintaining the family–state system and increasing the population (Miyake 1991: 267–8). We argue that these two processes were crucial to the production of the special Japanese military spirit and 'will to die' (Tsurumi 1970: 4), which contributed to Japan's successes on the battlefield and compensated, at least in the earlier stages, for the lack of finance capital for the war.

If Japanese soldiers were more willing to die on the battlefield than the enemy, they needed to be more rapidly replaced; hence the urgent requirement for women to remain in their domestic and reproductive roles in order to reproduce the military social capital of the state. At the same time as women were being pressed into reproductive service, however, the physical destruction and social devastation of the war forced the re-emergence of multiple class and gender roles which challenged and undermined these traditional models. This contradiction may be seen in the state's reluctance, despite the severity of the labour shortage at the start of the Pacific War in 1941, to conscript women for war work; this did not take place until 1944. Even then it was only for unmarried and widowed women between the ages of 12 and 40 – that is, those who could not legitimately reproduce, *not* those without families to look after. In fact, the population failed to increase substantially and the economy failed to meet the production needs of the war, while those young unmarried women who worked in munitions factories on a 'voluntary' basis were 'forced to work gruelling hours under miserable conditions to make up for the labour shortage' (Miyake 1991: 267–70).

Resolving contradictions

We have argued that the middle-class woman was effectively constituted as the representative of Japanese womanhood as a whole, as a way of resolving the contradiction between the needs of the political economy for paid female labour and those of the family–state system for women's domestic and reproductive labour, since the model rendered invisible the productive labour of working-class women. This contradiction became particularly acute in the phase of active expansionism during the war, when the demands of the military project threatened to break down the divisions between the classes by drawing middle-class women into production, thus undermining the construction of the ideal Japanese woman, and with it the unique institution of the family–state. This analysis helps to explain why there was such reluctance on the part of the state to conscript women, since forcing middle-class women into the factories would break down the image of the ideal Japanese woman, undermining the patriarchal family–state system and the class divisions themselves.

Thus the war led to a contradictory approach to the woman question. On the one hand, the state attempted to re-establish the gender categories structured by class and to repress the earlier struggles for emancipation, in order to preserve the family–state system and reproduce the military forces in the struggle with the West. At the same time the demands and devastation of the war compelled the emergence of gender roles which undermined these gendered class structures. We will argue that it was in the social spaces created by these contradictions that women were able to forge new identities and take up positions as social subjects, long before the USA instituted legal and constitutional reforms in the position of women.

'A Field of Struggles'

Bourdieu defines the social field as the social space in which a contest takes place between individuals or institutions who are competing for domination and a position of distinction in the social hierarchy. He conceptualises the social field as a system of objective relations, but emphasises that whilst the social positions within the field appear to be in a 'static order of discrete compartments', they are also 'strategic emplacements, fortresses to be defended and captured in a field of struggles' (Bourdieu 1984: 244). Andermahr, Lovell and Wolkowitz point out that the possibility of capturing dominant social positions in the field of power depends not only on the possession of cultural capital but also on the legitimacy of particular categories of contestant to compete in that particular field (Andermahr et al. 1997: 97). We will suggest that women captured some of these strategic emplacements from men during the war, and succeeded in defending them even after the men's return.

In addition to the idea of social spaces as positions signifying hierarchical emplacements in the social field, we will introduce the concept of 'social absences', referring to positions in the social field which have been vacated on a temporary or permanent basis, leaving those strategic emplacements undefended. Carolyn Steedman, analysing working-class children's writing in a British setting, suggests that children saw fathers as 'absences', and saw power in the home as female (Steedman 1982: 140–41). Although female power over children in the home is a subjugated form of power, it is still, as Lovell points out, a form of power, which prevailed largely in men's absence, albeit under men's overall authority in the family (Lovell 2000: 30). In peacetime, men's absence may have been less apparent to adult family members than to children, but in times of war the absence of men was both more comprehensive, in terms of long periods spent away at the front, and in many cases more permanent, in terms of death on the battlefield.

We use the concept of 'social absence' to refer not just to the physical absence of male bodies, but to their absence from the system of patriarchal social regulation in the family, as well as their inability to play the social roles and undertake the social practices which help to retain their position of power as men, and to reproduce the gender hierarchy in general. We also extend the meaning of the concept to cover men's physical return to the family in a state of injury or mental or physical incapacitation, which prevents them from performing these roles. In other words, we are referring to the social consequences of a physical absence or incapacitation, which in the case of war is deeply gendered, and may therefore have long-term implications for the organisation of gender relations.

Fragmentation of class and gender

In the rest of Part III we will show how middle-class women came to capture some of the fortresses defending male middle-class power in Japan, and how women increased their legitimacy as contestants in the struggle. We will argue that despite the fluctuations in the state's approach to women, and the harsh repression meted out to individuals and social movements, women took advantage of openings which allowed them to move from a position as social objects to a position as social subjects, whether inside or outside the family. We identify the sense of 'yearning' or desire – to acquire an education, take up a profession, or create an identity based on more than marriage – as an expression of women's agency in the struggle.

We will argue that, in opposition to the overwhelming state moves to consolidate and sustain a social structure based on gender, class and empire during the war, there was also a continuous process of fragmentation of these social divisions. In the period of Taisho 'democracy', women began to transcend gendered class identities; this seriously challenged the renovated forms of gendered class positions constructed during the Meiji period. During the militarist expansionism of the 1930s, the gendered social absences of men in the war, and the movement of women into male roles in the family and the factories, continued the process of disintegration of gendered class identities which had been a cause of concern in the 1920s, and undermined the patriarchal family–state system together with the class divisions on which it was based. This process of fragmentation was dramatically reinforced when the militarist project was defeated, as the authority of the family–state system under the emperor, which held gender, class and ethnic relations in place, was eroded by the failure to provide military victory. Finally, these changes in social relations were institutionalised, and in some cases extended, by the occupation reforms – not because of concern with the position of women, but for the political ends of the occupying power. We will identify the changes that came about in the social field, which opened up new social spaces and left undefended many of the strategic emplacements in the hierarchical social structures implicated in the family–state–emperor system. We will demonstrate the significance of women's agency in this process, inasmuch as the changes consolidated demands made by feminist activists throughout the first period of modernisation. We will show that women struggled to capture strategic emplacements vacated by men, and fought to retain them on the return of their former occupants after the war.

How, then, did the changes come about that enabled women of the middle class to transform themselves and re-emerge from their confinement in the home despite the suppression of the movements for women's liberation that took place during the war period? We identify three key moments which opened up spaces for changes to women's position that ran counter to the construction of womanhood promoted by the state: first, Japan's decision to engage in militarist expansionism in its struggle with the imperial powers; second, the defeat of the militarist project in 1945; and third, the reforms of the occupation period (1945 to 1952). We will show the processes by which these transitions happened, using interview material from the older respondents who were born before the war, as well as material from secondary sources.

Chapter 13

Militarist Expansionism

The decision to engage in a strategy of militarist expansionism had served Japan's cause well in the 1894–95 war with China and the 1904–05 war with Russia, as well as in the First World War. In all these conflicts Japan was on the winning side, emerged with its own colonies, and succeeded in improving its image in the eyes of the world. The previous success of the strategy was only one of the reasons why Japan adopted this approach in the 1930s. Others included the recognition that without a show of force and military gains, Japan could not hope to win symbolic capital in the eyes of the West, or compete with the West's own military strategies; and the fact that compulsory military training, including skills training and moral or spiritual training, was already in place for the purposes of disciplinary regulation of the adult male population. Further reasons included the heritage of samurai history and culture, which facilitated the ruling elite's return to military principles and ethics in the face of global challenge; and the belief that Japan's technical and financial inferiority in military strength could be compensated for by the unique 'military spirit' of Japanese tradition.

Each of the two dimensions of this project, expansionism and militarism, had a significant impact on Japanese women. The changes in the conditions of the social field of gender as a result of the strategy of militarist expansionism brought about changes to women's position which women seized and made their own. These changes in the social field comprised two important processes. First, new roles and activities for women developed along with the production of Japanese imperialism in the colonies. Second, a breakdown in the social regulation of women began to occur in Japan itself as the war effort was stepped up in the

123

1930s, arising from the gendered impact of the war. Both of these processes affecting the position of women were structured by class.

The Colonies: 'Civilisation and Enlightenment'

Japanese trading and bureaucratic activities in the colonies required a managerial and governmental labour force on the mainland consisting chiefly of middle-class men and their families. The growth of the colonies helped to expand the supervisory and administrative sections of the middle class as trade developed and state control increased. As representatives of the ruling power, the Japanese community in the colonies regulated the colonised population, and middle-class women used the opportunity to develop their own activities. Despite the repression of women's demands in the islands of Japan in the period after Taisho 'democracy', the colonies created spaces for new activities linked to the administration of colonised populations, and provided alternative models against which Japanese women could compare themselves. In a scene reminiscent of the English middle-class woman in India (Jayawardena 1995), Japanese women who travelled with their families to the colonies, or were born and brought up there, found that living in the colonies brought with it freedoms and opportunities to expand their own horizons away from the atmosphere of state regulation at home. These sources of change centred on the differing conditions of life for Japanese women in the colonies, and the opportunities for bringing 'civilisation and enlightenment' to the women there. Matsuoka Yoko describes the railway company, which was the equivalent of the British East India Company, as 'an empire in itself', which claimed to be 'the carrier of the light of civilisation into Manchuria' (Matsuoka 1952: 129). Nakatani Masako's father was a manager of the China Railway Company when Manchuria was a Japanese colony. She was born in 1924, the first of seven children, and spent all her childhood in China. At the time of the first interviews, she was a manager in Tokyo:

> My parents said I should do what I want so I should have no regrets. I was never told to do this or that because I was a girl. I was born and brought up in Tairen and Halpin, in Manchuria, and never knew life in Japan until I was eighteen. People in those cities had liberated ideas.

Like Nakatani-san, the women in our sample who had lived in the colonies during their youth had experienced a much more liberal environment than most of those who had lived all their life in Japan. Matsumoto Kuoko was born in 1921 in the Japanese colony of Korea, where her father was a businessman and her mother a full-time mother of eleven children. At the time of the interviews she was a divisional head in the civil service:

> My parents didn't think of anything consciously about what I should do, but I was told to make much of everyday life. Since I was raised in Japan's territory overseas, there was a freer atmosphere than on main-land Japan and individualism was thought much of, though it was so long ago. When I was in China I held the idea that agriculture gives us a splendid dream. I wanted to give others what I had. I taught sewing and weaving to women in the farming communities as part of the government's agricultural policy.

So the existence of colonial bureaucratic institutions and the feeling of greater freedom for women in a social milieu far away from the stric-tures of home created openings for ambitious and idealistic young women like Matsumoto-san to move into a teaching career as part of the project of bringing 'civilisation and enlightenment' to colonised communities. This experience also made it possible for her to enter the Japanese government bureaucracy when she left Korea for Japan at the end of the war. Matsuoka Yoko, reflecting critically on her two years in Korea as a child, writes about how she 'became convinced of the in-herent inferiority of the Korean people and took pride in the high principles and superior knowledge of the Japanese'. This conviction was bolstered by the fact that Korea provided a more comfortable life-style for Japanese officials and their families. As Matsuoka points out, people who 'could only afford one maid in Japan had two in Korea' (Matsuoka 1952: 43).

The myth of inferiority

This experience of the colonies was both divided by class and cut across class. In the case of lower-class Japanese people who had been encouraged to emigrate to the colonies, they too were able to raise their standard of living and experience a sense of national superiority, but the conditions in which they lived were dramatically different from the comfort and style of the government officials and company manag-ers. During a later visit as a young woman to the Japanese colony of Manchuria, Matsuoka went to see a community of peasant settlers, who had accepted a government subsidy to move from Japan. They now owned their own houses, and a piece of land much larger than any they had rented in Japan. Migration to Japanise the colonies was approved of and encouraged by the government and the railway com-pany, but Matsuoka was dismayed by the hostile conditions in which the settlers lived, and the inadequacy of the provision that had been made for them. Their houses and clothing were inadequate for the cold and desolate environment: 'I could feel their suffering in this dry, windy, sub-zero weather.... Behind their tired, strained faces, the men wore a harsh, determined look, and the women showed almost complete apathy' (Matsuoka 1952: 123–5). Matsuoka believed that many of the peasant settlers would have preferred to return home, even if it meant becoming tenants again, but they had been told that it was patriotic to migrate, and they would have lost face. But, as she points out, 'even the lowest and poorest Japanese had millions of lower and poorer people to look down upon here, and that no doubt sustained their superiority' (Matsuoka 1952: 44, 125).

Only on seeing Japanese people under US occupation behaving in ways which she had despised as 'inferior' did Matsuoka realise that the inferiority of the subjugated population was a myth. This realisation came about as she overheard a US journalist comment on the 'uncivilised behaviour' of the Japanese, which made her remember having the same thought about Koreans. Watching pickpockets, burglars, war orphans, paupers and prostitutes roam the streets of Tokyo, Matsuoka reconsidered the belief she had held in Korea that 'the Japanese would never [behave like] that' (Matsuoka 1952: 226).

So colonialism introduced a complex set of relationships for Japanese women. In some ways it reduced class divisions by eroding the restrictions which, in Japan, kept middle-class women in the home; but it also reproduced class divisions between Japanese women in the colonies by creating different standards of living and styles of life for peasant settlers compared with the managerial and administrative class. Imperialism also created national differences between colonised and coloniser women which cut across class, since every class of expatriate Japanese improved their social position compared with the conditions of life in the home country, and could feel that they belonged to a superior culture to the people of the colonies. Thus, the acquisition of an empire after the Restoration was a crucial part of Japanese women's national identity as the nation-state struggled for position with the western powers: refusing to be inferior to the West, but claiming superiority over the people of the colonies.

War: Repression and Opportunity

At the onset of war, state repression of women's opposition and resistance to subordination, and the extension of new forms of regulation over women through state-administered women's organisations, helped to maintain control of women in the family despite men's absence at the front. When we examine the position of women in wartime, however, there is a tendency to see only the repressive impact of the regulatory regime introduced by a militarised and unaccountable government. This neglects the ways in which war creates 'gendered absences' in the social field, which weaken established forms of social regulation and open up spaces for new activities through the destruction of the social and material fabric. In fact, despite state repression, the war significantly relaxed certain forms of social regulation, as well as providing opportunities for women to take up different activities and create new identities in the spaces where the established forms of regulation broke down. First, the war changed the pattern of middle-class marriage. Second, it legitimated the employment of young unmarried women of all classes. Third, it encouraged young women who were in a position to do so to continue their education as a means of avoiding war work in the munitions factories.

The war reduced the pressure on young women to marry. Ishihara Mayumi was born in 1923, the youngest of eight children. Her father was a doctor, her mother a full-time housewife. Ishihara-san graduated from Japan Women's College in 1943 at the age of 20:

> When I was at college I didn't think of marriage since it was during the war and there weren't many men to choose for marriage. Also I wanted to work. During the war the whole atmosphere wasn't for marriage, and it was considered just natural to work. So my wish was accepted as a matter of course. In those days we had to work. If you weren't doing anything you would be taken for requisition.

This is in stark contrast to Dr Ogino's experience. She was born only five years earlier, but this age difference was crucial, and by the time Japan entered the Pacific War she was already married. She, too, 'wanted to work', but she was not allowed to go to college or take up paid work until she was widowed. Her father was a professor, her mother a housewife:

> My parents hoped their sons would go to college and be professionals, and the girls would be ordinary housewives. My father and brothers didn't think girls should study. It was such an age. My teachers expected me to be a good woman, that is, a good wife and wise mother. In high school I liked astronomy, I had a yearning for the sky and the stars, I liked physics, but I spent my time doing handicrafts or arranging flowers. Such were my high-school days.

My elder brother became a university professor, my sister married a physics professor, I married a doctor. Soon after I had my first child my first husband died of illness. As a young widow I went to medical school and became a doctor. I received higher education after marriage, till then I only had high-school education. I went back to my own family with my child after the death of my husband. While I studied at medical school my parents looked after my son. They were co-operative, since I decided to study after my husband's death.

That marriage was not the choice of all Japanese women is shown by the fact that in the 1920s Japan had the highest rate of 'illegitimate' births in the world – partly because of concubinage among middle-class men, partly because common-law (naien) marriage was prevalent in rural areas, and in the expanding urban areas (Smith and Wiswell 1982; Nagy 1991: 210). Thus the war and the growing demands on the labour force enabled young middle-class women to choose to work rather than to marry.

U-turn by the militarists

War made demands on both sexes in the labour force. As men were conscripted to fight, it was necessary for more women to work outside the home. This had the effect of legitimating and sustaining the idea of the middle-class working woman which the government had tried to suppress since its emergence in the 1920s. Despite the state's reluctance to draft women for war work, in the later stages women who were not in legitimate reproductive categories were requisitioned. Matsuoka writes of how she had returned from Manchuria in the early stages of the war to see the slogan 'Bear more children and increase the population', whereas by 1943 the slogan had changed to 'Produce more aeroplanes': 'The militarists, formerly the staunchest supporters of "women in the home", now became the strongest advocates of "women in the facto-ries"' (Matsuoka 1952: 137, 178–9). As Matsuoka points out, this development was not welcome to all upper-middle-class families, who believed 'that it was shameful for girls to work after finishing school. The only occupations approved as ladylike until they were safely married were the arts of flower arrangement, tea service, cooking' (Matsuoka 1952: 179).

Nevertheless, this was the first generation of young unmarried women who were universally required to 'go out to work' and labour for the war effort. Even before the labour draft for women was intro-duced, most young women had to work, either through the efforts of voluntary organisations or through less organised social pressure. But here, too, social background could make a difference, and it was possible to avoid the worst jobs through the deployment of various forms of social capital such as family, educational or other networks. Takagi Yoshi was born in 1923, and came from a rich high-class rural family. She was fortunate to attend one of the best women's colleges, which provided her with the social capital to gain entry into a highly coveted job:

> After graduation from Japan Women's College I wanted to be a teacher but I couldn't find a job. I was wondering what to do, stay in Tokyo or go back to the country. I stayed home doing nothing, but not for long, since unless you were working you would be taken for military work as we were at war. By chance I saw an advert on the college board and heard from one of my seniors about a job. I applied to the company at the recommendation of my college alumnae and I've been working for them ever since.

Many young women whose fathers owned companies were given jobs in the family firm, or found office jobs through some other social connection which could provide an entry into the more congenial forms of employment (Matsuoka 1952: 179).

Class and war work

Young women without social or economic capital had little alternative but to make munitions in the factories. Kimura Hideko was born in 1928. Her father's political activities meant that he was unable to get regular employment despite his elite education, and his early death left his family with few resources:

> I was an only child. My father died when I was in primary school. He got involved with the leftist movement at Tokyo University, which was a very famous political movement amongst students and intellectuals in those days. Because of this he didn't have a stable occupation and earned a living translating French into Japanese. After her husband died, leaving her behind at a young age, my mother brought me up by working as a teacher. I was much influenced by her, a woman who could be so strong in spite of an adverse situation.
>   I went to a girls' high school under the old system towards the end of the war. Because it was during the war we studied for only two years, and for the rest of our school years we were sent to military factories to work. I wanted to go to pharmacy college, but was told to work.

Kimura-san was unable to go to college, despite the cultural capital of both parents' education, because of the war and her family's lack of economic resources or social connections. Yet for some of her more privileged counterparts, going to college was itself a way of avoiding war work. Kubota Fujiko was born in 1927; her father was a professor and her mother a housewife:

> I went to Metropolitan First Girls' High School – a famous school under the old system of education. During the war, when I was in tenth grade, my teacher advised me to go to college to avoid being mobilised by the army. I wanted to do liberal arts but medical colleges were the only places that classes were being held. That's how I became a doctor. In medical colleges girls were encouraged to study hard, since there weren't too many men around because of the war. I became a doctor mostly because of the social conditions of those days, and if we hadn't had the war, I would certainly have gone to a liberal arts college. Due to the war we couldn't study as we wanted but were working as factory workers. We were in a situation where going to school meant nothing, but I went to medical school more or less to avoid the war with which our nation was involved. The reality was that I had no other school to go to. There was no choice – you could study only at medical school.

But a college education was a choice that was not available to most young women, since only those from wealthy families were in a position to take this route out of monotonous, difficult or back-breaking manual work. These two processes through which war work could be avoided – that is, through the cultural capital of higher education and the social capital of a network of connections – helped to reproduce class divisions between women. The processes of change brought about by the war had a particular impact on young middle-class women, for they were released from early marriage, and their entry into education and paid work was made respectable and patriotic. These changes did not have the same significance for lower-class women, for whom marriage did not have the same compulsion, paid work was always a necessity, and higher education was beyond reach. Class divisions were reproduced in some ways, but in others the divisions began to erode as the middle-class model of the ideal Japanese woman was undermined in the rejection of marriage and the move into paid employment.

We should recognise, however, that it was not only young unmarried women who engaged in war work. Even women who were married and had children had to work, because of the devastation and chaos which the war created. The conscription of men for active service left women to keep the family together, to feed and clothe dependants, and to replace men in industry, including heavy engineering and munitions work. In addition, the loss of husbands, fathers, sons and brothers in the war, or their incapacitation, had the same effect of forcing women to become responsible for male as well as female roles in the upkeep and continuation of the family.

Contradictory Gendering

In order to understand the transitions in the perceptions of gendered identities, we will draw on Tsurumi Kazuko's (1970) and Carolyn Steedman's (1988) conceptualisations of the changing social relations produced by military hierarchies. We will argue that the process of militarisation in war produces a contradictory form of gendering in men. Alongside an extreme form of aggressive masculinity, in which soldiers were trained to kill on command, there developed a kind of feminisation which removed from the soldiers any sense of being in control of their own actions. Tsurumi argues that men in the Japanese imperial army were 'reduced to childhood roles' through the absence of privacy, the creation of anxiety and humiliation, and the use of arbitrary violence against them. These processes were designed to produce obedience to orders, dependence on the hierarchy, and submission to the 'ideology of death' (Tsurumi 1970: 124–5). They were particularly strong in the training of the Japanese military forces, because of the aim of creating the special military spirit or 'will to die', as a form of compensation for the technical and financial superiority of the western military forces. Steedman, in a different colonial context, also points to the infantilisation of the soldier, but hints at a kind of feminisation with her references to the 'domestic tone of soldiers' lives as they cooked, washed and sewed together', and to the 'female metaphor' of the 'caged bird' (Steedman 1988: 41, 48, 104). Steedman is referring to working-class British soldiers in India, but Tsurumi demonstrates that in Japan middle-class male students received the same treatment to produce obedience, dependence and submission (Tsurumi 1970: 113–20).

We argue that a similarly contradictory but opposite process of gendering was occurring with the women left at home. Alongside an extreme form of femininity, in which women were exhorted to reproduce new life continuously to replace the state's military form of social capital, women also had to take over men's activities in the home, moving middle-class women away from the feminine roles of obedience to the male hierarchy in the family, dependence on male relatives for survival, and submission to the ideology of male power. As men went to war and were subsumed in the military hierarchy to become obedient, submissive and dependent, women cast off these qualities to assume the role of father, husband, son and elder brother, undertaking what had been male activities, supporting children and old people, and going out to work to earn a living. This process entailed a degree of masculinisation, as middle-class women took responsibility for the protection and survival of others rather than being protected and supported themselves, and came to see themselves as proactive family members who could be reliable and decisive, rather than relying on others to take decisions and act upon them.

This process challenged specifically middle-class female identities and brought them closer to the less respectable lower-class women whom Matsuoka had admired with mixed feelings when she saw them challenging men: 'It hurt my pride that street girls and [female] black-marketeers would stand up for their rights when ordinary [sic] women could not' (Matsuoka 1952: 225). Just as Japanese women in the colonies began to take up positions as subjects in relation to colonised women's position as objects, so in Japan men's social absences at the front provided spaces for women to step into subject positions which had previously been reserved for men, acquiring new forms of capital in their own right. Thus class as well as gender divisions began to break down, as middle-class women took up new masculinised activities and roles which identified them with lower-class models of womanhood. They began to accumulate new forms of power in the family and outside it, including economic capital from paid work, cultural capital from education and social capital from new networks and connections – all affecting the way middle-class women saw themselves and their place in society.

These changes in the practices of middle-class womanhood, which largely ran counter to the new ideals for women promoted by the state, occurred as a result of the spaces opened up by Japan's decision to pursue the strategy of militarist expansionism in the struggle with global imperialism. They happened regardless of the outcome of Japan's imperialist war, as can be seen from the fact that countries on the other side of the conflict also saw women emerge into new fields (see Braybon and Summerfield 1987). In relation to Britain, however, Braybon and Summerfield's assessment is that 'even though there were many changes … the continuity in women's position at work and in the home between 1914 and 1945 is very striking' (Braybon and Summerfield 1987: 286–7).

We argue that in Japan it was the changes rather than the continuities in women's position which were more striking, and that the reason for this difference lay in the social changes which were consolidated by Japan's military defeat, rather than the US legal reforms which followed it. These social changes had a powerful impact in delegitimating the structures of social regulation and the system of ideas about women's place, resulting in a breakdown of authority in the entire edifice of the family–state–emperor system among significant sections of society. In Chapter 14 we look at how the defeat of the militarist project contributed to the erosion of the renovated authority systems of the family–state under the emperor system, which held gender, class and colonial relations in place before the end of the war.

Chapter 14

Defeat of the Militarist Project

How did these entrenched forms of institutional authority – the authority of the emperor as head of state and the authority of men as heads of the family units of the state – break down at the end of the war? We suggest that there were three main causes. First, the material losses imposed by the destruction of war wiped out much of Japan's economic capital in terms of both finance and property, and undermined the material basis of the class structure. Second, the social absences caused by the war's human casualties damaged the social fabric and eroded the practice of male domination in the family. Third, progressive discourses in the form of counter-hegemonic critiques of the class and gender hierarchies, which had been created by the prewar opposition movements and sustained at some risk within liberal families and educational institutions in the wartime period, were reactivated as a response to the material and social destruction of the war.

We argue that the imperial and patriarchal forms of authority embedded in the family–state–emperor system were integrated in a system of social regulation based on a hierarchy structured by gender, class and nation. The war caused both material losses and social absences, forms of destruction which were repeated on both sides of the conflict. But defeat transformed these losses and absences into culpable responsibilities, undermining the right of the emperor and the ruling classes to control the people, the right of the state to dominate other nations, and the right of men to determine the activities of the household. Thus we argue that, paradoxically, the creation of obedience, dependence and submission in men by the state in the production of military social capital eroded the obedience, dependence, submission, protection and confinement of middle-class women in the family, fragmenting the image of womanhood presented to the nation as the ideal model to emulate. This was later to have dramatic effects on the constitution and authority of the family–state system as a whole.

Material Loss and Social Absence

We will now describe the social and economic impact of the conflict on women's families at the end of the war. First, the loss of the empire meant material losses for young women whose fathers had made a career out of running the colonial system, rendering a protected middle-class life impossible. Saito Masako was an only child whose parents died prematurely:

> My father was an engineer in Korea, and I went to school and teacher training college in Korea. The family came back to mainland Japan after the war. The family wealth was lost abroad, and my parents died soon one after the other, so I had to support myself.

But losing the empire also meant cognitive transformations in the minds of young Japanese women who had thought they could teach 'civilisation and enlightenment' to the people of the colonies. Matsumoto Kuoko is the young woman we met earlier, who returned to work for the government:

> I took up this work from my experiences of coming back to Japan from China. In those days Japan was in a period of confusion. When I came back to Wakayama prefecture in Japan, I was shocked to see the low level of farmers' awareness, which made me realise the great gap between the reality and the idealistic idea I had of agriculture. I taught people in my village what I had done in China. I taught the people in my neighbourhood how to improve living conditions in the period of confusion right after the war.

Matsumoto-san's illusion of the superiority of Japanese civilisation and knowledge was shattered when she saw the conditions of agriculture and the peasantry in Japan at the end of the war.

The losses sustained by the nation were not limited to those returning from the colonies. The war brought agricultural chaos, economic collapse, the destruction of property and a loss of wealth for many people. Kohga Manae was a professor of home economics. Her father was a draughtsman, her mother a housewife:

> We lost our mother and all our property in the war. I had to take care of my younger brother and lost my chance and age for marriage. He

was very bright, but I was the only person with an income and we were too poor to give him an education. Now he's teaching at a junior high school and isn't content with it. He gave up hope halfway through. The war presented the greatest difficulties, and also our family circumstances. My father's property was all lost in the war, and I had to work to support the family. I fed my father too. My mother died early, and I worked to support my father and brother and looked after them. This mental, physical and economic burden was on me for fifteen or sixteen years. My brother had a side-job for two years at the US base when he was a student, which helped greatly. But still, just before payday we had very little money and not enough to eat, and we were very sad.

Because men were at war, it was mostly women who held the family together. Ninomiya Kimi was only eight when the war finished, but she recognised that the family would not have survived without the two 'mothers' who maintained it:

My real mother died three months after the cease-fire because of fatigue. The family would have collapsed but for my stepmother. I was evacuated. We lost our house and had to start everything again.

Survivors' consciousness

The war brought with it not only material destruction but also social devastations in the form of the death, sickness and injury of relatives, friends and community members, which had a profound effect on the way the survivors saw the rest of their lives and their obligations to others. Higashiura Hisami was 17 in the final stage of the war:

I was living in Nagasaki when the atom bomb dropped. Many of my classmates and friends were killed. Houses were lost, everything was burned. Women and children were supposed to leave the city, but my father said the Americans weren't brutal, so when the troops came in we didn't go. It made me think the rest of my life was something I couldn't expect to get, it was very valuable. So I had to live a special life, I had to do something with it as so many others had lost their lives.

Experiences like this had a profound impact on the consciousness of women and men of that generation who survived the war, and of the next generation to whom the same disasters had not happened. Tamura Mariko was born in 1925:

I took the decision to work because of the war. I was twenty after the war and most young men were dead, that's why I decided to work. There was very bad inflation. I decided I must have a career, it's necessary for women to have their own financial knowledge.

Kohno Chiyomi was born in 1944:

> A male teacher at school said women should have a job. He said so, I think, because he'd seen many women without jobs experience great hardship after the war. Such women had a really hard time after their husbands were killed in the war.

Inoue Yoshi was born in 1945:

> My mother wants me to be independent as a person. Human life is very contingent: you never know when you'll die, your husband may die, so you must be able to support yourself. My mother had difficulties in the war; that generation had many problems, psychological and physical, in the war. Women were forced into independence; many women had no husbands.

The impact on women of these gendered social absences in the family during the war legitimated the experiences of women whose male relatives had died and left them unsupported, not through war but through sickness – such as Onuma Youko, whose father died at an early age, Bando Yoriko, whose father had TB and could not work, and Dr Ogino, whose husband died of illness soon after the birth of their first child. In all these cases of death or incapacity, whether through war or sickness, it was predominantly women who were forced to take the place of men, to act as fathers as well as mothers to their children, sons as well as daughters to their parents and parents-in-law, elder brothers as well as elder sisters to their younger siblings, and to replace men as the economic supporters and protectors of their families. Although this process opened up new social spaces for women, it should be recognised that it did not guarantee a life of comfort and fulfilment, but often meant 'forced independence', hardship and overwhelming fatigue.

Progressive Discourse

These spaces for new activities and changing ideas were supported by the persistence and subsequent reactivation of counter-hegemonic discourses that had been constructed by the prewar oppositional movements, including the liberal reformist, socialist and women's movements. Left-wing and feminist activities were forced underground after 1931 (Mackie 1988: 58), but, regardless of the severe penalties for 'wrong thoughts' in the Peace Preservation Law, progressive discourses were maintained throughout the war period by relatives within the safety of the family, and by teachers in the more exposed arena of the educational system. The heavy state repression to which these systems of ideas were subject is indicative of the continued existence of the critiques, the threat they posed to the family–state system, and the importance of making them invisible. These minority oppositional discourses undermined the legitimacy of the systems of imperial and patriarchal authority, and helped women in their struggle to obtain and retain positions as social subjects.

Some of the older women who had been pioneers in the movement away from the domestic middle-class ideal came from liberal families in which progressive ideas of parents or grandparents made it possible for women to undertake activities closed to previous generations, or enabled them to follow non-traditional roles and practices that had first been explored by (or, indeed, denied to) their mothers. These women lived within a progressive family culture where they had no need to struggle against the established pattern of life for a middle-class woman. The discourses involved incorporated influences from different sources, including Japanese and western intellectuals: such as Miura Fumiko's father who was a scholar and senator educated at Tokyo University; Murakami Hiroki's father, who was a teacher of philosophy at a teacher training college; and Hitomi Yumiko's parents, who eloped together and went to the USA for their education. As Hitomi Yumiko says, 'It was easy for me because I'm the second generation of liberals. Most women of my generation had to fight the family.'

Class duties

Two major discourses contributed to the sustaining of progressive ideas and the breaking down of middle-class ideas of womanhood – one centred on the idea of class duties, the other on the notion of women's rights. The liberal discourse of philanthropic obligation recognised class differences and the duty to contribute to society as a kind of *noblesse oblige* for one's class privilege and as a means of repaying the lower classes, without developing into a demand for structural changes in class power. Hitomi Yumiko's family was a good example. She was born in 1928; her mother was a social worker and her father was a statesman who came from a privileged background:

> My parents are unique. Usually when a girl is of a certain age she is expected to marry. But from when I was a baby my mother used to say: 'Be exceptional, you're privileged, you should feel you owe something

to others, you're healthy and clever, you must repay the underprivileged somehow.' My parents were unusual because they were reform workers. They went to the USA and my father got his PhD from there; my mother and father eloped and got married as comrades. We are from a very old family; we had no financial troubles. My father is ninety and still active, my mother is eighty-one, she was a graduate of Tsuda College.

In this quotation, the discourse of philanthropic obligation creates a duty to 'repay what you owe to the underprivileged'. This acknowledges the interdependence between the poor and the wealthy, and recognises a social obligation on the part of the rich to show paternalistic benevolence to the less well-off. This discourse was oppositional because it is a reversal of the traditional idea within Japanese feudalism, whereby the subordinate's receipt of benevolence (*on*) creates a lifelong obligation of loyalty to the superior (Tsurumi 1970: 93–4), a concept which was renovated in the Meiji period into an obligation to the emperor for the good fortune of having been born in the empire. This alternative discourse was used to legitimate change and reform.

Women's rights

The other major discourse was a women's rights discourse. It may be suggested that the idea of rights is a western concept, based as it is on western liberal thought, but we have already shown that the notion of women's rights was developed within an indigenous Japanese context by the 'first-wave' Japanese women's movement as long ago as 1876. These ideas were influenced by both male reformers and Japanese feminists. The association of Kubota Fujiko's family with the women's movement went back two generations. She was a doctor, born in 1927:

I'd never been told in my own family to do this or that because I was a woman. Being the eldest child with two younger brothers, I'd been treated the best. I was perplexed at the attitude at work to my being a woman. My family was a little different from ordinary ones in that my grandmother was one of the so-called 'new women' who agreed with the ideologies of Hiratsuka Raicho and other women. She was a feminist, and everyone in the family believed in sex equality and never discriminated against its members for being man or woman. Therefore they thought that of course women should have higher education and take on a profession. My grandmother herself came to Tokyo to become a doctor, but couldn't due to being a woman. So she encouraged me all the more to be a doctor. The social conditions of the war were the major influence in my becoming a doctor.

Takahashi Kiyo is a senior civil servant, born in 1924. Her father was a lawyer, her mother a housewife:

> My mother influenced my awareness. She was in the women's suffrage movement. I was also reading *Shin Onna Daigaku* by Fukuzawa Yukichi. In the Edo period there was a famous book by Kaibara Ekken, a Confucian scholar who established a women's college which he named Women's Virtue. He taught that the wife must obey, etc. *Shin Onna Daigaku* is a criticism written in the Meiji period by the founder of Keio University [Fukuzawa Yukichi]. I read that book; it made me really angry about the old text. I was in the mood to criticise the prewar set-up, particularly the law, because my father was a lawyer. I naturally looked up jurists' records, judges' decisions – they also made me angry. I was very much influenced by the restrictions put on women. The change came when I was twenty, in 1945. But in my childhood women had no rights of any sort. So I and my friends felt angry – it was something of a movement. In prewar days women's status was low, legally and in fact. They couldn't enter university, there was no suffrage, married women had no right to property. All this changed after the war – they got rights. There was a very strong objection by the feudal elements – very strong. I wanted to improve that situation.

Progressive discourse in education

Progressive discourses were also maintained in certain schools and colleges, since many teachers had been part of the Marxist student movement of the Taisho period, although this was a more dangerous location than the family in which to express radical ideas. The teaching profession was a source of both reactionary and progressive ideas, despite the disapproval and surveillance of the state. Government officials could intervene to regulate the circulation of 'wrong thoughts', but many teachers continued to promote ideas about rights and freedom. William Cummings (1980: 5–6), referring to the postwar education system in Japan, argues that there is a gap between official educational policy and its implementation by teachers: what teachers do in the classroom cannot be totally controlled by the state, and this was true of education before and even during the war, as progressive teachers persisted in undermining government propaganda. At Yuwasa Yayori's school there was a strong feeling of sex equality in education, and this was put into practice in the educational process, albeit with unfortunate consequences for the principal. Yuwasa-san, a professor, was born in 1918:

> At high school before the war, the principal encouraged girls to go to higher education. The sexes were segregated at that time; in spite of that

we were encouraged to do academic work the same as the boys. For example, we had more maths and science, less domestic science. There were separate books for boys and girls, but we used boys' books. We had many competent teachers. A hundred and twenty students went on to higher education out of two hundred and forty in my year. Four out of a thousand overall went, but in our group a half went. We were always told to work equally with boys. I think school was a basic influence on me and my socialisation. The principal had been all over the world, and had preached equality; it was a very important influence on me. He taught us comparative religion – a different religion each year! This was a Metropolitan school. The principal was sacked after thirty-seven years because of his progressive ideas; it was considered dangerous to encourage women to be outgoing. But for me, to work outside was natural. We got the feeling women could do something.

In universities, too, progressive teachers flouted the rules which excluded women from a higher education equivalent to men's, and taught women along with men, even finding them places to do research, although officially this was impossible. Kanzaki Mieko, a professor, was born in 1919. Her father was a lawyer and her mother a college graduate:

I went to the First Girls' High School, a very special school in Tokyo before the war. They wanted women to learn a lot. I was influenced by it. There were three streams: the first leading to higher education, the second vocational, and the third for housewives. I was in class one. Women couldn't go to high-level university then. But if all the places weren't filled by men, a second exam was open to women. I wanted to go to Osaka University, but it wasn't open to women. But the professor allowed me to attend classes even though I wasn't a proper student and I wasn't entitled to a degree. Then he introduced me to a research institute, and there I was treated the same as men who had graduated. I had a friend in Paris who was with Madame Curie. She said if I wanted to learn I must choose a high-class university, but they were closed to women before the war.

Clearly the middle class was not a uniformly conservative social category (Crompton 1993: 204), and in Japan, too, it consisted of diverse political elements, for there were families who maintained minority oppositional ideals and made it easy for their daughters to take up a position as subjects.

We now go on to examine how the authority of the system of social regulation over women broke down. We will use the concept of authority to refer to the legitimate exercise of power, attained through the acquisition of symbolic capital, which Bourdieu defines as a 'reputation for competence, respectability and honourability' (Bourdieu 1984: 291).

Erosion of Authority Systems

We have argued that the regulation of women by men in the family–
state system was eroded through the gendered social absences occasioned
by the war. At least partly as a result of the special Japanese military
spirit or 'will to die', and partly because of the USA's willingness to
drop atomic bombs on large centres of civilian population, Japan
sustained high casualties, estimated at more than two million dead and
more than one million missing or injured (Tsurumi 1970: 80), and a
significant proportion of the population were affected by the loss of
family members. Around 80 per cent of these were military casualties,
meaning that many more men than women were killed. As men were
absent, incapacitated or killed in the war, these gendered social absences
meant the loss of women's protected status in the middle class, and the
necessity for women to take over male roles and activities in the family
and outside it. These gendered social absences also entailed the undermining of existing gendered structures of social organisation, social
relations and social hierarchies. The absence from the family of large
numbers of key men, leaving their positions in gendered hierarchies
undefended, eroded systems of social regulation and the enforcement
of gendered authority. The social spaces created by these absences were
willingly or unwillingly filled by women who were no longer in the
position of being protected, dependent, obedient and submissive, but
of protecting others, having others depend on them, taking family
decisions, providing a livelihood and articulating a sense of authority
themselves.

The authority of the family–state system was also, as we have seen,
undermined by the material losses sustained in the war. The effect of
these absences and losses on the systems of imperial and patriarchal
authority are crucially linked with the outcome of the war. Absence and
loss featured on both sides of the conflict, but to understand what
happened in Japan we need to understand the difference in the concepts
of accountability and honourability. In Japan the Diet was accountable
to the emperor, not the people. The authority of the emperor as head
of state emerged not from a democratic mandate, but from a divine
mandate to perform the ceremonial rituals of government and intercede
between the gods and the people to produce a benign environment in
which the people might flourish – an old idea revived when the Meiji
emperor was restored to the throne (Bocking 1996: 118).

At Japan's defeat, the head of state and officers of the armed forces
were shown to have produced detrimental outcomes in the form of the

destruction of the material and social fabric, which were neither compensated for by other valued gains, such as would be provided by victory or the extension of Japanese power, nor atoned for through the traditional means of accepting responsibility and restoring honour. As a result, the emperor's right to rule, to perform the ceremonials and to intercede with the deities, and the right of the military to enforce the power of the state and to direct the nation, were forfeited for significant sections of the population. Under the military code of honour, failure to produce a benign environment, or to provide victory, was viewed as 'dishonour', and could be erased by various actions which signified the acceptance of responsibility by those at fault.

Betrayal

Examples of the breakdown of state authority amongst different classes of the population are provided by Tsurumi Kazuko (1970) and Matsuoka Yoko (1952). In the first example, a rank-and-file member of the military forces, for whom the emperor represented the personification of the authority of the state, describes in physical terms his loss of respect for the emperor, whom he had been trained at school and in the military to revere as the earthly embodiment of the sun goddess. Tsurumi quotes Kamishima, who argues that the people lost respect for the authority of the emperor because not only did he lose the war, but he also refused responsibility for the defeat by failing either to commit suicide or to abdicate according to the traditional ethics of the military value system. She quotes the furious and even traitorous response of a disillusioned low-ranking sailor when the head of state failed to take responsibility for the defeat in the traditional way: 'I wish I could hang the emperor upside down ... and flog him with a club as hard as I was beaten up in the navy' (Tsurumi 1970: 186). A public opinion survey in 1954 by the Prime Minister's Office showed that 43 per cent of those questioned in Tokyo thought they had been betrayed by the government, although the figure was lower in less urbanised areas (Tsurumi 1970: 186–7).

In the second example, this loss of authority by the head of state was extended to the armed agents of the state by a group described on the basis of their 'appearance and language' as 'lower-middle-class travellers' (Matsuoka 1952: 201). Matsuoka writes of a train journey she took to Tokyo on 17 August 1945, two days after the emperor announced the surrender. Everyone in the crowded train was discussing what would happen when the US forces arrived. A Japanese army captain in uniform got into the carriage, clearly expecting to be offered a seat, as usual. But most people ignored him, while others stared:

Finding his way blocked, the captain became angry and shouted, 'Get up, you...'. 'I was amazed that no-one stood up to make room for him. With scorn in their eyes, the passengers ... watched him indifferently. A man in the back of the car shouted, 'Don't be superior. You lost the war, didn't you?' The captain was now outraged. He put his right hand on his sword and drew it. What he met ... was not fear and obedience, but hatred, scorn and defiance.... Without a word, he put his sword back and struggled out of the car. (Matsuoka 1952: 201)

In the third example, the conceptualisation of the state as a transcendent unitary organism with the emperor at its head was questioned by a member of the intellectual elite who thought in abstract terms. Tsurumi quotes the academic Okuma Nobuyuki:

In my mind there used to exist a concept of the state as an ideal or norm. I even considered the state as the source of morality....
    However, that concept of the state was destroyed [by ... Japan's defeat] ... [w]hen we observe everything that was done during the war by the state, we can see that they were only human actions exercised through the agencies of men.... And the men who occupied the upper stratum were ordinary men who were often controlled by ignorance, stupidity, and prejudice.... When we look at the state from the point of view of these actions, there is nothing transcendental about the function of the state. (Tsurumi 1970: 187–8)

Although each example portrays a different understanding of the state – concrete, embodied or abstract – what they all have in common is the demonstration of the dramatic decline in symbolic capital which had formerly attached to the system of state regulation. Bourdieu argues that once status has been conferred, and symbolic capital granted, the occupant of the honoured position is expected to rise to the respect which he embodies by exhibiting the capacities and attributes attached to it. It is in this sense *noblesse oblige*, since nobility has its obligations (Bourdieu 1984: 24). The Japanese emperor, high-ranking state officials and military leaders suffered a dramatic loss of the recognition on which symbolic capital depends. The emperor personified not only imperial and state power but also class and gender power, and the system of state regulation in the form of the family–state–emperor system was so completely saturated with the symbolic capital of masculinity, class and empire that the authority of the hierarchies of gender, class and nation also collapsed along with that of the state.

'I saw everything fall apart'

The erosion of the authority of the state impacted down through the social hierarchy of the family–state system. For women, men failed to deliver the return for their authority over them in the family. Just as the emperor could no longer protect the country, deliver victory over the enemy, or provide a benign environment in which the people might flourish, men could no longer protect women from foreign forces, provide their means of living, or ensure a benign environment in which they could reproduce life and bring up the next generation, eroding men's right to command and control women, and breaking down male authority in the family. Yoshioka Terumi was born in 1932. Her father was a landowner before the war and lost everything:

> I was twelve when the war ended and Japan was defeated.... I saw everything fall apart, including the emperor's authority and men's authority. I learnt the lesson that nothing is absolute in this world – only myself. I was awakened to myself when I was twelve. I discovered everything would change.

Like Yoshioka-san, Nakatani Masako discovered that the securities of class privilege for women were destabilised along with the collapse of imperial, patriarchal and state power. It is in this light that Nakatani-san's words, seamlessly linking the material losses sustained by her middle-class family in the colonies with the discourse of women's rights, may be understood:

> My family had to return to Japan when the war ended and our financial situation drastically changed. It happened when I was at Tokyo Women's Christian College, when Japan had its hardest time. To my regret, middle-class lifestyle underwent drastic changes due to defeat in the war. When the war ended I was twenty. I thought there should be less and less difference in the treatment of men and women in the future. Women had the right to vote, and universities were opened up to us. I thought sex discrimination would disappear, and it was important to be economically independent in order to establish a basis for speaking out.

With Japan's defeat, Nakatani-san's father lost his prestigious job in China, and as the eldest of six children she took up schoolteaching to support the family. This collapse of gendered, class and colonial authority changed both her world-view and her world.

Taking Advantage of Change

Finally, we will show how women took advantage of changes in the social spaces and systems of authority to move from a position as object to a position as subject. Hara Harumi was born in 1921, and wanted to be a doctor before the war. Her father was a company director, her mother a housewife:

> My parents wanted me to be a housewife. I passed the exam to enter a women's medical college recommended to me by my mother's brother, but I had to give it up because of objection from other family members. I became sulky, since I couldn't go to medical college, although I wanted to be a doctor. Instead I went to Metropolitan Women's College for two years, where I studied in a classical Japanese class. I thought if I couldn't be a doctor I could do anything else if I really tried. Then I went to a language school to learn French, and I worked for the Telephone and Telegraph Company for two years. My family told me I wouldn't be able to marry if I kept working. I tried to persuade them somehow to earn their sympathy, but it didn't work and I gave up.
>
> After the war I received a notice that my husband had died, so I took a job and left my three-year-old child with my mother. The three of us lived together. My mother's attitude was that it couldn't be helped, being at the time of confusion during and after the war. My in-laws weren't in a position to say this or that, since my husband was off to war and later his death notice was sent. We weren't in a position to pay much attention to what others were doing. Everybody had a hard time just surviving, and people were indifferent to what others were doing. Several years later my husband returned home from overseas, but he'd been seriously injured and I couldn't stop working. When he returned to Japan and was able to start working again, he asked me to stop, but I continued.

As a young woman, Hara-san wanted a career, but was forced to accede to family pressure in order to marry. In stark contrast, even after her husband's unexpected 'return from the dead', she simply ignored his request to stop working. Clearly it was not the simple fact of the war itself which changed her approach to family authority, but a complex set of influences including the social conditions outside the family, the impact of the war on the family circumstances, and the responsibilities she held for the survival and protection of her mother and son. The lengthy absence of the key male figure of support and protection – who finally returned but stripped of his authority to determine events in the household on his final recovery of fitness – undermined the ability of the husband's parents to control their daughter-in-law. Her son needed protection and had no father to provide it, just as her mother needed support and had no other children to offer it. The system of patriarchal regulation of women broke down in both the family and the community, as the key men who would have upheld it were absent at a time when the social organisation was in a state of disruption, and the systems of class, gender and imperial authority had forfeited their right to exercise power. Paradoxically, masculine 'honour' may more easily have been retained by those who did not return, since they had made the sacrifice which eradicated dishonour.

Losing symbolic capital

Thus, the family–state system under the divine mandate of the emperor was predicated on the hierarchies of nation, class and gender. The defeat of the militarist project eroded the authority of this system of social regulation, producing a sudden dramatic loss of symbolic capital in each set of social hierarchies, as military defeat transformed the in-evitable material losses and social absences of war into culpable respon-sibilities of the state, its military agents, its head in the form of the emperor and its familial representatives in the form of male heads of household. We argue that the decline in the authority of the system of state regulation as a whole eroded the legitimate exercise of power of each of the social hierarchies through the loss of symbolic capital.

First, the legitimacy of the emperor system depended both on the symbolic capital of the emperor in his position as earthly representative of the sun goddess, and on the existence of the empire as an embodi-ment of the superior military and cultural capital of the Japanese nation-state. The loss of the empire abolished the symbolic capital which had accrued to the Japanese state in its successful struggle for global dis-tinction, removing from Japan's sphere of influence the inferior com-parator in the form of the colonised peoples, and at the same time reinserting Japan into a subordinate relationship with the USA. This process produced a deficit of symbolic capital both in the abstract concept of the state held by the intellectual elite, and in the various bodily manifestations of the state held by the lower and lower-middle classes, such as the head of state, the agents of the state and the familial representatives of the state. In each case, recognition of the 'compe-tence' and 'honourability' of these manifestations of the state was withdrawn. Their incompetence in running the affairs of the family–state was demonstrated by the defeat of the military project, and found tangible form in everyday life in the disintegration of the material and social fabric in both the public and the private spheres, referred to by many of our respondents as 'the period of confusion after the war'. Their dishonour was located in the failure to abide by the traditional military code of honour whereby responsibility for defeat was accepted and atoned for through an honourable act of self-sacrifice which transformed dishonour into respect. In this way, the reputation for competence and honourability was erased from the physical embodiments of the state at the time of Japan's defeat by the West.

Second, the family–state system under the emperor depended on the symbolic capital of the class structure, and on the existence of the wealth and property of the middle and upper classes, which had been seriously undermined by the end of the war. The extensive material losses in the form of wealth and property left behind in the colonies, property damaged or demolished in Japan, and financial capital dissolved through inflation, fragmented the material basis for the class structure, and created a body of 'newly poor', which undermined the legitimacy of class power and seriously damaged middle-class women's ability to lead a protected life.

Third, the family–state system depended on the symbolic capital attached to the structure of patriarchal gender relations and the presence of the male head of household in the family. By the end of the war, however, many families had been left without functioning male heads, and the movement of women into these vacated social positions eroded the authority of the patriarchal family system and the legitimacy of male power. At the same time, the failure of those troops who did come home from the battlefield to return in glory, having earned the right to rewards and privileges, increased the right of women to emerge from the domestic sphere and compete in the public fields of education and employment, which also undermined the gendered authority of men, and contributed to the disintegration of patriarchal authority.

Chapter 15

The US Occupation

In this chapter we will argue that the transformations in gender relations which came about in the position of middle-class women after the war owed as much to events internal to Japan as to the legal and constitutional changes introduced by the US occupation authorities. While these legal changes were important in setting up a framework for the reorganisation of gender relations after the war, they were only a reflection of changes in thought, outlook, behaviour and practices that Japanese women had already made themselves as a result of their wartime experiences. Although it is true that the USA liberated the legal and political structure for women, we will argue – contrary to western views that the changes to women's position were handed to them as a gift by the more 'advanced civilisation' of the occupying force – that many Japanese women had already emerged into subject positionings, willingly or unwillingly, and had struggled to take up and retain strategic emplacements which men had vacated. We further argue that the USA, far from being an 'advanced civilisation' in terms of a commitment to women's rights, used the issue of women's rights to promote its own political aims in relation to Japan.

The Occupation Reforms

The aim of the US military occupation in Japan from 1945 to 1952 was to emasculate militarist nationalism, and to preserve capitalism in a form that would ensure Japan's subordination to US imperialism. This process was carried out using a discourse of liberalisation and democratisation (Halliday 1975: 162). The USA excluded its European Allies while carrying out reforms in their name, awarding the title of Supreme Commander of the Allied Powers (SCAP) to General MacArthur (Beasley 1990: 215). The exclusion of the European Allies demonstrated that the aim was to bring Japan into the US sphere of influence in the Pacific, as part of the competition with the other imperial powers. At the same time, Japan was condemned by the Allies for having attempted to bring neighbouring countries into the Japanese sphere of influence, as part of the competition with the West in East Asia (Halliday 1975: 167–8).

That the objective was demilitarisation can clearly be seen in the purge of 1946 and 1947, which was aimed mainly against the military, who constituted 80 per cent of those excluded from public office, followed by politicians mostly from the right-wing Progressive and Liberal Parties, which composed 16 per cent. This resulted in the promotion of the government bureaucracy, who comprised less than 1 per cent of the purge, and who took over many of the positions vacated by the purged politicians. Reform of the bureaucracy was never implemented because of disagreements in the USA and opposition from within Japan (Halliday 1975: 172–4).

Several important reforms with implications for women were initiated by the US administration in this first stage. Education was reformed by banning the nationalist ethics courses and militarist ideology, providing free compulsory education based on equal opportunity and the possibility of coeducation (Beasley 1990: 222). Land reform was instituted to eradicate the remnants of the feudal system and permit the free development of capitalism (Halliday 1975: 190–92). The initial proposals were weakened by landlord interests in the Diet, but the revisions were rejected by MacArthur, and a new draft was forced through a reluctant Lower House in 1946. This provided for compulsory purchase by the state of land held by absentee landlords, which was offered to existing tenants on easy terms. Owner cultivators and resident landlords could own an upper limit of 3 *cho* (hectares) or 12 *cho* on the less hospitable northern island of Hokkaido, not more than one-third of which could be let out to tenants. As a result of the reform, the area of tenanted land decreased from 40 per cent to 10 per cent, defusing rural radical movements and making Japan a country of owner-peasants whose interests became politically conservative (Beasley 1990: 222–3).

Other than the United States' desire to abolish the remnants of feudal class relations in order to allow capitalism to flourish, neither the USA nor the Tokyo ruling group wanted any change in the class struc-

ture or the capitalist mode of production, and both parties agreed to
retain the emperor as head of state, as the key to rebuilding the class
system (Halliday 1975: 167–8). The Constitution recognised the emperor
as the symbol of national unity, although he renounced his divinity in
1946 at SCAP's instigation (Beasley 1990: 220). The Constitution established the supremacy of the Diet and the independence of the judiciary,
renounced war as a sovereign right of the nation (Article 9), established a bicameral Diet with both Houses elected by universal adult
suffrage, and guaranteed US-style civil rights (Halliday 1975: 171; Beasley
1990: 219–20). The Japanese authorities had delayed producing a draft
Constitution, so SCAP drafted one and foisted it on a reluctant Cabinet.
It was promulgated in the emperor's name in 1947, with a few amend-
ments introduced by the Diet (Beasley 1990: 219). The speed with which
the Constitution was drafted was largely to avoid Allied input. The Allied
Far Eastern Commission, intended to oversee the occupation, responded
that they 'doubted that the pending draft Constitution expressed the
free will of the Japanese people … they were apprehensive that it would
be pushed through the Diet without adequate time for consideration',
which would result in hostility to its provisions (Halliday 1975: 171).

Japan becomes an ally

That democratisation was not the real or primary aim of the reforms
is clear from the second stage of the occupation, when US policy
changed from the deconstruction to the reconstruction of Japan. The
communist victory in China in 1949 had deprived the USA of its chosen
ally in East Asia, and the hostilities in Korea in 1950 made Japan the
only alternative. As Beasley says, Japan became more important to the
USA as an ally than as a democracy (Beasley 1990: 224). This second
stage is known as the reverse course, and involved a new 'red' purge
in 1949 which removed left-wing workers from their jobs in the public
and private sectors. In 1948, the newly established right to strike had
been prohibited for civil servants, and in 1950 this was extended to all
public-sector employees, including those in local government (Halliday
1975: 183–4, 227–9). These moves were motivated by the Cold War and
the desire to build up Japan as a strategic ally in East Asia against the
renewed threat from the USSR, as well as from the 1949 Chinese Revolution, which forced the USA to acknowledge the loss of China to the
capitalist system.

    The USA began to rebuild Japanese capitalism (Halliday 1975: 183–
4) to enable it to become the workshop of Asia and to provide an
arsenal for the Korean War against communism in 1950–53 and the

Vietnam War from 1965 to 1975. The USA also began to remilitarise
Japan from 1950 by using the Korean War to institute what was to
become a Self Defence Force, and to establish military bases. The USA
made the army and the bases the precondition for independence, and
the Peace Treaty was made conditional on the Security Treaty. The US–
Japan Security Treaty was highly unpopular with almost every country
in the world, and only 18 per cent of the Japanese population supported the retention of US military bases, with more Diet members
opposing the Security Treaty than they did the Peace Treaty (Halliday
1975: 196–202).

Equality and freedom

The political reforms which affected women included revision of the
election law, allowing female suffrage and the right to stand for political office, for which Japanese women had struggled for so long. The
new Constitution included a guarantee of sex equality in the family,
education, employment and political representation. Article 14 of the
Constitution states: 'All of the people are equal under the law and there
shall be no discrimination in political, economic or social relations
because of race, creed, sex, social status or family origin.' The new civil
code abolished women's subordination in the ie, eradicated preferential
treatment for men, regulated parental power and child custody, and
provided for the mutuality of marriage and equality in divorce (Hendry
1981: 26; Hunter 1989: 150). The code removed the legal basis for the
family system which had hampered women's freedom, made legal
incompetents of married women, and disinherited them from the right
to own family property, thereby opening the way for women to possess
economic capital in their own right. The Trade Union Act 1945 and the
Labour Relations Act 1946 provided the right to organise and to strike,
whilst the Labour Standards Act 1947 improved conditions at work, and
laid down equal pay for men and women employed on the same jobs
(Beasley 1990: 221).

The land reform, although it was not specifically directed against
women, had a dual effect on women of the landowning class, since on
the one hand it wiped out the large landowners together with the
material basis for the protected lifestyle of upper-class women, while
on the other it removed from power the feudal remnants which had
prevented political reform for women before the war. The loss of lands
and wealth meant that many upper- and middle-class families had to
sell what property and investments they had to survive (Beasley 1990:
222–3), breaking down the class divisions so that even women who

had belonged to landed families now had to earn their own living. The reform of education also had a dramatic effect, since it opened up higher education to women, and permitted their entry into educational institutions at all levels of the system.

The new Constitution was one of the most liberal in the world, and a comparable provision for sex equality has not been admitted into the US Constitution to this day. Why did the USA offer provisions for equal citizenship to Japanese women which are still not available to their own population? Part of the answer lies in the reason underlying US reforms of Japan, which was not to institutionalise democracy but to establish structures which would allow civilians to restrain the military. It is in this context that the labour movement's right to organise and the political rights for women may be understood (Halliday 1975: 178, 190–91). Susan Pharr argues that the reforms favouring women were initiated by the lower ranks of US personnel in the occupation administration who were in contact with Japanese women leaders (Pharr 1980: 113). We agree that the prewar campaigns of the Japanese women's movement were crucial to the introduction of these reforms in the occupation period, but suggest that it is unlikely such reforms would have been implemented if they had not also helped to fulfil US political aims. The motives behind these aims were neither democratisation nor sex equality, but demilitarisation and the restraint of militarist nationalism, for which purpose the establishment of liberal reforms for women performed admirably.

In the next section we demonstrate the ambiguities in the approach of the US administration towards women in Japan, showing that, far from being committed to sex equality, the USA, too, constructed women as social objects, and drew on a discourse of women's rights not with the aim of abolishing gendered power relations, but as a means of maintaining its own position in the struggle for global power.

The US Occupation's Approach to Women

The changes to the position of women brought about by the reforms of 1945 and after were far from insignificant, and those reforms were real enough. We will argue, however, that just as the process of democratic reform was not designed primarily because of the US commitment to a democratic Japan, so too the reforms to women's position did not stem from any democratic commitment to women's rights, or a concern with women's liberation. Rather, they were designed to assist the process of demilitarisation, and to consolidate US dominance. Two examples will demonstrate this.

Supporting women's organisations

First, the USA gave selective support to women's organisations in Japan as the occupation administration backtracked on its commitment to 'democratisation', giving and withdrawing support on the basis of the militancy or pliability of the organisations after the reverse-course strategy began to operate. Many women's organisations arose in the first few years after the war. Ichikawa Fusae led the New Japan Women's League, set up to inform women of their new rights. The left-wing Women's Democratic Club was started in 1946 by intellectuals such as Miyamoto Yuriko (Feminist Japan 1980: 87), supported at first by SCAP's Education Division and the newspaper *Asahi Shimbun*. Its aims were to liberate women from traditional attitudes, freedom for women to do paid work or housework by choice rather than compulsion, and promotion of the process of democratisation. But as SCAP began to retreat on 'democratisation' on the grounds that it was giving succour to communism, the Women's Democratic Club lost the support of the occupying power and became a leftist organisation for women, splitting off from the New Japan Women's League, which aligned itself with women from the Liberal Democratic Party, the Socialist Party and the Young Women's Christian Association (Tanaka 1977: 37–9). This example shows how the US administration divided the women's organisations, supporting those it considered politically innocuous and refusing help to those it thought militant or subversive.

Expanding prostitution

The second example relates to the development of prostitution in Japan under the US occupation. From the start, the US army took advantage of the system of prostitution organised by the Japanese authorities, both groups sharing the assumption that men, especially soldiers, had the right to sex with women of the occupied nation. According to a booklet published after the surrender in 1945, called 'Protecting Women in Metropolitan Tokyo', the Japanese Cabinet held a special meeting a week after the surrender on the question of sexual services for the officers and men of the occupation. The director-general of police then sent a notice to all district police chiefs in the country:

> You are urged to take measures that will enable the rapid expansion of
> sexual comfort facilities, restaurants and bars, and such places of leisure

as cafés and dance halls. It is suggested that women for these businesses be recruited mainly from among geisha, barmaids, waitresses, prostitutes and sexual offenders. (Yamazaki 1985: 154)

Matsuoka Yoko, in her position as translator to the police chief in the small town of Hanamaki, confirms that only a few days after the US forces arrived the lieutenant asked for prostitutes for the GIs (Matsuoka 1952: 206). George Hicks reports that in one location at the end of the war, the brothels 'continued to function until the entry of the occupation force, when a US officer requested the mayor and the head of the Female Entertainers' Union to supply 30 women for the use of occupation troops' (Hicks 1995: 72–3).

As Yamazaki Tomoko points out, the rationale behind the Japanese government initiative was primarily to assure that women from 're-spectable' families would be left unmolested by the occupation forces (Yamazaki 1985: 154), in an attempt to keep intact the gendered class system by which the middle-class Japanese woman was preserved sexually for the middle-class Japanese man. But the fact that the facilities were taken up and demanded by US troops clearly demonstrates that the US military men shared the approach to women and class adopted by the Japanese bureaucracy. Although the US administration abolished the licensed prostitution system in 1946 on the grounds that state regulation of prostitution was 'against democratic ideals', this essentially represented a form of privatisation of prostitution, as private brothels were allowed to continue, and individuals discharged from the public system continued to be employed by the US military both during and after the occupation (Yamazaki 1985: 154–5). The continuation of the military bases – and, later, the Korean and Vietnam wars – all provided a demand for prostitution for the US military in Japan, both internally and from the war zones. In this way the USA helped to continue and reinforce the system of prostitution in Japan.

Thus, while the reforms were important in institutionalising demands that had been made by women over the course of almost a century, we argue that the legal changes were largely only a reflection of the social changes that Japanese women had already made themselves as a result of their experiences of Japan's wartime history. The US approach to women in Japan was deeply contradictory, suggesting that the reforms stemmed not from a commitment to women's rights, but from a belief that they would support US aims. Thus the transformations in gender relations after the war depended as much on the social changes Japanese women had already made as on the legal interventions of the USA.

Women and the Reforms

We will look briefly at how women took advantage of the reforms to achieve a position as subjects. The ideas of Bourdieu and Lovell help us to understand the changes to women's position in the development of a modern capitalist society. According to Bourdieu, the various forms of capital in a modern society are initially inherited, and profits are accumulated through investments, the most significant of which is the investment in education, where initial capital stocks may be extended and accredited. Cultural capital and education are not exactly synonymous, but educational credentials can serve as an index of cultural capital, because education legitimates cultural capital and converts it into symbolic capital (Bourdieu 1984: 13). The cultural capital derived from education directs access to occupations, which provide both economic capital and social status, and 'occupation is generally a good and economical indicator of position in social space' (Bourdieu 1987: 4). Occupational fields are sited within the social space, which is the location for struggles for domination and position in the hierarchy, undertaken by social groups who are unequally armed with capital resources. Through the deployment of symbolic violence, some social and cultural capitals are denied recognition, while more powerfully resourced social and cultural capitals are given value as legitimate currencies that can be converted into symbolic capital (Bourdieu 1984, 1987).

In terms of female education, as Lovell makes clear, the campaign for women's education in Britain could not have succeeded without the co-operation of bourgeois parents, and this co-operation was given because the middle class began to see female education as 'a necessary preparation for marriage and motherhood, not an escape from it' (Lovell 2000: 27–8). This necessity was used by women to gain access to higher education, and the cultural capital thus acquired could then sometimes be invested, not in the production of symbolic capital for the men of the family, but in the creation of symbolic capital for the woman herself, through access to a career (Lovell 2000: 26–7).

But this move from trading on the marriage market to trading on the labour market is not unproblematic, precisely because women represent capital value for the investment strategies of family members who control access to education, and also because access to education and the labour market is structured by class and gender. In this case, families may block women from accruing enough cultural capital in the form of education to be able to enter the labour market (Lovell 2000: 25). But the move may also be supported by the family if an assessment is made that the family has a better chance of increasing its symbolic capital through women's investment in capital that is tradable in the labour market, rather than only in the marriage market, or in educational forms of cultural capital that provide a better rate of return in the market than more directly embodied forms such as physical beauty, reproductive ability or domestic skills (Lovell 2000: 23, 25).

Taking up new social spaces

In Japan, land reform finally demolished the feudal system of social relations which had tied women of the former landowning class into the structure of property relations, and confined them sexually and economically to the domestic sphere. The eradication of feudalism both released constraints on capitalist development, and compelled former landowning families to enter the labour market for their living. The US authorities compulsorily purchased land at fixed prices, which were artificially low because of the effects of inflation (Beasley 1990: 223). Having lost his land, Yoshioka Terumi's father sold his other assets to survive, and she became a journalist to support herself:

> My father was an intelligent person and quite westernised. He had been in France and told us a lot of what was going on. My father never 'worked', he just paints. He didn't have to sell his paintings in the beginning because he had land. But because of the war he lost everything – houses were burnt down and he couldn't keep the land. He sold everything, very cheaply too. During my schooldays it was an age when everybody had to work, everyone was so poor.

Nakagome Haruko recognised that accredited cultural capital was a more secure investment than economic capital, and although she had already acquired a qualification from Japan Women's College before the war, she continued to study when the higher education system was opened to women, and became a professor:

> My father died when I was ten, then my mother encouraged me because she was a widow, so she encouraged her daughters to be independent. When I was young we had no financial problems, so I could always do what I wanted. But after the war everything was lost, our land was confiscated by the government so we had to get money. Without this experience I may not have tried to get an education.
>   After the war society wasn't well organised, there was a lot of unemployment, so my teachers at university advised me to continue studying. It was my brother who suggested applying to Tokyo University. I was out of town, living in the country, and my brother phoned to say: 'Tokyo University has just opened to women, so why don't you try? You

have to work for your living, and women's college isn't enough, so try
it.' The social situation was the biggest influence.

Nakagome-san never married, which would have been unusual for
a young woman of her class before the war, but it is clear that not only
Nakagome-san herself but also her brother, the male head of household
since their father's death, realised that an investment in educational
capital would be of more benefit to his sister and his family than
marriage once the family land was lost. A similar feeling prevailed
amongst the less wealthy middle class, who had no lands to lose but
who would still in the past have expected their daughters to give priority
to marriage. Ryu-u Taeko's father was the owner of a small factory.
Ryu-u-san never married, despite her mother's anxiety that she should:

> I went to Metropolitan Girls' High School and Tsuda College, where I
> graduated with a teacher's qualification under the old system in 1951. It
> was the time of transition to the new education system. Society's mood
> was that women should go out and work, and both teachers and students
> thought it natural to go on to college and to work. At college most
> people went out to a career, and for financial reasons about 80 per cent
> of graduates worked while few stayed at home. The first half of high-
> school days was during the war, therefore the policy of high school was
> to make girls into good wives, wise mothers. But this changed com-
> pletely when the war ended. Teachers as well as students took it for
> granted that women would have careers. This atmosphere was also strong
> at university. My mother worried about my losing the opportunity to
> get married under the influence of such an atmosphere at college.

So despite the concerns of the older generation, family accumulation
strategies and the interests of women as capital-accumulating subjects
converged under the new circumstances of economic uncertainty.

Okazaki Teruko did marry, but had no children and found life empty,
so she took up a career after marriage:

> When the war ended I left Technical School and got married. We had no
> children. I hated staying home all the time, my husband too, so I went
> to university and graduated in 1952. At university in those days the
> atmosphere was favourable to trying out new things, and I was encour-
> aged by the teachers there. I wanted to apply to a newspaper company
> and my husband strongly encouraged me. I was the first woman jour-
> nalist. They wanted a woman journalist to take charge of the newly
> created women's section. I was fortunate to meet an egalitarian attitude,
> prevalent at the time the war ended, an understanding husband and a
> liberal father influenced by the democratic movement in the Taisho era.

The biggest influence on my having a career was that the times had changed.

Okazaki-san's encouragement by her male relatives points to the way family strategies for accumulating capitals shift in changing contexts, such that a daughter's educability may be of greater strategic value than her marriageability (Bourdieu 1990a). Whether out of necessity or desire, women from formerly protective families took up the new social spaces which were offered to them in education and employment, inventing for themselves new identities and ways of living.

Constant Quiet Struggles

In conclusion, we argue in Part III that the transitions which occurred in the lives of middle-class women from the Taisho to the immediate postwar period were brought about not primarily through the intervention of western legal reforms, which represented a consolidation of many of the transformations that had already taken place in the social field, but by women themselves in response to the changing social conditions in Japan. As we showed in Part II, before the intrusion of the West women had fought and won many battles to attain or maintain a position as social subjects, but the social space where this battle was finally lost was in the military class. It was partly by appropriating and deploying women's economic and social capitals as their own that military men were able to establish a position of dominance in feudal class relations. After the early period of Meiji liberalisation, as we showed in Part I, certain renovated forms of class-based gender definitions of Japanese womanhood were applied to the whole population as a means of social regulation under the family–state system.

As feudalism began to fragment in the face of capitalist development in the Taisho period, however, women's resistance and agency in the middle class emerged as a challenge to the renovated gender–class boundaries confining them to the family as repositories and transmitters of value for men, and separating them from the institutions of cultural and economic capital in the form of higher education and employment. During the wartime period, as the material and social destruction eradicated predictable forms of social relations and changed gendered class relations, women stepped into strategic locations which men could no longer defend, and developed for themselves new identities based on a position as social subjects. These new activities and multiple roles for middle-class women contributed to the continuing disintegration of the boundaries marking out the ideal Japanese woman, and began to undermine the family–state–emperor system and the patriarchal class divisions on which it was based.

As women captured some of the social spaces left vacant in men's absence, they were able to acquire capital of their own: economic capital through paid employment, social capital through new social networks outside the family, cultural capital through new knowledge and skills acquired in the course of performing men's social duties, and symbolic capital through determining what happened in the family. These capital resources, which women accumulated in their own right during the war, were then deployed, with or without the family's approval, to defend the subject positions they had gained.

The fragmentation of gendered class boundaries was exacerbated when Japan lost the war. Along with the material and social losses went the social structures and symbolic capitals upholding imperial power, class power and male power, bringing about the disintegration of the systems of authority which had held gender, class and national relations in place in the eyes of many sections of the population. The failure to provide military victory was crucial in eroding the power and authority of the family–state–emperor system, and in constructing the legitimacy of women to compete in the public field.

The reforms that the USA introduced for women consolidated the changes in gender relations that had taken place up to this point, but the idea that women's liberation in Japan was primarily the result of intervention by the foreign power is both misleading and oversimplified. Progressive legal reforms for women were instituted by the US administration not with the aim of abolishing gendered power relations, but in the belief that opening up access to public life to women would help to put limits on militarist nationalism. These moves were part of the struggle over symbolic capital, as the USA used the position of women in Japan in the competition for global dominance and distinction. It is this which helps to explain two widely held beliefs so common in the West: that women's emancipation was imported from the USA, and that Japanese women can be viewed as passive social objects. This neglects and diminishes women's constant quiet struggles to resist oppression, to take up subject positionings and to act as agents within the social field. The position of women and the constitution of gender and class relations are central components in the struggle for power and distinction on the global stage.

PART IV

Gender, Class and Power in Employment, Education and the Family

In Part IV we focus on the context of the lives of women who have achieved a measure of power in public life. Bourdieu sees education as the key to the reproduction of difference in a modern capitalist society, whereby the reproduction of class power takes place through the process of ratifying inherited cultural capital through educational credentials.

In Chapter 16 we discuss the significance of class in Japan, and set out the main concepts which underpin the analysis that follows. We then examine the distribution of power in the social fields of employment, education and the family. In each field, we look at studies which show how class power is distributed among men, and then ask what happens to the analysis if we introduce information on women, using our own data on professional women. We use statistical patterns to show how power is distributed in the field.

Our analysis focuses first on the position of women in employment, because it is in this social field that class relations are structured in a capitalist society. We use this discussion to explore the respondents' class origins.

We then examine the position of women in education, since this social field is a major site in which class is reproduced.

Finally, we look at women's position in the family, showing how entry to the field of professional employment changes their position of power in the family.

Chapter 16

Class and the
Reproduction of Power

The Significance of Class in Japan

The declining significance of class as an analytical concept and a political issue has been remarked upon by many academic writers in the late twentieth century. It coincides with the breakdown of communism in Eastern Europe, the process of deindustrialisation in western capitalist countries, and economic liberalisation and structural adjustment in many developing countries. It also coincides with a 'new international economic order' in which capitalist forms of social and economic organisation have gained supremacy, and the USA, Europe and Japan compete for power within it. These trends have been accompanied by the rise to dominance of poststructuralist and postmodernist approaches which eschew structural analysis and 'grand narratives' such as Marxism. The rejection of the idea of class is not new, however, and the attempt to deny or disguise class divisions has a history as long as that which has obscured the power and significance of gender. Despite the fact that material indicators of structured economic inequality across large areas of the globe have become more pronounced over the last two decades, and that material inequality is linked to both class and gender divisions, the idea of class in its various forms has been comprehensively eclipsed in much academic analysis, including feminist analysis.

Denial of class

In Japan, the denial of class has been reflected in debates which have suggested that class is a western concept with no relevance for Japan – as proposed, for example, in the work of the internationally known anthropologist Nakane Chie; and in the suggestion that while it used to be relevant, it is relevant no longer, since everyone is now middle class – as proposed by the economist Murakami Yasusuke. Nakane, while she conflates class as a social relation and class struggle as a form of class consciousness, argues that the organisation of Japanese society is based not on 'horizontal stratification by caste or class but [on] vertical stratification by institution':

> Even if social classes like those in Europe can be detected in Japan, and even if something vaguely resembling those classes that are illustrated in the textbooks of western sociology can also be found in Japan, the point is that in actual society this stratification is unlikely to function and that it does not really reflect the social structure. In Japanese society it is not really a matter of workers struggling against capitalists or managers but of Company A ranged against Company B. The protagonists do not stand in vertical relationship to each other but instead rub elbows from parallel positions. (Nakane 1973: 90)

Although we agree that the Japanese economy is vertically stratified on the basis of large-scale corporations and small-scale family enterprises, we would argue that in the struggle between Company A and Company B, Nakane's 'capitalists or managers' have no alternative but to compete in extracting the maximum output from the labour of the employees for the minimum cost, since it is through this process that each company produces its profits, and is thus able to struggle for power with others. The contest occurs not only between large- and small-scale enterprises but also within the large and the small sectors of the economy, and between those who control and manage each enterprise and those whose labour is controlled. Nakane further argues at an individual level that

> The society in which class distinction is least developed offers man [sic] more opportunities for free competition on the road to success than class or caste societies. In general, in Japan a man's personal ability and actual achievements count for much more than family background. Whether an individual was born into a reputable or rich family or into a poor peasant family matters little after he has once gained admission to a successful group or has been given the choice of being linked with a successful or promising man. (Nakane 1973: 108)

The problem with this argument is that admission into a successful social group or the circle of a promising man is not necessarily independent of origin in a rich or poor family, as has been demonstrated by Ishida Hiroshi's analysis (1993). The 'promising man' argument also raises the question of how far a 'promising woman' can follow the same trajectory as her male equivalent and find 'opportunities for free competition on the road to success'. To what extent is Japan a 'non-class' society, and how far do women share in whatever degree of 'classlessness' exists for men?

The centrality of class

Ishida shows that while Marxist intellectuals in Japan have seen class as central to inequality, other academics have questioned the idea that class is the basis of stratification in the debate over the new middle class (Ishida 1993). Murakami Yasusuke, writing on the 'new middle class', argued that more than 90 per cent of the population saw themselves as middle-class, as the postwar economic miracle produced a large middle stratum which was homogeneous in lifestyle, attitudes, speech, dress and other status dimensions (Ishida 1993: 18). The Marxist Kishimoto Shigenobu countered that the middle class consisted only of people with enough assets in the form of houses, land, savings or stocks to support themselves by disposing of the property which the majority of population did not have. For example, 62 per cent of those whose income was less than US$5,000 in 1984 said they were middle class. Such people were vulnerable to economic change, and the new middle class was therefore an illusion (Ishida 1993: 19). The sociologist Tominaga Ken'ichi rejected both Murakami's class homogeneity and Kishimoto's class polarities, and argued that since resources are distributed by pluralistic criteria in Japan, only a small proportion of the population consistently occupied a high or low status. The majority of people are in the middle; there is therefore a 'diverse middle class' (Ishida 1993: 19). Labour economists such as Koike Kazuo, on the other hand, argued for the dual structure of class and firm size in the determination of income distribution, suggesting that the size of the firm differentiates workers of the same class (Ishida 1993: 19). Ishida's own study tested these theses on the basis of evidence from the 1975 Japanese Social Stratification and Mobility National Survey (SSM), and concluded that class is far more important than either education or occupational status in explaining the inequality in income in Japan, and that Japan is not significantly more open or closed to class mobility than the UK or the USA (Ishida 1993: 255, 260), thus casting doubt on both the new middle-mass thesis and the idea that class is not relevant to Japan.

Feminism and class

When western feminist analysis entered the debate on class, it was recognised that both the concept and the measurement of class were gendered, and could not readily be applied to women in the same way as to men. For example, gender was not properly covered in employment schemes of class, because occupational segregation meant that schemes were centred on male, not female, employment, and employment-based measures of class could not easily be applied to non-employed housewives or part-time women workers (Crompton 1993: 96, 118). Such problems, together with the retreat from class in the wider academic community, contributed to the comprehensive eclipse of concepts of class in feminist analysis in favour of discourses of diversity and difference (Coole 1996: 17), tending to neglect or obscure the power hierarchies embedded in difference.

Despite the focus on diversity emerging from other significant social divisions such as ethnicity, sexuality and nationality, discussion of the differences caused by class has been notably absent. Rosemary Crompton has suggested that although the class position of women remains contentious, much of the discussion of women's class position in the occupational structure is a pseudo-debate, and does not provide grounds for eliminating class as an important concept in the understanding of gender relations (Crompton 1993: 94). Diana Coole has pointed to the need to reinstate class differences in feminist research, and has argued that despite the difficulty in measuring it, class cannot be dissolved into a linguistically mobile and simple diversity of equally valuable differences (Coole 1996: 23). Beverley Skeggs has responded to the challenge in a British context, and demonstrated both that the concept of class must be conceptually integrated with gender in order adequately to portray gendered power relations, and that the production of class as invisible is a mechanism which enables working-class women to refuse a subordinate class identity at the same time as tying them into it (Skeggs 1997: 7).

In Japan the debate has followed different lines. The AMPO collection has argued that Japanese feminism, particularly the dominance of housewife feminism, has played a significant part in the neglect of class, since its middle-class base has meant that the class specificity of much feminist analysis was not recognised (AMPO 1996). In the same collection, Inoue Reiko and Kanai Yoshiko have suggested that the Japanese women's movement is also concerned with diversity and identity, arguing that questions of nationalism, poverty and inequality in a global context are the crucial issues which have been neglected by Japanese feminism, and must now be addressed (AMPO 1996: xx–xxi). In Part IV we examine how far class divisions are significant in women's access to positions of power in Japan. We will argue that Japan has not uniquely succeeded in creating a classless society, and that class is crucial to women's access to power in a modern capitalist society.

Analysing Power

In Part IV we look at the context of women's lives, focusing on the fields of power to which our respondents struggled to gain access. We examine the structure of the social fields of employment, education and the family, the positionings of women within these fields, the capitals attached to these positionings, and the relationships between the fields. We examine the changing conditions which constitute the culturally and historically specific characteristics of the fields as the context for the production of social practice.

In Parts V and VI we will go on to examine women's own representations of their positionings within the fields, showing how the capitals within these fields shape the women's practices and subjectivities. In this Part, we set out the basis for that discussion by examining Bourdieu's claim that 'there exists a space of positions which cannot be occupied unless one possesses one of a number of forms of capital to a very high degree' (Wacquant 1993: 21). We will examine the social fields of employment, education and the family as sites in which gendered power is produced, and identify some of the mechanisms which reproduce the relations between the fields. We will ask how far changes in the gendered distribution of power within these fields represent an opening up of positions of power in society to a wider social base, or alternatively constitute a means for reproducing forms of power based on other social divisions such as class.

Fields of power: the 'uncrossable boundary'

The structural changes in the educational system, the employment system and the family system which took place after 1945 reconfigured the contest for power within Japan, as legitimate competition for power in the public arena was opened up to a broader cross-section of society. A struggle ensued over who could legitimately compete for positions of public power. This struggle included women. In assessing how far these changes represented a redistribution of power in society to a wider social base, we draw on Bourdieu's conceptualisation of the social field, the resources attached to positions in the field, and the relations between fields.

Bourdieu conceptualises social reality as the product of the interaction between the social structure and the ways in which that structure is represented (Bourdieu 1990b: 123). Through the concepts of the 'habitus' and the 'field', Bourdieu posits his understanding of social action as the interdependent production of subjective formulation, or representation (the habitus) and objective conditions, or social structure (the field). Social practice is produced by the habitus interacting with the objective contextual conditions of the particular social field (Pullen 1999: ch. 3). A field is a 'structured space of positions' (Bourdieu 1993: 72) which are located in historically and culturally specific relation to one another, and bounded and defined by the capital resources on which the field is based (Wacquant 1989: 39).

The focus of social analysis is the distribution of power between positions in the field, rather than individual social interactions. Bourdieu substitutes the term 'field of power' for 'ruling or dominant class', in order to stress the need to examine structures of power as systems of objective relations, as opposed to studying populations of agents. Although there is no alternative to studying populations of agents, since the properties which structure access to power are attached only to individuals, the aim in using statistical survey methods is to identify how power is distributed across the space of positions, rather than to analyse individuals or institutions (Wacquant 1993: 20–21).

The concept of the field emphasises the importance of context in the generation of social practice, and enables Bourdieu to place social relations at the centre, analysing not individual interactions but the distribution of power between positions in the field, and relationships between the fields. Bourdieu argues that there is a space of positions which 'cannot be occupied unless one possesses one of a number of forms of capital to a very high degree', and within this space are 'various fields: the intellectual ..., the field of higher civil service, the field of economic power ... etc.' (Wacquant 1993: 21). What must be analysed is the objective relations between these fields, and 'the mechanisms which tend to reproduce these relations by continually reproducing the agents who will occupy their positions, in such a way as to perpetuate the structures' (Wacquant 1993: 21). As we analyse the reproduction of power, however, it must be remembered that power is variably distributed in different social contexts, so a field is not just a space of static positions but also a space of 'forces and struggles' between those who do and do not control resources (Wacquant 1989: 38).

Reproducing power through education

The three fields of employment, education and the family are crucially interrelated in the reproduction of power. Bourdieu argues that in developed societies, the field of education has become the primary site in which the social position of the family is reproduced in the employment field, and that the significance of education is less the credentialising of technical knowledge and skills than the legitimation of the social reproduction of power: 'no power can be exercised in its brutality in an arbitrary manner, ... it must dissimulate itself, ... make itself be recognised as legitimate by fostering the misrecognition of the arbitrary that founds it' (Wacquant 1993: 25).

As a field of social and intellectual production, the education system is a space of power relations structured by the distribution of its particular forms of capital and a site of competition for these resources. Through this competition, the education system operates as a site for the production of gender, class and ethnic relations: 'What has to be reproduced is a *system of differences* which defines a historically given division of the work of domination' (Wacquant 1993: 22). The elite educational institutions create an uncrossable boundary between those who do and those who will never exercise power. It is these social uses that are concealed by the technical uses of education (Wacquant 1993: 33).

The elite[1] educational institutions produce a nobility whose members feel different, and feel that their differences entitle them to exercise power, and whose differences are recognised as such by others. Elite education creates the belief that the dominant possess natural characteristics and abilities that justify their positions of power and their right to rule. The reproduction mechanism of the elite academic institutions is very powerful, because the legitimating characteristics that they accredit are 'the most universal of the time' in terms of culture, and 'the most natural', since they are attributed to natural talent rather than cultural acquisition (Wacquant 1993: 28).

In familial social reproduction (what Bourdieu refers to as 'blood' or 'family nobility') the transmission of power is monitored by the family itself (Wacquant 1993: 26). In education-mediated reproduction (in Bourdieu's terms, a 'school' or 'state nobility'), the transmission of power depends on educational credentials, at least in developed societies

---

1. Harel van Wolferen (1989) argues that the most powerful group in Japan consists of three categories: top bureaucrats in some ministries, political clans, and certain leaders of business organisations. We regard these as 'elites' and do not include them in our study, partly because so few women can be found at this level. Instead we focus on women in the professional/managerial class (see Chapter 17). We do, however, refer to an 'educational elite' consisting of those who attended the top universities (see Chapter 18).

with advanced education systems. Family transmission of economic capital continues in capitalist societies, but more and more of this power is transferred under the mantle of educational qualifications. Academic credentials represent investments in the contest over social classifications, but they are also weapons in the struggle (Wacquant 1993: 27).

There are costs in the education-mediated system such that there is no guarantee that positions of privilege will be automatically transferred to the next generation. But reproduction operates statistically: the class maintains its position without all the individual members retaining their privileges (Wacquant 1993: 29). The eliminated heirs may rebel against the system of privilege, creating social protest movements in their wake, but there are enough exceptions in either direction – failures among those who should inherit, and success stories among those who should not – 'to create the illusion of independence and democratisation' (Wacquant 1993: 30). The academic transmission of privileged positions is preferable, despite its lower success rate, because of its superiority in dissimulating the process of reproduction (Wacquant 1993: 29–30).

Indiscernible power

Bourdieu argues that the field of power still reproduces itself, and sometimes does so genealogically. In the past, this was a family nobility through bloodlines; today it is a state nobility through education. One of the fundamental dimensions of the role of the state is to produce the symbolic power of the elite educational institutions (Wacquant 1993: 39). The state functions as a 'formidable instrument of naturalisation of the arbitrary' (Wacquant 1993: 39, 41). What education does is to extend, accredit and mask the dispositions that have been inculcated in the family. The school relies on the family to transmit the social and cultural capital that is linked with class of origin, and the family relies on the educational institutions to ratify and accredit the attitudes and aptitudes, accents, bearing and ways of being that are 'the hallmarks of their class of origin ... and destination' (Wacquant 1993: 31–2; ellipses in original). Technical competencies and bodies of knowledge must be acquired to occupy positions of power, but the characteristics that have to be transmitted cannot be reduced to technical skills, and they are not separable from the social dispositions which govern how the techniques are used and 'subordinate technical uses' to social uses. It is the 'indiscernibility of the technical ... and ... social dimensions which is at the root of the power' that educational credentials confer (Wacquant 1993: 32–3; original emphasis).

Thus Bourdieu sees education as the reproduction of a system of differences, where the reproduction of class power takes place *under the guise* of education credentials. One of the most important characteristics of the state is to accredit the symbolic power of the elite educational institutions, operating as the naturalisation of arbitrary power. It is this social function of education which is so effectively disguised by the learning of technical competencies, and explains why the idea of educational credentialism is so important in developed capitalist societies.

Although education represents the primary gateway – Bourdieu's 'uncrossable boundary' (Wacquant 1993: 33) – to women's access to power in employment, and subsequently in the family, we will first examine the field of employment, because it is here that the social relations of class are structured in a capitalist society. We will use this discussion to explore our respondents' class origins. We will then examine the field of education, as a means of understanding how class is reproduced. Finally, we will look at how women's access to positions of power in employment affects their position in the family.

Chapter 17

Employment as a Field of Power

In order to examine the structure of employment as a field of power, and women's positions within it, we will outline the changes to the Japanese economy since the war, and specify some of the historically and culturally distinctive features of female employment in Japan. We will identify four forms of sex segregation within the structure of employment which help to organise women's positionings in the field. Two of these, the horizontal and vertical segregation of occupations by sex, are common to other industrialised countries such as the UK and the USA. The other two, which we have termed contractual segregation and sectoral segregation, may be specific to Japan, in the sense that they form a coherent pattern of practices consistent with the specific structure of the Japanese economy.

Postwar changes to the economy

The end of the 1950s saw Japan's recovery from the devastation of the war, and the start of rapid economic growth and industrialisation. From the late 1950s to the early 1970s, known as the 'rapid industrialisation period', Japan's growth rate was 10 per cent per annum. In the mid-1970s industrial growth was restrained by the oil crisis, and the annual growth rate was 5 per cent per annum thereafter up to the late 1980s, according to the National Institute of Employment and Vocational Research (NIEVR). This latter period, from the mid-1970s to the late 1980s, is characterised by NIEVR as 'post-industrialisation', or the move to a service economy. In the rapid industrialisation period, increasing demand for industrial labour drew people from the agricultural sector, whereas in the post-industrialisation period the demand was for professional knowledge and technical expertise. This demand for specialist expertise, together with the need for management personnel in the public and private sectors, became a basis for power in the field of employment. Before the war, most female employment had consisted of agricultural family labour, notwithstanding the dominance of female labour in the textile industry. But the rapid growth of the 1950s and 1960s reduced the size of the rural petty bourgeoisie (the independent small farmers created by the land reform), especially agricultural and family labour, and new urban communities formed. These changes were accompanied by an increase in nuclear families and a corresponding decline in the extended family, a fall in the birth rate and a greater proportion of students going into higher education (NIEVR 1988: i, 2, 3).

Women's Positioning in the Employment Field

Norman Stockman, Norman Bonney and Sheng Xuewen, in their comparative study of women's work in Japan, China, the UK and the USA, give a clear picture of the specificities of the four different labour-market structures. Although they conclude that gender differences in the structure of employment were most pronounced in Japan (Stockman, Bonney and Sheng 1995: 59), they also argue – against Lam (1992) and Brinton (1993), and with Saso (1990: 51) – that there was more variation among Japanese women than was generally apparent in the literature (Bonney, Stockman and Sheng 1994: 403–4), a view with which we concur. They challenge both Brinton's thesis that graduate women dropped out of the labour market because they could not make a financial return on their educational investment (since many of Bonney et al.'s graduate respondents did make such a return), and Lam's thesis that most women in managerial careers could reach and retain their positions only because they had no family responsibilities (since many of Bonney et al.'s graduate respondents had both families and long-term careers) (Bonney et al. 1994: 403).

We will later address the question of why the image of the homo-geneous Japanese woman, primarily orientated towards a domestic career (the 'professional housewife'), is so popular within and outside Japan (Bonney et al. 1994: 390). For the present, however, following Bourdieu's conceptualisation of the social field, we will argue that while the structure of employment places women in locations where they cannot compete within the field as equals to men, the field must never-theless be seen not as a site of 'static positions' but as a 'site of struggle' in which significant numbers of women are engaged in a competition to increase their capital and improve the return on their investments.

The fact that there was more differentiation between men's and women's positionings in the employment field in Japan than in the other three countries analysed by Stockman et al. (1995: 15) does not mean that Japanese women were not engaged in the struggle, although it may mean that many of them decided to engage in a field, such as the family, where their positionings were more advantageous. The important point is that women in Japan, contrary to many of the assumptions and arguments in the literature, were not homogeneous, and different groups of women engaged in the struggle in different fields and in different positionings within the fields.

We will first examine the structure of the employment field to ascertain women's positions within it. From this analysis we will identify the characteristics of the Japanese labour market as a gendered field of power. We will show that women's participation in employment was comparable with that of other industrialised countries; that there was less 'horizontal' occupational segregation by sex in Japan than in other countries, although women were still clustered into sex-typed, 'feminine' jobs, as in other countries; that women were overrepresented in small and medium-sized enterprises (SMEs) and underrepresented in large organisations; that women were more likely to be engaged under informal employment contracts in jobs without a career structure; and that there was a significant degree of 'vertical' occupational segregation. We will then focus on women in professional and managerial positions, and assess how far those who had reached positions of power in management and the professions had done so independently of the class positioning of their family of origin, and the capitals attached to it.

Women's Participation in the Employment Field

The percentage of women in the total labour force (including the unemployed) showed a small but steady fall from 41 per cent in 1960 to a low point of 37 per cent in 1975 during the rapid industrialisation and labour-force shortage period. Then from 1975 there was a steady rise to 41 per cent in 1990, as the slowdown in the economy reversed the previous trend (Ministry of Labour 1994: 5).

If we exclude the unemployed, women's share in the workforce rose from 31 per cent in 1960 to 38 per cent in 1990 (Ministry of Labour 1994: 5). This was broadly comparable with – though slightly lower than – female employment in the UK, where women constituted 32 per cent of total employees in 1961 and 43 per cent in 1988 (Hakim

1981: 524; Gapper 1988). The proportion of female employees in Japan (excluding agricultural workers) who were married increased significantly over the period: from only 33 per cent in 1962 to 58 per cent in 1990 (Ministry of Labour 1994: 23). Since 1983 there have been more married women part-time workers than full-time housewives and mothers (Sugimoto 1997: 145). Between 1970 and 1985, significantly fewer women were retiring from paid work after marriage or childbirth (NIEVR 1988: 6).

As Bonney et al. point out, women's participation in the labour force in Japan was not particularly low compared with other industrialised countries (Bonney et al. 1994: 390). The predominant image of the Japanese woman as the full-time 'professional housewife' is not supported by the evidence of women's participation in the employment field.

Horizontal occupational segregation

Horizontal segregation of jobs, as practised extensively in the UK, is an important mechanism through which positions in the employment field are gendered. If we use the OECD definition of job segregation as the difference between women's representation in the workforce as a whole and their representation in a particular occupational category, Japan emerges with the least horizontal segregation (Saso 1990: 54–5).

In 1980, women constituted 34 per cent of all employees. They were overrepresented in Clerical work (51 per cent), Security and Service (51 per cent), and Professional and Technical (48 per cent). They were massively underrepresented in Management (5 per cent), which we will consider later in the discussion of vertical occupational segregation (Ministry of Labour 1994: 17).

A detailed examination of each of these categories reveals the specific types of jobs in which women predominated, representing over 70 per cent of the workforce. In Clerical occupations, women were mainly typists and accounts clerks. In Protective and Service work they were largely domestic workers, waitresses, barmaids, beauticians and entertainers. Women in the Professional and Technical category were mainly nurses, kindergarten teachers, nutritionists and musicians (NIEVR 1988: 57). Almost all these categories may be seen as 'feminine' activities based around women's domestic support and service roles.

Stockman et al. have shown that 'the occupational patterns of women in each country are a product of the structure of each society and of gendered processes of allocation to positions' (Stockman et al. 1995: 73). In Japan, although women were less concentrated into particular occupational categories than women in certain other industrialised countries, they were nevertheless mainly clustered in sex-typed work. There are, however, other forms of sex segregation in Japan which affect the positions of women in the employment field, and reflect the different structure of the Japanese economy.

Sectoral segregation

Cummings identifies three sectors of production in Japan: the agricultural, the entrepreneurial – meaning SMEs – and the large-scale organisational or corporate sector (Cummings 1980: 42). A greater proportion of the workforce was employed in the entrepreneurial sector in Japan: 78 per cent, compared with 59 per cent in the UK and 53 per cent in the USA (JSBRI 1998: 8). Small businesses, workshops and family firms were still a significant and stable section of the Japanese economy, but they could not compete in wages, status or employment benefits with the state or the corporate sectors. A blue-collar worker in a large organisation could expect to earn 25 per cent more than in a small one. The owner of a small business would earn just over half that of a manager in a large organisation (Cummings 1980: 47).

Sectoral segregation was also structured by gender. If we adapt the framework used in horizontal job segregation, we find that in 1980 the 34 per cent of women in the workforce were overrepresented in the smallest organisations of 1–29 employees (39 per cent) and underrepresented in organisations of 500+ (28 per cent) (NIEVR 1988: 104). Nevertheless, the differential between men and women was not great, and a majority of men also worked in the less privileged small-business sector.

Contractual segregation

Contractual segregation refers to different forms of employment contract. Stockman et al. (1995) delineate these into 'standard' and 'nonstandard'; Saso (1990) and Lam (1992) into 'regular' and 'irregular'. Although her figures relate to a later period than our study, we have chosen Shima Satomi's terms 'formal' and 'informal', since her analysis was the most useful in clarifying the confusion and ambiguity surrounding the issue of contractual segregation and the structure of employment (Shima 1997).

Shima analysed the employment structure as consisting of: inner-core workers with formal contracts inside the long-term employment system; outer-core workers with formal contracts outside the long-term employment system; and peripheral workers made up of employees with informal contracts, plus family workers and the self-employed (Shima 1997: 77).

In 1992, women constituted 41 per cent of all workers in employment and self-/family employment. Women were heavily overrepresented in peripheral forms of work (55 per cent) and, within this category, particularly numerous in part-time work (68 per cent) and as family workers (82 per cent). Peripheral workers made up 50 per cent of all female workers, but only 28 per cent of male workers (Shima 1997: 78).

The low status of part-time work was clearly reflected in lower pay and inferior conditions. Pay was less than 50 per cent of full-timers' pay, despite similar hours (Stockman et al. 1995: 78). In Stockman et al.'s study of working mothers with preschool children, only a tiny minority (4 per cent) of part-timers had formal contracts. The minority of mothers who retained full-time employment whilst having children maintained an advantageous employment position, but most women who took a break were unable to return to formal contractual status, and re-entered work with less protected employment conditions under informal contracts (Stockman et al. 1995: 77–8).

Although women graduates in Japan, alone amongst OECD countries, were more likely than other women to withdraw from paid work when they had children (Saso 1990: 356), there was an increasing trend for women seeking employment to move away from two-year to four-year higher-education institutions (Lam 1992: 74). These women were far more likely to have a continuous work pattern (78 per cent in Bonney's sample: Bonney et al. 1994: 397), representing an increased willingness to compete with men for privileged positions in the employment field. Nevertheless, twice the proportion of graduate men had been continuously employed for over thirty years (55 per cent) compared with graduate women (27 per cent) in 1985 (NIEVR 1988: 11), revealing the different working patterns of men and women overall.

Another form of contractual segregation operated by the corporate sector was almost entirely based on gender: the division of qualified full-time women workers with formal employment status into the career track (*sogo shoku*) or the routine track (*ippan shoku*) (Sugimoto 1997: 145–6). Career-track workers had to have four-year degrees, work long hours of overtime, transfer to other locations and work without interruption to their careers. Less than 1 per cent of women graduates entering the labour market got on to this track (Sugimoto 1997: 146–7), in contrast with 'almost all the male employees…as a matter of course' (Saso 1990: 66). Women predominated in routine clerical jobs without the challenges offered by promotion opportunities. Some jobs, in care and service roles, required high levels of those elements of cultural capital which are compatible with femininity, but they also required the least cultural capital in terms of education. This contrasts with the positions dominated by qualified men, which required much higher levels of educational capital.

Vertical occupational segregation

The final form of sex segregation in the employment field is vertical segregation, whereby men were positioned in jobs located at the top and women in jobs at the bottom of the occupational hierarchy. In manual work, women were more likely to be in lower-status blue-collar jobs, making up only 13 per cent of craft and production workers, but 42 per cent of operators and labourers in 1980 (Stockman et al. 1995: 67). In non-manual work, women were concentrated in routine lower-status jobs (Stockman et al. 1995: 70–71). Women were also heavily underrepresented in managerial positions.

Table 17.1 shows that the proportion of women in management had risen to 8 per cent by 1990, but compared to women's representation in the workforce as a whole (38 per cent in 1990) the 1 per cent of women workers who were managers was still very small.

If we look at the way women managers were distributed according to hierarchical ranking, we see that their proportion decreased the higher the position. In 1985, only 1 per cent of women employees were 'position-holders', compared with 16 per cent of men (NIEVR 1988: 40, 42). Of all position-holders, 98 per cent were men, and only 2 per

Table 17.1   Distribution of women in managerial occupations

Year	% women in management	% managers in all women workers
1960	3	0.3
1970	4	0.5
1980	5	0.8
1990	8	1.0

Source: Ministry of Labour 1994: 17.

Table 17.2   Distribution of women in the professions

Year	% women in professions	% professionals in all women workers	% women in total workforce
1960	33	9	31
1970	41	9	33
1980	48	13	34
1990	42	14	38

Source: Ministry of Labour 1994: 17.

cent women (NIEVR 1988: 39). Even within this tiny minority of position-holders, 70 per cent of women were in the lowest category.

A study of government employees in 1989 showed that only 58 out of 5,600 civil servants (1 per cent) in the top four levels were women; and a 1993 study of nearly 40,000 directors in more than 2,000 corporations listed on Japan's eight stock exchanges found only 48 women – just over 0.1 per cent (Sugimoto 1997: 147–8).

NIEVR concludes that while male workers in privileged positions in the employment field achieved promotion as part of the seniority-orientated promotion system, women workers were in effect excluded from this framework, and achieved promotion only as exceptions. This was attributed to management policies which denied career development and promotion in the internal labour market to women (NIEVR 1988: 45).

The exception to this pattern of women's underrepresentation in jobs with authority and decision-making power seemed to be their contribution to professional jobs based on educational qualifications.

Table 17.2 suggests that women were overrepresented in professional work compared with their numbers in the total workforce. Professional occupations constituted 13 per cent of paid employment for women in 1980. If, however, we look at the specific occupations where women were located in the professional classification, we find that the three largest categories in 1985 were nurses, teachers and social workers (NIEVR 1988: 51); this follows the pattern of women's occupations being associated with female domestic and caring work. Analysis of

Table 17.3   Women in the higher professions

	%	Date
Medical doctors	9	1975
University teachers	8	1977
Career civil servants	4	1978
Managers*	0.3	1975

* Defined as section chief or above in 1,396 private companies listed on the Tokyo stock exchange and 101 corporations with special status.

Source: Hirano et al. 1980: 19.

data presented by Ishida using Standard International Occupational Prestige Scores (IPS) shows that women's professional work was clustered in the bottom half of the range for the Professional category (45 to 62, out of a possible range of 45 to 78), with five out of the six occupations being concentrated in the bottom third of the range (Ishida 1993: 265–73).

Table 17.3 shows the percentage of women in the higher-prestige professional occupations covered in our study (scoring 65 to 78 on the IPS scale) (NIEVR 1988: 51). Again we find that women were under-represented, compared with the 1980 figure of 48 per cent of women in the professions.

The impression that women were approaching parity with men in the professions is extremely misleading, masking their underrepresentation in higher professional occupations. The low-status professional occupations in which women were overrepresented indicate the low symbolic capital attached to their position in the labour market, whereas the professions which have high prestige were heavily dominated by men.

As Stockman et al. point out, pay reflects the different values attached to men's and women's occupations (Stockman et al. 1995: 73). Women's salaries were about 50 per cent of men's overall in 1985, although this varied by age, position and education. Women's earnings for formal full-time workers in continuous service in the same company since leaving school were 85 per cent of men's at age 35 for university graduates, and 74 per cent at age 45, suggesting that women were not promoted in proportion to their numbers in the privileged sector of the workforce. Among Stockman et al.'s sample of working mothers with preschool children in 1987, only 6 per cent had an income equal to or higher than their husband's salary, the average being 48 per cent of the husband's salary (Stockman et al. 1995: 74–5). Clearly women's positions in the employment field had significantly less economic capital attached to them than did men's positions.

Power Distribution in the Employment Field

The structure of employment as a field of power was made up of a complex pattern of crosscutting divisions which stratified the workforce into more and less privileged positionings. These divisions consisted of the entrepreneurial and corporate sectors of production, the formality and informality of contractual status, the long-term and short-term employment systems, and the routine-track and career-track trajectories. The entrepreneurial sector was particularly large because of the historical circumstances of the late but rapid development of capitalism in Japan, while the long-term employment system was a culturally specific form of constructing privileged employment positionings. Economic, cultural, social and symbolic capitals were attached to the social spaces where the privileged divisions overlapped, which was also where men predominated: in employment positions on the executive track, with formal contractual status in the long-term employment system and in the corporate or state sectors.

The employment field both structured and was structured by class divisions, but this class stratification was also gendered. Men were systematically distributed in greater numbers into positions to which capitals were attached, while women predominated in positions which lacked capitals. The level of women's participation in the employment field was high, and there was less horizontal segregation of occupations by sex than in some other industrialised countries. But women were clustered in jobs which were sex-typed as feminine, overrepresented in smaller firms, and heavily overrepresented in informal contract and short-term work. The routine track for qualified personnel with a full-time formal contract of employment was almost exclusively female, while the career track, with opportunities for promotion in the internal labour market, was almost entirely male. The career track was based on male work patterns of continuous employment, while women who joined it were obliged to follow male career patterns in order to retain the privileges of the system. Since less than 1 per cent of new women graduates entered this trajectory, it was clear that positions of class power in the field of employment, which the career track represents, were deeply gendered. Positions of power were constituted by full-time formal executive-track contracts in the long-term employment system within the corporate and state sectors. The bar on employees returning to privileged contractual positionings if they left for any reason ensured that most positions of privilege were held by men, although it should be recognised that a majority of male employees were also outside the privileged sector.

In terms of economic capital in the employment field, women's salaries were half of men's overall, although the difference was less among women graduates in full-time continuous service. In terms of symbolic capital, women were positioned in lower- rather than higher-status jobs in each category: in lower-status forms of manual work rather than skilled or craft production; in routine clerical and service work rather than managerial work in non-manual jobs; in lower-status rather than higher-status professional work. Managerial positions which had power in terms of authority, decision-making and control over others' labour had one of the lowest proportions of women amongst all the occupational categories, and their proportion declined the higher the position in the managerial hierarchy. A total of 98 per cent of all holders of managerial positions, and 99 per cent of all career-track personnel, were men. In other words, women were statistically negligible in employment positions to which economic, cultural and symbolic capitals were attached, and vastly overrepresented in labour-market positions where these capitals were absent.

The question this raises for an examination of gender, class and power is: how did women who achieved employment positions to which capitals were attached gain access to them? When the structure of the employment field placed women in positions of low economic, cultural and symbolic power, what capitals did women need to bring to the labour market in order to gain access to positions of power? We will argue that the social class of the family of origin was an important factor in women's access to positions of power in the employment field. To explore this, we first look at the changes in and characteristics of the class structure, and then present our own data on women's class origins, comparing our evidence with studies of class based on men.

Employment Position and Social Class

There are several different approaches to the understanding of class, but broadly we will use the term as a descriptive concept to refer to a number of aspects of social life which differentiate hierarchically ordered groups in society materially and culturally. Both Sugimoto Yoshio (1997: ch. 2) and Ishida Hiroshi (1993: ch. 6) refer to various different approaches to understanding class in the context of Japan. These are based largely on the two major western approaches of Weberian social stratification and Marxist social relations. The former perspective uses class as a description of social status or prestige, a concept which has emerged from Weber's ideas of status groups. This is often measured by occupational prestige scales – which, as Crompton points out, measure the relative distribution of rewards, reflecting the outcome of class processes, rather than explaining the structure of class relations which brought these outcomes about (Crompton 1993: 10, 13, 57). The latter, Marxist, perspective uses class as a description of relations of structured social inequality, where material differences are stable over time and reproduced within a group (Crompton 1993: 119). Bourdieu understands class in terms of social relations, and conceptualises class divisions as differing conditions of existence, systems of dispositions produced by those conditions and different endowments of capitals (Brubaker 1985: 761). Although he recognises occupation as a good indicator of position in social space, he does not regard it as determining, and is more interested in processes of class formation than in class structures themselves (Bourdieu 1987: 7). We will use Ishida's model for understanding class structure in Japan, and Bourdieu's approach for looking at class processes.

Sugimoto (1997) and Ishida (1993) use ideas from both Marxist and Weberian models to understand class, while drawing attention to the specificities of class in the Japanese context. In relation to the debates and ideas concerning the middle class, Sugimoto suggests that the term *churyu*, which refers to a 'middle domain of social status, respect, and prestige', is the most appropriate concept in Japanese for the Weberian sense of middle class; and the term *chusan*, meaning the 'middle to upper positions in the economic hierarchy' for the materialist sense of middle class, although this term contains no reference to class as social relations. Sugimoto refers to research which shows that the largest proportion of the population categorises itself as *churyu* (middle class in status terms), followed by a considerable section which identifies itself as *chusan* (middle class in economic terms) (Sugimoto 1997: 49). Both writers rely on their own studies or those of other researchers which analyse data from the Japan Sociological Association's Social Stratification and Mobility Survey (SSM), which has collected data every ten years since 1955.

Although the frameworks adopted by Sugimoto and Ishida result in some differences in classification, there is broad similarity between the

Table 17.4   Historical changes in class structure (percentage)

Class	1955	1985
Capitalist	5	6
Old middle		
farming	39	7
self-employed	19	18
New middle	17	32
Working	20	37
Total	100	100

Source: Hashimoto's SSM analysis, cited in Sugimoto 1997: 37.

two views of the size and structure of the class system. In both analyses, the working-class category taken as a whole is the largest single class, at nearly 40 per cent (Sugimoto 1997: 37). Given that an absolute majority of the population (60 per cent) can be categorised as middle-class by these criteria, and that many clerical workers consider themselves to be middle class because of the non-manual nature of their work, it is clear why some surveys show up to 90 per cent of Japanese classifying themselves as middle class.

We will now use Hashimoto's analysis to show historical changes in the class structure since the war, and Ishida's analysis of comparative class distributions to show the cultural specificities of the class structure in Japan. Hashimoto divides Japanese society into four major classes: capitalist (corporate executives and managers), old middle class (declining independent farmers and stable independent small businesses), new middle class (professionals, middle managers and clerical workers), and working class (skilled and unskilled blue-collar workers plus temporary and part-time – mainly women – workers) (Sugimoto 1997: 36–7).

Table 17.4 clearly demonstrates the enormous decline in the 'old middle' farming class, with both the working class and 'new middle' class almost doubling over the thirty-year period. It is clear that most class mobility would be expected from the rural petty bourgeoisie (small farmers), with little mobility out of the professional and managerial class ('new middle') or the working classes.

Ishida (1993) compares class distribution figures from Japan in 1975, the USA in 1973, and the UK in 1972, to show the cultural specificity of the class structure in Japan. He identifies a set of Marxist class categories, based on control over the means of production (employers and petty bourgeoisie) and control over labour (professionals and managers), and further breaks down the working class according to Weberian ideas of the prestige ranking of the nature of work and marketable skills (non-manual, skilled and unskilled). The Japanese class structure is characterised by a higher proportion of petty bourgeoisie and a lower proportion of professional/managerial and manual working classes than the class structures of the USA or the UK, because of late rapid industrialisation. In Japan, blue- and white-collar employment grew as agriculture declined, with no historical period of stable reproduction of an unskilled manual working class (as in the UK). This helps to explain why there is little working-class consciousness, and why a large sector of the population identify themselves as middle-class (Ishida 1993: 168, 202–3).

Japan's rapid change from a predominantly agricultural society to a highly industrialised society accounts for a significant proportion of the social mobility which has taken place. Ishida makes the distinction between *structural* class mobility ('forced' by these sorts of changes in society) and *unforced* class mobility, which is independent of structural changes. According to Ishida's calculations, the total amount of social mobility is remarkably similar in the three countries at around 68 per cent, which means that two-thirds of the population changed class compared with the class position of their parents. Ishida shows that whereas only one-fifth of this mobility in the UK and USA is due to structural (forced) change, half of all class mobility in Japan has been as a result of these enormous and rapid postwar structural changes (Ishida 1993: 173, 177, 202–3).

Gender and Class Origin

These patterns, however, are based on data which examines men's position in the class structure. Our study presents a range of indices connected to class positioning based on women in the professional/ managerial class. We will examine this data to see how far women's access to employment positions in professional and managerial occupations was independent of class background.

Ishida's analysis of the SSM based on the employment position of the total male workforce differentiates between class *origin* and class *destination* (Ishida 1993: 173). Using Ishida's analysis, we will now examine the class origins of, first, the total male workforce and, second, of male professional and managerial workers. We will then compare these figures with the class origins of the professional and managerial women in our sample.

Ishida points out that in his analysis, the assessment of the employment position of the respondents, which he terms 'class destination', is a reasonably accurate representation of the class composition of the male labour force at the time of the surveys. However, the assessment of the employment position of the respondents' fathers, which he terms 'class origin', does not represent the class composition of fathers at a specific point in the past. For this reason, this measure must be understood as the 'class origin of the respondents', not the 'class composition of the fathers' (Ishida 1993: 172). We will first examine the class origins of the total male labour force, and then of men in professional and managerial work, using Ishida's analysis based on the class positions of fathers. We will use the term 'professional' to refer to the 'professional and managerial category'. We will first compare professional men with the whole male labour force, to identify what is distinctive about the social origins of male professional workers. We will then compare the class origins of professional women against the distinctive class origins of professional men, using data from our sample of 120 women employed in management and the professions in Tokyo in 1977.

Class origins of the male workforce and male professionals

As Table 17.5 shows, more than half (53 per cent) of the male labour force had its origins in the petty-bourgeois class, and nearly one-fifth (19 per cent) came from the employers' class (including small-business owners). These were the two largest categories of class origin of the male workforce as a whole; the remainder (17 per cent) came from the working classes taken together, and the professional class (11 per cent). The petty bourgeoisie was by far the largest class origin for male workers, as would be predicted from the historical changes in the class structure outlined above. The working and professional classes, as we would expect, were the two smallest categories of class origin.

Of all male workers in 1975, 68 per cent had experienced a change of class (Ishida 1993: 177), compared with 80 per cent (the total of male professionals who came from classes other than the professional class) of male professional workers from the same study, indicating a higher level of class mobility for professional men compared with male workers as a whole. If we compare the class origins of the male professional class with those of the male labour force as a whole, we can

Table 17.5 Class origins based on father's employment position (percentage)

Employment category	Total male labour force*	Male professional/ managerial†	Professional women‡
Employer	19	20	31
Petty bourgeoisie	53	41	14
Professional/ managerial	11	20	48
Non-manual	5	7	4
Skilled	3	4	1
Unskilled	9	8	2
Total	100 (n = 2,043)	100 (n = 458)	100 (n = 109)
Class mobility (% changed class)	68	80	51

Sources: * adapted from Ishida 1993: 173; † adapted from Ishida 1993: 177; ‡ Our data is from 120 professional women, excluding 11 who did not specify the employment category of their fathers.

see that the proportions of professional men coming from the employers' class and the three working-class categories (non-manual, skilled manual and unskilled manual) were very similar to the proportions of the total male workforce coming from those origins. What is distinctive about the class origins of the male professional class, however, is that fewer of them came from the petty bourgeoisie compared with the total male workforce (41 per cent compared with 53 per cent), although this was still the largest single category of class origin; whereas twice as many professional men came from the professional class itself compared with the whole male labour force (20 per cent compared with 11 per cent). Professional men were therefore twice as likely to have fathers in the professional class compared with male workers as a whole, and less likely to have fathers from petty-bourgeois origins. This suggests that it was easier for men coming from professional families to become professionals themselves than it was for the male workforce in general. Clearly, being a member of a professional family proved a significant advantage to men in achieving professional class status in their own right, and a considerable degree of class reproduction was occurring between fathers and sons of the professional class. For men, it seems, access to power in the employment field in terms of achieving a professional or managerial position was not independent of class position of the family of origin.

Class origins of female professionals

We have just seen that professional men had more class mobility than male workers as a whole, but professional women had less class mobility than either group. Based on the employment positions of our respondents' fathers, Table 17.5 shows that only half of the respondents (52 per cent: all those not coming from the professional class) experienced a change of class over two generations, compared with 80 per cent of male professionals and 68 per cent of all male workers (Ishida 1993: 177), suggesting that it was much more difficult for women than for men to move into professional and managerial occupations from a different class background. The largest category of repondents who did change class came, significantly, from the employers' class (31 per cent), which represents the highest class position. But by far the greatest proportion came from the professional class itself: nearly half of all respondents (48 per cent) had fathers in the same class, compared with only a fifth of male professionals (20 per cent) and a tenth of the whole male workforce (11 per cent). Far fewer respondents came from the petty bourgeoisie and the working classes compared with either professional men or the male workforce as a whole. So it was much easier for a woman to become a professional herself if her father was from the professional rather than from any other class, and there was considerably more class reproduction between professional women and their fathers than between either professional men or male workers as a whole and their fathers. This does not mean, of course, that the daughters of professional men found it easier to become professionals than the sons of professional men, since the actual numbers of women were much smaller, but that a professional background was much more important for a woman to gain access to the professions than it was for a man.

A third (31 per cent) of respondents came from employer-class families; this, together with the 48 per cent from professional families already mentioned, means that these two powerful classes accounted for 79 per cent of the social class origins of our professional women, compared with only 40 per cent of professional men from these two classes. This tends to support Bourdieu's claim that the reproduction strategies of the dominant classes may be changing, placing a premium on the educational and professional status of daughters, which may pay dividends in terms of the class's ability to reproduce itself (Bourdieu 1990a). The distinctive features of our professional women's origins compared with professional men's are that they were more than twice as likely to come from the professional class itself, and twice as likely to come from the two middle-class categories of employers and professionals. As a corollary, respondents were only a third as likely to come from the working classes and a quarter less likely to come from the petty bourgeoisie. Thus there was a much higher level of class reproduction among our professional women than among professional men, the inflow coming largely from the higher classes, suggesting that it was much more difficult for women to become professional workers if they came from petty-bourgeois or working-class backgrounds than it was for men to do so.

Professional women's much stronger class reproduction, their greater recruitment from within the middle classes, and their lesser recruitment from lower-class backgrounds suggest that women specifically required the various forms of capitals that were attached to a middle-class background in order to break into the ranks of the more privileged forms of employment. Thus for women, access to the higher positions in the labour market in the form of professional and managerial occupations was even more dependent on the class position of the family than it was for men. What is distinctive about the relationship between gender, class and power for women is that the connection between a position of power in the employment field and the social origin of the family was so much greater than it was for men.

Mothers' positions and class origins

Since the analysis of class positions based on the SSM refers to male respondents and their fathers, we do not have comparable data on mothers' occupations. The debate on how women fit into class categories based on employment position is contentious, since many are not employed at various periods of their lives, and when they are employed it is unclear how their own employment position should be assessed in relation to that of their fathers or husbands (Crompton 1993: 96). Nevertheless, the employment position of respondents' mothers can tell us something about the social origin of the family.

Table 17.6 shows that two-thirds (66 per cent) of our respondents' mothers were not employed, but worked as full-time housewives either at the time of the study or up to their deaths, compared with 54 per cent of the general female population who were housewives at that time (Ministry of Labour 1976: 29). Since these women were the

Table 17.6   Distribution of employed women and housewives (percentage)

Employment status	Women in general population*	Mothers of professional women†
Housewife	54	66
Employed	46	29
Not specified	n/a	5
Total	100	100

Sources: * Ministry of Labour 1976: 29; † Our data from 120 professional women.

mothers of our respondents, they were not strictly comparable with the general population because they were older and may have been less likely to engage in paid work because of generational differences in middle-class women's participation in the labour market. However, their age also means that they were less likely to have young children, and therefore did not have the same restraints on undertaking paid work, counterbalancing any greater tendency to stay out of the workforce. If we understand being a housewife as a full-time occupation in the display and transmission of family capital, and thus as signifying the extent of economic, cultural and symbolic capital available in the middle-class family, then we can see the overrepresentation of mothers who were housewives, compared with the proportion of housewives in the general female population, as another index of the more privileged class position of the respondents' families of origin.

This class position is confirmed by the employment categories of mothers who did engage in paid work, since employed mothers were very heavily clustered in the professional and managerial category.

Table 17.7 shows that more than two-thirds of employed mothers (69 per cent) worked in professional or managerial occupations, compared with 48 per cent of fathers and a mere 13 per cent of all women workers in 1980, indicating an even greater degree of class reproduction between working mothers and their professional daughters than between fathers and daughters (although of course the actual number of working mothers was much smaller). Most of the professional-class mothers were in teaching, nursing or social work, these three categories covering 83 per cent of mothers employed as professional workers.

Table 17.7 Distribution of mothers' and fathers' employment categories (percentage)

Employment category	Respondents' fathers	Respondents' mothers (employed only)
Employer	31	0
Petty bourgeoisie	14	14
Professional/managerial	48	69
Non-manual	4	17
Skilled	1	0
Semi-/unskilled	2	0
Total	100 (n = 109)	100 (n = 35)

The proportion of working mothers in the petty-bourgeois category was very similar to the proportion of fathers. None of the working mothers was an employer, compared with 31 per cent of fathers; and none was a manual worker, compared with 3 per cent of fathers, although considerably more mothers than fathers were in the non-manual working-class category (17 per cent, compared to only 4 per cent of fathers). The 17 per cent of working mothers in clerical work, however, constituted almost half of the 33 per cent proportion of all women workers in 1980 (Ministry of Labour 1994: 17), again suggesting that professional women's mothers were more likely to be in higher- rather than lower-class employment categories compared to the general population.

Clearly, an even greater degree of class reproduction was occurring between mothers and daughters than between fathers and daughters. If a mother was employed at all, employment in the same category of occupation as the daughter was much the most common pattern. But by far the greatest number of mothers in our sample did not engage in paid work: they were full-time housewives. We have argued that this may be understood as a full-time occupation in the display and transmission of the family's cultural, economic and symbolic capital, and thus an index of a more privileged family background. It is through the transmission of family capitals to their children in the position of full-time housewife that the mothers of our respondents reproduced the class. Thus the pattern of professional and managerial women coming from more privileged class backgrounds was confirmed in relation to the positions of mothers as well as fathers.

Class Origins and Women's Access to Power in the Employment Field

We have demonstrated that the families of origin of women who have gained access to privileged positions in the employment field were from significantly higher-class positions than those of comparable men, that there was less social mobility and a higher degree of class reproduction than for men, and that women from lower-class backgrounds were much less likely than comparable men to gain professional and managerial positions.

It is clear from the evidence that the distribution of positions in the field of employment was not independent of the social origins of the family for either men or women. While men's access to professional and managerial positions was affected by the class position of the family of origin, this pattern was intensified for women, so that class background was much more important for women than for men. We would argue that professional- or employer-class origin was crucial for – though not completely determining of – women's access to a privileged position in the field of employment.

Chapter 18

Education as a
Field of Power

Since privileged positions in the employment field are based on educational credentials as well as family background, we look next at education as a field of power. We will suggest that although educational credentials were statistically necessary for access to privileged employment positions, they were rarely sufficient in themselves, for access to educational credentials was no more independent of social origin than was access to employment positions. In order to examine the structure of education as a field of power and women's positionings within it, we will outline the differences between the prewar and postwar education systems. We will identify two forms of sex segregation within the structure of education which help to organise women's positionings in the field. We will then show how education constitutes a process of class reproduction, and identify some of the mechanisms through which this takes place.

The Development of Education

Education before World War II

The system of education in the 'first' modernisation period (1868–1945) was a major site for the production of gender, class and nationality. Although universal education was designed to produce a literate populace who could compete with the West in the industrialisation of the economy, this democratisation of learning was restricted, as in the West, to compulsory levels of schooling. Higher education was designed to produce a 'system of differences', to distinguish those with legitimate access to power from those without (Wacquant 1993: 19).

Class differences were created through the selection of an elite which was trained in the university system as a ruling class; an intermediate class consisting of a technically competent labour force trained in the vocational schools, teacher training schools and technical/semi-professional schools; and a labouring class trained in the primary schools to read and write (Cummings 1980: 21).

Ethnic differences and the creation of a national identity were also produced in the education system through morals training, which emphasised loyalty to the emperor and allegiance to the national purpose; by the daily repetition in every school class from 1891 of the Imperial Rescript on Education, which stressed the 'glory of the empire' of which all Japanese were subjects; and the teaching of gratitude for the privilege of being born in the empire (Cummings 1980: 19–21). These practices clearly demarcated those who were and those who were not ethnic Japanese.

Gender divisions were created through the morals curriculum and through the practice of sex-segregated schooling. The morals training set out the different patterns by which men and women could fulfil the nation's goals: men were destined for the army and the workplace, while women were trained for the home (notwithstanding the number of women who entered paid work) (Cummings 1980: 19). Boys and girls were segregated after second grade, and the curriculum diverged, with girls being taught domestic skills including cooking, sewing and flower arranging. The secondary education that was available to girls was of a lower level than that offered to boys, as girls' high schools were equivalent to boys' middle schools (Inoue 1971: 28). Women were barred from the universities, and most of those in higher education went to women's colleges or teacher training colleges. As an official report stated: 'Our female higher education may be said to have the object of forming character in women and of imparting knowledge well-calculated to make good wives and wise mothers, able to contribute to the peace and happiness of the family into which they marry' (Cummings 1980: 20).

Thus, although the state promoted the idea of equal opportunities for the whole population, education was not equal. The state made sure that every child attended primary school, which was both compulsory and free, but secondary schooling was neither. Girls' secondary schools were mainly private, and the tuition fees were substantial (Inoue 1971: 21). Scholarships were rare, except for military and teacher training schools; as a result, women of ability but without means were largely confined to schoolteaching (Cummings 1980: 28).

Tokyo Imperial University was established in 1886 as the premier learning institution for men. Admission was based on the national competitive examination. The aim was to select a national elite, and provide a broad education appropriate for the ruling class. Kyoto University was established in 1897. These two universities may be regarded as Japan's equivalent of Oxford and Cambridge, although Tokyo was – and is – clearly the leader. The state ratified the symbolic power of the elite universities by providing generous financial settlements for their operation, and offering their graduates favourable treatment in the competition for government jobs. As other sectors of the economy began to recognise the symbolic power granted by the state to the universities, they too increasingly selected personnel from among their graduates. In time, an education at an elite university was recognised as a preparation for an elite career in government service, business and the professions (Cummings 1980: 21, 26).

In 1918, more universities were set up, and there were thirty altogether by the end of the 1920s (Cummings 1980: 28). The University Ordinance 1918 expanded higher education, and allowed local governments and private organisations to set up universities. Japan Women's College (*Nihon Joshi Daigaku*) and Tokyo Women's College (*Tokyo Joshi Daigaku*) applied for recognition as universities, but only male institutions were accredited, and women's colleges had to remain 'special schools'. The state withheld symbolic power from women's educational institutions, thus marking an elite education as an exclusively masculine social space. No national higher-education institutions were established for women, although a few universities gave women limited access. Hiroshima University, for example, opened its doors to women from its foundation in 1929, and Tohoku Imperial University opened some faculties to women in 1913 and 1922 (Inoue 1971: 34–5).

Since 1900, when compulsory education was made free (Stephens 1991: 32), the proportion of the population attending compulsory-level schooling has been more than 98 per cent (Hendry 1987: 87). In the early part of the twentieth century, around 1 per cent of this age group went on to post-compulsory education (higher school and above), 96 per cent of whom were men. Cummings quotes the figure of less than 0.1 per cent of the age group who went to Tokyo University, all of whom were men. After the expansion of higher education in the 1920s, 4 per cent of men and 0.5 per cent of women went into post-compulsory education (Ichibangase 1971: 64).

Education after World War II

After the war, the Occupation Authorities purged or accepted resignations from 120,000 teachers (a quarter of those in the profession), appointed liberals in their place, and extended compulsory education. The 1947 Education Law specified nine years of compulsory education from age 6 to 15, followed by non-compulsory upper-secondary school of three years, and then either two-year junior college, or four-year university. The three-year lower-secondary school was compulsory, free and co-educational. Higher secondary school was also free and mixed-sex, and open to all who wanted it. Higher education was to be meritocratic, but for the many, not the few (Cummings 1980: 32–4, 88).

The Occupation Authorities tried to level the university hierarchy by reducing financial differentials between the universities; the resource allocation to Tokyo University, for example, shrank to 8 per cent of the total budget for national universities. But by the late 1960s this allocation had almost doubled again to 15 per cent of the total budget. Cummings argues that the occupation reforms failed to alter the government's favourable treatment of elite universities, and also failed to change the central element of the examination system, which was the link between elite universities and the prestigious employers of the corporate and state sectors (Cummings 1980: 208–9). But it is precisely this recognition of the symbolic power of an elite university qualification by the state and the major employers that guarantees the cultural capital through which the class is reproduced, and is thus a crucial process in an advanced capitalist society, which the Occupation Authorities could hardly be expected to abolish.

Women's Positioning in the Educational Field

Education in Japan is designed to be egalitarian at the compulsory level and meritocratic at the post-compulsory stage. Cummings sees education as a transformative process which has undermined the state's promotion of social stratification since the war. He argues that the teachers' unions have successfully resisted government attempts to reverse democratising reforms, through the daily practice of an inclusive education in the schools. As a result, 'Japan's distribution of cognitive skills is probably more equal than that of any other contemporary society' (Cummings 1980: 6, 88, 233–4, 273). While we agree that education has been a site of struggle, we also argue that education is a site for the production of gendered power, and that women's access to educational opportunities has not been equal to men's at the higher levels.

The mechanisms through which gendered power differences are produced include the vertical and horizontal segregation of education by sex. There has been a remarkable expansion of secondary education since the war, for both girls and boys. In 1950, nearly a half of boys (48 per cent) and more than a third of girls (37 per cent) went on to upper-secondary from lower-secondary school. By 1985, girls had not only caught up with but overtaken boys, with 93 per cent of boys and 95 per cent of girls going on to upper-secondary school. But at this stage there is a marked divergence in the routes which young men and women take into higher education.

Vertical segregation of higher education

Vertical segregation is evident in the fact that most women go to junior college, whilst a majority of men go to university. Junior colleges were set up in 1948 to replace the higher vocational schools and provide training in liberal arts. In 1955, 2 per cent of men and 3 per cent of women went on to junior college, but 13 per cent of men and only 2 per cent of women went on to university. By 1985, if one looks at the number of students entering higher education, the sexes seem fairly evenly divided – at 55 per cent men and 45 per cent of women – but there was a startling sexual segregation based on the level of institution attended. Whereas 21 per cent of women went on to junior college, a negligible 2 per cent of men did so. And while 14 per cent of women went to university, the proportion of men was almost three times as great, at 39 per cent. Of men in higher education, 95 per cent were at university, whereas the majority of women (60 per cent) were at junior college. Women made up only 25 per cent of university students, but 91 per cent of junior college students. At postgraduate level the discrepancy was greater, for whereas women constituted 25 per cent of total university students, they made up only 13 per cent of postgraduates (Ministry of Education 1986: 11–13). This pattern of segregation based on the level of institution would suggest that women's representation at the most exclusive university would be tiny. This is borne out by the proportion of women attending Tokyo University, which rose from 0.5 per cent (9 women out of 1,804 students) in 1949, to 3 per cent in 1960 and 6 per cent in 1977 (Tokyo University 1986).

Horizontal segregation of higher education

Horizontally, too, women and men are segregated in education. Between the junior college and university systems, sex segregation by subject was almost complete. At junior college (91 per cent female), 77 per cent of women took the three most popular 'women's courses' in Home Economics (29 per cent), Humanities (25 per cent) and Education (23 per cent), whereas 83 per cent of the men took the three most popular 'men's courses' in Engineering (45 per cent), Social Science (29 per cent) and Agriculture (9 per cent) (Ministry of Education 1986: 14).

At university the segregation was not quite so marked, but there was still a clear difference. Here 52 per cent of women took the two most popular 'women's subjects' in Humanities (35 per cent) and Education (17 per cent), whereas 71 per cent of men took the two most popular 'men's courses' in Social Science (mainly Law, Economics and Management) at 46 per cent and Engineering at 25 per cent. Men confined themselves mainly to subjects which facilitated entry into secure professional occupations. Women were more likely to choose subjects which interested them, but had more limited direct occupational value (Ministry of Education 1986: 14).

Power Distribution in the Educational Field

The structure of higher education as a field of power is made up of the junior college, the university and the graduate school. This stratification of higher education is gendered. Women's participation in higher education was almost equal to men's, but women were clustered in the lower-quality institutions, taking subjects which were non-vocational or sex-typed as feminine. Compared with their proportion in higher education as a whole, men were overrepresented in the higher-quality institutions, and heavily overrepresented in the higher-level academic degrees. Men were also concentrated into subjects which had direct relevance for the labour market. The vertical and horizontal segregation of education acts as a mechanism for producing gender differences. In terms of the acquisition of cultural capital, women were positioned in lower- rather than higher-status educational spaces, and in locations which were loosely rather than firmly attached to labour-market positions. In other words, women were statistically underrepresented in positions in the higher educational field to which the most cultural and symbolic capitals were attached, and overrepresented in higher-educational positions to which the least capitals were attached.

It is clear from this analysis that education is a mechanism for the production of gendered power, and that women's positioning within the educational field locates them in the less privileged spaces in terms of the quality of their education, their access to elite positions in the educational hierarchy, the value of their education for occupational status, and their access to privileged positions in the employment field. The question this raises for an examination of gender, class and power is: how did women who did achieve positions of privilege in education gain access to them? When the structure of the educational field places women in positions of low economic, cultural, social and symbolic power, what capitals did women need to bring to the field of education in order to gain the educational credentials that would qualify them for a privileged employment position?

We will argue that the cultural capital of the family of origin was important in women's access to higher education. To explore this, we will first look at the links between education and social class, particularly the education offered by the elite universities. We will examine the relationship between higher education and privileged positions in the labour market, and then between higher education and class background, in order to show the mechanisms of class reproduction. We will then present our own data on the cultural capital of our women respondents and their families of origin, and compare the evidence with studies of educational credentials based exclusively or predominantly on men.

Education and Social Origin

In the context of Japan, both Ishida Hiroshi (1993) and William Cummings (1980) have used Bourdieu's ideas on education, but with rather different emphases. Ishida uses statistics from the Social Structure and Mobility Survey (SSM) to argue that the social effects of education are to reproduce inequality. He is, however, unable to answer the question of why the thesis of educational credentialism is so popular, since the idea of Japan as an educational credentialist society (whereby those with most intellectual merit gain access to positions of power) is not supported by his evidence (Ishida 1993: ch. 8). Cummings, on the other hand, sees education as a site of struggle between the state and the teachers' unions, leading to a transformative process which has undermined the state's production of social inequality and stratification. We will argue that both arguments are correct, but at different positions in social space. At the level of primary and secondary schooling, a democratisation of education and more egalitarian cognitive achievements have been produced since the war; whereas at tertiary level, although the quantity of higher education has expanded and therefore included more people in its scope, the creation of an elite among the university-educated has been retained. We will answer Ishida's question using Bourdieu's argument that the thesis of educational credentialism is so popular because what higher education is doing is not producing a purely meritocratic system, but *disguising* the reproduction of privileged social backgrounds. We will demonstrate that educational credentials are not independent of social origin; that an elite education in particular is productive of privileged positions in the employment field; and that cultural capital, acquired in the family of origin and credentialised in educational qualifications, is much more important for women than it is for men.

Secondary education and social origin

Despite the egalitarianism of education, many authors have argued that post-compulsory education is not independent of social origin. In relation to secondary education, Cummings suggests that managerial and professional families have made the greatest gains in education in the twentieth century, and proposes that family support for children is the key component in this. Average-ability children from professional and managerial families continued their education, while more able children from farming and blue-collar families gave up school at the end of compulsory middle school. Ushiogi's 1972 study of post-compulsory-school dropouts showed that among high-achieving children, 10.3 per cent from rural and 8.4 per cent from blue-collar families dropped out, compared with only 1.7 per cent of children from white-collar and 0.4 per cent from managerial families (Cummings 1980: 222–3). Clearly, educational achievement is not the sole determinant of access to post-compulsory education even at high-school level.

The most prestigious high schools are those which are most successful in sending pupils to the high-quality universities, since attendance at a prestigious university strongly determines employment opportunities (Hendry 1987: 91). Rohlen found a significant correlation between the prestige of the high school attended by the pupil and the level of the parents' education, as well as the extent of facilities at home for academic study. He also found that practice, and the ability to pay for expensive private tuition and repeat years, were factors in gaining access to the high-prestige universities (Rohlen 1983: 86–7, 129). Hendry argues that 'a wealthy elite is being separated off at an ... early age' (Hendry 1987: 93–4).

Tertiary education and social origin

To make the connection between educational position and class reproduction, we will first show that higher education, particularly at one of the elite universities, facilitates access to privileged positions in the employment field. We will then demonstrate that access to higher education, particularly in one of the elite institutions, is affected by the social class of the family of origin.

Higher education and the employment field: where do graduates go?

Cummings argues that, at the higher educational level, two trends were evident over the course of the twentieth century. First, university education became much more important in gaining a privileged position in the employment field. This is clear from the inexorable rise in the proportion of university graduates among what he terms 'elite occupations': from 28 per cent at the beginning of the century to 94 per cent in 1964. Second, the importance for a high-status employment position of an education at the premier university remained stable, and even increased slightly from 12 per cent in 1903 to 17 per cent in 1964 (Cummings 1980: 27). As a result of these two trends, the contribution of Tokyo University graduates to all graduate 'elites' declined, particularly following the expansion of higher education after the war (from 34 per cent in 1955 to 21 per cent in 1964), but it was still a significant percentage overall, especially in professions like government service (41 per cent) and university teaching (36 per cent) (Cummings 1980: 27). So we can say that a university education has become increasingly important for a privileged position in the employment field, and that an education at the top university still accounted for more than a fifth of such positions in the 1960s.

Higher education and the family: where do graduates come from?

Since 1960, a growing proportion of students at university level have come from higher-income groups, despite the expansion of higher education. Among national universities the proportion of students with family incomes in the top 40 per cent bracket increased from 45 per cent in 1961 to 60 per cent in 1976. In private universities the disparity between the proportions of rich and poor was much greater, for obvious economic reasons. While there have always been significantly more students from higher-income families, this pattern has been intensifying. In 1961, 43 per cent of students were from the top fifth income level, compared to 11 per cent from the bottom fifth. In 1976, 47 per cent were from the top fifth and only 7 per cent from the bottom fifth (Education Ministry report, cited in Cummings 1980: 226). Table 18.1 compares the class origins of Tokyo University students with Ishida's analysis of class structure.

Table 18.1   Class origins of Tokyo University students (percentage)

Father's employment position	Students' class origins (1970)*	Ishida's class structure (1975)†
Employer	6	13
Petty bourgeoisie	27	25
Professional/managerial	41	22
Working classes	20	40
Other	6	–
Total	100	100

Sources: * Cummings 1980: 227, adapted from Table 8.4; † Ishida 1993: 173.

The greatest discrepancy was the overrepresentation of the professional and managerial class, by almost 100 per cent, and the underrepresentation of the working classes, who had half their expected proportion at the top university. On the basis of such analyses, Cummings argues that class background affects access to elite institutions, especially Tokyo University. Although official data on the social background of students is no longer released by Tokyo University (Cummings 1980: 223, 225), Cummings's conclusion is confirmed by a 1991 study, which showed that three-quarters of Tokyo University students came from the professional and managerial class (Sugimoto 1997: 10).

Ishida, too, argues that education is not independent of social origin, and that the higher levels of academic qualifications have become the means of reproducing inequality from generation to generation (Ishida 1993: ch. 3). His analysis of SSM shows that men's access to tertiary education was affected by economic, cultural and social capital. On the basis of an assessment of the father's class as an index of economic capital, a man whose father was in the top category of economic capital was six times more likely to attend university in Japan than a man whose father was in the lowest category. On the basis of the father's occupational status and size of family as indices of social capital, a man whose father had the highest social capital was ten times more likely to go to university. And on the basis of parents' education as an index of cultural capital, every year of increase in the father's and mother's education as an index of cultural capital increased the chance of the son attending university by 1.4 (Ishida 1993: 67–8).

So in terms of social origin in general, and the specific economic, cultural and social capitals attached to social origin, family background was crucial for men's access to education in Japan. Ishida also shows that access to higher education has become statistically *more* dependent on social origin over time. Economic capital was less important than in earlier times, but social and cultural capital were more important, especially mother's education, father's occupation and family size. Ishida concludes that the attainment of academic degrees became less equal and more dependent on social origin in the twentieth century: higher levels of academic qualifications 'are becoming the means for reproducing inequality from generation to generation' (Ishida 1993: 69–73, 77–8). As Bourdieu suggests, there is no perfect reproduction of educational elites between generations, but economic, social and cultural capital are all crucial in access to educational credentials.

But if social origin affects access to higher education, both social origin and education affect access to high-status occupations in the employment field. Social origin affects occupational position directly, but also indirectly through the mediation of education. Neither the effect of social background on occupational position, nor the role of education in transmitting the effect of social background, can be overlooked, especially the effect of cultural capital in the form of father's education (Ishida 1993: 90,127). Ishida's statistical data clearly shows how a man's occupational status is affected by cultural capital in the form of his father's (but not his mother's) education, social capital in the form of his father's occupational status, and economic capital in the form of his family's wealth. Social capital is the most important of the three, and the major determinant of this is father's occupation. As Ishida makes clear, although there is no perfect reproduction of occupational hierarchy, families with prestigious occupations, on average, successfully transfer their advantaged positions to the next generation (Ishida 1993: 94–5, 100).

Elite Education and Class Reproduction

Both Cummings and Ishida argue that privileged positions in the employment field were filled disproportionately from a small number of elite universities. Indeed, the most dramatic effect of stratification in higher education found by Ishida was in the formation of an elite (Ishida 1993: 133, 159). In 1980 there were 436 universities and graduate

Table 18.2   Universities and top jobs (percentage)

University	Higher civil service (1980)*	Company presidents (1985)†
Tokyo University	39	23
Other elite universities	42	39
All elite universities	81	62
Non-elite universities	19	38
All universities	100	100

Source: * Koyama 1981, cited in Ishida 1993: 154; † Nihon Keizai newspaper 1986, cited in Ishida 1993: 153.

schools in Japan (ESCAP 1984: 181). There is a high degree of consensus on which are the elite universities, and Ishida identifies twelve as in the 'top league'.[1]

Table 18.2 shows that Tokyo alone provided almost 40 per cent of higher civil service recruits, and that all the elite universities accounted for four-fifths of successful government service applicants in 1980. Tokyo accounted for 23 per cent, and all the elite universities 62 per cent, of company presidents in 1985.

Thus the link between the top of the educational hierarchy and the top of the professional/managerial hierarchy is very strong in Japan. Privileged positions in employment are filled disproportionately from a small number of elite institutions (matching the contribution of Oxbridge in the UK). The educational pathway to the top corporate and bureaucratic elites shows a high degree of closure. The stratification of higher education does differentiate the occupational success of graduates, but its most dramatic effect is on the attainment of privileged positions in employment (Ishida 1993: 160).

Ishida argues that the effect of education as opposed to social background on occupational position is not simple, because of the dual effect of education on access to high-status occupations. Education both

1. Ishida identifies the top league of universities as consisting of the seven former imperial universities (Tokyo, Kyoto, Hokkaido, Tohoku, Kyushu, Nagoya and Osaka), plus three other prestigious universities (Tokyo Kogyo, Hitotsubashi and Kobe), and the two high-status private institutions (Waseda and Keio).

affects occupational achievement directly, independently of social background, and is used indirectly to pass on privileged positions to the next generation. We may understand the direct effect of education as the acquisition of technical knowledge, and the indirect effect as the ratification of cultural capital acquired in the family. Indeed, when a wide range of social background characteristics are included, the effect of social background surpasses the effect of education on access to high-status occupations (Ishida 1993: 241–4, 248). Advantaged families ensure higher occupational status for their sons by sending them to elite universities, and part of the effect on occupational success of the stratification of higher education is due to the elite universities being attended by people who already have advantages. Ishida claims that previous studies have overemphasised the direct impact of the quality of the university, because they failed to control for social background. Ignoring the impact of stratification in higher education in reproducing inequality leads to an overemphasis on the effect of higher education on social mobility and an underemphasis on the effect of social background (Ishida 1993: 159).

Ishida concludes that the idea of educational credentialism cannot be supported as an explanation for who achieves privileged positions in Japan, since access to educational credentials is not independent of social background, and access to higher education has become more dependent on social origin, despite the expansion of higher education (Ishida 1993: 247). The distribution of education has widened, but access by people from disadvantaged backgrounds has not improved. Secondary schooling is becoming more equal, but higher education is increasingly affected by class background, and universities and academic qualifications are increasingly becoming a mechanism for reproducing inequality (Ishida 1993: 241).

Since the statistics do not support the idea of educational credentialism, Ishida (1993: 249) asks why the thesis is so popular, and indeed why education is so popular if education itself is not what brings occupational benefits? The answer, using Bourdieu's insights, is that the significance of education is not that it produces social mobility based purely on merit and ability, but that it disguises the fact that it is actually reproducing privileged social backgrounds.

Thus educational credentials are not independent of social origin for men, particularly among those reaching privileged positions in the employment field. Instead educational qualifications ratify the cultural capital that is acquired in the family of origin, thus reproducing class power while simultaneously disguising this reproduction. In particular, an elite education facilitates access to positions of occupational privilege. So both family background and education affect men's access to privileged positions in employment.

Gender, Cultural Capital and Class Reproduction

The above patterns are based on data from male respondents (in the case of SSM), or from total populations (in the elite studies) in which women were a very small minority. They therefore represent male educational patterns, and obscure any differences that may be found in female patterns. Our study presents evidence on educational positioning based on data from women in the professional/managerial class. We will examine the data to assess, first, how far women's access to higher education was independent of class background; and second, how far women's access to privileged positions in employment was independent of an elite education.

We will assess the cultural capital of the family of origin by looking at father's and mother's education. This is not exactly synonymous with Bourdieu's concept of cultural capital, which he defines as an inherited linguistic and cultural competence, but he regards education as sufficiently close to be useful as a measure, since it is through the process of acquiring educational credentials that the cultural capital of the family is ratified (Bourdieu 1984: 13).

Table 18.3   Fathers' education

Highest educational level	% of respondents' fathers
Primary school (compulsory)	8
Secondary school	18
College	7
University	58
Military academy	1
Not specified	8
Total (n = 120)	100
All post-compulsory	84
All higher education excluding higher school	66

Our respondents were aged from 23 to 67 at the time of the first study in 1977, and were born between 1910 and 1954. The education of their parents took place between the 1890s and the early 1940s (although education was limited after Japan entered the Pacific War in 1941). If we compare the education levels of our respondents' fathers with the proportion of the population who received higher education before the war, we can see that our respondents were from a highly select group of families. Before the war, higher education consisted of higher schools, higher normal schools (teacher training colleges), colleges (including women's colleges) and universities (ESCAP 1984: 180).

Taking for comparison 1920 as a midpoint in the parents' education, and 1940 as the point when higher education reached a peak, we see that in 1920 only 2 per cent of men received higher education (including higher school), rising to 5 per cent in 1940 (Ichibangase 1971: 64). The estimated proportion of the population who went on to higher education *excluding* higher school was 1 per cent in the 1930s (Cummings 1980: 21). In contrast, Table 18.3 shows that two-thirds (66 per cent) of respondents' fathers had been educated at college, university or military academy. A further 18 per cent had been educated beyond compulsory level, and a mere 8 per cent had been educated only to primary level. Thus fathers with higher education were vastly overrepresented among respondents' families of origin compared with the general population.

If we look at the proportion of fathers who went to the elite universities, we find that almost one in eight (12 per cent) had attended the top institution (Tokyo University), and one in six (18 per cent) had attended one of the twelve elite institutions. These figures are shown in Table 18.4.

Table 18.4 Percentage of fathers who attended elite universities

Tokyo University	12
Other elite universities	6
All elite universities	18
Other universities	40
Non-graduates	42
Total (n = 120)	100

Table 18.5   Mothers' education

Highest educational level	% of respondents' mothers
Primary school (compulsory)	15
Secondary school	46
College	30
University	2
Not specified	7
Total (n = 120)	100
All post-compulsory education	78
All higher education excluding higher school	32

The educational levels of respondents' mothers were less conclusively clustered in the higher reaches of the university system, but were still remarkably high considering the proportions of women who had access to higher education before the war.

In 1920, a negligible 0.1 per cent of women received post-compulsory education, but even taking as a comparison the highest figure of 0.6 per cent in post-compulsory education in 1940 (Ichibangase 1971: 64), Table 18.5 shows that an extraordinarily high proportion of respondents' mothers had received higher education by comparison. Nearly four-fifths (78 per cent) had received post-compulsory education, while nearly a third (32 per cent) had received higher education at college or university. Most of the higher-educated mothers had attended women's colleges. Of the three mothers who went to university, one went to a women's medical college and became a doctor, another studied at Tohoku University and became a lecturer, and the third studied maths at Hiroshima University and became a professor. It is clear from these figures that mothers with post-compulsory and higher education were also vastly overrepresented in the families of our professional women in comparison with the general population.

Thus the evidence suggests that professional women came from families in which there was a remarkably high degree of educationally credentialised cultural capital on the part of both parents. Indeed, we may say that professional women came from an educational elite.

Professional Women's Education

Taking the highest figures for comparison, in 1970, when the youngest of our sample was moving on to university, only 6 per cent of girls went on to higher education (Ministry of Education, Science and Culture 1986: 11).

Table 18.6 shows that 96 per cent of the respondents were qualified, while 83 per cent were graduates, including 10 per cent with doctorates. The two unqualified respondents were both managers who had risen through the company. The respondents with vocational qualifications consisted of thirteen managers and three of the older civil servants, whose educational credentials were mostly in teaching, nursing and languages, but also included subjects like pharmacy, dietetics and home economics: these subjects were relevant to the manager's job in most cases. Thus the vast majority were educationally qualified, and it was mostly those in management who had pre-degree-level qualifications. This is consistent with the lower proportion of graduates in management generally.

Table 18.7 shows that a third (33 per cent) of the whole sample had attended Tokyo University, and more than half (53 per cent) had been to an elite university. By comparison, 20 per cent of the total population of graduates in Japan came from the twelve elite universities (Ishida 1993: 34). Thus graduates of elite universities were overrepresented by more than 250 per cent among the women in our study in professional employment, compared with the proportion of elite graduates as a whole.

Table 18.6   Respondents' education

Educational qualifications	% of respondents
No qualifications	2
Vocational qualifications	13
Graduate	73
Doctorate	10
Not specified	2
Total (n = 120)	100

Table 18.7   Respondents' universities

Place of study	% of respondents
Tokyo University	33
Other elite universities	20
All elite universities	53
Other universities	30
All graduates	83
Non-graduates	15
Not specified	2
Total (n = 120)	100

Next we will break down the Tokyo University graduates into professions and compare the numbers with the proportions in the profession as a whole. The figures on the profession as a whole comprised large majorities of men, and therefore represent male statistical patterns (see Table 17.2 for proportions of women in the professions).

Table 18.8 shows that Tokyo University graduates constituted 33 per cent of the whole sample of professional women (including those who were and were not educated at university) compared with 17 per cent of all professional 'elites' in Aso Makoto's 1967 study (Cummings 1980: 27). In Table 18.8 we also examine the position of graduates, comparing the proportion of Tokyo University graduates among graduate men and women in each profession. We can see that with the exception of academics, Tokyo University graduates were more highly represented among professional women in the study who were educated at university than among graduate professionals as a whole. Among doctors, 23 per cent of the women respondents were Tokyo University graduates, compared to 17 per cent of the profession as a whole in 1964. In the elite cadres of the civil service, 64 per cent of our graduates in 1977 were from Tokyo University, compared with 41 per cent of the whole profession in 1964, and with 39 per cent of successful applicants to higher civil service positions in 1980 (see Table 18.2). Among business leaders, 43 per cent of our women were Tokyo University graduates, compared with 14 per cent of qualified members of the profession in 1964, and with 23 per cent of company presidents in 1985 (see Table 18.2). Overall,

Table 18.8 Tokyo University graduates out of all professionals

Profession	Tokyo University graduates as % of			
	all respondents	all professionals‡*	graduate respondents	all graduate professionals‡*
Civil service	53	–	64	41
Doctors	23	–	23	17
Academics	33	–	33	36
Managers	20	–	43	14
All professions	33	17	39	21

‡ predominantly male.

Sources: * Aso Makoto 1967: 217–9, cited in Cummings 1980: 27, Table 2.1; other columns, our data.

we find that 39 per cent of our graduate respondents were Tokyo University graduates, compared with 21 per cent of all graduate professionals, consisting mainly of men. Thus almost twice as many of our respondents were educated at the leading university compared with those in privileged professional occupations as a whole.

It appears that an elite education was generally more important for women's access to professional occupations than it was for men's, and this was particularly marked in relation to government service and corporate management (although management was more open to non-graduates in general, while it was less open to women). We suggest that this was because government service and corporate management were non-traditional professions for women, and women required significantly more cultural and symbolic capital in the form of an elite education to be recognised as legitimate contenders in these fields of employment. Although medicine and university teaching were also high-status male-dominated professions, they did have associations with women's caring and childrearing roles; indeed, women's representation in these two professions was significantly greater than in management and the civil service (Hirano Takako et al. 1980: 19). Next we assess how far an elite education produces a greater likelihood of promotion to the top of the profession for women.

In 1989, we traced 66 of the original respondents. Between 1977 and 1989, 28 had been promoted to the top of their profession. Of these,

43 per cent had been educated at Tokyo University compared with 35 per cent of the whole 1989 sample; 65 per cent had been to the elite universities compared with 61 per cent of the 1989 sample. Thus, the top universities, and particularly Tokyo University, were overrepresented amongst women who had reached the top of their profession between 1977 and 1989, suggesting that an elite education facilitated women's career progression.

Class Origins and Women's Access to Power in the Educational Field

We have seen that educational credentials, particularly from an elite institution, are necessary for access to a privileged employment position, but access to educational credentials is not independent of social origin. The stratification of higher education is a mechanism of class reproduction, and the vertical and horizontal sex segregation of higher education is a mechanism for the production of gendered power. These two mechanisms are not separate, but interlocking. The reproduction of class through the stratification of higher education is a gendered process. Men dominate elite university education, while few women are able to access an elite education for themselves.

Men who gain access to a position of privilege in the educational field are able to move more easily into privileged positions in employment, and they come disproportionately from families with higher class backgrounds and greater economic capital. Their educational credentials are themselves dependent on the social background of their families of origin. Although there is no perfect reproduction, as Bourdieu acknowledges, we can see here the mechanism through which advantaged families pass on their accumulated economic, cultural and social capitals to men of the next generation, and the way in which the fields of employment, education and the family are linked in this process.

For women who gain access to privileged positions in the higher-education field, these patterns are intensified. Women who receive an elite education represent a highly select group. Our study showed that, compared with the general population, they came from families with significantly higher levels of education, and they were distinguished from comparable men by the vastly superior levels of cultural capital among not only their fathers but also their mothers. Professional women's social origins lay in the educational elite. With respect to their own education, graduates of elite universities were overrepresented among women achieving privileged employment positions, and they were more likely to be promoted to the top of their profession than women from other universities. In comparison with male professionals, twice the proportion of women professionals in our study were graduates of the leading university. Clearly, an elite education is much more important for women's access to privileged positions in the employment field than it is for men's.

In answer to Bourdieu's claim that 'there exists a space of positions which cannot be occupied unless one possesses one of a number of forms of capital to a very high degree' (Wacquant 1993: 21), we conclude that while this is true in general, one must first identify the sex of the individual seeking access to the social space before one can establish the degree of capital required. We concur that privileged positions in the fields of employment and education cannot be occupied without a high degree of economic, social and cultural capital in the form of a privileged family background and a high level of education. These capitals both define and are defined by class divisions, but they are gendered class divisions: the legitimate contestants in the fields are middle-class men. Women who attempt to enter these fields must bring with them significantly more of these capitals if they are to be given the opportunity to enter the 'space of positions'.

As Bourdieu acknowledges, there are costs in the education-mediated system of class reproduction such that there is no guarantee that positions of privilege will automatically be transferred to the next generation (Wacquant 1993: 29). But there are also costs in the education-mediated system of gendered power production. If gendered positions of class power are to be breached, and women are to be admitted to positions of power in the field, the cost is, we would argue, that the class is more tightly reproduced. In this sense, Bourdieu's characterisation of fields of power as 'sites of struggle' rather than as spaces of static positions must be taken seriously, and the struggle must be recognised as composed of crosscutting social relations. Women's admission into new sites of power must be seen as a struggle that revolves around both gender and class.

In view of the context of the fields as sites for the production of gendered class power, women's access to privileged positions must be problematised rather than taken for granted as a natural process of increasing meritocracy and opportunity for all. The patterns we have identified suggest that statistically the price of female admission to privileged positions in the employment and educational fields which are identified as legitimate for middle-class men is a more closed and inwardly defined reproduction of class power, rather than an opening-up of positions to women of all classes. We have shown that women cannot occupy the space of privileged positions without possessing economic, social and cultural capital, as well as technical knowledge and intellectual ability, to a greater degree than men. Thus it seems that women who win recognition as legitimate contestants in the field do so at the expense of any opening-up of positions to a wider class base.

Chapter 19

The Family as a Field of Power

Finally, we examine the effect of women's access to privileged employment positions on their position in the family. We have already referred to the family in terms of the social class and educational backgrounds of the respondents' families of origin, but the family is also a field of power in which women's positions change according to age, marital status and parenthood. We will ask how far women's access to privileged positions in education and employment enabled them to increase their power in the social field of the family. In order to examine the family as a field of power, and women's positionings within it, we will first outline changes to the structure of the family since the war, and briefly identify some of the specific ways in which women's positionings in the family are determined. Using data from our study, we will look at how changes to the position of professional women in the fields of employment and education had laid the conditions for changes to the family.

Postwar changes to the family

Although the Occupation Authorities abolished the old family–state system, the idea of the family, or the *ie*, as the basic unit of society has been retained in different forms and sustained by different regulatory practices. The most significant of these, according to Sugimoto, are the *koseki* family registration system and the *jumin-hyo* resident card system, together with the discourses of *seki* and *ie*, which create meaning on the value attached to family life. This family registration system keeps full personal details of every individual in the local government office, and the resident card system obliges every household to register its membership and current address. The system controls the behaviour of family members through practices of surveillance, for government officials have access to the records, and on occasions like marriage or recruitment into an organisation employers or prospective spouses can request individuals or family members to submit copies of the *koseki*. The surveillance of the family by the state, employers and potential marriage partners is reinforced by the notion of *seki*, the idea that there is no proper place in society for a person who is not registered in an institution or organisation (Sugimoto 1997: 136–7, 141–2).

Women's Positioning in the Field of the Family

The family registration and resident card system creates gender divisions in the family through a number of legal and symbolic practices. The *koseki* requires each household to nominate a household head, and specifies who this should be under a variety of circumstances. In the majority of cases, the rules specify males. A wife may become household head only when she earns a living and the husband has no income. Of the marriages that took place in 1990, the husband was registered as the household head in 98 per cent of cases. The system also requires that a married couple must take the same surname at marriage, which must be one of their unmarried surnames. In the vast majority of cases it is the wife who changes her name to that of the husband. Women's groups demanding a change to the surname system succeeded in 1996 in getting a recommendation for a revision of the civil code (Sugimoto 1997: 138–41, 166–7).

The family registration system identifies both divorced members and children born out of marriage, thus deterring single motherhood and marital separations, since shame has been attached to both in the twentieth century. The divorce rate is remarkably low in Japan compared with other industrialised countries and compared with Japan itself a century ago. In 1883, when people still married and divorced according to local customs, the divorce rate was twice its level in the 1980s, when it reached a postwar peak of 1.51 per thousand persons. As Sugimoto points out, divorce is kept low through the requirement of the *koseki* system for two separate family registers to be created upon divorce, into one of which the children must be entered. Since children usually go to live with their mother, their change of register will be recorded and the stigma attached to divorce will be passed on to the children whenever they have to show the *koseki*. This deters many women from leaving an unhappy marriage (Sugimoto 1997: 138–40).

A national survey in 1992 showed that 78 per cent of women had experienced violence from their husbands, while a survey in 1989 in Kanagawa prefecture showed that 49 per cent of married men admitted to hitting their wives (Sugimoto 1997: 156), but this is not reflected in the divorce rate. Although divorce has been increasing since the 1980s, the rate is still low because of women's economic dependence, the shame attached to divorce, the effect on the children, and the difficulty for women of remarrying. Sugimoto argues, however, that the stigma of divorce is weaker in the cities because of feminism, especially amongst educated middle-class women, and lower-class women (Sugimoto 1997: 142, 159–60).

Women's economic dependence also sustains heterosexual marriage and the family system. The Ministry of Health and Welfare study of married women aged 50 showed that more than a quarter left employment at marriage or childbirth, and never returned. Nearly a half left and then returned to paid work after raising their children, comprising almost three-quarters of married women who had no source of income for a significant period of their lives apart from the husband's earnings (Sugimoto 1997: 143). Women who do have paid work are often partly dependent on the husband's income, since their earnings are significantly lower: on average 50 per cent of men's (NIEVR 1988: 33). So women's position in the employment field is a potent factor in keeping women in unhappy marriages.

In these ways, the family registration and resident card system keeps track of the whole population, provides a mechanism for penalising single motherhood, 'illegitimacy' and divorce, and legitimates male leadership of the household. These ideas and practices construct the family as a gendered institution in which men hold positions of sexual and economic privilege.

Biological and Class Reproduction

Marriage and children

We will first examine our respondents' rates of marriage and divorce, and compare them with those of the general population. This will enable us to assess how far a position of privilege in employment affected women's approach to decisions about marriage.

Table 19.1 shows that a third of our respondents (34 per cent) were unmarried in 1977 compared with 21 per cent in the 25–29 age group and 8 per cent in the 30–34 age group, going down to 4 per cent in

Table 19.1   Women's marital status (percentage)

Age group	Single	Married	Divorced
General population (1975)*			
25–29	21	78	1
30–34	8	90	2
35–39	5	91	3
40–44	5	89	3
45–49	5	85	4
50–54	4	–	4
Respondents (professional women) (1977)†			
all ages	34	60	4

Note: Rows do not add to 100 per cent as figures for widows are not given.

Sources: * ESCAP 1984: 64, 65, 72; † our data.

the 50–54 age group. Only 60 per cent were married, compared with 78 per cent to 91 per cent of the general population. These figures suggest both that respondents married later than women in general, and that significant numbers did not marry at all.

Of our respondents 4 per cent were divorced, compared with 1 per cent in the 25–29 age group, 2 per cent in the 30–34 age group, rising to 4 per cent only in the 45–54 age groups. In 1989 the divorce rate among the respondents went up to 6 per cent. These figures show that our respondents were more willing to separate and divorce compared with the general population. With a combined single and divorced rate of 38 per cent, it is clear that a very large section of our respondents had taken decisions against marriage. This suggests that they had both more alternatives and more control over marriage decisions than the general female population.

Table 19.2 shows that the birth rate among married respondents was lower than that of the 25–29 group in the general population, although the respondents' ages ranged from 23 to 67. Of married respondents, 17 per cent were childless. Given that a further third of the women were single, it is clear that our professional women were less likely to reproduce the family and the class biologically.

Table 19.2 Number of children born by wife's age

Age	Number of children
General population (1977)[*]	
25–29	1.35
30–34	1.99
35–39	2.15
40–44	2.19
45–49	2.33
Respondents (1977)[†]	
all ages	1.29

Sources: * ESCAP 1984: 28, Table 21; † our data.

Family structure

We now compare the respondents' family structures with those of the general population. It is clear that fewer respondents lived in extended families compared with the general population, and this pattern intensified between 1977 and 1989. Fewer lived in nuclear families, too, and this was also a growing trend; while many more of our professional women lived alone compared with the general population. These patterns were clearly connected with the decision of large numbers of professional women not to marry, and suggest a greater degree of both sexual and economic autonomy from the family. We would argue that the distinctive marriage rates and distribution of family structures among respondents reflected a position of greater power within the family, which was contingent upon a privileged position in the employment field.

Next we look at the men whom the respondents married. Given that professional women appeared to have more power in the family and more control over whether to marry, or stay married, what kind of husbands were chosen by those who did marry? In particular, what class of husbands did professional women marry?

Table 19.3   Distribution of family structures

Family structure	% of general population* (1985)	% of respondents (professional women)† (1977)	(1989)
Extended	31	23	19
Nuclear	64	62	59
Living alone	5	15	19
Not specified	–	–	3
Total	100	100 (n = 120)	100 (n = 64)

Source: * Sugimoto 1997: 163; † our data.

Class reproduction

Sugimoto presents evidence that people chose spouses from the same class, whether they were arranged or 'love' marriages, showing that marriage was an important site of class reproduction. This pattern occurred most markedly in the professional and managerial class, suggesting that class reproduction was particularly important amongst the higher classes. Perhaps surprisingly, class origin was more diverse for arranged than for 'love' marriages, showing that individual choice in love marriage has consolidated rather than loosened class reproduction (Sugimoto 1997: 158–9). Table 19.4 looks at the class position of our respondents' husbands, based on employment status.

Our respondents' spouses were even more solidly grouped into the higher class categories than the women's fathers. Of those with partners, 75 per cent of husbands were professionals and 17 per cent were employers. There were no petty-bourgeois, non-manual or manual workers, suggesting a significant degree of upward class mobility as the women moved from the natal to the marital family. The figures suggest that women in privileged employment positions overwhelmingly married within the class, thus reproducing it: marriage decisions were an important site for class reproduction, even when – or particularly when – women had more control over the selection of marriage partner. However, the fact that women tend to lose status by 'marrying down',

Table 19.4   Husbands' class

Employment category	% of respondents' husbands
Employer	17
Petty bourgeoisie	–
Professional/managerial	75
Non-manual	–
Skilled	–
Unskilled	–
Not specified	8
Total (n = 77)	100

whereas men generally do not, suggests that professional women may have had more limited choice of partners if they wished to retain their status gains from education and employment.

Finally, we look at the individual and household earnings of our professional women, to assess how far their access to privileged positions in employment was reflected in the economic capital they brought into the family.

Economic capital

Table 19.5 shows that respondents' average income was ¥342,000, ranging from ¥110,000 for a junior doctor to ¥700,000 for one of the senior managers. The lowest average wage was for civil servants at ¥298,000 and the highest for managers at ¥424,000. This compares with an average wage of ¥234,000 for men and ¥127,000 for women in 1977. The respondents earned almost twice as much as graduate women in general, although these figures covered all qualified workers including the 'lower' professions in which women predominate. Average total family income was ¥708,000 compared with an average family income of ¥330,000 in 1980 for the working population in general.

Professional women earned high salaries, and dual-career families produced extremely high levels of economic capital. Families where both men and women had a professional, managerial or employer's

Table 19.5   Average earnings (Yen per month)

Workforce	Individual	Household
Male workforce[*]	234,000	
Female workforce[*]	127,000	
Graduate men[*]	289,000	
Graduate women[*]	181,000	
Respondents[‡]	342,000	
Working population[†]		330,000
Respondents[‡]		708,000

Note: Figures for the late 1970s, £1 = approx. ¥450.

Sources: * Ministry of Labour 1977: 2–7; † Statistics Bureau 1989: 113; ‡ our data.

income had significantly higher living standards than families where the husband was the main breadwinner and the wife worked part-time or not at all. The accumulation of economic capital by our respondents enabled them to reconfigure their positions of power in the family, and to attain a measure of both sexual and economic independence. The consolidation of economic capital among professional women who married within the class also realigned their power within the family, but at the same time helped to reproduce divisions between the classes.

Power Distribution in the Family and the Connections between the Fields

In conclusion, we have argued in Part IV that neither employment position nor educational credentials are independent of social origin, and that both family background and education affect access to positions of power in employment. These patterns are greatly intensified for women. Women who succeed in gaining access to the employment field are required to bring with them higher levels of economic, social and cultural capital than comparable men if they are to convert these capitals into symbolic power in the form of recognition and respect as legitimate players in the field. This suggests that the exchange values on these capitals are lower for women than they are for men. Although Bourdieu acknowledges that there is no perfect class reproduction in the 'school' or 'state' nobility, he does not recognise that the mechanism through which advantaged families transmit their capitals is gendered, that women need more capitals to reproduce the class in their own right rather than through marriage, and that it may be more difficult for such women to pass on their capitals to the next generation, because it is more difficult for them to *produce* the next generation than it is for men.

The connections in the distribution of power between the different fields are very clear, and it is true that the capitals which are required in order to enter a field cannot be properly understood without 'grasping them in their mutual relations' (Wacquant 1993: 21). The fields of education, employment and the family are intimately tied together, such that powerful positions in the employment field are based on cultural capital acquired in the family and credentialised through the higher education field, whilst access to educational credentials is dependent on the social origin of the family.

We argue, however, that the mutual relations of class and gender production must also be grasped, for a position of power in education or employment occupied by a woman has completely different capitals and meanings attached from one occupied by a man. This can be seen in the effect on her position in the family of a woman attaining a position of power in employment. Our study suggests that fewer women in privileged employment positions agreed to marry, more of them married later, those who did marry had fewer children, more left unhappy marriages, and more lived alone compared with the general population, showing that our professional women were able to reconfigure their power in the family. But, equally, our study shows that women in privileged employment positions who agreed to marry tended to marry more closely within the class, thus reproducing the class. Being in a professional job enabled women to compete for power in the family and in the class structure − a consequence which would make no sense for a professional man, since his position of power in the family is already assured. It must therefore be recognised that women's access to positions of power in employment both changes gender relations and consolidates class divisions.

We began Part IV by asking how far changes in the gendered distribution of power in the fields of employment, education and the family represent an opening-up of access to power to a wider social base. We may answer that access to power is widened in gender terms, but narrowed in class terms. Women's access to power, in effect, constitutes a means for statistically reproducing a distribution of power based on class divisions. It is unclear, however, how far women who have gained entry to the field of power in education and employment will be able to compete with men in the field of the family in passing on their gains to the next generation.

Part V

Becoming a Professional Woman:
The Struggle for Change

In Part V, using the subjects of our study, we examine women's own understandings of their position within the fields of employment, education and the family, showing how the capitals within these fields shaped their practices and subjectivities.

We begin by setting out some key concepts which underpin our approach. We then identify competing discourses of gendered class identity, showing how the discourses of the 'professional housewife' and the 'corporate warrior' positioned middle-class women in the household sphere and middle-class men in the public sphere.

Next we show how these discourses were both enacted and reinforced through regulatory social practices in the fields of education, employment and the family, producing gender difference, class distinction, and the respectability of the middle-class family.

While we recognise the two discourses as hegemonic, we also acknowledge the circulation of alternative discourses which competed with and ran counter to the dominant constructions of middle-class femininity and masculinity, and that these alternative discourses were linked with changing social practices.

We then explore the contradictions of middle-class femininity that arose for women in professional occupations, when their everyday life was in conflict with the dominant definitions of gendered class identity, suggesting that these contradictions were a potent source for social change.

Chapter 20

Gendered Class Identities

We argued in Part IV that the struggle for power in the public arena in the postwar period was dominated largely by men; that women struggled, less successfully, for legitimacy to enter the contest; and that the opening up of the field of power to women was significantly influenced by the class positioning of those who gained access to it. In Part VI we will go on to examine the strategies women used to achieve power in the field, and how they legitimated their right to compete, arguing that the symbolic capital attached to class positioning played an important part in the process of legitimation.

Here, in Part V, we identify the hegemonic discourses and practices in the fields of power which constructed gendered class identities and produced middle-class women as social objects for the embodiment and display of family position and class respectability. We then examine the contradictions of middle-class femininity which create the conditions for change. We will draw on Bourdieu (1977, 1990b) for a general understanding of how social reality is produced through structure and representation, but will use Wendy Hollway's (1984) approach to subjectivity to understand change, and Dorinne Kondo's (1990) ideas on social relations and social processes in the context of Japan.

As indicated in Part IV, Bourdieu attempts to move beyond the division between subject and object, and to conceptualise social reality as neither structure nor representation, but as the interdependent production of objective conditions and subjective formulation (Bourdieu 1990b: 123). Social practice is produced by the dispositions of the habitus, which express subjectivity, in interaction with the contextual conditions characteristic of the specific social field. These dispositions are acquired experientially, produced through childhood socialisation, shaped by the social circumstances of their production, and therefore differ by class, gender and ethnic positioning (Bourdieu 1977: 72–95; Thompson 1980: 12; Moi 1991: 1030). It is through the dispositions that people perceive, categorise, understand, evaluate and act upon the social fields to which they belong. The dispositions provide social actors with the cognitive, affective and practical resources for living everyday life, and structure their strategies for action in specific social settings (Bourdieu 1990b: 61). This conceptualisation allows Bourdieu to examine both the resources or capitals attached to positions in the social space, and the individual strategies of agents, without giving epistemological priority to one or the other (Pullen 1999: ch. 3).

Contradiction and change

To help us understand how women change from a position as objects to envisaging and positioning themselves as subjects, we draw on Wendy Hollway's approach to subjectivity as a set of positions in discourses which are both constituted by and constitutive of contradictory social practices. Hollway sees subjectivity as non-rational, non-unitary and contradictory, with systematic differences in subjectivity being reproduced through power relations. Discourses provide the powers through which people position themselves in relation to others, but the discourses themselves – as well as the multiple positionings offered to people within them, and the social practices associated with them – are often in contradiction; it is these contradictions which provide sources of resistance and change (Hollway 1984: 227–8).

Fusing class and gender

Gendered subjectivity is produced by, and produces, gender difference, which is itself produced by everyday practices and the meanings attached to them – that is, discourse. These practices and discourses contribute to both the continuity of and the changes in gender difference. Hollway focuses on heterosexual relations as the primary site for the production of gendered subjectivity (Hollway 1984: 230), but traditional discourses on work relations are also gendered, and men and women have available to them different positions and powers in discourses on work and employment; to be a woman means not to be like a man, and masculinity is defined in opposition or in negativity to being a woman. Gender difference is thus also produced and reproduced in labour relations, including paid and unpaid work. Further-

more, labour relations are a primary site for the production and reproduction of class differences.

We therefore argue that work and employment activities are a major
site for the production of gendered class difference and gendered class
subjectivity. Work practices and discourses both maintain and modify
gendered class differences, and these discourses provide the powers
through which men and women position themselves in relation to
each other and in relation to other classes. As Hollway (1984: 227–8)
suggests, the regulatory power of discourses and practices is important
to their reproduction, but the contradictory nature of meanings, positions and practices is central to explaining how they are subject to
continuous change and modification.

The importance of the attempt to fuse class and gender in a Japanese
context is demonstrated in Dorinne Kondo's analysis of women workers
in a small, family-owned factory producing cakes and sweets in 'down-
town' (*Shitamachi*) Tokyo, where she clearly shows how the middle-class
'uptown' (*Yamanote*) population constructed themselves in opposition to
the lower-class factory workers:

> Yamanote and Shitamachi were vibrantly alive as facets of my Tokyo
> friends' and co-workers' identities … the bourgeois respectability of
> Yamanote by and large looks askance at the 'vulgarity' of what it considers
> 'déclassé' Shitamachi culture. For in the eyes of an elite, a semiotics of
> 'class' and 'distinction' defines both Shitamachi men and women as a
> lesser 'other', united by their common characteristics. Their occupations
> were necessary for the functioning of society, yet they were not per-
> ceived as equal. They were … less possessed of the polished social surface
> required of the respectable middle-class sensibility. (Kondo 1990: 71)

Similarly, the women factory workers identified themselves as distinct
from the middle-class women of the Yamanote area:

> Many of the part-time workers defined themselves as occupying quite a
> different social location from that of the middle-class housewife.…
> Hamada-san made a disparaging remark to me about one of my neigh-
> bours, a housewife who did not work for wages outside the home. 'You
> see, women like that don't know what the world is like; they're just in
> the house all the time. They're narrow.'
>
> In this context, wifely accomplishments such as tea ceremony or
> flower arranging had little place. They were a luxury.… 'We here in
> Shitmachi don't do things like that. We'd rather have a good time.' …
> Hamada-san, in her refreshing way, pointed out the class bias of these
> pastimes when she called the tea ceremony … snobbish. (Kondo 1990:
> 282–3).

Challenging identities

We will argue that class is of crucial importance in understanding the production of gender relations and the connection between gender and power in Japan, as it is in many other developed capitalist countries (Liddle and Michielsens 2000a, 2000b), although it may manifest itself in different ways in different cultures. In Part V we examine the fusion of gender and class – not for working-class women, as in Kondo's study, nor for the middle-class housewives against whom Kondo's factory workers compared and distinguished themselves, but for professionally employed women who challenged these dichotomised categories of class-based gender identities. Although they form a minority group, these women are important partly because they have broken into positions of responsibility and power normally reserved for men, and partly because they have challenged the gendered class identities established in postwar Japan which construct middle-class men as 'corporate warriors' and middle-class women as 'professional housewives' (Kanai 1996: 7). They have also demolished ideas about Japanese womanhood constructed in the West.

Our respondents constituted the first two generations of women to be allowed to compete with men for privileged positions within the public arena. Their ages ranged from 23 to 67 when we first interviewed them in 1977. In 1989 they looked back over lives, which collectively spanned much of the twentieth century. They spoke of the struggle to take up positions which became available to women only after 1945. The span of their lives coincided with a key period of world history when women's movements, including those in Japan, began to organise to improve women's conditions, struggle for social mobility and escape from historical emplacements. The span of their careers coincided with important changes in the international political economy and in Japan's history, when the development of capitalism and the expansion of the economy opened up opportunities for new social groupings to challenge the monopoly on power of dominant groups in society.

When we retraced the women in 1989, they were aged from 35 to 79, and many of them had reached, or nearly reached, the summit of their career trajectories, whilst most of those who intended to have children had done so. Thus the study covers the life-cycles of a cohort of women, looking mainly at the 1950s to the 1970s, and then re-visiting them at the end of the 1980s. During this time, they had negotiated the natal family and other conditions of their social situation to strike out into education and employment, while also negotiating, or declining, families of procreation. In Parts V and VI, we attempt to show how these women's life-cycles represent a moving structure framed by a significant moment of history. We hope both to allow the women to tell their own stories, and to analyse their experiences within the social and historical framework which we have developed. For this reason, we rarely report the women's narratives in the third person, but quote their words directly.

Chapter 21

Discourses of
Gendered Class Identity

Competing discourses of gendered class identity can be seen to be circulating in the educational system, in the labour market, and among the families of our respondents. Many authors (Kanai 1994; Hendry 1993) refer to the gendered roles of the 'professional housewife' and the 'corporate warrior'. We will look at these roles as discourses which, when they are combined with regulatory practices in education, employment and the family, produce gendered class identities through the enactment of middle-class femininity and masculinity.

The prewar idea of the 'good wife, wise mother' is visible, but in a modernised form, in the professional housewife discourse, but there are clear distinctions between them. The good wife, wise mother discourse draws attention to the gendered social relations in the family: the woman's identity as partner to her husband and mother to her child. The professional housewife discourse highlights the woman's work as a long-term career within the institution of the household, construing housework as a parallel occupation to that of the professional man. The 'professionalisation' of household work emphasises the significance of and need for an extended education as both the production of technical knowledge and a credentialised legitimation for the performance of the duties and responsibilities of housewifery.

The concept of professionalism in housework represents a specifically middle-class understanding of the non-earning wife, who 'works for' and is economically supported and rewarded by the husband. This is in contrast to the 'working mothers' of the working-class areas of Tokyo studied by Kondo (1990), who worked in both the home and the factory. This discourse of the professional housewife should not be seen as producing a necessarily subordinate position of power even in relation to the husband, since, as Hendry argues, middle-class professional housewives are often 'rather privileged', 'reluctant to change places with their husbands', and 'enjoy the freedom to plan, organise and carry out their lives in their own time' (Hendry 1993: 239).

Competing Discourses of Femininity

Education

Kuba Taeko, a company manager, finished her schooling in 1958 and obtained her degree at Tokyo University in 1962:

> At high school sixty per cent of the teachers thought women's happiness is in housework. So even if you were a very good student, the ultimate goal was marriage.

Kuba-san *was* a good student: she was first out of five hundred pupils at secondary school, and second in her class at Tokyo University. But as a young middle-class woman, she encountered contradictory messages. Her schoolteachers were divided, but at university, although there were few women students, it was 'taken for granted we would have a career'.

Family members, too, were divided: some saw the goal of education as marriage, while others saw alternatives. Otahara Atsuko, a science lecturer, took her graduate, master's and doctoral degrees at Tokyo University in the 1950s and early 1960s:

> One of my aunts told me: 'If you study like that, you won't be able to get married.' But my mother encouraged me to do as I liked, and said she was responsible for what would become of me. My high-school days were just after the war, and the atmosphere was rather liberal.

Both the accommodation and the containment of female education within the framework of heterosexual gender relations can be seen here, as women's access to higher education became incorporated into the professional housewife discourse for the purposes of marriage. This incorporation entailed the recognition of female education as an important part of a young middle-class woman's training for marriage, but it also imposed qualitative and quantitative limits, for a woman's education should be appropriate for her activities as a housewife and mother. Qualitatively, this meant home economics, liberal arts or teacher training. Quantitatively, it meant a lower level of education than her husband's, to reflect their differential symbolic values.

We argue, with Bourdieu, that higher education was important for middle-class women not merely because it provided a technical training for marriage, since many women did not take the technical house-wifery subject of home economics, but because female higher education legitimated women's class position, credentialised their knowledge of middle-class cultural values, and acted as a signifier of their ability to reproduce the class distinction of their husband's family. Thus female higher education represented not merely a qualification for a marriage of distinction, but a marker of a wife's ability to sustain, reproduce and increase the class positioning of the next generation. The professional housewife discourse, together with the practice of female higher education, produced the meaning of women's education as the accumulation of cultural capital for middle-class marriage and the reproduction of the family's social positioning.

Given the limits on female education within the professional house-wife discourse, women used various strategies either to avoid marriage or to compete for the right to enter both labour and marriage markets. Shimizu Fumiko, a civil servant, implicitly invoked the professional housewife discourse when her father opposed her plans. He had no objections to her taking paid work before marriage, but saw 'too much' education as a problem:

> When I was going to university my father said I should find a job at a first-rate bank rather than go to college, because he thought it would be a barrier to my getting married. I got his permission to go to university by emphasising my desire for education, not for getting a job.

Here we can see that female education did possess value for men, provided it was not linked to professional employment. The key to breaking down the father's opposition was the unstated association linking education with a domestic career.

The meaning of the professional housewife discourse was hegemonic, but it was not completely determining, since it was countered in many quarters by what may be termed the oppositional discourse of 'women's entitlement'. This discourse was related to old arguments about women's entitlements which arose during the first-wave women's movement, themselves linked back to ideas about civil rights in the popular rights movement. The notion of popular rights and women's entitlements had grown during Taisho 'democracy', and been kept alive by progressive individuals in schools and families in wartime. As Kondo points out, 'hegemonies are never simply put in place, but are always contested and therefore must always be reasserted' (Kondo 1990: 203).

The competing discourses in the educational system and the family, and the incorporation of female education within the professional housewife discourse, left open the possibility of women resisting the pressures to conform. Sato Taeko graduated as a doctor in the early 1960s:

> In junior high school most teachers advised us to do something all through our lives. It was three years after the war when democracy was imported from the USA, so teachers had democratic ideas. Most teachers were leftists. But the careers advice we got at high school was that higher education is bad for women because women are inferior and women's ability is inferior, and they'd marry late so people would worry about that. Teachers at high school advised us girls to leave now and not to go to university, because we were inferior to men and the chance of marriage would be lost. These were men teachers. We didn't resist at all, but we didn't take it seriously either. It went in one ear and out the other. Girls who wanted to go to university didn't leave; *none* of them left.

The circulation of the counter-hegemonic discourse on women's entitlement, though seen by many as a US import and claimed as such by the Americans, actually represented a change in practice and subjectivity which had already been established by Japanese women themselves before the US occupation.

Employment

The competing discourses of femininity also circulated in the employment field. Just as teachers and parents both reproduced and challenged the professional housewife discourse in education, so too employers, colleagues and subordinates took up alternative positions in the discourses of femininity in employment. Iwasaki Keiko was accepted as a management trainee after graduating from Tokyo University, but her right to a place on the management track was constantly questioned, drawing on the professional housewife discourse:

> When I was looking for a job in the 1950s, only three companies out of fifteen hundred allowed women to take the exam. There was much discussion whether women should be employed as managers. The personnel manager's wife was a doctor at that time, and he insisted women could be accepted. In my first job as a management trainee, I was given the job of writing the decisions and circulating them to the rest — the lowest job. My boss said this job was too important for a woman to be doing! He kept telling me that happiness is to be found in marriage.

Iwasaki-san's boss categorised women's work as unimportant, valorising men's work by contrast. This helps to explain why men refused jobs defined as women's work, either in employment or in the family, while women struggled for the right to do men's work: the symbolic capital attached to women's work was too low, and would impose dishonour on men. It was acceptable for middle-class women to do menial service jobs in the office in the period before marriage, since it protected men from performing work with symbolic capital deficits. Inokuma Ryoko, a civil servant:

> Men think some jobs can only be done by women, such as serving tea. A woman's job is to serve tea until she gets married.

Such jobs constituted enactments of femininity, but could only emasculate men.

Family

Competing discourses of femininity also operated in the family. Okazaki Teruko, a section head at a newspaper publishing company:

> My father wanted me to be a good wife, wise mother. He also thought of making me a teacher, but gave it up, thinking a career woman would have difficulties getting married. Although he was a liberal, my father worried that a working woman tended to miss the chance of marriage.

Even where family members accepted counter-discourses of women's entitlement, the need for girls to marry was paramount. Some parents thought that femininity could be stretched to include working in a job closely connected to the wife-and-mother role. Ninomiya Kimi, a government servant:

> My father wanted me to be a teacher; he was in education, he thought it was good for women. He didn't necessarily want me to go to work, he wanted me most to be a good wife. But he had many women working around him, so he thought it would be okay, that I could still be feminine if I was a teacher.

The key components of the professional housewife discourse were that to be feminine, first, a woman must marry, and second, marriage, home and children must constitute the profession. The women's entitlement discourse influenced the professional housewife discourse to accommodate not only female higher education but also women's short-term employment, and even extended to a longer-term career consistent with and secondary to marriage and child-raising, such as teaching.

We can see here the changing construction of middle-class femininity as the meaning of the discourse moved from 'no paid work', to 'paid work as a short-term interlude', to 'longer-term secondary paid work'. But the failure to marry under any of these conditions was understood as a failure to perform femininity. Thus not only a commitment to being a career woman but also singlehood and childlessness constituted a challenge to the dominant discourse. Saito Nobuko was an unmarried university teacher who had experienced 'social oppression towards unmarried women':

> My father expected me to be a housewife; my mother thought I was more suited to professional life. Besides, she thought I wasn't feminine enough. My father knew he couldn't do anything with me. I was strong-willed. When I was very small I thought I wouldn't be an ordinary woman. I have no qualifications to find a husband. I thought I wasn't pretty enough, and I was more interested in academic work than women's accomplishments. I hated flower arrangement. The general opinion that women should be at home hinders us, and social oppression towards unmarried women as if I'm not human, for example, 'Can you cook at all?' or 'Can you iron your own clothes?' In fact some career women are better cooks than housewives.

Saito-san that felt her lack of femininity left her unqualified for marriage. Other people saw her as 'masculine' and unable to perform simple domestic chores. Being feminine meant performing or enacting wifehood through domestic work tasks. This approach to femininity understood not only the performance of domestic tasks but also the married state and heterosexual relations in general as a crucial means through which femininity was enacted.

Femininity also meant the bearing and raising of children, which is where women's natural talents were seen to lie. Shimizu Ayuchi, a civil servant:

> Childcare is an extension of the mother function, so it requires women. In this sense, if it's not the mother, it should preferably be other women, I believe.

Women who had no children may have felt that they lacked the 'natural talents of femininity', but some of them felt nevertheless the absence of children as a loss. Okazaki Yumiko was unmarried, but living with her partner, who didn't want children:

> I feel I've stepped outside ordinary women's happiness to bear and raise a child. The reason is that one of my relatives, who influenced me on

philosophies of life, praised me once for not being sweet and feminine, and for having the great characteristic of being unfeminine and highly motivated. Contrary to the compliment, this leaves me some room to desire being sweet and feminine like ordinary women.

Femininity meant that women's happiness lay not only in marriage but also in motherhood. But the compliment paid for being 'unfeminine' made clear that although the profession of wife and mother was highly valued, it was not accorded as much symbolic value and respect as the masculine characteristic of 'motivation'.

Femininity meant recognising the subordination of women to men in the family. Takahashi Yoshiko was a doctor at a university hospital:

> There's an atmosphere in this country which says women should be behind men and put up with it, not only in their own nuclear family but also for keeping good human relations with other families.

Kakuta Masako taught German:

> The idea in Japan that women should stay at home and help the man achieve his career makes it harder for women.

The man's career had priority, and he could improve his social position by drawing on her cultural capital.

The 'professional housewife'

Thus the crucial aspects of middle-class femininity in the professional housewife discourse were to marry and not to have a competing occupational commitment, but to use the cultural capital of a female higher education to enhance the social position of the husband. For women, there was an intimate relationship between the heterosexual relation invoked through marriage and the employment relation enacted in paid work. Here we can see how sexual relations and labour relations are inseparable in the construction of gendered class identity, in the way that Bourdieu's 'yellowness of a lemon' is inseparable from its 'acidity'. For it is precisely through the organisation of gendered class relations that we can understand the professional housewife discourse as the production of respectable middle-class femininity. Miura Fumiko, a manager in a media company:

> I never had any pressure myself, but my mother sometimes suffered from her relatives about why I don't get married. Relatives thought I had to stay single to earn for the family – a sacrifice. In Japan, girls from respectable families must not work.

Tsuzuki Kimiko practised medicine at a cancer hospital:

> The disadvantage of being a professional woman lies in the old concept of a working woman. Women should stay in the background. If a woman works, she's not a lady.

Commitment to marriage and the performance of unpaid work devoted to the family marked out a woman as feminine, contrasting her to middle-class men who devoted themselves to salaried work for the organisation. Not undertaking a paid profession marked her out as 'respectably' middle-class, in contrast to lower-class women who performed paid work throughout their lives out of necessity. Thus the construction of middle-class femininity through the hegemonic discourse of the professional housewife was crucial to the production of gender difference and class distinction.

Competing Discourses of Masculinity

The 'corporate warrior'

If middle-class femininity was defined, according to the professional housewife discourse, as enacting domestic work, performing wifehood and a natural talent for childcare, middle-class masculinity according to the corporate warrior discourse was defined in opposition to these characteristics. Takahashi Yoshiko again:

> I don't find housework so troublesome, but it seems a man has limitations. For childcare, before school age the mother or a woman in her place is necessary. Some aspects can't be divided equally between mother and father. I couldn't leave my young child to my husband or father.

Masculinity meant a lack of natural ability in childcare. Masculinity also meant being incapable of domestic work. Matsumoto Toshie was a hospital anaesthetist:

> Most men over thirty-five can't cook and don't know how to clean the room or wash their clothes. Most people think housework and childcare are women's jobs. It's hard for her to work; she has all the home responsibility too. Women stay at home because it's easier for them. They can be their own master at home, and be more accepted socially.

Dr Matsumoto positioned men as the objects of women's domestic work, and conceived femininity as the performance of household work. This conceptualisation of domestic work as the enactment of a gendered identity helps us to understand the complaint of Saito Nobuko, the single woman who felt that she was treated *as* a man because she failed to perform wifehood for a man, and who herself felt unfeminine because she lacked interest in domestic tasks. Wifehood was not just a set of tasks but a form of femininity, while Saito-san's failure to perform wifehood was constituted as a masculine identity.

Women who positioned themselves within the hegemonic discourse on gendered identity felt tremendous resistance to any encroachment of men into household spaces construed as feminine. Sato Ikuko was a doctor:

> I don't think housework is a woman's job, but women are fit to do certain things and men other things. If a man can do something it should be done by him, but I don't think men and women are equal in everything. I don't like men hopping into the kitchen.

Dr Sato construed masculinity as exclusion from domestic activities, with the notion of men 'playing' at housework − a parallel to the conceptualisation of middle-class women's paid work as an 'interlude' between the two serious aspects of a woman's life. Domestic work created femininity, but undertaken by men it both destroyed masculinity *and* threatened the femininity of the wife. Men's failure to perform domestic work was inseparable from their commitment to the performance of paid work. We will look at this role as the 'corporate warrior' discourse.

The corporate warrior discourse originated in the masculinity of the military ruling class in the pre-Meiji period, which was extended to the conscripted male population of the imperial army after the Restoration, and then transposed from the military setting to the political-economic struggles taking place within global capitalism at national and international levels in the postwar period. The institutional focus of the discourse was on the employment organisations producing commodities for profit in the corporate sector of the economy, as well as the public-sector organisations servicing and regulating the corporate sector such as government, education and health.

The renovation of the concept of the 'warrior' evoked the notions of military discipline, endurance under hardship, a strong spirit, loyalty and commitment to the organisation, and sacrifice for the cause which is greater than the individual. Devotion to the company encompassed the goals of the nation in the struggle for political-economic power and global honour. Loyalty to the organisation and the nation brought with it the power of capital and the state, and imbued the corporate warrior with the symbolic capital necessary to legitimate a position of honour and respect in the community. In return for his devotion, he was metaphorically armed with the authority of the company or state institution by whom he was employed, producing the corporate warrior's power as a man as well as the social positioning of his family. Bando Yoriko was a cardiologist:

> Men work from morning till midnight. I really feel in Japan men don't feel any responsibility for family life. My husband is a man of ability in medicine, he looks after patients, does his research, three or four days a week he doesn't even come home. All the family responsibility is on me. If they felt some responsibility and women were equally respected, they could change and divide the family chores and the responsibility. They think if they do tiny things in the house, they're helping. If my husband does this, he thinks he won't become an important man in his job. Social thinking, especially that of the husband, makes it difficult for women. Freedom and equality are truly not respected.

The main characteristics of the corporate warrior discourse were not doing domestic work, displaying physical strength and mental energy by working at the office 'from morning till night', and exercising the authority of the corporate executive or professional man. Middle-class masculinity meant carrying none of the day-to-day responsibility for the family. The corporate warrior stayed away at the 'front', fighting the battle in the competition with other organisations and nations, and a man who resisted would be left behind in the contest.

The modernised discourse of the corporate warrior should not be seen as producing a uniformly privileged position of power. The middle-class professional or managerial man held a position of authority within the organisation, and received domestic services in the family. But the demands in time, stamina and mental resources made on him in enacting his devotion and company loyalty meant that he was often absent from the family, experienced little or no leisure, and had limited opportunities to enjoy family life. For the reproduction of his family line and class position in the next generation, he relied almost entirely on his spouse as the professional housewife. Heroic self-sacrifice at work gave a man power, but his absence from the family created women's power. This self-denying devotion to the organisation was a largely middle-class form of masculinity, although there were exceptions. The 'heroic' approach to employment was on occasions adopted by working-class male artisans, and was similarly rewarded with symbolic power as evidence of the 'strong spirit' valued by the culture of the corporate warrior (Kondo 1990: 216).

Men's resistance

The symbolic capital of the corporate warrior did not mean that no men resisted. Some men were unwilling to submit to long hours and constant transfers at short notice. Nojiro Chiyoko's husband refused to transfer, and started his own company, which he now subsidises with a salary from another job. So he still spends little time at home:

> My husband worked for an import–export company and was once or-dered to transfer to Germany, but I wasn't willing to give up my work, so he refused the transfer. As a result, he left that company. He is now an employee of another company and earns a salary, but doesn't bring it home. He started a small company of his own and he's having a hard time paying his workers' wages, so he doesn't put any money into our living expenses.

Nojiro-san's job as a director in a media company made her husband's resistance financially possible. Nakane Misa was a manager in a food company:

> My husband was an ordinary office worker. After our marriage he moved to a job with no transfer, and has been in head office ever since. Still we worried at transfer time. He was asked to transfer occasionally, but he refused. It disadvantaged him, but he's not ambitious for promotion.

These women's husbands invested not in the corporate warrior dis-course, but in an alternative which we may term the corporate recusant discourse. This was not because they were unwilling to work hard but because, out of respect for their wives' careers and the desire to keep the family together, each has sacrificed his own opportunity to rise and become 'an important man in his job'. It is no accident that their wives were from small-business backgrounds, allowing both families to con-template a lack of corporate success without fear. In Bourdieu's terms, the *desire* to take power – the drive and motivation to give, and to give up, whatever was necessary to maintain a position of social distinction – had not been created in them from childhood. This had facilitated a more egalitarian approach to married and working life. But the alter-native discourse of the corporate recusant was not a position of power for middle-class men, for it could not be converted into symbolic capital and a position of honour and respect, whereas the alternative discourse of women's entitlement *was* a position of power for middle-class women.

In this case, women's entitlement could be construed as counter-productive to the interests of corporate capital and the nation. It had the effect of producing 'slippage' for middle-class men, resulting in a failure to sustain social positioning. For this reason, men who had invested in the corporate warrior discourse did not want working women as wives. Sato Ikuko:

> My mother strongly wanted me to marry because of our family background and my father dying young. When I decided I was willing to marry, I realised for the first time that some men and their families dislike my working as a doctor. I actually don't have much to complain about, since I met a nice person and am happily married to him. But by becoming a doctor I worried my mother over my marriage prospects.

Hattori Hisako was the public relations director of a private company:

> When I was twenty-four I was making more money than men. Men expected a woman to stay at home unless she was especially talented. All the men I met were upset because I wanted to work and because I earned more than them.

The professional housewife was clearly a tremendous social asset for a middle-class man: an accumulator of cultural capital for the family, and a provider of moral and material support to the husband's life of self-sacrifice for the organisation. Ninomiya Kimi, a civil servant:

> Men work too hard here; work occupies all their time and interest and concern. So women must stay at home, otherwise they can't do it. Sometimes we have meetings at midnight. Sometimes we sleep overnight at the office at budget time, and have to compete on this. Before we look at women, men's conditions must be examined.

In the husband's absence at the global contest for political–economic power, the professional housewife has taken responsibility for running the household, raising the children and reproducing the class. Middle-class women have acted as social reproducers of the family's class position, and this role has been a central aspect of their identities. Having such a wife to perform this role has also been an important part of middle-class men's identities. The capitalist organisation of production has drawn upon this gender division of labour, to enable men to devote their lives to the organisation in the global struggle for power. Middle-class women have adopted a subject positioning in the professional housewife discourse because it has imbued them with feminine respectability. Women could also adopt a position in the alternative discourse of women's entitlement, and perform professional work saturated with the symbolic power of middle-class masculinity, thereby enhancing their respectability. But men could not perform domestic work, saturated with the symbolic capital deficits of femininity, nor could they refuse a subject position in the corporate warrior discourse without losing respect.

Chapter 22

Regulatory Social Practices

We now go on to identify some of the social practices in education, employment and the family which were linked into the discourses of middle-class masculinity and femininity, and which together produced hegemonic gendered class identities.

Social Practices in Education

The professional housewife discourse in the field of education has produced gender difference, vertical and horizontal sex segregation in the educational process, and the construction of women as housewives. These regulatory practices comprised gendered selection policies, gender differentials in teaching quality, and the gendered use of social capital in the search for employment.

Gendered selection

Nagayama Junko went to Tokyo University in the early 1960s, then became a university teacher:

> Local government schools in Tokyo don't accept students in the order of their academic achievement, but a fixed number of students to be accepted is set separately for boys and girls. Within each sex group, students are accepted in the order of their academic achievement. This results in differences in the level of academic achievement between the two groups.

This practice was similar to the setting of gender quotas in Britain when the 11-plus examination selected children for the more academic grammar-school education. Although statistically girls performed better than boys, the quota allocated equal numbers to the grammar schools. But whether or not one sex was systematically privileged in Nagayama's example, the point is that girls and boys were admitted to selective higher education not on merit, but against criteria which directed them into different social purposes.

Gendered admission into educational programmes was achieved not only by explicit selection policies but also by a subtle undermining of female abilities as well as a positive construction of women's suitabilities. For example, compulsory home economics for girls at school ensured that they spent time learning professional housewifery, but the practice of discouraging them from 'male' subjects at university and from higher levels of study also had a profound effect. Nagayama Junko again:

> At university the teachers were strongly against my going to graduate school and being a researcher because (a) there's no precedent; (b) it's difficult for a woman; (c) she would inevitably lead a dehumanising life if she wants to combine marriage and a career as a researcher. I was told a woman has neither a clear sense of the problem which she can study throughout her life, nor the ability to construct the research; therefore she shouldn't be a researcher.

Similar practices were apparent in the other professions, although in medicine the justification for women's inability was constructed in physical rather than intellectual terms. Respondents were told by their professors that women were not wanted in surgery because women are 'physically weak', and were advised to specialise in areas which did not require 'physical strength'.

Gendered teaching quality

The second practice consisted of gendered differentials in teaching quality, affecting the kind of education received. Tano-oka Hisako, a public-relations manager:

> I went to a local government high school which had been a girls' school before the war. So boys studying at the school weren't first-rate students. The school told us to go to a private preparatory school if we wanted to go to college, because they didn't do anything special for this.

Tano-oka-san's school had low educational standards and poor preparation for higher education precisely because it had been a girls' school, which only second-rate boys joined. The alternative of a 'private preparatory school' points to the economic resources necessary for girls to go into higher education.

The quality of teaching was also gendered in terms of how subjects constituted as male were taught at girls' schools; this particularly affected women who wanted to be doctors or scientists. Fujita Michiko got her medical degree in 1974:

> I wanted to take physics for one of the electives in an entrance exam, but I couldn't because the content of the physics class was too poor. Most of the teachers were men, and male teachers have no enthusiasm for teaching girls. Teachers don't try to teach it seriously because they think girls can't understand it anyway.

Nashimoto Tomoko got her PhD in 1967 and became a biology lecturer:

> Since it was a girls' high school, the standards of maths and science were low. I went to a college preparatory school to take extra classes in these subjects. I also searched for more advanced knowledge because I wasn't satisfied with what I was taught at school. There were no specific pressures, but the whole atmosphere was that girls should get married and stay at home. I also thought that way.

These practices produced in many women a feminine subjectivity constituted through the professional housewife discourse, even though some of them sought out 'more advanced knowledge'.

Gendered deployment of social capital

The third practice was the assistance provided to students by their tutors and professors in finding employment, which was often withheld from women. Kato Atsuko got her PhD from Tokyo University in 1970, and became an academic:

> At university I did chemistry, where all the students go on to graduate school. But they don't have a positive attitude to women scholars. They are still wondering how to treat women. They are very earnest in helping male students find jobs, but they seem indifferent to women. After I got my PhD I worked as an unpaid researcher and part-time lecturer for five years before getting this post. Although the professors approved of my wish to work, they never tried to find a job for me.

So too with Ohashi Kimiko, who studied sociology at Tokyo University and got her MBA from the USA in 1975:

> At junior high school there were high expectations of me; they thought me a bit different and encouraged me to compete against men. At university my professor gave a good academic training but was prejudiced against women. My professor said I should try something myself because he didn't know any way.

The social capital and professional networks upon which professors drew to help their male students to find privileged positions in the employment field were not always made available to women.

Thus we can see that regulatory social practices, in articulation with the discourses of the professional housewife and the corporate warrior, created both gender difference and sex segregation in education: horizontally, in terms of women's and men's preferences for feminine or masculine subjects; vertically, in terms of men's desire to compete intellectually and women's desire for educational moderation. And they constructed the meaning of male and female higher education as having different social purposes: long-term professional employment for men; preparation for the social reproduction of the middle-class household for women.

Failing to reproduce exclusion

As Cummings (1980) argues, however, education was not only a form of state regulation reproducing hegemonic discourses and exclusionary practices but also a source of innovation, change and resistance. Although few institutions had formal practices which included rather than excluded women, there were individuals who undermined the power game. They allowed spaces for women to move into new social arenas, by ignoring formal barriers and failing to reproduce exclusionary practices. These new social spaces in education were articulated through the discourse of women's entitlement. An example was Kagayama Mariko, whose father was a professor of physics and whose mother lectured in maths, having studied at Hiroshima University. Kagayama-san got her PhD from Tokyo University in 1966, and then became a chemistry lecturer:

> My parents were scientists; I was brought up in an atmosphere of scientific inquiry. It influenced me a lot. I was raised from primary-school days to have a career like a man. My university teachers gave advice on the entrance exam for postgraduate work, and graduate-school teachers helped me find this job. Many universities were establishing or strengthening their engineering departments, but there weren't many people with PhDs. So they said I was lucky.

Kagayama-san *was* lucky – not only because of the expansion of the universities, but also because she was able to draw on the cultural capital of her family and the social capital of her teachers to find employment.

Kitamura Masako's parents were teachers who adopted a critical approach to education. She got her degree in 1973, and practised medicine at a city hospital:

> Both my parents were teachers; I thought I would be a teacher. I was influenced by my mother – she had her own thoughts about education, and she firmly and often criticised the education of the time. I thought she was a great, thoughtful woman.

Ohara Masako got her PhD at Hitotsubashi University in 1967, and then found an academic job:

> I was told by a teacher in junior high school to pursue what I wanted to do. At university I consulted a professor who was close to me. As this professor didn't have sexist ideas, his encouragement positively affected my choice of career.

Otahara Atsuko studied chemistry at Tokyo University in the 1950s and 1960s, then became an academic. Despite specialising in a masculine subject, she was supported by her supervisor, who used his social capital to ask the help of 'a great figure related to this university to get me employment'.

Of the four professions, doctors and academics relied more on social capital for gaining access to professional jobs than managers and government officials. A total of 53 per cent of the doctors and 40 per cent of the university teachers had found employment through the personal recommendations of their supervisors. In the other two professions, the proportions gaining employment through this route were in single figures.

The counter-hegemonic discourse of women's entitlement, used by parents and teachers, provided a position in discourse which enabled women to claim the right to study masculine subjects, to reach the highest levels of education, and to be considered for long-term professional careers. This discourse, together with practices which failed to reproduce exclusion in education, enabled women to compete for places in the elite universities, to continue to the highest level of postgraduate work, and to move into professional positions in the employment field previously reserved for men. Counter-hegemonic discourses and inclusionary practices coexisted with dominant discourses and practices of exclusion, and helped to legitimate women's movement into positions constituted as masculine entitlements.

Social Practices in Employment

We now examine how the professional housewife discourse in the employment field was linked to social practices which produced gender difference, occupational sex segregation and the exclusion of women from positions of power in the labour market. These practices included the 'domestication' of women, the gendered placement of men and women in work constructed as masculine or feminine, and the exclusion of women from positions of authority.

Domestication

'Domestication' of women at work covered a range of practices which constructed women workers as domestic, with natural abilities in tasks related to household work, and servicing and caring for others. The first of these practices consisted of the marriage or pregnancy bar, which shaped the ideas of those hiring graduates. Nojiro Chiyoko, having studied law at Keio University, applied to a broadcasting company and a stock company in 1958, and was accepted by both. But the stock company imposed a condition that she would stop working on marriage, and different salaries for women and men. The broadcasting company imposed no marriage bar, and had an equal salary scale, so she accepted their job.

Even when the conditions of selection were the same, however, the conditions in the job were sometimes different. Shimizu Yumiko was a personnel manager at a department store. She applied for her first job in retail in 1955:

> The exam at the department store was the same for men and women, which I liked very much. In those days it was very rare for any organisation to give the same exam to men and women, and to hire them under the same conditions. But I was excluded from meetings or planning because I was a woman. I was ignored. Though qualifications were the same at entry, it wasn't really so. I wasn't included in meetings for years.

These practices were not confined to the 1950s. Ohashi Kimiko got her first job in management consultancy in 1975:

> They didn't let me see clients for the first year. But when they did I was good, and I was accepted. I got fewer opportunities than men for good projects. It's been like that for two years. I only get a third of men's choices, so I have to utilise them and I have to make a hit.

Another facet of the domestication process for women workers was sexualisation. Women were construed as the sexual objects of men's desire, undermining their position as serious professional workers. Kanamori Yasuko was professor of physics:

> When I was younger I was annoyed by the differences which were caused only because I was a woman. For example, a professor who was a co-worker on a paper wanted us to attend a conference together. This trip could be misunderstood by people. Another example: overnight experiments. Some men wanted to run overnight experiments with an underlying intention, which I hated very much. When I was still a research associate I was disgusted at the attitude of my colleagues and the students. They looked at me more as a female than as a person. If I was constantly critical of a student, he thought it was because I loved him especially, and became more arrogant rather than more obedient.

Nagayama Junko taught sociology, and began her job in 1975:

> The students were terrible in my first year. Now they had a young woman teacher they wanted to tease her. They talked sexually in class deliberately, or some male students came to class wearing lipstick. Such attitudes have disappeared lately.

The sexualisation of women workers was undertaken not only by colleagues and superiors, but by men over whom the women had a degree of power. The sexualisation of women in a work context, particularly by subordinates, may be understood as an expression of the threat to masculine identity posed by women entering a field in which the right to compete was reserved for men, and as resistance to women's claim to legitimacy.

The third way in which women were constructed as domesticated was in terms of 'seclusion' within a framework of gendered time and place. Women's work incorporated restrictions which confined them to a narrow area of the workplace and a limited set of time constraints: women could not range freely in time and place, as men could. The gendered limits on 'place' varied from an unmarried woman's parents wanting her to live at home, like Takahashi Noriko, restricting where she could work, to employers refusing to send women out on fieldwork trips or assignments abroad because they might 'cause problems', as happened to Watanabe Nobuko. The gendered limits on time varied from the legal restriction on night work – often ignored by professional women like Inokuma Ryoko, and abolished only in 1999 (Asian Women Workers' Centre 1999: 4–5) – to employers' demands for excessive overtime, with which women who had children, like Shimizo Fumiko, found it extremely difficult to comply.

Gendered placement

The practices outlined above which attempted to confine women in time and place and into sexual, marital or domesticated roles are related to practices of gendered occupational placement. Such practices positioned women in jobs which were constructed as feminine. Takahashi Noriko was a civil servant:

> Because I'm a woman I was sent to the section for the Improvement of Living Conditions for Women Agricultural Workers. Out of the six qualified women in the Ministry of Agriculture, four are in the women workers' section. What's more, more than two-thirds of the workers in this section are women.

In the civil service, women were found mainly in the Ministries of Education, Health and Welfare, and Justice, and the Ministry of Labour, especially the Women and Minors Bureau. In other ministries they were often heavily segregated into feminised jobs, like Takahashi-san above. In medicine women were physicians rather than surgeons, and were found in lower-status specialisms like dermatology and geriatrics rather than high-status ones like cardiology. Women academics were found largely in humanities, especially languages, and the 'soft' social sciences. In management women were mainly in media jobs in publishing and broadcasting catering to female audiences, and in 'feminine' industries such as cosmetics, fashion, baby food and retail store management. Miyazono Yoriko worked as a civil servant:

> Superiors have subtle feelings, for example: 'How about giving her this kind of work although she's a woman?' or 'She has done well in spite of being a woman.' I haven't experienced promotion yet, but I believe personnel will come up with a womanly or feminine position.

The practice of gendered occupational placement helped to construct professional and managerial positions in the employment field as masculine or feminine jobs. But these jobs were not equally valued. Feminine jobs were both limited in number and bound by the deficit in symbolic capital attaching to femininity.

Exclusion from authority

Several practices operated to exclude women from positions of authority, including direct reluctance to promote them, on the assumption that they were not as competent or reliable as men. But several indirect practices also reduced women's likelihood of gaining promotion. The first was the practice of not transferring them because of their 'seclusion by place'. It was taken for granted that men were transferred, and these experiences of transfer were used as a criterion of promotion. Horiguchi Kinko was one of the earliest woman career civil servants, and the only one holding a post at the highest level in 1977:

> The National Personnel Authority had a problem with me; they didn't know what to do with me. I was put in a women's bureau and not moved around like the men. But what could they do? After ten years, at a party, the Vice-Minister found out I was still at the same bureau. He ordered them to put me elsewhere. Today, with younger women who encounter the same problem, I encourage them to complain.

Nagasaki Chizuko was a manager with a national media company:

> In promotion there is obvious discrimination. To be sure, if I were a man I'd be in a supervisory administrative position, judging from how long I've worked here. Women are pushed out of the seniority system. Institutionally women and men are equal, but in practice women are about three years behind men in terms of job ranking. This is because men are transferred soon after hiring to local press and are promoted on returning to Tokyo. Women aren't transferred to local areas.

In 1989, Nagasaki-san reported that her promotion to the administrative post of chief director took seven or eight years longer than for men who were employed in the same year.

Second, the system of assumed overtime was also used as a criterion of promotion. Watanabe Tokiko, a director in a government ministry:

> The problem is, in the Japanese government officials work too long – till midnight often. It's a very important problem for women.

Shimizu Fumiko was a section head in the civil service:

> To get promoted you must work a hundred hours of overtime a month. I find it hard to finish work quickly, since I can't stay late to do overtime.

Four or five hours of overtime per day effectively excluded mothers from the right to compete with others for promotion.

Third, the practice of promotion by seniority was problematic for women, since it meant that they could not take time off to raise children without losing their right to return to a career-track position. Miyazono Yoriko again:

This practice of promotion by seniority is disadvantageous to women. It prevents them from finding a job again once they give up their work initially.

These social practices resulted in the exclusion of women from positions of authority, and helped to create positions of power in the employment field as the exclusive preserve of men. Tano-oka Hisako showed how some of these exclusionary practices combine. Tano-oka-san worked in a Japanese subsidiary of a multinational company:

> I wanted to work for a publishing company for women's magazines, but it was very difficult to get in. In those days women graduates weren't needed by most companies and were given very low evaluation. In principle this company should be considered understanding, since they made me a manager in spite of my being a woman, but I regret to say that I have handicaps in salary scale and promotion. Men can get promoted much sooner. Companies are organised in such a way that each time you change your work section you get promoted one step. My managerial position is limited to just one field. Women are never incorporated into the competitive route for promotion through changing sections. Also I'm not given a chance to go abroad. In the case of a man, his turn will come even if he can't speak a foreign language.

Tano-oka-san was unmarried, and had no family ties to prevent her from becoming a 'global employee' (Lam 1992: 177), and her example illustrated how women's professional work was regulated through gendered forms of work experience, irrespective of the actual conditions of the employee's life. Despite these social practices, she nevertheless made a successful career: although promotion came later than for men, by 1989 Tano-oka-san had become director of public relations.

Here we can see that regulatory social practices in employment in the form of the domestication of women, their placement in feminised work and their exclusion from positions of authority rendered marriage and parenthood incompatible with professional work for women, though not for men, constructed qualified women workers as sexual objects rather than serious professionals, and created feminised work as constrained by time and place, and reflecting the association with domesticity, while simultaneously constituting positions of power and authority as masculine. These practices, in association with the dominant discourses of gendered class identity, created gender differences and the sex segregation of occupations in the field of employment. They also perpetuated women's subordination to men through women's exclusion from positions of power, constituting men as the legitimate agents of institutional authority in employment organisations.

Social Practices in the Family

We will now look at how the professional housewife discourse was linked to regulatory social practices in the family. These practices constructed the centrality of marriage for the continuity of the household, created the wife's obligation to care for the family, and produced the symbolic and material importance of a full-time housewife and mother devoted to the prosperity of the family. The practices included: arranged marriages organised through parents and go-betweens (*miai*); the practice of marrying at the appropriate age (*tekireiki*), usually translated as the 'marriageable age'; and the duty of care for older and younger family members, held especially – though not exclusively – by the eldest son, which in all but financial terms meant the eldest son's wife.

The marital code of the 1947 Constitution states:

> Marriage shall be based only on the mutual consent of both sexes and it shall be maintained through mutual cooperation with the equal rights of husband and wife as a basis. With regard to choice of spouse, property rights, inheritance, choice of domicile, divorce and other matters pertaining to marriage and the family, laws shall be enacted from the standpoint of individual dignity and the essential equality of the sexes (Article 24). (Hendry 1981: 26)

This concept of marriage and family life was in conflict with the idea of the *ie*, the family or household, which, although legally abolished after the war, still influenced the organisation of family life in the period of our study. The main feature of the *ie* was the idea of the continuity of the household, with individuals expected to sacrifice their personal interests for the good of the household community. Marriage was understood as the entry of a new wife into the *ie* rather than simply a relationship between two individuals (Hendry 1981: 15–16). The low status of a young wife often meant that the strength and solidarity of the family rested on a considerably greater degree of self-sacrifice on her part than on that of the men or the older women. Thus, the individualistic approach to marriage in the postwar Constitution challenged the authority structure of the family, and was the subject of much contentious debate.

Marriage practices

Arranged marriage attempted to select a spouse who would fit well into the *ie*. There is much debate about how far this had spread into the lower classes before the war, but as Hendry points out, the possession of property made it much more important for middle-class families to select a suitable spouse. She also makes it clear that figures on the extent of arranged (*miai*) or love (*ren'ai*) marriages are unreliable because of the overlap between the two (Hendry 1981: 30, 146). We did not ask our married respondents how they found their partners, but it was clear that both methods of selecting a spouse were used. It was also clear that many middle-class families did not want a working wife, and that career women could have difficulty in finding a husband. Tano-oka Hisako again:

> In the past I had several opportunities to get married, but each time the question was whether I could combine marriage and a career. I always had to choose between them. Each time I chose career.

Ohashi Kimiko met her husband, a leader of the radical student movement, when they were both students at Tokyo University. Her mother had mixed feelings about their love marriage:

> My mother was unhappy at first because I didn't marry a member of the elite, but she changed her mind because of her bad experience with her own husband – he had mistresses, etc. – and my husband didn't seem to be like that.

Ohashi-san's choice of husband undermined the reproduction of the family's social position, but meant that she married a man in a mould unlike her father's.

The idea of an appropriate age for marriage, particularly an upper age limit, was still important in Japan. Amongst the Tokyo middle classes it was around 25 for women and slightly older for men. Shimizu Yumiko reached marriageable age in 1955:

> I was working as a clerk in a department store. Around that time I approached the marriageable age, and my brother said it was no use looking for promotion. He advised me to stop working and get married. His opposition to my working hurt me.

The practice of organising marriage by a particular age applied to both men and women. For men, marriage posed no bar to their employment, but for women it was often the time when pressure to leave work came from all sides.

Duty of care

Article 900 of the postwar Constitution made all the children equally responsible for the care of aged parents (Hendry 1981: 27). In practice, as we have said, this responsibility was still often shared by the eldest son and his wife. Kitamura Masako again:

> My husband is the eldest son. His parents want him to go back to the countryside to live with them and take care of them because he's the eldest. They also insist that since I'm a doctor, I must be able to come back with him and open a clinic there.

Dr Kitamura and her husband and children did not go back to the countryside. By 1989 she had been promoted to director of internal medicine at the same hospital.

The duty of care for the family was divided between husband and wife. The husband's obligation was to provide financial support, while the wife's was to perform the day-to-day labour. Ohara Masako had two young children and taught at a university:

> Interpersonal relationships in the family, views on childcare and old people's problems are the biggest factors working against professional women. Also traditional views on femininity reinforce rigid sex-role stereotyping. The myth of motherhood is very strong. Mothers are expected to bear all the practical responsibilities for childcare. And views on old people. The family structure is organised in such a way that the care of old people falls entirely on women in the family.

Higashiura Hisami lectured in English; her husband was also an academic. Her profession led to her exclusion from the wider family:

> My in-laws strongly objected to the wife working. They didn't like an educated woman; they prefer a dependent, subservient woman. My husband is the only son with five sisters; he has heavy responsibility for the family, financially and emotionally. But my income helped him send five sisters to college. My son is seventeen now, but the sisters still oppose my working; they don't visit me; two sent me letters saying they don't consider me their sister-in-law, even though I'd helped them at college. They haven't changed, in fact they've got worse. Not only in Japan but in the whole world, the family set-up affects women unfavourably. How the family operates is important. If the home is well organised, it doesn't have to be a hindrance. In my family my husband helps a great deal in the house. I picked this up in the USA. It's one of the reasons his sisters are furious against me.

The hostility of Higashiura-san's in-laws suggests that the symbolic meaning of the professional housewife was of central importance to the larger family. Despite the lack of any 'family duty' to fulfil at that time, her husband's family essentially disowned her. In this case, the symbolic power and material benefits of a 'professionally employed wife' were not sufficient to compensate for the deficit in symbolic capital produced by the absence from the family of the 'professional housewife'.

Bando Yoriko was a cardiologist, her husband was a surgeon, and they had two small children:

> I'm struggling now with my husband's conservative attitude. I want another baby, I want to get someone to look after it, but my husband wants me to give up my job. He's changed since marriage, maybe because of his social status. When I had the first baby, my in-laws wanted me to stop work until it was twenty. I took leave for three years, and had two children close together. Now I have a babysitter, but it's expensive. When I returned after three years, I felt the change of atmosphere because my cohort had six years' experience and I only had three. I had different experiences and a much lower position. I felt a struggle in my mind because of it. But there will be no problem over the next baby: if my husband doesn't change, I won't have one.

Dr Bando's husband became more conservative as his social status increased. But by 1989 Dr Bando had had her third baby and been promoted to a teaching post at one of the best teaching hospitals in the country:

> In terms of continuing my work, my husband and mother-in-law refused to give me any support from 1971 to 1985. However, I managed to continue working through the co-operation of my children and a very good nanny. Although we are in the same profession, I do not think I had an equal opportunity with my husband. But since I was promoted to Lecturer, my husband's and mother-in-law's attitude – which used to be 'The family has been sacrificed by the mother having a job' – has changed.

The reason for the family's change of heart was the high level of symbolic capital attached to the teaching position. Nothing else had changed. The children were still being looked after by paid childcare. But Dr Bando had finally reached a level with sufficient symbolic power to convert her dishonourable course of action into a mark of respectability.

We can see that regulatory social practices in the family in the form of arranged marriage – preferably by a certain age – and the wife's full-time duty of care produced both the centrality and the urgency of marriage for the continuity of the household. In articulation with the professional housewife discourse, these practices helped to construct gender difference in the family, and produced the meaning of middle-class womanhood as the reproducer of the family's social position and class distinction.

Reproducing Family and Class Distinction

We have argued that the professional housewife discourse established separate spheres for women and for men, and constructed gender difference in the fields of education, employment and the family. It produced women's work as based in the home, concerned with house-work, childcare and family life, while excluding men from domestic work and preserving for them paid professional employment in the public arena: a class- and gender-specific discourse which was pro-duced as normative and hegemonic, was legitimated as a 'respectable' feminine identity to which symbolic power was attached. It was of-fered as a model for the lower classes to aspire to in the search for social mobility, thus constructing the meanings and affecting the prac-tices of the lower as well as the middle classes.

This discourse also constructed the meanings and affected the prac-tices of men as well as women, for men were the objects of women's domestic 'profession', the recipients of the goods and services pro-duced by the housewife's domestic labour, as were children, and old people. Family members were the 'products' of women's domestic labour, through whom the family continuity was sustained; and wom-en's reproduction of the family was social as well as biological.

Changes in the discourse and practice of women's work have oc-curred to account for – but also to contain – middle-class women's entry into the labour market, such that middle-class women could undertake paid work before, and possibly after, but not during the major period of family care, thus constructing their paid employment as short-term interludes surrounding their long-term professional careers as housewives. If, however, discursive changes have recognised middle-class women's limited involvement in paid work, they have not ac-knowledged men's entry into domestic labour. Men's masculinity was still defined by their positioning as the objects of domestic work, and performance of household labour was demeaning for them because of its association with femininity and the low symbolic capital of wom-en's work. Thus the professional housewife discourse and the practice of reserving domestic labour exclusively for women were crucial to gender difference, and the production of masculine as well as feminine identity.

We have argued that the hegemonic discourse of the professional housewife has constructed the meaning of the work activities of the non-earning middle-class wife as an established 'career path' with the goal of reproducing not just the family, but the class position of the family in the next generation. For this task, women required the cultural capital obtained from a middle-class education. The professional housewife's responsibility was to pass on to the children the necessary knowledge and values for reproducing the class position of the husband's household. This required creating in the next generation not only technical skills and cultural knowledge but also – in Bourdieu's terms – the desire to take one's place in the class system, to enter the field of competition and to step into the social positionings of one's parents.

This desire was itself gendered. If we compare the demands made on women and men of the middle class, it is not hard to see why many young women preferred the professional housewife route rather than competing with their male colleagues to become corporate warriors. For sons it involved entering the competition for an elite higher education from an early age, as a qualification for access to professional or corporate life. For daughters it involved acquiring a modest and refined higher education as a qualification for marriage.

We argue that the professional housewife discourse produced the meaning of female higher education not only as a technical training for marriage and housewifery, but as a programme of cultural capital development for the purpose of class reproduction. The middle-class woman as represented in this discourse was still the model of Japanese womanhood as a whole, as seen from both inside and outside Japan. Nevertheless, interwoven in the discourse was the counter-hegemonic discourse of women's entitlement, which was sometimes construed as a more effective means of reproducing class privilege, and sometimes as subversive of the system of class and family reproduction.

Chapter 23

Contradictions of Middle-Class Femininity

When we talked to women in professional employment, the most remarkable feature requiring explanation was the contradiction in the definition of the subject. If one examines professional women's experience of the way they are seen by others, it is apparent that a woman and a professional worker are seen as contradictory concepts. We will attempt to explain this with reference to gendered discourses within specific class locations.

Having examined the hegemonic definitions of gendered class identity, we now turn to the contradictions of middle-class femininity which women in professional occupations encounter in their everyday life – in education, in employment and in the family. We will argue that these contradictions are a potent source for change.

Contradictions in Education

First we will look at the contradictions of middle-class femininity in the field of education. Sugimoto Yumiko studied sociology at Tokyo University and became a manager:

> I was at high school in the early 1960s. Girls wanted to be very feminine and lovable. I felt certain pressures from girl classmates that it's better to be a 'girl', 'feminine' – that is, you shouldn't score good grades, you should carry a needle and thread, so if a boy dropped a button you could sew it on. I thought about it, maybe it's better to be dumb and innocent, but I didn't carry a needle and thread. Later I was in the USA as a schoolgirl. I found new books on women at that time. They had a great influence on my way of thinking. But there was a big

difference between myself and my younger sister. She would think the needle-and-thread business a big joke. I was in some conflict.

Being feminine meant pretending to be stupid and displaying ignorance at school – Sugimoto-san's 'dumb innocence' – and taking care of boys' bodily needs rather than one's own intellectual development. We will see in the next few quotations how ideas about academic ability were deeply gendered and saturated with notions of masculinity. Wakabayashi Yasuko was a civil servant whose father ran a small business:

> My father said, 'I wish you were a boy.' He had a son, but he thought I had ability and could do more.

Ideas about academic ability were also tied up with practices of sex segregation in education. Kurokochi Mei was a dermatologist whose father was also a doctor:

> When I was very small, the headmaster told my father that if I was educated just like a boy, I would go very far.

To educate her 'like a girl' clearly meant the opposite. In some cases, a girl who did not fit with the dominant definition of femininity was thought of as being a boy. Kohga Manae was a university lecturer whose father was a draughtsman:

> My father didn't want me to enjoy hobbies and he drove me only to study. So I didn't like him. My mother sometimes let me do something else. I had a good relationship with her, but my father was sorry I wasn't a boy. Even though I had a younger brother, he wished I had been a boy and taught me boys' games and dressed me like a boy. That I was a girl was against his desire, and we were in constant antagonism.

The gendering of intellectual ability helps to explain why Tsuzuki Kimiko's teachers were so surprised at her achievements:

> I was a good student. I know because I asked. At school they were flabbergasted at my ability.

Dr Tsuzuki's view that she was seen as unusual was not just because of her exceptional intelligence, but because she was an exceptionally intelligent *girl*.

Within the definition of femininity as 'dumb innocence' and limited intellectual ability, the contradictions for girls who excelled academically were apparent. Ohara Masako's understanding of how she was seen by others at school was clearly based not on her intelligence alone, but on the link between her femininity and her intellect, a feature that continued into adult life:

> As I was different from the others at school, they didn't think I'd get married but thought I'd do something. There was no active obstruction, but people started to see me as a special person. This has two meanings: she is a bright person, and at the same time she is not normal. It was proof of being a special person to study in a high-achievers' class at school and prepare for college entrance exam. For a girl to be in this class meant a departure from the group of ordinary girls. My friends regard me as a special person: both very bright and abnormal – as strange. After all, I'm also a housewife with children. I share certain feelings with them, but our relationship is only in the range of being a housewife with children. I still feel the same way: that I'm considered abnormal. I'm considered as a person who has both normal and abnormal elements.

This 'strangeness' or abnormality may be understood as a contradictory form of gendering in which girls displayed characteristics defined as masculine. The same reaction was encountered by girls who expressed an interest in certain subjects or professions identified as male. Fujita Michiko went to school in the 1960s:

> When I said in high school that I wanted to go into medicine, some teachers encouraged me to do my best, but some women teachers said I was a rather strange girl to want to go into such a field. Some friends also said I was strange as a girl, since women doctors were few.

Watanabe Tokiko's father saw engineering as unfeminine:

> My father studied engineering and specialised in electronics. I wanted to be an engineer too, because I was good at maths and physics, but my father said no. He had no conception of a woman engineer. He thought engineering was too hard work for a woman and it didn't have good conditions, too much fieldwork and machines.

So besides ignorance, modest intellectual ability, and the servicing of male bodily needs, femininity was constituted as opposed to mechanisation, technology and science, and as confined to the inner space rather than associated with the open air and physical mobility of 'fieldwork'. Although a degree of intellectual ability was necessary for higher education, intellectual excellence in women was not normal; thus the active development of the female intellect was both deviant and strange. These contradictions, all familiar to women in the West, represented powerful forces for change for women with intellectual ability.

Contradictions in Employment

We now go on to show what middle-class femininity constituted in the field of employment. The idea of women as dumb innocents, as un-tutored and unteachable, was continued in the employment field, and extended into ideas about physical strength, competence in work performance, and recognition for professional authority. Watanabe Nobuko was a section head in the civil service:

> My superiors belong to the older generation who can think of women in no other way than just inferior and weak beings. Their brains are occupied by old ideas about women. They are doubtful whether a woman can actually do a good job even if she is given the opportunity. They feel I'm too pushy if I talk with foreigners in English since I'm taking English conversation lessons. When a woman has special knowledge and uses it at work, they judge her impertinent. As long as she plays up to men's ego, retiring a few steps back from them, they think she is 'feminine'. Because of our sex, we women must always stand at a little distance and watch ourselves in everything. Since society is mainly men, I am often asked by men who phone me to let them speak to a man, since being a woman I cannot deal with his business. There's a problem of position for women. Men can be sent to any position, but for women, positions which can be given are quite limited.

Middle-class femininity stood in an opposing relationship to both middle-class masculinity and professionalism. In relation to masculinity it meant a lack of physical stamina, inferiority and subordination: Watanabe-san's 'inferior and weak beings'. In relation to professionalism it meant incompetence and a lack of expertise in arenas defined as the preserve of men. Demonstrating knowledge or expertise was un-feminine, and represented a challenge to men's masculinity. Watanabe-san's final sentence indicates the extent to which 'positions' in the field of professional employment were constituted as qualitatively masculine. Middle-class femininity also stood opposed to working-class femininity, for paid work was not seen as anomalous in the same way for Kondo's part-time women factory workers (Kondo: 1990).

    Femininity also meant subordination to men, as was evident in the experience of two government officials when traditional gender relations were reversed in the work context. Takahashi Noriko explained that on business trips a man sent from central office would be treated with respect:

> But when I go accompanied by a male subordinate, I'm mistaken for a 'tea server' or 'business-case carrier'. When they find I'm the person sent to see them, they're so surprised, I feel sorry for them.

Inokuma Ryoko:

> When I go to see factories on business, people in the factory get very curious about a woman official. If I take a young male subordinate with me, they take me as his subordinate, and get embarrassed to know which is which. Usually I'm taken as a maid or secretary.

Femininity evoked ideas which were in contradiction to the competence and authority required of a professional worker in a 'masculine' profession. Femininity implied ignorance as opposed to knowledge, incompetence as opposed to capability, subordination as opposed to authority. These features were intricately woven together in the meanings attached to gendered identities in professional employment.

Femininity also connoted weakness as opposed to strength. Several women doctors discussed how female colleagues had less strength and stamina for surgery. Medicine was the site of other contradictions. Takahashi Yoshiko:

> I'm in my forties now, and have no trouble, but I did when I was younger. I worked at Tokyo University for ten years. There were some people who asked why a woman was examining patients in Tokyo University Hospital, or they automatically thought I was a nurse, or some demanded to see a 'real' doctor, since they'd come all the way to Tokyo University Hospital. I was once told by my own son: 'I've always thought you were a nurse, but Grandma said it wasn't true, and you're a doctor. I was very surprised to know there are women doctors in this world, and that you mother are one of them.'

Matsumoto Toshie was an anaesthetist:

> If I say the same thing as a male doctor, they don't take my word. Male doctors don't want to discuss a case with a woman, even a case where I will be the anaesthetist. This is dangerous for the patient. For example, I had one patient who had an asthmatic attack after the operation. I told the surgeon what should be done, what medicines to administer, etc. He didn't even listen, but took the patient to the ward and asked the ward doctor what to do. He gave exactly the same instructions as I did. Only then was the patient treated. I've been working fifteen years as a doctor and nothing has changed, in fact it's getting worse. Men don't like to be told what to do by a woman. Patients have more trust in male doctors than women doctors. Some don't even realise we can be doctors.

In academic work, students may feel that women teachers' intellectual ability is not of the same standard as that of their male tutors, and male staff may be reluctant to employ women teachers for the same reason. Ishihara Mayumi was a law lecturer:

One male colleague said that however great a theory might be, students would be unlikely to give it complete trust if it's formulated by a female scholar. It seems this is a common opinion of men in general.

Yamaguchi Kyoko lectured in economics:

Since I came to this university I've seen many bright students whose academic level is high. They feel something lacking about me as a teacher. They want to improve by serious study with their teachers, they want to have discussions with them and join in their talks, but they feel dissatisfied because they have an idea women can't do such things after all. The other day a woman applied for a teaching post at this university, but was turned down for the following reason: according to the university administration, students would feel dissatisfied about the faculty if we had another female teacher of economics.

Management, too, had its contradictions. Iwa-o Shigeko was a manager in an airline company:

Before coming to this department I was in another section. When clients telephoned and heard a woman's voice, they said, 'Can I talk to a man?' They assumed I was a minion. I used to explain that though I'm a woman, I'm in charge of certain areas and might be able to help them. Little by little my name became known among the customers.

Tagaki Yoshi, a manager in a publishing company, complained that a male subordinate working for a woman 'won't take it even if he was hired yesterday':

When I was chief editor for a women's magazine, an article was sent to me through an editor written by a young male journalist. I ordered the article to be rewritten because I thought it would stir up strong anxieties in mothers. He looked quite angry, but rewrote it next day. The second version was much better, and was included in the magazine. At the end of the year, when we went out for drinks, he told me, 'When the article was rejected by a woman chief editor, I felt so insulted, I wrote a resignation letter. But then some of the points you made seemed reasonable, so I decided to rewrite the article first and then hand in the letter. The rewritten article was accepted without trouble, so I decided not to resign.' For this incident to happen, there was only one reason and nothing else: that I'm a woman.

The changes happening over a generation can also be seen, but it is significant that the change began in a 'feminine' area of medicine. Ogino Fumiko was an obstetrician:

When I came to this hospital as the first department head, I only had one subordinate. I heard that the head of the hospital said to this young doctor that he would hate working under a woman. But he said he had never felt that way.

The doubts about women's professional competence and specialist knowledge raised questions about their placement and promotability, so that femininity was construed as occupationally 'capable' in relation to forms of work associated with traditionally feminine, but not masculine, occupations. At the same time, traditionally feminine occupations were often associated with low status and a lack of symbolic capital. The attempt to produce the meaning of femininity as ignorance and incompetence was constantly re-enacted by demands that women refrain from displaying their competence or expertise, and by the practice of characterising women who insisted on demonstrating it as 'pushy' or 'impertinent'. The conventional construction of femininity created the stark contradiction experienced by professional women. By displaying and exercising their strength and competence, women demonstrated their abilities and claimed the right to professional authority, but such displays denied their femininity.

However, it was precisely in the social spaces caused by the ambiguity, doubt and uncertainty of these contradictory gendered identities and social practices that changes and challenges to orthodox ideas and traditional practices could be mounted. We will use as an example a particular office ritual referred to by many of the women civil servants. This ritual has been used by western authors to invoke a traditional image of the Japanese woman worker: we use it to challenge this image.

To many of the women in government service, the serving of tea in the office was saturated with symbolic meaning of a gendered nature, and they referred to it without any prompting on the part of the interviewers. However, no consistent meaning, or even practice, was attached to the ritual. Its significance was in flux, as the meaning of middle-class femininity at the workplace was being negotiated and reconstituted. The fact is that people often did not know what to do or how to behave when new social practices were in contradiction with gendered identities. What was socially appropriate was unclear. It was in these spaces that new social practices, discourses and identities could be forged. Some groups in privileged positions may have resisted this because of what they had to lose, but for those who had something to gain, the uncertainty opened up possibilities for experiment and initiative.

Mitaka Teruko:

> There's a custom that women should serve tea to people at work. There's nothing wrong with serving tea, but the question is that they think women should do it.

Mitaka-san recognised the ritual as an expression of gendered identity and women's domesticity, but questioned both its association with femininity and its low symbolic value. Sonoda Yuriko recognised that the ritual was also associated with a class position:

> There's a special atmosphere in the office in Japan; most women only serve tea and clean the office. When I began working, I thought, 'I'm a woman, not a man', so I should do the same work as women – serving tea, cleaning the room. Now I think it's bad for me. If I started again, I wouldn't make so much effort to be like other women.

Sonoda-san linked the ritual with 'cleaning', a task with such little symbolic capital that it is virtually invisible. These tasks were what 'most women' working in offices did: domestic tasks which set women apart, as low-level subordinates, from the 'important' work of the men. But at the start Sonoda-san acknowledged only the connection with femininity, and performed the womanly tasks which located her with 'the women' and set her apart from 'the professionals'. This enacted all the feminine characteristics of subordination and inferiority, and undermined her ability to establish the 'masculine' characteristics of professional competence and authority: serving tea diminished any symbolic value she held as a woman in the position of a professional civil servant.

Hayashi Kouko:

> Last year I worked for the Civil Affairs Bureau. My main job was to examine applications for naturalisation – about two applications a day. But I was always having to serve tea to my colleagues, and it was too much work, so I couldn't apply myself properly to the job.

Hayashi-san recognised that the practical effects of the ritual were to reinforce not only women's domesticity but also the idea of women's inability to do the job.

Hara Yosiko:

> Men don't serve tea to guests. My boss told me not to serve tea, and that I should work equally to men. I was lucky. One of my friends was told she had to do it. It depends on the boss's attitude. This friend has left already.

Hara-san and her boss both recognised the ritual as *creating* inequality for women, while her friend felt undermined enough to leave the job.

Ninomiya Kimi was a deputy head in the civil service:

> I shouldn't be too conscious of the fact that I'm a woman. For instance, men serve tea to us. When I did it once, my subordinate said I shouldn't because it embarrassed them. So I stopped and decided to behave like a man in my position.

In Ninomiya-san's case, her male subordinates were more disturbed by the contradictions caused to the organisational hierarchy than by the gender implications. Clearly, gender contradictions caused uncertainty on how to behave, but both the women and their male colleagues took initiatives, deciding whether to reproduce or undermine established power relations. In questioning the tea-serving ritual, both women and men were challenging and changing gendered class identities.

Contradictions in the Family

In the family, the contradictions are for men. It is not that women lack credibility or authority in the home, or that their femininity challenges and is in conflict with their presence and position in the family. The problem is that women's *absence* from the family is not legitimate, and that they are not entitled to take on responsibilities outside the family which would develop their capacities, provide an income, or pose a challenge to men's exclusive right to compete in the employment field. Nor is it acceptable for women to negotiate the sharing of family responsibilities with men. The problem for women is excessive workload, and in this situation the complex arrangements necessary to perform and organise two workloads are awe-inspiring.

Problems for women

Shimizu Fumiko, a civil servant, lived in a joint family with her husband, mother-in-law, daughter of 6 and son of six months:

> I do my best, but I regret I can't work as fully as I wanted during the period of having children. At home I feel sorry for my children at times, since I can't look after them enough. Childcare is a problem. This is the toughest period. The baby is taken care of by my friend, housekeeping by a neighbour, and my daughter by a day-care programme at elementary school. My two sisters help me to look after my children; I've been greatly helped by my sisters. The family's attitude is basically favourable. The difficulties in the future will be what to do if my husband is transferred to a faraway place, and how to manage a demanding job schedule. I can't cook food, can't spend enough leisure time with the children like an ordinary mother. I can't be relaxed because of the

strain of work. In reality it costs money for women to work. Now I pay ¥70,000 for the baby-sitter and ¥50,000 for the housekeeper out of my salary of ¥170,000 every month, which leaves only a little to spend myself. It's hard. It would be a lie if I said I never think about giving up work. But if work is what a woman wants, she should do it. The point is to choose one's own life. Today women lose many other things by working. If it's only for money, they should think it over again.

Shimizu-san did not give up work, and by 1989 she had become director of a department. Shimizu-san solved her workload problem through family relations and employment relations, all reliant on women.

Inokuma Ryoko had similar problems. She was married with a 7-year-old son:

I'm living separately from my husband because of our work. I had a hard time trying to find someone who would take care of our son after the day-care centre was closed. I didn't have time for it physically. Now he's in first grade and an after-school care centre. At night a neighbour takes care of him. Work in this section especially continues until late at night, and I find it hard to cope with it. My youngest sister-in-law is very understanding, and tells me not to give up my career even if it leads to living separately. I leave my child with a housewife in the neighbourhood; I couldn't have continued work without her. I also have someone who helps with housekeeping; I can't keep working without them. Whether by chance you can find such people determines whether you can continue with your career or not.

Inokuma-san, too, depended on female employees to replace her at home, paying neighbours and day-care centres to do the housework and childcare, as did Moriyama Ichiko, an obstetrician:

One child goes to a nursery, the other to primary school. Fortunately my family live close to us, and I have a good housekeeper. These people's help is great. When I'm too busy my housekeeper works after her assigned time. When I have a hard time I need to call a housekeeper regardless of expenditure, or I go back home early to study at home beside the children rather than stay in the office to work overtime. If an urgent call comes from the hospital, my niece, who is a college student, baby-sits for my children. If there's an emergency patient my mother helps me working at home. Lunch boxes for my children are prepared by my brother's family. My mother is totally supportive; my brothers are also co-operative. My husband is the eldest son, which often means he would have lots of obligations in Japan, but fortunately in his case it's not so. Only if the in-laws get sick, I can't foresee what will happen to us. I may have to take care of them.

Women like Dr Moriyama who used other women's labour were often subject to criticism – from family members, from their employment organisation, from the state or the community – for not being proper wives and mothers, for not being feminine, and for not acting out the ideal model of the middle-class woman. Higashiura Hisami, a lecturer in English:

> After I had my son there was some feeling – not pressure, but Japanese society felt I should give up. I had guilt feelings. I took him to the kindergarten attached to the college; well-to-do leisured families send their children there, so there was a lack of sympathy and co-operation for working mothers. I had to work for the kindergarten as well as my own work. There was particular pressure from women.

And Sugimoto Yumiko, market research manager:

> The model role for woman is very stereotyped. It sets limits, and con-scious or unconscious pressures. Every morning when I come to the office I meet young mothers sending their children to kindergarten. People say, 'Oh, I envy you, you're going out', but it's not a compli-ment, it's a criticism.

Women themselves recognised the extent to which domestic work was constituted as feminine, and saw the need for a 'wife' of their own. Horiuchi Tokiko was a physician:

> It's difficult to be a housewife and to have a profession at the same time. It's a matter of time. I wish I could have a wife for myself who keeps the house. I have no time for study. I rely on electrical appliances as much as possible to be efficient with the housework, and that's the only way. Housework is merely drudgery.

And it was not only married women with children who felt this way. Tsukamoto Tokiko was a gynaecologist:

> After I came here I had a hard time with my work because it involved research too. It even made it difficult to do housekeeping just for my-self. Till then I'd thought men were superior to women, but I came to feel that after all it wasn't so hard for a man to get a high position. When he works he's completely supported by a woman. I concentrated on my research for three months without doing any housework. It was really horrible.

In fact professional women did get themselves a 'wife' – or several wives – but it was rarely a 'spouse'; rather, the unpaid labour of women relatives, and the paid labour of women housekeepers, babysitters, nannies and cleaners.

These problems for women were not caused by double workloads alone, but also by organisational practices which assumed priority over family needs, even for men. Niimura Misako was in government service:

> Five years ago my husband was transferred to another prefecture. I asked to change my job to there. My husband and I entered the Ministry at the same time, so the government could change my job too. But they changed it to yet another prefecture a hundred kilometres away. So I lived on my own for two years, and the rest of the family lived with my husband.

Kuba Taeko was a company manager:

> It's not mental but physical pressure. My husband works for Nippon Iron and Steel Company. He gets transferred. He's moved five times since our marriage, including to the USA. They give short notice, only ten days. We have to change the children's school. Every time I wonder whether I should quit. Usually I have some important project, he goes ahead, I find another way to manage.

To argue that femininity meant weakness, inferiority and incompetence in these circumstances would be to deny the evidence of women's immense organisational abilities. But the excessive workload at the office and at home, combined with the devaluing of women's contribution to economic life, could have serious deleterious effects. Tamagawa Kazuko was a lecturer. She was visibly upset when she related her story:

> I have been excluded from work, caused by personal factors, not the work itself. I was almost excluded from the position I had. I had many miscarriages. On those occasions young people offered me a lot of assistance, but men who spent their childhood and adolescence in the war didn't show such understanding at all. What bothered me most was being told women can't deal with physics while doing housework and childrearing, since it takes a man's whole life even if he concentrates on it. In order not to be told such a thing, I had to watch myself very carefully.
>
> When I gave birth I was forced to stay in bed, since I wasn't doing well. I had to take six months' leave in addition to legally approved maternity leave, which caused other teachers great trouble. One professor said such happenings are the result of mixing up private and official matters. He tried to cut my research expenses and decrease the number of students who would take my classes. With the help of women colleagues, his attempts were thwarted. But as shown in this incident,

staying in bed due to complications after giving birth did not receive social recognition as sickness. I myself can't understand why such an abnormal childbirth couldn't be regarded as sickness, and why it is viewed as confusion between official and private matters. It's a total lack of understanding.

When the child was sick I took her to my parents, worked all night and tried really hard, almost sacrificing my own health. Looking back to those days is really painful. It's painful to think that women's problems are put into a special category and are yet to be taken up as a general problem area.

Women have to work harder for the same recognition. For example, our child had to have an operation. If this happened to a man, people around him would say, 'That's too bad, go home as soon as possible for your child. Your wife must feel helpless when she's alone.' But if it happened to a woman teacher, she would hear people say, 'That's why we don't want women with us.' We women work harder not to be talked about in such ways.

When I was giving birth to my daughter, I was prepared for my own possible death. I could give up neither my work nor my maternal instinct. I wanted to bear a child and rear it myself. It was really painful to be torn between the two. My aunt and mother-in-law helped me most. When the child gets sick my mother-in-law often stays overnight to take care of her. I hired a maid. But there were times no one was available to help, and I stayed up all night to finish work. I didn't want to hear people say women can't work. When I was in trouble, the biggest help came from other women.

As Anne Marie Goetz writes: 'one aspect of the gendering of public space is the way the sexed body is perceived in that space … women … can be devalued by invoking the symbolic significance of the public–private divide to associate their presence … in the organisation with their private identities' (Goetz 1997: 21). The reproductive female body is an incontrovertible statement of femininity in the public space. Pregnancy and childbirth represent the bodily manifestation of femininity. No matter how much a woman may attempt to behave like a man in order to be accepted as a professional worker, maternity poses a challenge to this strategy.

In these circumstances a woman must counter the construction of professionalism as masculine, insist on the right to be different, and claim entitlement to enter the field of professional employment *as a woman*. Tamagawa-san's superior categorised her abnormal childbirth as 'confusion between official and private matters' because her lengthy maternity-related illness forced the intrusion of her femininity into the professional sphere which had hitherto been constructed as a masculine social space. Tamagawa-san's giving birth represented femininity's challenge to the masculine constitution of professional employment.

Contradictions for men

The different conditions of professional women's lives, and the organisation of employment around the conditions of men's lives, caused not only difficulties for women but practical contradictions for men. Ninomiya Kimi worked in a government ministry:

> My husband has double standards. He approves of my working very positively because he has a responsible position and gets annoyed when women quit. But as a husband he's dissatisfied and wants to be waited on, especially when he comes home late.

Matsumoto Toshie was a doctor:

> The reason working women don't like to work overtime is that they have to prepare food for the family, etc. Men can't blame women when they want to leave work, because they expect their wives to prepare dinner when they get home.

Kakuta Masako taught German:

> Before marriage my husband said he prefers a woman with a job, but now he doesn't. He still recognises my job, but doesn't actually like how it affects him. My husband is not particularly happy that I have a job to occupy my time, but prefers me to stay at home, do translation work or part-time lecturing. At present he's giving minimum co-operation.

Although professional men benefited from the organisation of work which privileged male lifestyles and working patterns, middle-class men, in their roles as both superiors and husbands, encountered practical contradictions between the capitalist organisation of labour relations, which employed women's professional skills, and the organisation of gender relations, which required women's services at home. Similarly, although parents may have admired a daughter who worked as a professional, when it came to choosing a daughter-in-law they would refuse a career woman because they were seeking a 'wife' who could perform domestic work, undertake the duty of care, and reproduce the social position of the family. Matsui Noriko, a maths lecturer:

> My parents were very pleased about my working as a teacher. My mother was pleased to see her child become a teacher because she has a simple

belief that to be in the educational field is a great thing for any person and it serves society. But she wouldn't select someone like me for her son's wife.

The other contradiction for men was that if they did take on domestic work, they were considered just as abnormal as a career woman. Ouchida Mariko was an anaesthetist:

> If there's a male member of the family who can keep house, let him do it. But generally speaking, the conditions are such that it's easier for women to do it. People have a traditional idea that housekeeping should be done by women. A man would find it hard to keep house, since he would be considered strange for a man.

Housework and childcare constituted performances of femininity, and were thus in conflict with masculinity. Kitamura Masako was a doctor:

> I don't think housework is women's work. Only historically it's been part of women's role. For myself I don't like to see my husband doing housework, just because we've been told men shouldn't work like a wife. But it's not true. Men as well as women should be educated so they can do everything well at home.

Dr Kitamura challenged her own feelings of unease about men doing housework, and demanded equality at home as well as at work. Clearly masculinity meant being non-domestic, and performing housework constructed men as conceptually anomalous.

The Struggle for Change

In conclusion, we have argued in Part V that the discourse of women's entitlement defining women as legitimate contestants in the fields of higher education and professional employment, and represented in the practices of the professional woman, undermined the gender differences established in men's and women's work, and contradicted the masculine and feminine subjectivities produced by these differences. A professional woman often excelled in academic performance, and in this sense she could not be termed ignorant or unintelligent. A professional woman was competent and authoritative in the skills and knowledges required to sustain a responsible job; she was therefore neither subordinate nor inferior to a man. A professional woman worked outside the home and did not devote her entire working life to domestic labour; in this sense she could be termed undomesticated. But these qualities constituted a form of middle-class masculinity, the opposite of middle-class femininity.

Thus a middle-class woman and a professional worker were seen as contradictory because middle-class work was gendered, and because gender difference in paid and unpaid work was crucial to the production of masculine and feminine subjectivity. In line with Hollway's understanding (Hollway 1984), women's knowledge of the alternative discourse on female entitlement, and of their contradictory practice as professional workers, could be empowering for them, showing how contradictions in the discourses and practices of femininity could be a potent source of change. These contradictions could also, however, produce enormous pressures, resulting in distress and disempowerment. The positive impetus to change was how to manage the contradictions and seek resolutions to the pressures, but equally the tensions could be intolerable and produce despair.

These contradictions also opened up new social spaces when 'appropriate' practices had not yet been developed in situations involving contradictory identities. At this point alternative practices became available as people made choices about how to act, some of which closed down new possibilities and reproduced old relations of power, while others undermined existing power relations and created spaces for change. Here economic demands could be a force for change, where the efficient performance of professional work took precedence over the reproduction of gendered power relations.

PART VI

Becoming a Professional Woman: Achieving the Right to Compete

In Part VI, we look at the way professional women managed the contradictions and challenged the conceptual anomaly of their social identities to achieve changes in social practice and subjectivity. Using the data from our study, we analyse their strategies and the representations of their actions as social subjects. We begin with the concepts which underpin our approach, drawing on Lovell (2000) and Kondo (1990). The latter provides important perspectives for understanding the context of social relations in Japan.

To understand how transformations in social practice were achieved, we examine the women's strategies for change, looking at the way they deployed the various capitals available to them in the field, in order to establish a professional career and negotiate new ways of living in the family.

We then explore women's changing subjectivities, looking at the way they legitimated their right to compete, by identifying how they understood their position as middle-class women with professional careers, and how they approached housework and childcare as gendered labour.

Finally, we assess how the respondents had fared twelve years on, looking at the changes to their lives identified by the women themselves at the start of the new Heisei era which began in 1989. We will compare their own representations of the changes to their lives with images of Japanese women produced in Japan and in the West, and ask why these representations are so starkly at odds with the picture presented in this study.

Chapter 24

Transforming Gendered Class Identities

To examine the strategies adopted by women in achieving changes in social practice, we draw upon Lovell's framework, which understands women as simultaneously subjects and objects specified in terms of the capitals possessed, and the deployment of these capitals. This allows us to raise questions about the kind of investment strategies employed by women, and under what conditions; and how women's object positioning as repositories of capital for others facilitated or hampered their position as capital-accruing and capital-deploying subjects (Lovell 2000: 23). Bourdieu argues that (men's) right to exercise power is legitimated through the conversion of social, cultural and economic capital into symbolic capital (Bourdieu 1984: 291). We will show how women's legitimacy to compete in the fields of public power drew significantly upon the symbolic capital attached to their class positioning.

In order to understand changing subjectivities in a Japanese context, we will draw on Kondo's understanding of the centrality of social relations and social context in defining both identity and social practice. Kondo, like Bourdieu and Lovell, deconstructs the binary between subject and object, and argues that selves and society are not separate identities in Japan, but that persons are constituted in and through social relations and obligations to others (Kondo 1990: 22, 24). She suggests that this is a fundamentally different way of thinking about the self and the social world from that which predominates in the West, which is precisely the problem with which Bourdieu is engaging (arguably less successfully than either Kondo or Lovell). Instead, 'contextually constructed, relationally defined selves are particularly resonant in Japan', where the self is permeable, 'determined by context and boundaries ... constantly shifting' (Kondo 1990: 26). As Kondo puts it: 'You are not an "I" untouched by context, rather you are defined by the context. One could argue that identity and context are inseparable.... Pronouns ... [shift] with social positioning and the relations between "self" and "other"' (Kondo 1990: 29). One of the criteria of maturity is not independence, as in the West, but the ability to read, interpret and manage the social relationships and interdependencies appropriate to different social situations. In Japan, Kondo argues, 'awareness of complex social positioning is ... *inescapable* ... for it is *utterly impossible* to form a sentence without *also* commenting on the relationship between oneself and one's interlocutor' (Kondo 1990: 31; original emphasis). Despite the differences between the Japanese and the western concept in the valuing of and the attention paid to social relations and social interdependence, the crucial point common to Bourdieu's and Kondo's understandings of social reality is that 'connectedness is never beyond power' (Kondo 1990: 305), meaning that social relations are inseparable from power relations.

The development of mature personhood in Japan may be understood as occurring through the increasing integration of the individual with the social structure: 'Japanese women portray themselves as accommodating to duties and to the needs of others, rather than as independent decision-makers [and this] ... makes them fully mature human beings' (Kondo 1990: 33). The path to mature selfhood is through the difficult process of developing a sensitive awareness of human social relations and obligations to others. The path to maturity and self-realisation can include fulfilling social obligations, meeting the demands of a job, or the performance of a social role such as bride, mother, student or worker. Maturity is especially found in a role *outside* the natal home, where hardship may be involved, where desires must be held back, behaviour monitored, and awareness maintained of the need to create harmonious social relations. From the experience of hardship can be claimed powers of endurance, fortitude and power, whereas without this one remains childlike, permitting the indulgence of selfish desires and allowing antisocial behaviour to disturb social relations. Thus self-realisation represents the process of becoming a mature adult, participating in and being aware of one's place in the world, taking one's place in society and constructing the self within the context of a network of human social relationships (Kondo 1990: 105–9, 230–37).

Kondo argues that the family unit and the work organisation are centres of both dutiful obligation and emotional attachment. The meaning of work is not exhausted by the economic relationship, but commitment to the work and participation in society are important too. Equally, emotional attachment does not completely define the meaning of family, for the duty of social obligation and the enthusiastic performance of a social role for the productive unit of the family is also important (Kondo 1990: 159, 198, 235–7). Work and family are thus two major sites of symbolic struggle and the assertion of identity. Selves and society are inseparable, as identities are subject positions created within relations of power, are constituted in social relations and obligations to others, and are constructed through practice rather than through the expression of essential inner traits (Kondo 1990: 10, 22, 33, 300–301).

In addition, Kondo argues that the family and the organisation are sites of historical struggles, the context for which is delineated by changes in the international political economy, and the meanings of which can be understood only in this context. The development of global capitalism, the outcome of the war and the westernised Constitution, the attempt to reinstate class hegemony, and the creation of a Japanese identity as a counterpoint to western expansionism have all contributed to the organisation of work and family life in Japan. Gender, labour relations, and the construction of gendered class identities have all been framed by the culturally and historically specific development of capitalism in the global political economy, within which western influences are seen as producing increasingly individualistic attitudes amongst the younger generation (Kondo 1990: 50–51, 114, 197).

Within a social framework which could be a 'profoundly conservative' means of 'producing disciplinary subjects' (Kondo 1990: 109, 112), then, how did our respondents produce and justify the changes in their social positions and social practices, which differed radically from those of the hegemonic identities of middle-class femininity?

Chapter 25

Changing Social Practice

In this chapter we look at women's strategies for achieving changes in social practices, in terms of establishing a professional career and negotiating new ways of living in the family. Although our respondents were from diverse social backgrounds, a majority were from more privileged families. We will argue that it was through the deployment of various forms of capital that these middle-class women were able to achieve changes in social practices and move into subject positions. We examine how they deployed their capitals to establish a professional career. We then go on to look at how they use their capitals to negotiate new family lifestyles.

Establishing a Professional Career

Economic capital

The purpose of education for middle-class women was clearly differentiated from that of men's education. Murakami Hiroki was a manager:

> I graduated in Home Economics in 1953. The teachers didn't expect me to get a job. They expected women to become good mothers at Japan Women's University. Only ten students did biology at my university. Only I got a job. The others were rich upper-class girls.

Inoue Yoshi obtained a teaching qualification in the 1960s, and later studied for her MBA. She was a manager in a large international bank:

> The college I went to was a special sort, a private girls' college in Tokyo. The students came from rich families, so we weren't expected to work. There was psychological pressure not to work, because graduates of this college always got married straight after. That discouraged me; I wondered if I should too.

Clearly, these high-class educations were not an automatic route to employment. So how did women transform their education for 'marriage' into education for 'professional employment'? For some, the transition was actively managed by their fathers, who recognised the potential enhancement of family respectability. Takahashi Yoshiko completed her medical training at Tokyo University Medical School in 1965:

> We were a middle-class family; my father ran a small advertising business. He said his children, male or female, had to go to a university which leads to a profession. He wouldn't approve of less than a four-year course. At high school I loved literature and wanted to study English. The teachers thought I'd go to an elite women's college, but my parents objected. So I went to a pharmacy college, but I couldn't stand it. When I was a senior I took an entrance exam for medical college and moved there. It was a big gamble in my life. My father said he couldn't support me unless I went to medical college after pharmacy, so I got in and went.

Dr Takahashi was an ideal candidate for an arts degree as preparation for marriage and the cultural capital necessary to reproduce class distinction, but her parents' support was conditional on her education delivering the symbolic capital of a professional career, suggesting the development of greater flexibility in the gender division of labour, whereby women could contribute economic as well as social capital to the family.

However, not every woman's family could afford to pay for two professional training programmes, and some respondents were from quite modest backgrounds. Saeki Takuko's family was unable to provide the economic capital for her education, but she overcame their opposition by applying for a scholarship:

> Our family had financial difficulties because of my father's sickness. I wanted to go to university, but they suggested I give up the idea. For myself I wasn't planning on going to medical school, but to a college in Kofu. But since the family advised me to give it up, I decided to try my ability by taking an entrance exam for medicine at a first-rate university. I passed it, which was a first event at our high school. The teachers were so impressed that they persuaded my parents, who felt they could not help but accept it.

Intellectual ability could overcome lack of economic capital, but crucially it was the symbolic value of passing for a 'first-rate' institution that made the difference. The teachers' action meant that Dr Saeki's intellectual success reflected honour, respect and achievement for the school, as well as for herself and her family.

Cultural capital

Although economic capital could be used as a resource, the experience of Takahashi Yoshiko illustrated how its deployment depended on older family members, and was not in the control of younger women. For this reason, cultural capital was more useful for young women, since it made the family appreciate education, and produced the desire to educate women. It could also compensate for the absence of economic capital. After the war, Tomita Kazuko's family had lost their wealth, but retained substantial cultural capital. Dr Tomita's father was a company president with an engineering degree, and she went to university in the 1960s:

> For economic reasons I had to pass the exam for a national university. I was fourth among six children. At around ten I admired my aunt, who was a doctor, as a great woman. At that time she was a very famous doctor who was one of the first twelve or thirteen women with a medical degree. Her father, my grandfather, was also a doctor. I respected my aunt as a figure who helped the poor. This thought was in my mind for a long time. With this background, and because we were hard up economically after the war, I made up my mind to be a doctor and give my parents some relief. Those family circumstances led me to be a doctor.

Dr Tomita's familiarity with the profession, and the male and female role models in her immediate family, enabled her to see medicine as an acceptable professional identity for a woman of her background.

Kato Atsuko was born into an academic family in similar economic circumstances. Her father had studied at Tokyo University before her, and was a professor of medicine. She completed her PhD in 1970:

> We weren't well-to-do, but my parents managed to buy the books I wanted. I didn't hesitate to enter academic life, thanks to my family circumstances. We were a big family, and from a financial point of view I was expected to go to a national university because they cost less than private ones. I studied hard and had good results. I was top among the girls at high school, and the teachers expected me to enter Tokyo University, which I did. The family atmosphere influenced me greatly; the idea of being a scholar had penetrated deeply into me.

Kato-san's academic family provided the knowledge, familiarity and desire with which to develop her intellectual ability and excel.

Kiuchi Fumie's father died in 1946, when she was a child, but he had been educated at Tokyo University, and managed a film company. His daughter was more than compensated for the financial hardship following his death by her inheritance of cultural capital, of which the desire to enhance it through education was a key component:

> Both my parents were university graduates. It was regarded as natural that I would work: our family background was such that women go to university. Somehow it was just natural for me from my childhood that I would work. Our grandparents were university professors. This was even though our financial background was severe because my father died when I was ten. He left lots of books when he died. Just after the war there was nothing else for us to do, no toys, just books. My father encouraged me to write a diary from the age of five or six, and he used to correct it. My father's father was a journalist, my grandmother was a poet. There was an atmosphere of literature in the house.

For Kiuchi-san, it was 'somehow just natural' for her to go to university and become an academic herself. But in fact this attitude was learnt and absorbed through the 'literary atmosphere', the house full of books, her father's training, and family role models. The family's lack of economic capital gave the daughter an opportunity to credentialise her cultural capital and convert it into a source of economic capital on the labour market, a strategy which might otherwise have been denied her. Indeed, although her grandparents gave support, her brother objected to her education, since she would then be able to compete with him for distinction.

The loss of family wealth after the war made many people realise that the return on the investment in cultural capital could be more valuable than the return on economic capital. Kinoshta Mitsuko studied economics at Tokyo University, and graduated in 1953:

> My parents expected me to do something – that was the war period, when many people lost money. If parents gave their children money it would be lost, but education was not lost, it was an investment, so they gave me higher education.

Here the family strategy converged with the daughter's in enhancing her cultural capital and facilitating her move into the labour market as a primary actor.

Social capital

The strategic use of social capital was a valuable bridge between higher education and a professional career. Kiuchi Fumie again:

I was a good student, and there were high expectations of me. I went to a famous girls' school, St Margaret's Girls' High School. I wanted to go to a women's college, but the teachers advised me not to, but to go to a coeducational university because it's better if you are a serious student, so I went to Waseda University. When I graduated, companies didn't recruit women. I had a relative in an airline company, and I applied and got in, but the salary was much below that of a man of the same history. When my professor at university read my dissertation, he told me to go to graduate school. But I had already got a job as a clerk at a company – very much below my ability, and with no chance to rise for women. I was timid in those days, but I went on a trip to the UK thanks to the cheap flights from my job, and it gave me confidence. After five years I went back to graduate school. At first I didn't think I could become a university lecturer, I thought maybe a school teacher. It wasn't until my professor offered me a job that I thought I could be an academic. In Japanese universities you can't find a job without your professor's help. If he encourages you, it means he will find you a job. I was the first woman to get a job in this school.

Despite her reduced circumstances, Kiuchi-san was able to draw on the cultural capital of her literary family to get an education, the social capital of her teachers and relatives to get employment, and the opportunity for travel to improve her confidence. These forms of capital were available to her because of the family's social background, regardless of their economic position. Through strategic deployment of these capitals she was able to regain her family's former distinction. By 1989 she had become a full professor.

In contrast, another academic, Kanamori Yasuko, lacked both economic and cultural capital, and therefore took a much more circuitous route to higher education and professional employment than Kiuchi-san. Kanamori-san was the youngest of seven children. Her mother was illiterate, her father a sheet-metal worker with a primary-school education. She started her university job after finishing her PhD in 1963:

At high school it was the middle of the war, and I was advised to go to teachers' training college. Fortunately or unfortunately, my parents were virtually ignorant about higher education, so I persuaded them I could go to college. My parents were just ordinary old type of people, and said nothing about what I should do. They were too busy raising lots of kids. They don't understand what it means to get the highest education, and what my profession is. My sisters were indifferent to my work except one who asked me what my purpose was in going to college. None of my sisters went to college.

I went to what is now Tokyo Metropolitan University under the old system, and got the teacher's qualification in 1948. I went to night school for two years after college. I was intending to be a high-school teacher or work at an experimental institute after college, but I was asked to stay at my teachers' college. I worked as an assistant researcher, and that was the start of my career as an academic. Nine years later, in 1957, I got my BSc in physics under the new system at Tokyo Science University, and then three years after finishing my BSc I went back to Tokyo Metropolitan University to do my PhD in the 1960s. I think I was rather lucky. I had good teachers and good luck. Some years ago science and technology faculties were added to many existing universities. The increase in teaching staff made it possible for me to get a teaching post here.

Kanamori-san took twenty years to get qualifications which should have taken ten. She had no cultural capital, and received little support or encouragement from her family. She attributes her early success to the social capital developed at her college, and her progress since then to the expansion of higher education in the 1960s.

Both Kanamori-san and Kiuchi-san were single and without family responsibilities, and entered the expanding labour market of the 1960s. Both were introduced to an academic career through the social capital of teachers impressed by their intellectual performance. The crucial difference was that Kanamori's personal recommendation was based on the educational credential of a PhD, gaining her employment in an ordinary university. Kiuchi-san's recommendation was based only on a master's degree, yet it gave her access to one of the elite universities. Nothing could more clearly illustrate the difference in the effect of their respective social backgrounds. The fact that so few of the respondents were from families like Kanamori-san's, where cultural capital was absent, compared with women from families like Kiuchi-san's, where it was in abundance, suggests that the inheritance of cultural capital played a crucial part in the legitimation of women's access to a professional career.

In Part IV we showed that women from manual-labourer backgrounds constituted a mere 3 per cent of the respondents, with a further 4 per cent from non-manual backgrounds. Intellectual ability, a scholarship as a replacement for economic capital, the expansion of both higher education and the economy, and the development of newly acquired social capital and educational credentials opened the doors to a professional career for such women. For the great majority of the women in our study, far more effective was the strategic deployment of the economic, social and cultural capitals available to women from middle-class backgrounds, ratified by educational qualifications. This supports

Bourdieu's view that educational credentials are favoured as a system of class reproduction – not because of the perfect reproduction of individuals in the social position of their parents, but because of legitimating and disguising an arbitrary system of power.

Thus, the main resources called upon by our respondents to access educational qualifications were the cultural capital of the family in appreciating the value and understanding the processes of higher education, together with the symbolic capital of an elite institution or the possibility of a high-status professional career if the family was opposed. These were invoked when women lacked economic capital, or lacked control over it. For gaining access to professional employment positions, social capital was the most important resource, together with the cultural capital credentialised by educational qualifications, although again social capital was not always directly controlled by individual women. For women without access to 'inherited' capitals, structural change in the form of economic expansion in higher education and employment was crucial to developing new social networks, new bodies of knowledge and expertise, and new sources of economic accumulation.

Negotiating New Family Lifestyles

We now look at how women who were able to acquire capitals through their professions might use them to negotiate new family lifestyles and relationships.

Negotiating singlehood

In Part IV we saw that just over a third of our respondents were unmarried – a significantly higher proportion than women's rate of singlehood in the general population. Among the older women, this was partly the result of male wartime deaths. Among the majority who undertook their education after the war, singlehood was often a choice – either because they preferred a career to marriage, or because they were actively opposed to marriage, as we saw in Part V. Men, of course, did not have to choose.

Kiuchi Fumie started working as an academic in 1967:

> I live in a joint family with my mother, my brother and his family. There's antagonism between my brother and me – very subtle irritating factors. Men don't like women to be superior to them. That's the problem between my brother and me, and also the reason I can't get married. I plan to live alone soon.

By 1989, Kiuchi-san had moved out of the family home and was living alone. The only reason she had been able to refuse marriage and set up her own household was the fact that she was financially self-supporting. Nagasaki Chizuko started her career in the media in 1960:

> My mother is a lawyer and a college lecturer; I thought it natural to work after university. I lost my father at the age of six and my mother was very busy rearing four children. Up to ten years ago she sometimes advised me to think about marriage, but since she was terribly busy she couldn't do as much as other mothers might. Whenever a marriage proposal was brought in, it had a condition that I would have to stop working.

In her forties Nagasaki-san found her own partner, and by 1989 she was married.

Negotiating marriage

Some women resisted an arranged marriage and successfully negotiated a 'love match'. Nojiro Chiyoko got her job in a media company three years before reaching the marriageable age:

> I took the decision to have a career for economic reasons. I didn't follow my family's advice about whom to marry. I wanted to support myself so I could lead my own life freely, such as to marry my present husband.

Women also resisted their parents' opposition to their own choice of partner. Yamaguchi Kyoko was a professor:

> My husband is a Christian minister; we fell in love and got married. My parents opposed me when I wanted to marry a minister. They were against me for three years. When I found a job as an assistant lecturer, I declared I would leave home. At this point they finally compromised, and I was allowed to get married.

The economic independence provided by Yamaguchi-san's first job was the crucial factor in enabling her to marry the man of her choice. Women also chose to marry late, often well after the marriageable age – either because they preferred to remain single rather than give up their career, or because they preferred to make their own choice of husband.

Kikuchi Ieko wanted to be a doctor, but her training would take her beyond the age of marriage. She started work in 1970:

My father opposed my wish to be a doctor at the time of the entrance exams to medical college. The reason was I would miss the marriageable age. I compromised and took the exams for Tsuda College and Tokyo Christian Women's College. But I also applied to do medicine at a university. Fortunately I passed all the exams, and my parents didn't lose face. Then I decided to take medical college.

Dr Kikuchi's strategy of applying to her own and her parents' choice, and then choosing the university with the most symbolic capital, enabled her to complete her training and marry later.

Hosaka Hisako got her PhD in 1957 from the USA, and was a lecturer in English:

I married late, and on the basis that he would cooperate, otherwise I wouldn't have married. Since I'd married late, I'd established my name, so my in-laws had to respect me.

Kuba Taeko, a director with a large company, finished her education in 1964:

I wasn't much interested in marriage. But I told myself I'd only marry someone who'd want me to continue working. That was the first condition. My husband conceded this – he was my classmate at Tokyo University.

Hosaka-san and Kuba-san negotiated their right to paid work as a condition of marriage. It was the economic capital and symbolic power of a professional career that enabled them to challenge their position in the family, to choose whom, when and under what conditions they married, or to decide against marriage altogether.

Some women who had negotiated the 'career' condition before marriage found that the agreement broke down after childbirth. Iwasaki Keiko was a manager:

Before we married my husband said it was good for women to work. After marriage he said different. After I had a baby he wanted me to stay home. I wouldn't, so we got divorced. He changed after marriage. Pressure came from my husband and the child. Now I live with my mother and my son. The pressure on my husband came from the working environment – we both worked at the same place.

Iwasaki-san was willing to divorce rather than give up her career, and her husband was willing to break their agreement rather than save his marriage. Hattori Hisako wanted to marry a foreigner because she thought it would solve the problem of the attitude to a working wife.

She was public-relations director for a Japanese subsidiary of a US company, and finished her education in 1964:

> I wanted to marry a foreigner because I think women should be treated equally. My husband is American. I married a non-Japanese because when I was twenty-four all the men I met were upset because I wanted to work and because I earned more than them. I thought a foreigner would be better. I was sick of the framework of Japanese society. This American's outlook on working women fitted with mine, so I married him. My husband was proud of presenting me to his family as a successful career woman.
>
> Now we're getting divorced. My husband was affected by the Japanese influence – he's been here seventeen years. My social environment changed me too. He works in a Japanese company, I in an American company. He stays in this Japanese environment; I change and develop. Divorce is sad, but I had to choose my way. Women need security too. I have to work, it's my life. Work is like my two arms and legs, it's me, I can't give it up. He complained because I work. He was threatened because I did better than him.

Although Hattori-san's husband appreciated the symbolic capital of a 'successful career woman', when her achievements excelled his own he became resentful of her success. The myth that western men were 'liberated' and 'treated women equally' by virtue of being foreign was exposed here. Although Hattori-san blamed the 'Japanese influence', it was clear from our examples that some Japanese husbands behaved more 'equally' towards their wives than did Hattori-san's.

There were also women who had rejected the formality of marriage and chosen to live with a partner outside wedlock. Okazaki Yumiko was a manager in a department store:

> I was already working in the department store when I met my partner. When I was around twenty-five or twenty-six my mother often told me to get married and stay at home, since that's where she believes women's happiness lies. I wanted to stay free. You can't be free to do what you want unless you have a job. But when I was thinking I must listen to her and meet men introduced as prospective grooms, I met my partner. I chose him feeling all my doubts were cleared. His mother came to accept our lifestyle as a new way of life and didn't interfere with us. She thinks we are quite different people from her generation.

Shimizu Kyoko was single, and by 1989 she had chosen to have a child. She was an academic and lived with her mother, a businesswoman, and her son:

I don't think I intentionally acted to take up professional work, but what I thought was, I'd be happy if I could get economic power by doing what I like. I wanted economic power. I also felt strongly against the traditional consciousness of people concerning sexual divisions and men's and women's sex roles, which led me into this profession.

Renegotiating the family hierarchy

A wide variety of different arrangements were negotiated by our respondents to deal with the demands of home and work. Each strategy had implications for changing power relations in the network of social relations within which this group of women was embedded.

Many women negotiated new ways of co-operative living, based on more egalitarian joint families as opposed to the traditional hierarchical structure based on gender and generation. Sato Ikuko practised medicine; her children were 5 and 3:

I don't take the children to a day-care centre; I didn't like it from my own childhood experiences, and I have my own beliefs about childrearing. Though everything was not satisfactory, I left it all to my mother-in-law. At first she wasn't very understanding, but I was very patient to educate her. I was a little afraid whether I could raise children well if I left them to the care of my mother-in-law, but I did. The process of bringing it to this level was very hard. But the children love their grandmother and lead a happy life. When my mother-in-law doesn't feel very well or the children are sick, I try to come home earlier. Since the children have grown up a little, it's now a little easier.

Yoshioka Terumi worked at a publishing company, and had two children:

The joint family structure helps. We needed domestic help, so I asked my aunt, who's a widow, to live with us when my daughter was born. We pay her. My parents live next door and can visit us easily.

These more egalitarian joint families were based on new relationships between women – sometimes paid relationships, but mostly unpaid female family labour. Previously the mother-in-law had exercised power over the daughter-in-law by virtue of her age and position as head of the female hierarchy in the household. In the new form of joint family, the mother-in-law (or mother) provided the duty of care to the daughter-in-law, breaking down the traditional authority structure and creating networks of female solidarity across age divisions.

Reproducing class relations

Although almost a quarter of the respondents lived in joint families, the majority (61 per cent) lived in nuclear families. Most of those who did not have access to family labour relied on the market for domestic work. Kitamura Masako had a young son; she had been working as a doctor since 1973:

> The child is a demanding creature, but I didn't know a baby brings joy and fulfilment to home life until I had him. The baby goes to a nursery, then a neighbour takes care of him until 9 p.m. I don't cook. The baby is fed by the neighbour; my husband and I eat out. It makes me more free. I don't clean the house often. There's no help from either family, so I look for a helper myself. Usually one of my patients helps me with the housework, so it's an advantage to be a doctor to find a housekeeper easily. The problem lies in the social structure where women have to struggle themselves without social or institutional help.

Nojiro Chiyoko, who worked at a media company, had one child:

> Before my daughter went to primary school I got a housekeeper, which took most of my salary. I did no housework at all. Although my daughter was sometimes unreasonably demanding, I didn't take too much notice. I brought her up using my own mother as a model. Though she was a latchkey child, I asked neighbours and relatives never to call her a poor child. It would be hopeless if she thinks of herself as a poor girl. She's now twelve, and may have some opinions about her mother not staying at home, but she never complains about it. Women should do the childcare to a certain degree, but I'm an exception! I left it to the housekeeper by day and my husband at night. He has no resistance against men doing housework or women working outside. This company is famous as one of the biggest industries in the country, and my family are proud of me working for it.

The economic capital attached to Nojiro-san's profession allowed her to employ domestic labour, but it was the symbolic capital of a career in the media that enabled her to persuade her husband to take a share of the childcare, and legitimated her failure to perform household work herself.

Women also used paid help in joint families. Ishihara Mayumi was a professor of law with two children:

> When I got married, my husband and I lived with his parents. They were sick in bed for two years and died one after the other, but we hired two people who were very helpful, which was a great help to me. In the year my parents-in-law died I gave birth to my second child, and the person who looked after my mother-in-law also took care of the baby. I overcame the difficulties with the help of these kind maids, but it was entirely by individual effort, and I don't want to see young people of today and tomorrow have the same experience.

Ishihara-san used her economic capital to delegate her duty of care, but she saw the solution in a new infrastructure rather than individual arrangements. Wakabayashi Yasuko was a government servant with two children:

> There was pressure from the family; my mother-in-law didn't like me working, especially after I had the children. Sometimes there were difficulties finding a maid. She lived with us, and kept saying I should give up because of the problems. But gradually she came round, because I got a better job than her son. When I had only one child I had a living-out maid; when I had two I had a living-in maid, and my mother-in-law helped at that time. Sometimes I considered giving up, but I managed. My mother-in-law helps me when the maid doesn't come, but it's good for her too. If I'm at home there are quarrels. Sometimes she oppresses me mentally. But her attitude is changing. She's getting older, so she's more dependent on me; therefore she's getting better. With my family I didn't ask for my husband's help, I did everything, so my husband thought I *could* do it. I asked him later and it was too late.

Wakabayashi-san attributed her mother-in-law's changing attitude to the symbolic capital of her job, but unlike Nojiro-san she failed to deploy this capital to change her husband's approach to household work.

These women, rather than developing new relationships within the female hierarchy, were reproducing old ones, deploying their economic capital to resolve the double workload through the use of domestic servants. Both strategies, however, rested on the labour of other women, redistributing the duty of care either amongst unpaid women family workers or paid female employees, and leaving middle-class men in the same position of privilege within the family as before. Neither strategy challenged men's relationship to domesticity. Many women wished to share housework and childcare, but only a few had managed to induce their husbands to participate in family labour. The factors ranged against such a strategy were formidable: the demands of capitalism and the global economy; the construction of masculinity; and the deficits in symbolic capital attached to the performance of household labour, which had much greater significance for men than they did for women.

As we argued above, women could take on men's professional jobs because they were saturated with symbolic capital and brought respect, but men could not easily perform women's work because it was deficient in symbolic capital and evoked disrespect. This was both the reason that the struggle to change gender relations seemed at times to be so intractable, and a cause for appreciation and celebration when change was achieved.

Thus, a third strategy involved envisaging and working towards changes in the gender division of labour, and more egalitarian relationships between men and women. The fact that this strategy involved challenging the value of the symbolic capitals attached to different social practices meant that it may have been less open to resolution through negotiation, and did not exclude the possibility of conflict and confrontation.

Challenging power relations

Onuma Youko challenged gendered power relations in the family, this time between husband and wife. She finished her medical training in 1971:

> I have two children; the little one is only eleven months old, and childcare hinders my career very much. My mother supported me, but I don't have much contact with my mother-in-law and can't guess how she feels. She complains I don't care much about my husband, and suggests I work part-time while the children are little. I get upset when I hear this. Why blame only the wife? I can't imagine giving up work. When we moved from Fukuoka to Tokyo I stayed at home for three months before I was employed at this hospital. I felt I might go insane then.
>
> I insist my husband must do the same amount of housework, and he's quite co-operative; he tries to do his best, but the fact is I'm responsible for the housework in most cases. Nurseries only open till 6 p.m. I always stop working so I will get to the nursery in time. The two children go to different nurseries and my husband and I take one each back home.
>
> Being married to my classmate, I think I have the same ability, academic background and experiences as my husband. But after years of married life it's quite clear my husband is more advanced academically and socially. We are personally unequal, and the cause is that I'm spending much more time on housework and childcare. Since both of us have the same profession, what makes the difference?

Dr Onuma had achieved some success in changing gendered power relations in her marital relationship. But she had not by any means achieved an equal sharing of household duties, and felt deeply aggrieved by the effect of this on her profession.

Takahashi Yoshiko, who practised as a doctor, had a son. She challenged the structure of power relations in the family based not only on gender but also on generation:

> I married while at graduate school. My husband is also a doctor. He promised to give me full support to my establishing a career. When I

married, my in-laws thought I would give up work if I had a child, but I didn't. My husband was the eldest child and only son, and we were prepared to live with his parents, but they told me they didn't like my working. When I consulted my father, he said it's okay for my family to look after my son. So I left my husband's house. But he then left his own family too, and we lived in a small apartment, leaving the child with my family until he started primary school. Since then the three of us have been living together. I couldn't get along with my parents-in-law, but my own family gave me full support. My parents fully supported me without criticism. Most of the time my mother took care of my son; when she wasn't available my brother's wife or sister did it. These three women took all the care.

My in-laws thought at first that taking care of the child was something they couldn't help with, but faced with the reality they realised they wouldn't want to make such a sacrifice. After that my husband's youngest sister was left a widow when her husband died young. Previously my mother-in-law had thought daughters should be brought up for marriage and family, but after that, and seeing me, she changed to the extent of advising her daughter to go to technical school. Now I have no trouble with the parents-in-law; rather they see me as a good example to follow.

Dr Takahashi used the social capital invested in her natal family, and the economic capital deriving from her profession, to change the power relations in her marital family based on gender and generation. Her challenge to the traditional authority structure of the family was ratified first by her natal family, then by her husband, and finally by the tragedy involving her sister-in-law, which together produced not only a change in family practice but a radical change of perspective by the older generation.

Finally, many women recognised the need for an infrastructure which would enable women as well as men to contribute to their profession. Matsumoto Mie worked as a civil servant:

Unless we have a system which allows women to get a job, take leave and then come back, there will only be a few women who can continue working throughout their lives. The problems that mothers face are the problems that all of us in society should face. They are not individual matters.

Matsumoto-san argued for change in the organisation of work at a structural rather than individual level, on the grounds that the reproduction of the family was a social issue rather than a personal problem.

Thus, the main resources called upon by the respondents in changing social practices in the family were the economic capital produced by a professional job, or the symbolic capital attached to the prospect of such a job. The generation of an independent income was a vital source of power for women, and enabled them to decide whether, when and whom to marry, to stipulate conditions for marriage, and to negotiate a new position of power in the family. They also deployed their economic capital to delegate their duty of care in the family to paid female employees, which introduced or maintained relationships of inequality between women in a domestic setting. They drew on their social capital within the family and their cultural capital in the form of skill in social relations to renegotiate more egalitarian relationships with other, often older female relatives, and in some cases negotiated new domestic relations with their husbands, to redistribute household work; and they invoked the symbolic capital of the profession to legitimate these redistributions. They used all these forms of capital to challenge power relations based on age and gender, successfully asserting their entitlement to a family and a career. Although women had effected structural change in the family, however, structural change in the organisation of employment to accommodate women's new patterns of life was strictly limited.

In terms of class reproduction, the entry of middle-class women into professional and managerial positions, and their partial withdrawal from and renegotiation of their position in the family, had several effects. First, it increased the differential between the classes, both in terms of the accumulation of economic capital in a two-career professional family, and in terms of the deployment of that capital to delegate the duty of care for the family. Second, it increased the ability of the class to reproduce itself across generations, particularly under circumstances of adversity when daughters' enhancing of their inherited cultural capital through education could facilitate the regaining of lost economic capital and class distinction, or where a high-profile working wife could add cultural, economic and symbolic capital by virtue of her success in a profession. What was visible in these changing social practices was an increasing flexibility in the sexual division of labour, which formerly made men responsible for economic and women for cultural capital accumulation. Thus, in line with Bourdieu's view, gender relations *within* the class may have enhanced the division *between* the classes.

Chapter 26

Changing Subjectivities

In this chapter we examine women's own representations of their subjectivities, looking at how they understood and legitimated their position as middle-class women with professional careers. First, we argue that social relations, obligations to others, and appropriate ways of acting were in flux, and were defined in different and variable ways. Second, while our respondents took up a position in the discourse of women's entitlement, they linked this position to family duty, the development of a mature selfhood, and obligations to society.

Supporting the Family

Most of our respondents gave a combination of explanations for their position as professional women, invoking family, self and society to legitimate the anomalous position of a professionally employed woman. The justification provided by the largest number of women was economic. Two-thirds (68 per cent) claimed that economic necessity was a major reason for working, although few gave this reason on its own. This constituted 34 per cent of women who were single, 4 per cent who were divorced and 30 per cent who were married. The latter were helping to support family members in their natal or marital families, including dependants who did not live with them. The financial obligation to the family was invoked here as a fundamental justification for women's professional employment, even in the middle class. There were also women whose husbands or fathers had died, and whose earnings had enabled the family to survive. Among younger women such family histories lived on, justifying their desire for a job which could provide economic security. Onuma Youko, a doctor:

The early death of my father made me think I had to get a career for economic stability. I wanted a career with no sex discrimination, with equal wages and long-term duration. To be a doctor was the best way. If my husband dies I won't be at a loss. If I were divorced I could work equally like a man. I looked at my mother and got the idea.

In a reversal of gender roles, other women provided financial support for their spouse. Ohashi Kimiko, a management consultant:

My husband was a radical student leader when we were at university. I wasn't politically radical, but I was radical about women. This drew us together. I helped him out of trouble. When we were first married my husband was still at university so I worked to support him. His family were so grateful because I helped him financially and got him out of trouble. When he got a job he sent me to business school in the USA in return.

More interesting in a middle-class context is the invocation of a better lifestyle. Kato Atsuko was a physics lecturer with two young children:

My salary is 100 per cent necessary because we bought a new house and have to pay for the loan. We can live on my husband's income, but it's not possible to buy a house without my help.

Nagayama Junko taught sociology, and also had two young children:

I'm 100 per cent dependent on my income. My husband's salary isn't enough even if I tried to be very economical. A lecturer's salary isn't enough to support a family if you want to do anything.

The idea of the professional wife's devotion to the family through the provision of a salary to improve living standards had a rather different meaning here from that of Kondo's women factory workers contributing a part-time wage to make ends meet (Kondo 1990: 284). It represented a new means of moving up in the world, producing or reproducing a new form of social respectability, and constructing class distinction.

Developing a Mature Self

The next major reason for working, claimed by 42 per cent of the respondents, was for self-development and self-realisation. This was a potent motivation and it was often defined as part of the 'hard path to maturity' (Kondo 1990: 108–9). Kimura Hideko was a manager in an airline company:

My husband and I are now living separately to continue our respective jobs. He was transferred to Kofu some years ago. The difficulty is to combine family and career. If women neglect responsibility for the family, there's no meaning to their working. I think doing both perfectly is very important, so combining career and family was very hard. I couldn't leave one job half done. I overcame these difficulties with good health and a hard spirit. Even now I get up at 5 a.m. to get breakfast, I see every member leave home and then I go to work. We have our breakfast at 6 a.m. I leave work around 6 p.m., arriving home about 7.30 p.m., and then take care of the housework. I go to bed around 12.00 after organising things. My mother stays at home. As to cleaning the house, I ask someone else. I do grocery shopping on days off. When I started working for this company I usually stayed at work till about 8 p.m., and then did housework after that. Housework is definitely a woman's job; you can't leave it to others because you have a job. It's not good to work outside and do no housework at all. Childcare, too, is a woman's job; it's important to bring them up with close physical contact without leaving the care to others. I'm two different people at home and work. I myself think it's strange, but even when I exhaust my energy at work, I never worry about it at home. I can keep a good balance using my head at work and my body at home.

Kimura-san sustained a double workload through 'good health and a hard spirit', but this was not a position available to the faint-hearted, since it required prodigious resources of energy and feats of organisation, modelled on those of the professional or managerial man. If the 'corporate warrior' achieved maturity and power through long hours of devotion to the organisation, the performance of a double workload by the 'woman warrior' showed that she was even stronger than a man. The two jobs of the full-time working mother became a mark of endurance, an index of fortitude, and a manifestation of power marking out the professional woman as displaying even greater stamina and maturity than her husband.

There was a fine line, however, between the economic contribution to the family and the development of the mature self on the one hand, and the more individualistic justification of financial and social independence and the 'selfish' fulfilment of personal desires on the other. Sato Taeko was a married doctor with no children:

From being a very small child I wanted to be independent. It was very natural. It's unusual for a woman, but I'm not interested in what other people think.

Ouchida Mariko was an unmarried doctor:

In high school I had the following idea and since then tried hard to build it up into a steady and solid one. First I have a rather selfish aspect in my personality, so I thought I would not be able to stay at home and do housekeeping, following the husband's ideas. I wanted to work.

The identification of independence with selfishness was one with which respondents struggled, posing the 'individualism of western influence' (Kondo 1990: 114) against the pleasure of a personal identity and the demands of a professional job. Many of them valued independence, and felt that it was one of the most satisfying aspects of being a professional woman. Ohashi Kimiko, a management consultant:

I want to be independent above all things. I'd go crazy if I had to stay in the house. I work for independence and a feeling of accomplishment. No one asks me about my husband, they're interested in *me*. I have my own friends, not just his. I have a personal identity – I enjoy that more than the job.

Shimizu Ayuchi justified her career by sacrificing career ambitions to the family, and choosing instead a 'balanced life':

I don't have many aspirations. I live day by day. In theory I'd like to see areas opened up for capable women, but not for myself. I don't think about career ambitions for positions I would have if I were a man. For I'm a woman and want to move ahead balancing family and career.

Sato Ikuko:

I'm in favour of women working, but I don't think it's good for them to push too hard on the surface. I don't like to work denying I'm a woman. I don't reduce the amount of work, but I work under the premiss that I have a family and children. I wouldn't accept an opportunity for promotion even if it were offered. If I did, family life would be affected.

Here the sacrifice of personal ambition for the well-being of the family was seen as a means to achieving self-realisation *as a woman*, as opposed to proving oneself stronger than a man.

Contributing to Society

Kondo argues that the idea of work as a 'service to the group' held currency amongst Japanese employment organisations in the late 1970s, and one of the main reasons for working was the desire to contribute to society (Kondo 1990: 198). Of our respondents, 38 per cent claimed as a reason for working the desire to return the benefits of a professional education to society; this also gave them a sense of belonging and participation in the community. Fukao Mitsuko:

> I don't need the money; we can live on my husband's salary. I work to be a member of society, to contribute as much as possible to the welfare of others. There's a sense of belonging to society.

Kagayama Mariko:

> I have to work for an income. I like using my talents. I'm 50 per cent economically dependent on the income. But I love this work. I had a large part of my education at government expense, so I feel I must return it to society in some way. The benefit is an equal salary and a sense of fulfilment.

The contribution that one could make to society was interpreted in different ways, often shaped by one's background. Shishiba Fumiko, the daughter of a judge, studied at Tokyo University, took a postgraduate degree in the USA, and then joined government service. Her entire outlook was international:

> When I was very young I wanted to be equal with men, and I wanted to do something for society, so I joined the civil service. I had aspirations since I was very young; I wanted to be in the civil service since primary school. Working for the government isn't for private profit. We all have a sort of confidence that we work for the nation, although we don't know how much we really do. I value the sense of participation.

Inokuma Ryoko, in contrast, took a degree in economics and then joined government service. Her father was an ivory craftsman who was educated only up to primary school. She saw society as fragmented, justifying her position in terms of bringing benefits to disadvantaged groups within the collectivity of the nation:

> I wanted strongly to make some contribution to improving the standard of living of low-class labourers. I thought even a woman could do something from the administrative aspect. I didn't have ambitions, but I wanted to make administration meet the needs of workers. My aspirations are to create an administration which can improve the working conditions of low-income workers, small household industry workers, including women. To do this I have to hold an appropriate position.

This contribution to society was also construed in terms of developing, improving or changing it. Niimura Misako:

I want to make women's position in Japan higher by working myself – it's an individual thing. It's very difficult to make society better for women by revolution; it must be done step by step individually. Women working is a very good thing for the development of society.

And Iwasaki Keiko:

I'm a hundred per cent dependent on my salary. I'm divorced, and I support myself, my mother and my son. I've also done a lot and contributed to changing Japan – that's what motivates me. According to history, in the Meiji Restoration, there were three stages. First, the pioneers were all killed. Second, the next cohort were unfortunate, but stayed longer and got good positions. We need the sacrifice of pioneers, and I decided to be a pioneer. I don't expect a position of high prestige, but I want to open up the jungle for followers. That's my aim, dedication to the cause, and I've been successful. I'm satisfied when I can change Japan! I devoted this and the last year to the welfare of single-parent families. The government started a new system of subsistence grants: for up to one year a mother can train without charge, and the public employment office finds her a suitable job. So a mother on her own isn't destitute. I put this idea to the government. When mothers are happy with this system, I'll be happy.

Okazaki Teruko:

I want to think of how we can change society. I want to appeal to housewives that they must act after giving thought to what kind of society they really want. For everyone to lead a happy life, society must change. I hope in the end women can develop their own abilities and individualities without being locked inside the home. When I first started working it was the meaning to my life, but I realised economic independence brings spiritual freedom, and it's such a wonderful thing to have financial power through my work experiences. I can develop myself as a person and my abilities through work.

Niimura-san understood her contribution to society as changing gender relations through the personal performance of a new role. Iwasaki-san's contribution, as a divorced mother, was to draw on Japanese history for a model of how to transform a personal gender problem into a public issue. Okazaki-san's was to use her job in the media to campaign for changes to women's position in society. All three were working for change in social relations and social structures, and in doing so were achieving self-realisation, contributing to the development of society, and exercising power as social subjects.

Being, and Failing to Be, the Professional Housewife

Kondo argues that part-time women factory workers defined themselves both with and against the professional housewife discourse (Kondo 1990: 280). Our professional women did this too, although on this question there was a marked distinction between the older and younger women, and between the single and married women.

Approximately half our respondents thought that housework and childcare should be shared between husband and wife, and a quarter thought it was women's work. A further quarter were unsure or unclear in their answers, reflecting the ambiguity and uncertainty of social practices and identities in a state of flux. Among those who thought that these tasks belonged to women, older women who received most of their education before or during the war, and single women who had not experienced trying to cope with work and home, were significantly overrepresented. Younger mothers who took up this position, however, often construed domestic work as both a 'disciplinary' means to self-realisation, and a source of pleasure through the provision of the duty of care. Kikuchi Ieko, born in 1945, was a married doctor with one daughter:

> As a discipline, anyone can do housework. I'm not for the idea that mundane work is women's business, although it might be true that women have more aptitude for it. But generally women keep things cleaner than men, and there are more women who love to cook than men. Besides, many women find it satisfying and pleasant to please men they love by making something for them.

Among those who thought household work should be shared between husband and wife, many positioned themselves within the professional housewife discourse in practice, but against it in principle. Ishihara Mayumi was born between the wars, in 1923. She was a professor with two children:

> Housework isn't necessarily all women's job. It should be shared by men and women as much as possible. Women in my generation are absolutely incapable of doing so, but I expect young men will get better from now on. Whether a woman is working or not, the man and the woman must both be involved in childcare. For example, at PTA meetings the school addresses only mothers and children, and doesn't take fathers into consideration from the beginning. We must think something is wrong with this situation.

Onuma Youko was born after the war, in 1946. She was a doctor with two children:

I want to be able to vote for a person who insists that housework should be a required subject at school for both boys and girls. Why can't a man do housework? I get mad when I think about this problem. Husbands can't do any housework thoroughly without the help of a wife. They need to be trained from childhood too.

Respondents also justified their position by the changing demographic patterns of family life. Kawase Sekiko was married with two children, lectured in physics, and was born in 1934:

My husband said housework is just as worthwhile as work outside the home, but I couldn't agree. If I had ten children maybe, but with two children it wasn't enough for me. Moreover, housekeeping doesn't satisfy one's intellectual needs, and I was afraid my intellectual abilities might become weak. I wanted to work where I could make use of my education. I couldn't get rid of the curiosity to pursue my interests. I tried many times but couldn't. These days the number of children per family is getting small, and women have more and more free time. So they take care of their children too much. They have so much energy left over, they spend it to prevent children being independent.

Kiuchi Fumie was single, a lecturer in English born in 1936:

Now women have too much free time, but men don't let them go out to work, so they concentrate all their energy on the children. It makes the children very competitive. Mothers are overprotective; children are less independent.

Okazaki Yumiko, deputy manager in a department store:

I live in a workers' housing complex, where many housewives have twenty-four hours all for themselves but lead an idle life. I feel sorry for them. Women should work. Anyone should pass through such a hurdle in life if they are to be called a human being.

Although in practice women were mostly responsible for the housework and childcare, and delegated it to the paid or unpaid labour of other women, many of them envisaged a gender redistribution of household responsibilities. They demonstrated their maturity and capacity for hard work by performing the duty of care alongside their professional work. But they also legitimated failing to act as full-time housewives with reference to demographic changes, seeing the professional housewife as underemployed, leading a 'boring' life, overindulging her children and creating too much 'dependency'. In this way women employed in a profession distinguished themselves from full-time professional housewives and created distinctions between women *within* the middle class.

Being a Working Woman

If professional women created an identity separate from that of the full-time professional housewife, how did they distinguish themselves from working mothers in part-time factory work or short-term clerical jobs? Kondo argues that the discourse of male artisanal work as self-realisation and aesthetic creativity was a way of creating cultural difference and legitimating hierarchical relations in the workplace (Kondo 1990: 230–31). The narrative of professional employment as creativity, self-development and self-realisation was also a way of creating hierarchical relations between women. In a similar manner to the construction of skilled craft work, professionalism was based on the exclusion of those who were not qualified as professionals. Yamaji Atsuko was a sociology lecturer:

> My having a PhD influenced people's treatment of me as equal to men. Without it, like most women, I wouldn't have been someone noticeable. I wouldn't have been satisfied as an average person. Because people don't think women are 'people', they'd ignore women's work. The fact that I got a PhD from the USA influenced my friends – they gave me more respect. I knew I would become a professional so society would treat me as someone. Being a girl isn't someone. I used to work for a publishing company; clients would say: 'Aren't I important enough that they send me a woman editor?' I wanted professional knowledge to get respect. I was mad at men outside the company; I felt angry towards the clients. It was a shock to me how clients treated me. But if I were a professional, people would treat me as independent and a proper person. I became a professional for independence and respect. I like having a professional job because of the autonomy and independence. If I gave up I'd go crazy, I'd be an impossible person to live with.

Invoking the symbolic power of an elite education, and the respectability due to the holder of a professional position, was a way of establishing professional women's distinctiveness compared to other working women.

The discourse of professional work created power and hierarchy through the economic capital of a professional salary, but also through the social capital of a network of important people. Nojiro Chiyoko worked for a media company:

> It's valuable to live a life related to society. It's fantastic to meet many great people in this life and listen to them talk so that we can produce a programme. I can meet or talk on the phone to almost anyone if I identify myself by my name card as a member of this organisation. I doubt if I could stay quietly at home.

The discourse of professionalism also created power through the symbolic capital attached to a woman in a high-profile job. Shishiba Fumiko:

> I experienced an advantage at the UN. You have to be known – being one of the few women, I had a great advantage.

Having a name and being known was a mark of the respect deriving from the symbolic capital of a professional position. And just as full-time housewives questioned the professional woman's commitment to the family as they dropped their children off at the same kindergarten, our respondents emphasised their own commitment and questioned the commitment to work of other women. Shishiba-san contrasted herself with 'younger' women –

> The younger generation take work lightly; they give up very easily on marriage. This makes it difficult for women who want to work seriously.

– while Higashiura Hisami, who taught English, drew a distinction between middle-class women who worked only 'for money' and those who were 'well-motivated and prepared':

> The present trend of many women working outside the home is very welcome, but I'm partly opposed to it. Some work merely to get money and neglect the family. I'm referring to middle-, not working-class women. They are wasting their time. But if they are well-motivated and prepared, it's very good for women to have work and home at the same time.

Thus, the discourse of professionalism as creativity, the exclusions of educational qualifications, and the economic, social and symbolic capitals attached to women in the professions, enabled our respondents to distinguish themselves from other women, who worked 'only for money', or were 'wasting their time'. It also enabled them to create power and hierarchy between different classes of working women, and to legitimate their own positions as middle-class, professionally employed women.

As well as legitimating by various means the discourse and practice of women's professional entitlements, and the construction of hierarchies of power in women's employment, our respondents linked the meaning of gendered employment relations to Japan's position in the world community. As Kondo has suggested, work and family are sites of historical struggles in the changing international political economy, and questions of global capitalism, class relations, westernisation, and the creation of a Japanese identity formed the backdrop for the organisation of work, family, gender and labour relations (Kondo 1990: 197). Japan's dual positioning in the global contest for power was reflected in its economic success and its cultural 'difference'. In attempting to account for Japan's place in the global community, our respondents adopted opposing approaches to how gender relations linked into their position in the world.

Takita Fumiko was a professor of psychology, educated at Keio and Yale:

> I think Japan is one of the most free countries. A great deal of options are open to women. Women who want to be career women can; house-wife is not a dirty word. She can be happy and perhaps more liberated. American women have a lot of constant pressure to work.

Iwasaki Keiko was a company manager, educated at Tokyo University and in the USA:

> Men are supposed to be old-fashioned, but I don't agree. I think Japa-nese are very good at adopting new ideas.

Takita-san positioned Japanese women as 'more liberated' and with more choice than western women; while Iwasaki-san constructed Japanese men as 'modern' and open to new ways of thinking.

A contrasting position was taken by Yoshioka Terumi, a manager in a publishing company, educated at Tokyo University and Iowa, USA:

> Compared to western countries Japanese men aren't liberated enough. Without men's co-operation, women can't be fully liberated. So Japan is very strange, an island country not aware of world trends.

Okazaki Yumiko was a deputy manager in a department store, one of only two managers with no qualifications:

> Our society has the traditional idea that women should stay at home, but it has no basis at all. By this thinking women are disadvantaged in this old-established system, since sex-role differentiation is very strong and explicit. But if we continue to maintain such a system, we'll be left behind in the world.

Yoshioka-san positioned Japan as unfree, 'unaware' and globally back-ward because men were 'not liberated' compared to those in the West; while Okazaki-san understood this 'old way of thinking' as detrimental to Japan's place in the world, 'left behind' in the contest. Whichever way the comparison with the West was made, the two opposing approaches concurred that gender relations positioned the nation on the scale of civilisation, for both perspectives saw gender relations as playing a crucial role in the construction of Japanese identity and its symbolic capital in the global field of power.

Different Worlds

We have examined in some detail the changes in social practice and subjectivity undertaken by the professional women in our study. We have argued that these changes were of sufficient significance to 'make a difference' to the construction of gendered class identities in Japan. Finally in this chapter we look at the way these changes have created 'different worlds' in terms of the social relations of gender, age and class.

Sato Taeko worked as a pathologist; she began her career in 1961:

> In the beginning, when I started work, most of my colleagues were very kind to me, but as time passes they are changing. The first reason is that I'm not so ladylike! My superiors didn't find me compatible. It's because I don't behave in the way they expect me to – femininely. Professional women have to lose their woman-like character, which men expect to see, such as a feminine manner and mood. The speaking speed of professional women is very high, with a very businesslike tone. The facial expression is different: more masculine, cooler. We become more logical, less emotional.

Our respondents' identities had changed in a way which was visible on the body and in the behaviour of the women concerned, creating a world in which many men did not know how to respond.

Kawase Sekiko taught physics; she began her career in 1962:

> When I talk with Americans or Europeans I'm impressed that women talk to men on equal terms. In Japan the way of talking between men and women isn't equal. My children often wonder why I change my way of talking to my husband, not to mention my manners in front of his parents or my mother. When I have my husband do the housework she gets so surprised she does it herself, in spite of her old age.
>
> I take care of my two homes, my own and my mother's, but I think it's better for the two not to live together, since their ways of thinking are so different. My family lives in Tokyo, but I have to go to Kamakura to take care of my mother. I spend three days a week in each city, and do all the commuting. My husband is co-operative, but can only do so much.

The change in Kawase-san's world compared with that of her mother's generation was such that both of them preferred to keep the two worlds apart. Kawase-san was a different person with her husband, when she was in the presence of the older and the younger generations. Although she could enact both subjectivities, the problem was not to keep the generations apart, but to prevent her fluctuating marital relationship from being simultaneously framed by two contradictory social contexts.

Ouchida Mariko has practised as an anaesthetist since 1975. Her change of worlds was based on social mobility and an approach to work based on a different class position. Dr Ouchida's father was a carpenter:

> Since I became a medical student and then a doctor, my family has gradually been feeling, as time goes on, as if I were no longer a daughter in their family. They can't understand what in the world I'm doing. At first I tried to explain, but gradually I find it hard to talk about my work, since I'm afraid they don't understand. They've come to feel not only that they don't understand my work but also that I'm doing some work which has no relation to them whatsoever, living in a completely different world.

Despite her mother's familiarity with medicine through her work as a rural nurse, the family experienced Dr Ouchida's rise to a high-prestige profession as deeply alienating. As she talked about the person she was in her family and the person she has become in her profession, there was a strong sense of the social distance she had travelled, and continued to travel each time she moved from one context of gendered class positioning to the other. These women inhabited different worlds, but they were also partly worlds of their own making.

Chapter 27

Women in the New Heisei Era

Continuity and Change

In 1989, when we interviewed our respondents again, a new era of Japanese history had begun. The close of one period and the start of another also marked a period in the life-cycle of our respondents when the older women were reaching or had reached the end of their working lives, and the younger women were approaching the completion of their reproductive lives and the pinnacle of their professional careers. In this chapter we look at how the women had fared during the twelve-year period, how they assessed the changes they had brought about, how they had restructured the field, and how they had transformed gendered class relations.

At the time of the second study, the respondents were aged between 35 and 79. Our choice of a longitudinal study, following up the same group of women at a later period in their life-cycles, meant that their assessments of the changes in Japanese society and in their own lives were seen through the particular lens of this cohort of pioneering middle-class women who had struggled for and won the 'right to compete' in male-dominated professions. Their particular perspectives on the changes were delineated by the period in their lives when few had young children, increasing numbers had older relatives to care for, and some had moved into a more leisurely period of the life-cycle.

The women's perspectives were framed by changes in the social structure, including a new equal employment opportunity law in 1985 (with no enforcement provision), and governmental recommendations to reduce working hours. In terms of the labour market, from the mid-1980s onwards more women were employed than were full-time housewives, whilst the 1989 election showed that gender was a live political issue. The women's assessments of their lives took place against this background of changes in work organisation and in the family, and wider changes in the political and global economy.

Of the 66 respondents we were able to trace, 19 were civil servants, 14 were doctors, 17 were academics and 16 were managers. Of these, 2 had died, 14 had retired (some to take up a new career), 6 had become self-employed and one had left work to become a housewife, which left 43. It is possible, of course, that those who had left to become housewives were overrepresented among those who could not be traced, although many were also likely to have left Tokyo because of their own or their husband's transfers. Among the 43 who were still employed in their professions, 28 (65 per cent) who had not previously been at the top of the career structure were now in top positions. This included 5 civil servants in senior government posts, and another 2 who had become Members of Parliament after retirement, one of whom had reached a very senior position. Nine of the doctors had become consultants or held teaching posts in university hospitals. Seven of the university teachers had become full professors, and 6 of the managers had risen to senior positions. It is clear that significant inroads had been made into some of the bastions of male power in professional life.

The respondents' views of the changes and continuities in their lives and in society varied. The largest single group of 24 (42 per cent) thought that discrimination against women had not altered; the next-largest group of 20 (35 per cent) thought there had been unambiguous improvements in women's lives, and 13 (23 per cent) thought changes had been mixed. Civil servants were the most optimistic and managers the most pessimistic. The complexity of social continuity and change was best expressed by Sasaki Shizuko's ironical comment on gender relations:

> Though many men are suffering from the change of women's status and attitude, women are now more free and demanding what they think they deserve. Still strong prejudice exists, but there has been a tremendous change in favour of women.

Continuity and change in the family

Many of the women felt that household labour was still largely defined as women's work. Housework, childcare and care of the elderly remained a feminine role in many of the respondents' families, including those in the younger age group, such as Nagayama Junko, who was 47 in 1989 and a sociology professor:

> As my husband believed and expected that women should work from home, I had to limit my activities. It's much easier now that my children are older, but my relationship with my husband remains the same: I am not very free.

Nevertheless, the women identified significant changes in their position. The development of commercialised services for domestic labour and the establishment of private nursing homes for older people had allowed women with sufficient economic capital to redistribute some of the servicing and caring work for which they were formerly responsible to the market rather than to individual domestic employees.

Some of the respondents' husbands had started to do more in the family, although this change in the gender division of labour was partly a result of men retiring from work while their wives were still employed, and the changes were limited by the continuation of intensive work pressures. Oguchi Taeko, a consultant anaesthetist aged 40 in 1989:

> When I am on night duty, my husband looks after our two children. He is very helpful, but, being a surgeon himself, he is often called out at night and leads a hard life.

Continuity and change in employment

In many ways the women saw professional and managerial employment as still shaped by – and helping to shape – the definition of masculinity as incompatible with practical parental responsibility and an active participation in family life. The pressures of competition within global capitalism continued to define the gender division of labour, directing men to paid work and women to domestic work, constructing work as the priority for men, and making professional employment incompatible with femininity. Onoe Kazu was 47 in 1989, and practising as a doctor:

> Work is extremely busy: long hours of work, irregular meal times, late returning home, work during holidays, overseas duties and living far away from the place of work.

Moriyama Ichiko, 59 in 1989 and a consultant obstetrician:

> Working hours have become extended because the new director of the hospital is young and a hard worker. Housework has started piling up.

If the children had still been small I would have had a difficult time
sending and collecting them from the nursery.

Clearly, shorter working hours were not necessarily implemented, and
women with young children working in these two hospitals would not
benefit from any change in ideas of 'gendered time'.

Respondents still found it difficult to combine work and home, or
to redistribute domestic work to men. The relentless need to compete
with other countries in the capitalist economy through long hours of
work highlighted the continuity of both the sexual division of labour
and the masculine organisation of employment.

Although many of the conditions of women's professional employment remained the same, certain changes in gendered concepts of place
and time were acknowledged by our respondents. Women were now
transferred in the same way as men, including being sent abroad. Small
changes in the long working hours had been implemented in government service. Tuchiya Sachiko was 53 in 1989, married but with no
children:

> As two Saturdays per month are now non-work days, I have more free
> time. An amendment to the Labour Standards Law has encouraged a
> reduction in working hours and the taking of two days off per week
> instead of one. Consequently, it has become easier to combine work and
> home.

Although the change of hours made some difference to family life, it
did not address the problem for women with children, and the trans-
ferability of two-career couples did nothing to resolve the splitting of
families when both partners were liable to relocation.

Partly as a result of these changes, however, women had begun to
be employed in new positions and to be promoted to higher levels in
the hierarchy. Okazaki Teruko was 61 in 1989:

> In 1979 I became the first director ever of a Japanese newspaper com-
> pany. The company had had a women's column since 1914, and after
> being employed in 1951, I worked under eleven male women's depart-
> ment directors. When I became the first woman director, people around
> me and my staff made a great fuss at first, but they soon got used to
> having a female boss, and naturally started accepting me.

Again partly as a consequence of the changes mentioned above, the
respondents saw modifications to the discourse of women's work, acknowledging women's right to professional employment. This represented a consistent change identified by the women, suggesting that

our respondents no longer experienced their identities as professional women as a conceptual anomaly. They no longer felt strange, abnormal or unfeminine. All of them agreed that in their experience, professional women's identities had been transformed from a construction as unusual and abnormal to one of 'natural acceptance'. This transformation in the construction of femininity had affected not only their work identities but also marital and sexual identities in the family, for those women who were single or divorced no longer felt peculiar or unfeminine. There were women who still experienced a deficit of symbolic capital attached to their femininity, such as Ohashi Kimiko, who was 44 in 1989, and had been made a partner in her firm:

> Although society is changing and acceptance of working women is becoming more widespread, I'm not sure whether the heads of large companies recognise me as being a management consultant on a par with the male consultants.

This deficit of femininity was likely to be felt more strongly by younger women, since the pressure to enact femininity was probably less amongst older women who had established themselves in a professional career. Nevertheless, for most of this middle to older age-group, what had been a radical counter-hegemonic discourse on women's identity appeared to have entered mainstream thinking, not necessarily in opposition to, but co-existing with the dominant discourse of middle-class femininity.

Continuing struggles for change

Several of the respondents identified changes in consciousness and continuing struggles for change in society. These changes covered a variety of areas, including the sexual division in the labour market, and politics and medicine. Moriyama Ichiko again:

> The sense of existence has changed. Female gynaecologists are in increasing demand because women have started to want to understand about their own bodies. I have increased requests for my lectures at places of work, workers' unions, women's groups, private meetings, public health centres and for health managers of private companies.

Takahashi Kiyo had retired from the civil service and become an elected politician. She was 65 in 1989:

> The notion that politics belongs to men is strong in Japan, and for female candidates to run is not readily accepted. The participation of

women in politics has increased rapidly over the last two or three years, and this has made it easier for me to function.

The settlement

In the context of our study, the significance of 1989 as the start of a new era may be understood as the point at which this cohort of educated women could look back at their struggle to achieve the right to compete with men in the field of power. In some respects, the settlement which these women had managed to achieve was being reinforced; in others it was subject to challenge. However, as Lovell says: 'It is an error to suppose that the possibility of moving onto the pitch as a legitimate player alters anything if it does not alter the terms and conditions of the game itself' (Lovell 2000: 32). Although we cannot offer an answer as to how far the terms and conditions of the game had changed, we can present the respondents' own assessment of their entry into the game.

According to their view of their lives, certain limited changes had occurred in the gender division of labour in the family, but larger changes to the domestic sphere had taken place in the commercialisation of domestic labour, of which professional women, unlike working-class women, were able to take advantage because of their greater economic capital. There were gains for some in the organisation of employment in terms of a move to shorter working hours, and local gains in individual organisations – which may nevertheless prove significant – by women employees organising against discriminatory practices. Although women were less restricted by notions of gendered place, in that they were subject to transfer in the same way as men, the transfer system itself still posed a problem for dual-career families.

The women's view after a lifetime in a male-dominated profession was that they had achieved significant changes in their own identities and practices, but that the same levels of change could not readily be attributed to men, since it was still rare for domestic work to be shared equally. The organisation of global capitalism and the symbolic capital deficits in work identified as feminine made it even harder for men to accommodate household duties into a new definition of masculinity than it was for women to move into the symbolically powerful positions of professional employment. Changes to organisational practices had been both modest and of mixed benefit to women. The capitalist organisation of employment still operated according to the terms of the global contest for power, and although the changes achieved by professional women to their own position had been extensive, the transformation of men and organisations had been more modest. Women entering the field of professional employment still had to rely largely on their class position to release them from full-time household duties through paid domestic labour. Nevertheless, the settlement these women had achieved consisted of a transformation in the recognition paid to a professional feminine identity, and acknowledgement of women's right to enter the game.

Representing Women's Subjectivities

Given the extent of change that women had achieved for themselves in Japan, this final section examines the question of how far these changes have been recognised within Japan and the West, and what accounts for the apparent discrepancies. To do this, we discuss some contemporary images of women from Japanese and western sources, taking examples from actions of employers and the state in Japan, and from western writers publishing for a popular audience in Britain. We ask how far these images coincide with our evidence on women's changing subjectivities and lived experiences.

Modern Japanese views of the middle-class woman

The view of Japanese women currently put forward by employers and government in Japan reflects the postwar changes in women's position and their large-scale entry into paid work. There is still, however, a view of women as naturally peripheral to the world of work, and defined primarily by their relationship to domesticity, reproduction and the family. Two examples from the 'new Heisei era' will demonstrate this.

In 1990, the Ministry of Health and Welfare produced a report predicting serious economic consequences from Japan's declining birth rate. The government then decided that women should produce more babies in order to redress the labour shortage, avoid importing foreign labour, and provide for the growing number of old people. The Finance Minister's comment, in an all-male Cabinet meeting, that fewer women should go into higher education, and instead fulfil their basic biological function, was widely reported in the press. Because of the outrage this caused amongst women, he later contradicted a government spokesman and claimed that he had been misinterpreted. But the Prime Minister also told his party's women's conference that the birth rate must be increased (McGill 1990: 11). The government subsequently launched the 'Campaign to Create an Environment in which Women can Bear More Children'. Reasons given for the declining birth rate included women's marrying late or not at all, their participation in public life, the difficulties of combining paid work and childcare, the high cost of children's education, and poor housing conditions. The first three of these reasons attribute the cause of the problem to women. The *Asahi Newspaper* quoted a female obstetrician who criticised the government for attempting to control women's reproductive rights, rejected the cataclysmic predictions for the economy, and attributed the blame for the difficult conditions women encounter to government policies (Asian Women Workers' Centre 1990: 9–11).

The second example is a case taken for arbitration in 1992 to the Women and Minors Bureau of the Ministry of Labour by twenty-one women claiming discrimination against married women by Sumitomo Life Insurance Company. They argued that the two-track career system instituted by Sumitomo in 1986 (soon after the new sex discrimination law), in which men and a majority of single women are allocated to the executive track, but a huge majority of married women are placed on the clerical track, was illegal. They also found evidence of direct and indirect pressure on women to leave their jobs on marriage and/or pregnancy. The Ministry of Labour, however, found against the women on the grounds that the jobs of the men in the executive track and the women in the clerical track could not be compared (Asian Women Workers' Centre 1993: 11). This case still continues.

These examples suggest that the view of women currently promoted by the state in Japan is one which accepts their working lives and recognises their changing identities, but is attempting to hold back or reverse the changes that have come about. The idea conveyed is that women should continue to give first priority to marriage and the family; they should bear as many children as the state thinks is desirable; they should regard their paid work as marginal to the economy, and take up jobs only to fill in the empty spaces in their lives when they are not servicing the family. The state does not promote an image of women contributing to the family, developing themselves through work or participating in the economy. Nor does it wish to develop and utilise women's talents, skills and creativity as an industrial or social resource, except as peripheral workers. This means that women's identities should be redefined as primarily housewives, reproducers and carers.

Employment organisations may hold a slightly different view, in that it is in their interest for women to be employed, but often in low-level, low-paid work without job security. This means that women's identities should be defined as workers *and* housewives to facilitate a flexible labour force. Thus although representations of women produced by capital and the state in Japan may be conservative, they do recognise women's shifting identities.

Western views of Japanese women workers

Western views of Japanese women have of course been influenced by the images presented from within Japan itself. But they have been overlaid by an additional factor arising out of the West's orientalist approach to nations of the East (Said 1979). Historically, the West saw Japan as 'other', positioning it as 'less civilised' because of its cultural difference and its economic backwardness. But Japan's economic success has challenged this definition, and given rise to fears that Japan will dominate the West culturally and economically. This fear underlies a tranche of popular English-language writing published in the 1990s by western journalists who have lived in Japan. We will look at the portrayal of women in two of these works, bearing in mind that they are not exceptional examples.

Brian Reading's book *Japan: The Coming Collapse* (1993) argues, according to the outline on the cover, that Japan is 'a nation of tax cheats ruled by venal politicians and paralytic government, its industry riddled with corruption, its finances with inequity, and its society with latent violence'. Beginning with this vitriolic condemnation of a nation, Reading goes on to repeat the tired stereotypes about Japanese women, particularly women workers. Two features stand out in the quotations below: the view of women as universally passive, uninformed and un-interested in their rights; and the implicit western norm with which all statements about Japan are compared, suggesting that the West is not like this, the West is normal, and the West is best.

'As yet few women are attracted to a career rather than marriage, and married career women are almost unknown' (Reading 1993: 195). It is simply not true that married career women are almost unknown: two-thirds of our respondents were married. In addition, the use of the words 'attracted to a career' in this statement implies that the lower proportion of women than men in careers is caused by women's lack of ambition rather than the excessive demands of the global economy.

'No man in Japan could be bossed around by a woman superior.... [Women's] way ahead is firmly barred. But nor do they do much about it' (Reading 1993: 198). It is untrue that no Japanese man could tolerate a woman boss, as indicated by many of the women in our study; nor that all the women with male subordinates encountered difficulties. The final sentence explicitly portrays working women as passive, and content with the discrimination they experience.

'Female emancipation is still only partial. Apart from a brief wave of interest in 1989, when Mrs Doi was leader of the Japan Socialist Party, most Japanese females are not interested in politics. They make no effort through the ballot box to change Japan's male-oriented society, nor are they much concerned by the discrimination (illegal) which they suffer at work' (Reading 1993: 197). Again women are presented as passive victims, but what is startling is the implied comparison with the West, suggesting that female emancipation in the West is *not* 'still only partial', and that western women *have* changed their male-oriented societies through the ballot box.

The second book is *The Japanese: Strange but not Strangers*, by Joe Joseph (1993). The title reflects the western view of the Japanese as 'other', and the paradox of familiarity and foreignness which is raised by this non-western nation beating the West at its own economic game. Joseph has an entire chapter on women entitled 'A Woman's Place (is in the Wrong)', in which similar sentiments to those of Reading are expressed. For example: 'Nobody could suggest that women are particularly liberated in Japan.... Women in politics are rare, women in boardrooms almost non-existent' (Joseph 1993: 13). Each of these sentences implies that things are different for women in the West, that women *are* liberated in the UK, and that many women enjoy careers in British boardrooms and in the Houses of Parliament. After the 1989 election, women constituted 5 per cent of women MPs in Japan (Nuita 1989: 2). The Hansard Society Commission reported 6 per cent women in the UK Parliament in the same year. The same report estimated that women accounted for 0.5 per cent of executive directors on main boards of UK companies (HSC 1990: 28, 60). These figures support a statement that in the UK, too, 'Women in politics are rare, and women in boardrooms almost non-existent.'

'Japanese women ... have tended to make the best of being ideal wives and caring mothers and have taught themselves to tolerate their husbands' drinking and philandering as long as those husbands bring home a fat pay packet every week' (Joseph 1993: 40). This implies not only that women have been passive in fighting for their rights and defining their own roles but also that they are prepared *en masse* to be bought off by unfaithful husbands and to overlook sexual deception. Yet one reason why Mrs Doi's Socialist Party did so well in the 1989 general election was the disgust of women voters at the sex scandals and corruption surrounding the governing Liberal Democratic Party (Nuita 1989: 2–3).

The passivity of Japanese women and the oppressiveness of Japanese men compared with western men are presented in the following quotation about one of these sex scandals in which Prime Minister Uno was found to have consorted with prostitutes:

> Many Japanese women, particularly the younger ones, were galvanised by the foreign media coverage given to Uno's hanky-panky. They started asking aloud why Japan, the world's newest superpower, was several decades behind its major western allies in giving women equal rights and freedoms and in allowing women access to the top jobs. Many people, inside and outside Japan, thought a quiet revolution had begun. It was so quiet that little has been heard of it since. (Joseph 1993: 41)

First, the credit for galvanising women into action is given to the *western* media. Second, it is explicitly stated that the West is more advanced in relations between the sexes. Third, the words 'giving' and 'allowing' suggest that western nations are so civilised that they *granted* women their rights, rather than that women fought for what freedoms they have. Fourth, Japanese women's questioning of their subordination is discredited by the claim that it was fickle and short-lived, when in fact Japanese women have been actively fighting for their rights since the nineteenth century.

What both these authors are doing is setting up an image of gender relations in Japan from which neither the Japanese woman nor the Japanese man emerges with any credit. Their criticism is not for the purpose of evaluating the culture and institution of gendered power relations, but to demonstrate, by implicit or explicit comparison, the superiority of western civilisation.

How can this extraordinary portrayal of Japanese women be understood, bearing in mind that our main study was conducted in 1977, and these authors were writing in the 1990s? We are not suggesting that women in professional occupations are representative of Japanese womanhood as a whole; in fact we have explicitly positioned them in a specific class context. But they do demonstrate the existence of diversity among Japanese women, and their experiences reveal evidence of changing ideas and practices which western authors seem determined to ignore. Our explanation for the discrepancy in these representations is that gender is a key stake in the contest for global power. Gender is used as a means to construct distinction in the global political economy, and its deployment for this purpose is recognised as legitimate by all parties to the contest. But it is used in different ways in Japan and in the West.

In Japan, the discourse of women's entitlement and the emergence of the professional woman have ambiguous connotations. On the one hand, they reflect the struggle of Japanese women to position themselves as social subjects with the potential for accumulating and deploying capitals in their own right. On the other hand, the Japanese state sees the middle-class full-time housewife as the model for Japanese femininity, a representative of a unique cultural identity, a resistance to the globalisation of western cultural forms and a bulwark against the social dislocations and destruction of communities which are visibly manifest in economically successful western countries. This is a specifically class-based formulation, since lower-class working women are not in a position to be full-time housewives, yet such women are rarely alluded to as an ideal model for femininity.

Japan's construction of a culturally and historically unique form of capitalist society includes a unique family structure, a distinctive approach to employment, and a specifically Japanese set of social values and gendered class relations. Japan sees these as what Porter (1990) calls the 'competitive advantage of nations' in the global contest for power: a means of attaining economic growth without the negative effects of global capitalism, which may be termed a form of cultural capital for the state. Japan's attempt to build a more effective form of capitalism than the West means producing higher-quality commodities with greater efficiency, a more contented workforce, no class divisions, a strong family, and women's satisfaction with their place within it. For Japan, the dominant image of the full-time middle-class housewife is an index of economic development not only for the family but for the nation. She is the cornerstone of the Japanese family, and the very symbol of national economic success without the corresponding social problems. Thus, the full-time housewife and mother is a mark, of a culturally unique social organisation and of national distinction: a symbol of a superior civilisation. This is why Japan, while it recognises the emergence of the professionally employed woman, does little to assist her passage; on the contrary, capital and the state attempt to hold back this transformation in the model of middle-class femininity.

The West, however, has its own agenda in relation to women and gender positioning in Japan. As we argued in Part I, in the late nineteenth century the position of women was seen by the West as a crucial part of the explanation for Japan's economic weakness. But at the beginning of the twenty-first century the West is deeply threatened by Japan's success and seeks reasons why it cannot be sustained. In the face of Japanese economic development, the image of the submissive oriental woman lives on in the western imagination as the primary remaining area of unreformed and unreconstructed social backwardness, representing to the western mind the cultural inferiority of non-western societies, regardless of their economic successes. In the West, the middle-class Japanese housewife is also a deeply significant symbol, but with quite different connotations. She is seen as a symbol of the repression required for any non-western country to compete economically with the West. Rather than a bulwark against social disorder, she is herself seen as a social disorder: as the symbol of a lack of freedom, evidence of an absence of liberality and democracy, the completely oppressed embodiment of social coercion and the nonexistence of free choice. We would argue that this is why the Japanese woman is seen so one-dimensionally in the West.

Such an image enables western countries to claim cultural superiority and national distinction through the position of women and the form of gender relations. So the discourse of women's entitlement, or women's rights, has been and still is used as a weapon by the West in its games of distinction with Japan. Kipling and others referred to the nineteenth-century imperialistic struggle between Britain and Russia for political ascendancy in central Asia as 'The Great Game' (Hopkirk 1982: 3). In the struggle between the West and Japan, parallel 'games', in which gender is a 'clandestine' aspect, are still played out. We would suggest that neither the Japanese nor the western states are concerned about the rights of women in relation to men, but both are concerned to invoke gender to demonstrate cultural superiority and national distinction. Thus, while women in the nineteenth century were used as an explanation for Japan's weakness, at the beginning of the twenty-first century they are posited as an explanation for the fragility of Japan's economic success. What links the two periods in relations between Japan and the West is the crucial part played by gender in the competition for global power and distinction.

Achieving the Right to Compete

In conclusion, we have looked in Part VI at how women entered new fields of power, and how they legitimated their right of entry, arguing that this gender mobility must be seen in terms of both class relations and global positioning. We have identified competing discourses and social practices in the fields of education, employment and the family, and demonstrated how hegemonic discourses of gendered class identity are enacted through regulatory social practices to produce gender difference, class distinction and the respectability of the middle-class family. While the contradictions of middle-class femininity for women in professional occupations have opened up social spaces and created subjective conditions for change, the strategies through which change in social practice has been achieved have relied heavily, though not exclusively, on the capitals inherited by women from 'enriched' family backgrounds.

The process of legitimating women's right to compete in new fields of power has drawn on the symbolic capital attached to their social positioning, in terms of both their class of origin and their occupational destination. In taking up new subject positions, women have created new feminine subjectivities, justifying their anomalous position as professional women in terms of realising a mature selfhood, contributing to the family, taking their place in society and developing an awareness of their place in the world. In so doing, they have established a distinctive place for themselves within a set of social relations structured by gender, class and nation, and have contributed to the diversification and transformation of the position and identities of middle-class women. They have also radically challenged the West's image of Japanese women, and its use of gender in the struggle for global distinction with Japan.

Conclusion

Rising Daughters

The conceptual framework we have developed begins from the perspective of class divisions and the establishment of class distinction through the 'judgement of taste' (Bourdieu 1984). Here women are identified as objects in the struggle for power between men (Bourdieu 1990a). This framework 'travels' (Said 1983) through gendered social space to a context in which women struggle for the right to compete with men (Lovell 2000). It also travels across cultures (Kondo 1990) and into a global context. Here our new framework helps us to understand how the international contest for distinction rests on particular formations of gendered class identities as markers of symbolic capital for the nation-state. In the context of Japan, we have shown how, in the feudal period, women were used as repositories of value for the ruling military class; and, after Japan's entry into the global capitalism, how middle-class women were used by both Japan and the West as repositories of value for the state and as markers of progress on the scale of civilisation.

In all these periods of Japanese history – under feudalism, under the transition to capitalism with feudal remnants, and under the development of fully fledged capitalism – the position of women has been intimately connected with the class to which they belong, although the form of gendered class relations has varied in different social formations and historical moments. In feudal times, the rise of the dominant class was built upon the subordination of the women of that class, which became a mark of class distinction. In the transition period, after Japan entered the global contest for power, the articulation of gender and class was reconfigured as a means of maintaining class position at home and gaining recognition as a civilised nation abroad. Under the development of full capitalism, the hegemonic discourse of middle-class femininity has acted as both a signifier of class positioning and a symbol of a more socially sophisticated form of capitalist economic development.

Japan has not, however, succeeded in producing a uniquely classless capitalist society, nor has it produced a society in which women are uniquely devoted to the family, and men alone occupy positions of power in public life. The invisibility of the production and reproduction of class relations is a mechanism which legitimates the claim of the middle class in Japan to have built a fairer and more effective form of capitalism, and refutes western claims that Japan is a more repressive and oppressed society than western capitalist countries. The construction of middle-class professional women and lower-class working mothers as invisible, the dominant image of Japanese femininity, and the denial of the diversity of Japanese womanhood are also mechanisms whereby Japan can lay claim to a more civilised form of capitalist development, contained within unique forms of social fabric, family organisation and gendered social relations. These hegemonic representations of Japanese womanhood are both confirmed and reproduced in the West, but their meaning is subverted to invoke historical definitions of the East in terms of 'oriental despotism' (Said 1979), masculine oppressiveness and feminine servility.

Middle-class women, however, not only exist as objects bearing symbolic capital for the family, the class and the nation-state, but also act as subjects who struggle for the right to compete with men for access to fields of power in public life, organising collectively and strategising individually to improve their social conditions, achieve social mobility and acquire more control over their lives. Class divisions act as a powerful influence in structuring women's access to new fields of power, as middle-class women draw on 'inherited' capitals from 'enriched' family backgrounds to effect the move from objects to subjects, while those few women who enter the field of power from families with capital deficits have obtained release from their historical emplacements through the expansion of the economy, which has created openings for the employment of intellectual labour. Thus women's entry to the field of power represents a reproduction of the class between the women and their parents as much as a disruption of gendered entitlements. It may, however, constitute a dilution of class reproduction between the women and their descendants, given professional women's lower rates of marriage and childbirth and the constraints on their investment of emotional capital in the next generation. The entry of middle-class women into new fields of power also creates new or reshapes old class differences and forms of social distinction between women in terms of the accumulation of economic capital, the development of new lifestyles, the delegation of gendered domestic labour to paid female employees, and the production of different 'kinds' of working women through the performance of intellectual rather than manual or routine non-manual labour.

The movement of women into new fields of power, the legitimation of their right to compete in the field, and the changes in middle-class femininity achieved by professionally employed women have diversified formerly dichotomised gendered class identities, so that middle-class femininity can no longer be construed (if it ever could) as a homogeneous category. A new category of working women who hold symbolic capital must be distinguished, thus dismantling the polarisation between the symbolic power of the middle-class housewife and the symbolic capital deficits of the lower-class working mother who earns to make ends meet. The agency and social mobility of this new category starkly negate western stereotypes of oppressed Japanese womanhood, and disrupt the production of western civilisation as superior on the basis of cultural differences in gendered power and traditional images of gendered class identities.

We have shown how, in the struggle to gain and sustain acknowledgement as elite nations, particular gender–class articulations represent a vital form of symbolic capital for the state which must be constantly reproduced on all sides of the global contest for power. Bourdieu argues that 'a class is defined in an essential respect by the place and value it gives to the two sexes' (Bourdieu 1984: 107). We extend this, and propose that a *nation* is defined by the place and value it gives to the two sexes, as well as by the way it differentiates and positions the social classes, and by the way it configures the articulation between gender and class.

Specific articulations of gender and class are invoked to represent the nation, and to construct cultural difference and national distinction. These articulations are used to justify economic dominance and to legitimate positions of power in the global political economy in terms of the cultural distinctiveness of uniquely civilised societies. Gender is used as a form of symbolic capital in the struggle for recognition as an elite nation, as states compete for respectability and distinction on the global stage. Gender is also transformed by competing states into a form of symbolic capital deficit to undermine the respectability of other powerful nations and to rationalise their imminent demise, particularly those conceived of as culturally 'different'; and these same unique,

culturally specific formations of gendered class identity are reinterpreted
to produce meanings which are incompatible with the definition of a
successful, modern nation-state.

We have demonstrated that women's escape from historical
emplacements into positions of power in public life is largely, though
not entirely, class-mediated, and that the legitimate opportunity for
particular categories of women to compete in the field of power is
strongly influenced, though not completely determined, by class. This
minor breakthrough in gender–class diversity gives some cause for hope
that future expansion of the gender basis of power will include women
from a greater variety of social backgrounds. In a post-colonial context,
Ryang argues that women's positions 'are often eroded and compromised by the existing socio-political institutions that are becoming more
and more deceptively accommodating by way of privileging certain
groups of women and illusorily presenting their achievements as the
achievements of women at large' (Ryang 1998: 2). Perhaps, in the new
Heisei era, women in Japan will continue the struggle to break down
gendered barriers to the fields of power, and thus alter the way these
fields are configured. In so doing, they may also produce a more socially and globally diverse representation of womanhood in positions
of power. As Iwasaki Keiko said back in 1977: 'I'm satisfied when I can
change Japan!'

Bibliography

Ackroyd, Joyce (1959) 'Women in Feudal Japan', *Transactions of the Asiatic Society of Japan* 30, 3, 31–68.

Ahn Yonson (1996) 'Out of the Darkness', *Indian Journal of Gender Studies* 3, 2, 225–32.

AMPO–Japan Asia Quarterly Review (eds) (1996) *Voices from the Japanese Women's Movement*, New York: M.E. Sharpe.

Andermahr, Sonya, Lovell, Terry and Wolkowitz, Carol (1997) *A Glossary of Feminist Theory*, London: Arnold.

Asakawa Kanichi (1929) *The Documents of Iriki*, New Haven, CT: Yale University Press.

Asian Women Workers' Centre (1990) *Resource Materials on Women's Labour in Japan* 7, December.

Asian Women Workers' Centre (1993) *Resource Materials on Women's Labour in Japan* 11, March.

Asian Women Workers' Centre (1999) *Resource Materials on Women's Labour in Japan* 24, October.

Asian Women's Liberation Committee in Japan (1977) *Asian Women's Liberation* 1, May.

Bacon, Alice (1891) *Japanese Girls and Women*, New York: Houghton Mifflin.

Beasley, W.G. (1990) *The Rise of Modern Japan* London: Weidenfeld & Nicolson.

Bernstein, Gail Lee (ed.) (1991) *Recreating Japanese Women, 1600–1945*, Berkeley: University of California Press.

Bocking, Brian (1996) *A Popular Dictionary of Shinto*, Richmond: Curzon.

Bonney, Norman, Stockman, Norman and Sheng Xuewen (1994) 'Shifting Spheres', *Work, Employment and Society* 8, 3, 387–406.

Bourdieu, Pierre (1977) *Outline of a Theory of Practice*, Cambridge: Cambridge University Press.

Bourdieu, Pierre (1984) *Distinction*, London: Routledge.

Bourdieu, Pierre (1987) 'What Makes a Social Class?', *Berkeley Journal of Sociology* XXXII, 1–17.

Bourdieu, Pierre (1990a) 'La Domination masculine', *Actes de la Recherche en Sciences Sociales* 84, 2–31.

Bourdieu, Pierre (1990b) *In Other Words*, Cambridge: Polity.

Bourdieu, Pierre (1993) *The Field of Cultural Production*, Cambridge: Polity.

Braisted, William (trans.) (1976) *Meiroku Zasshi*, Cambridge, MA: Harvard University Press.

Braybon, Gail and Summerfield, Penny (1987) *Out of the Cage*, London: Pandora.

Brinton, Mary (1993) *Women and the Economic Miracle*, Berkeley: University of California Press.

Brubaker, R. (1985) 'Rethinking Classical Theory', *Theory and Society* 14, 6, 745–75.

Caplan, Jane (1991) 'Afterword', in Bernstein, Gail Lee (ed.) *Recreating Japanese Women, 1600–1945*, Berkeley: University of California Press.

Chabot, Jeannette (1985) 'Takamure Itsue', *Women's Studies International Forum* 8, 4, 287–90.

Chaudhuri, Nupur and Strobel, Margaret (eds) (1992) *Western Women and Imperialism*, Bloomington: Indiana University Press.

Coole, Diana (1996) 'Is Class a Difference that Makes a Difference?', *Radical Philosophy* 77, May/June, 17–25.

Crompton, Rosemary (1993) *Class and Stratification*, Cambridge: Polity.

Crump, John (1983) *The Origins of Socialist Thought in Japan*, London: Croom Helm.

Cummings, William (1980) *Education and Equality in Japan*, Princeton, NJ: Princeton University Press.

di Leonardo, Michaela (1987) 'The Female World of Cards and Holidays', *Signs* 12, 3, 440–453.

Economic and Social Commission for Asia and the Pacific (ESCAP) (1984) *Population of Japan*, New York: United Nations.

Feminist Japan, The (1980) *Feminist International* 2, Special issue on 'Asian Women '80'.

Fujiwara Keiko (1988) 'Introduction', in Kiyooka Eiichi (ed.) *Fukuzawa Yukichi on Japanese Women*, Tokyo: Tokyo University Press.

Fukuzawa Yukichi (1899) in Kiyooka Eiichi (ed.) *Fukuzawa Yukichi on Japanese Women* Tokyo: Tokyo University Press.

Gapper, John (1988) 'Taking Women Seriously', *Financial Times*, 9 September.

Goetz, Anne Marie (1997) *Getting Institutions Right for Women in Development*, London: Zed Books.

Gomi Fumihiko (1982) 'Josei-shoryo to Ie' ('Women's Territory and Housing'), in Joseishi Sogo Kenkyukai (eds) *Nihon Joseishi* (*The History of Japanese Women*), Vol. 2, Tokyo: Tokyo University Press.

Hakim, Catherine (1981) 'Job Segregation', *Employment Gazette*, December, 521–9.

Halliday, Jon (1975) *A Political History of Japanese Capitalism*, New York: Monthly Review Press.

Hansard Society Commission (1990) *Women at the Top*, London: The Hansard Society for Parliamentary Government.

Hara Nobuko (1989) 'Manifesto of Japan's Madonnas', *Guardian*, 18 November, 6–7.

Havens, Thomas (1973) 'Frontiers of Japanese Social History During World War II', *Shakai Kagaku Tokyu (Social Science Review)* 18, 3, 1–45.

Havens, Thomas (1975) 'Women and War in Japan, 1937–45', *American Historical Review* 80, June–December, 913–34.

Hayakawa Noriyo (1991) 'The Development of Women's History in Japan', in Offen, Karen, Pierson, Ruth and Rendall, Jane (eds) *Writing Women's History*, London: Macmillan.

Hayashi Reiko (1982) 'Choka Josei no Sonzai Keitai' ('Conditions of Existence of Women in Tradesmen's Houses'), in Joseishi Sogo Kenkyukai (eds) *Nihon Joseishi (The History of Japanese Women)*, Vol. 3, Tokyo: Tokyo University Press.

Hendry, Joy (1981) *Marriage in Changing Japan*, London: Croom Helm.

Hendry, Joy (1987) *Understanding Japanese Society*, London: Routledge.

Hendry, Joy (1993) 'The Role of the Professional Housewife', in Hunter, Janet (ed.) *Japanese Women Working*, London: Routledge.

Hicks, George (1995) *The Comfort Women*, London: Souvenir Press.

Hirano Takako, Kanda Michiko, Kobayashi Koichiro and Liddle, Joanna (1980) 'Josei no Shokugyo-Seikatsu to Sei-Yakuuwari' ('Women's Occupational Life and Sex Roles'), *Shakaigaku Hyoron (Japanese Sociological Review)* 30, 4, 17–37.

Hollway, Wendy (1984) 'Gender Difference and the Production of Subjectivity', in Henriques, Julian, Hollway, Wendy, Urwin, Cathy, Venn, Couze and Walkerdine, Valerie *Changing the Subject*, London: Methuen.

Hong Kong Standard (1989) 26 August.

Hopkirk, Peter (1982) *Trespassers on the Roof of the World*, Oxford: Oxford University Press.

Howard, Keith (1995) *The Stories of the Korean Comfort Women*, London: Cassell.

Hunter, Janet (1989) *The Emergence of Modern Japan*, London: Longman.

Hunter, Janet (1993) *Japanese Women Working*, London: Routledge.

Ichibangase Yasuko (1971) 'Women's Status and the Task of Education', *Education in Japan VI*, 59–68.

Igeta Ryoji (1982) 'Meiji-Minpo to Josei no Kenri' ('The Meiji Civil Code and Women's Rights'), in Joseishi Sogo Kenkyukai (eds) *Nihon Joseishi (The History of Japanese Women)*, Vol. 4, Tokyo: Tokyo University Press.

Inoue Hisao (1971) 'A Historical Sketch of the Development of the Modern Educational System for Women in Japan', *Education in Japan VI*, 15–36.

Ishida Hiroshi (1993) *Social Mobility in Contemporary Japan*, London: Macmillan.

Iwai Sachiko (1993) 'Hataraku Onna-tachi no Sugata' ('Aspects of Working Women'), in Sogo Joseishi Kenkyukai (eds) *Nihon Josei no Rekishi: Onna no Hataraki (The History of Japanese Women: Women's Labour)* Tokyo: Kadokawa.

Japan Small Business Research Institute (1998) *JSBRI Report 7*, September.

Japanese Women Speak Out (1975) Tokyo: Pacific Asia Resource Centre.

Jayawardena, Kumari (1986) *Feminism and Nationalism in the Third World*, London: Zed Books.

Jayawardena, Kumari (1995) *The White Woman's Other Burden*, London: Routledge.

Johnson, Linda (1992) 'The Feminist Politics of Takako Doi and the Social Democratic Party of Japan', *Women's Studies International Forum* 15, 3, 385–95.

Joseph, Joe (1993) *The Japanese*, London: Viking.

Kaibara Ekken (1905) 'Onna Daigaku (Greater Learning for Women)', in Cranmer-Byng, I. and Kapadia, S. (eds) *Wisdom of the East*, London: John Murray.

Kanai Yoshiko (1994) 'Josei to Seiji: Seiji no Orutanatibu ni Mukete' ('Women and Politics: Towards an Alternative Politics'), in Inoue Teruko, Ueno Chizuko and Ehara Yumiko (eds) *Nihon no Feminizumu: Kenryoku to Rodo (Feminism in Japan: Power and Labour)*, Vol. 4, 225–37, Tokyo: Iwanami.

Kanai Yoshiko (1996) 'Issues for Japanese Feminism', in AMPO–Japan Asia Quarterly Review (eds) *Voices from the Japanese Women's Movement*, New York: M.E. Sharpe.

Katakura Hisako (1993) 'Nichijo wo Koeta Onna-tachi' ('Unusual Women'), in Sogo Joseishi Kenkyukai (eds) *Nihon Josei no Rekishi: Onna no Hataraki (The History of Japanese Women: Women's Labour)* Tokyo: Kadokawa.

Kawahara Chizuko (1962) 'Awakening of the Meiji Woman', *Asia Scene*, January, 45–47.

Kidd, Yasue (1978) *Women Workers in the Japanese Cotton Mills: 1880–1920*, New York: Cornell University East Asia Papers.

Kiyooka Eiichi (ed. and trans.) (1988) *Fukuzawa Yukichi on Japanese Women*, Tokyo: Tokyo University Press.

Kondo, Dorinne (1990) *Crafting Selves*, Chicago: University of Chicago Press.

Kubo Takako (1993) 'Seiji no Sekai to Josei' ('The Political World and Women'), in Sogo Joseishi Kenkyukai (eds) *Nihon Josei no Rekishi: Onna no Hataraki (The History of Japanese Women: Women's Labour)*, Tokyo: Kadokawa.

Kuroda Hiroko (1993) 'Minshu-josei no Hataraki Kurashi' ('Labour and Life of Women in the Rank and File', in Sogo Joseishi Kenkyukai (eds) *Nihon Josei no Rekishi: Onna no Hataraki (The History of Japanese Women: Women's Labour)*, Tokyo: Kadokawa.

Kurushima Noriko (1993) 'Sengoku no Onna-tachi' ('Women in the Civil War Period'), in Sogo Joseishi Kenkyukai (eds) *Nihon Josei no Rekishi: Onna no Hataraki (The History of Japanese Women: Women's Labour)*, Tokyo: Kadokawa.

Lam, Alice (1992) *Women and Japanese Management*, London: Routledge.

Lebra, Joyce (1991) 'Women in an All-Male Industry: The Case of Sake Brewer Tatsu'uma Kiyo', in Bernstein, Gail Lee (ed.) *Recreating Japanese Women, 1600–1945*, Berkeley: University of California Press.

Liddle, Joanna and Joshi, Rama (1986) *Daughters of Independence*, London: Zed Books.

Liddle, Joanna and Michielsens, Elisabeth (2000a) 'Gender, Class and Political

Power in Britain', in Shirin Rai (ed.) *Gender and Democratisation*, London: Macmillan.

Liddle, Joanna and Michielsens, Elisabeth (2000b) 'Women and Public Power', *International Review of Sociology* 10, 3, 207–22.

Liddle, Joanna and Rai, Shirin (1998) 'Feminism, Imperialism and Orientalism', *Women's History Review* 7, 4, 495–520.

Lovell, Terry (2000) '"If I was a lad, do you think I would say I'm a lass?": Bourdieu and the Feminist Project', *Feminist Theory* 1, 11–32.

McGill, Peter (1990) 'Women Ordered to Lie Back and Raise Workforce', *The Observer* 24 June, 11.

Mackie, Vera (1988) 'Feminist Politics in Japan', *New Left Review* 167, 53–76.

Matsui Machiko (1990) 'Evolution of the Feminist Movement in Japan', *National Women's Studies Association Journal* 2, 3, 435–449.

Matsui Yayori (1975) 'Protest and the Japanese Woman', *Japan Quarterly Review* 22, 1, 32–39.

Matsuoka Yoko (1952) *Daughter of the Pacific*, New York: Harper

Ministry of Education, Science and Culture (1986) *Women and Education in Japan*, Tokyo: Social Education Bureau.

Ministry of Labour (1976) *Hataraku Josei no Jitsuju (The Actual Condition of Women's Labour)*, Tokyo: Nijusseiki Shokugyo Zaidan.

Ministry of Labour (1977) *Chingin Kozo Kihon Tokei Chosa Hukoku (Statistics of Wage Construction)*, Tokyo: Statistics and Information Division.

Ministry of Labour (1994) *Hataraku Josei no Jitsuj (The Actual Condition of Women's Labour)*, Tokyo: Nijusseiki Shokugyo Zaidan.

Miyake Yoshiko (1991) 'Doubling Expectations', in Bernstein, Gail Lee (ed.) *Recreating Japanese Women, 1600–1945*, Berkeley: University of California Press.

Miyashita Michiko (1982) 'Noson ni okeru Kazoku to Kon-in' ('Family and Marriage in Farm Villages'), in Joseishi Sogo Kenkyukai (eds) *Nihon Joseishi (The History of Japanese Women)*, Vol. 3, Tokyo: Tokyo University Press.

Moi, Toril (1991) 'Appropriating Bourdieu', in Lovell, Terry (ed.) *Feminist Cultural Studies*, London: Edward Elgar.

Molony, Barbara (1991) 'Activism Among Women in the Taisho Cotton Textile Industry', in Bernstein, Gail Lee (ed.) *Recreating Japanese Women, 1600–1945*, Berkeley: University of California Press.

Molony, Barbara (1993) 'Equality versus Difference', in Hunter, Janet (ed.) *Japanese Women Working*, London: Routledge.

Nagahara Keiji (1982) 'Josei-shi ni okeru Nanboku-cho Muromachi-ki' ('The Nanbokucho-Muromachi Period from the Viewpoint of Women's History', in Joseishi Sogo Kenkyukai (eds) *Nihon Joseishi (The History of Japanese Women)*, Vol. 2, Tokyo: Tokyo University Press.

Nagano Hiroko (1982) 'Bakuhan-ho to Josei' ('Bakuhan Rules and Women'), in Joseishi Sogo Kenkyukai (eds) *Nihon Joseishi (The History of Japanese Women)* Vol. 3, Tokyo: Tokyo University Press.

Nagashima Junko (1993) '"Shufu" no Kurashi' ('The "Housewife's" Life'), in Sogo Joseishi Kenkyukai (eds) *Nihon Josei no Rekishi: Onna no Hataraki* (*The History of Japanese Women: Women's Labour*), Tokyo: Kadokawa.

Nagy, Margrit (1991) 'Middle-Class Working Women During the Interwar Years', in Bernstein, Gail Lee (ed.) *Recreating Japanese Women, 1600–1945*, Berkeley: University of California Press.

Nakane Chie (1973) *Japanese Society*, Harmondsworth: Penguin.

National Institute of Employment and Vocational Research (1988) *Women Workers in Japan*, Report No 4, Tokyo: NIEVR.

Nishimura Hiroko (1982) 'Kodai Makki ni okeru Josei no Zaisan-ken' ('Women's Property Rights at the End of the Ancient Period'), in Joseishi Sogo Kenkyukai (eds) *Nihon Joseishi* (*The History of Japanese Women*) Vol. 1, Tokyo: Tokyo University Press.

Nitobe Inazo (1905) *Bushido*, New York: Putnam's Sons.

Nolte, Sharon (1986) 'Women's Rights and Society's Needs: Japan's 1931 Suffrage Bill', *Comparative Studies in Society and History* 28, 1, 690–714.

Nolte, Sharon and Hastings, Sally (1991) 'The Meiji State's Policy Toward Women, 1890–1910', in Bernstein, Gail Lee (ed.) *Recreating Japanese Women, 1600–1945*, Berkeley: University of California Press.

Nuita Yoko (1981) *Japanese Women* 45, March.

Nuita Yoko (1989) *Japanese Women* 62, September.

Ochikubo Monogatari: The Tale of the Lady Ochikubo, Whitehouse, W. and Yanagisawa, E. (trans.), London: Peter Owen.

Ooi Minobu (1977) 'Chusei-Shakai to Josei' ('Women and Society in the Middle Ages'), in Miyagi Eishoo and Ooi Minobu (eds) *Shinko Nihon Josei-shi* (*Newly-written History of Japanese Women*), Tokyo: Yoshikawa Kobunkan.

Ootake Hideo (1979) *'Ie' to Josei no Rekishi* (*Women and the History of the 'Family'*), Tokyo: Kobundo.

Oufuji Osamu (1989) 'Kindai' ('The Early Modern Period'), in Sekiguchi Hiroko, Suzuki Kunihiro, Oufuji Osamu, Yoshimi Kaneko and Kamata Toshiko, *Nihon Kazoku-shi* (*The History of the Japanese Family*), Tokyo: Azusa-Shuppan-sha.

Pettman, Jan (1996) 'Boundary Politics', in Maynard, Mary and Purvis, June (eds) *New Frontiers in Women's Studies*, London: Taylor & Francis.

Pharr, Susan (1977) 'Japan', in Giele, Janet and Smock, Audrey (eds) *Women: Roles and Status in Eight Countries*, New York: Wiley.

Pharr, Susan (1980), in *Feminist International* 2, Special issue on 'Asian Women '80'.

Porter, Michael (1990) *The Competitive Advantage of Nations*, London: Macmillan.

Pullen, Elaine (1999) 'Feminism and Sociology', University of Warwick: unpublished PhD thesis.

Reading, Brian (1993) *Japan: The Coming Collapse*, London: Orion.

Robins-Mowry, Dorothy (1983) *The Hidden Sun*, Boulder, CO: Westview Press.

Rodd, Laurel (1991) 'Yosano Akiko and the Taisho Debate over the "New Woman"', in Bernstein, Gail Lee (ed.) *Recreating Japanese Women, 1600–1945*, Berkeley: University of California Press.

Rohlen, Thomas (1983) *Japan's High Schools*, Berkeley: University of California Press.

Ryang, Sonia (1998) 'Love and Colonialism in Takamure Itsue's Feminism', *Feminist Review* 60, 1–32.

Said, Edward (1979) *Orientalism*, Harmondsworth: Penguin.

Said, Edward (1983) *The World, the Text, and the Critic*, London: Vintage.

Sansom, George (1962) *Japan: A Short Cultural History*, London: Cresset Press.

Sansom, George (1978a) *A History of Japan to 1334*, Folkestone: Dawson.

Sansom, George (1978b) *A History of Japan 1334–1615*, Folkestone: Dawson.

Saso, Mary (1990) *Women in the Japanese Workplace*, London: Hilary Shipman

Shima Satomi (1997) 'Part-time Employment in Britain and Japan', University of Warwick: unpublished PhD thesis.

Shingoro Takaishi (1905) 'Introduction', in Cranmer-Byng, L. and Kapadia, S. (eds) *Wisdom of the East: Women and Wisdom of Japan*, London: John Murray.

Sievers, Sharon (1981) 'Feminist Criticism in Japanese Politics in the 1880s', *Signs* 6, 4, 602–16.

Sievers, Sharon (1983) *Flowers in Salt*, Stanford: Stanford University Press.

Silverberg, Miriam (1991) 'The Modern Girl as Militant', in Bernstein, Gail Lee (ed.) *Recreating Japanese Women, 1600–1945*, Berkeley: University of California Press.

Sinha, Mrinalini (1995) *Colonial Masculinity*, Manchester: Manchester University Press.

Skeggs, Beverley (1997) *Formations of Class and Gender*, London: Sage.

Smith, Robert and Wiswell, Ella (1982) *The Women of Suye Mura*, Chicago: University of Chicago Press.

Statistics Bureau (1989) *Statistical Handbook of Japan*, Tokyo: Management and Coordination Agency.

Steedman, Carolyn (1982) *The Tidy House*, London: Virago.

Steedman, Carolyn (1988) *The Radical Soldier's Tale*, London: Routledge.

Stephens, Michael (1991) *Japan and Education*, London: Macmillan.

Stockman, Norman, Bonney, Norman and Sheng Xuewen (1995) *Women's Work in East and West*, London: UCL Press.

Sugano Noriko (1982) 'Noson-josei no Rodo to Seikatsu' ('The Labour and Life of Women in Farm Villages'), in Joseishi Sogo Kenkyukai (eds) *Nihon Joseishi* (*The History of Japanese Women*), Vol. 3, Tokyo: Tokyo University Press.

Sugimoto Yoshio (1997) *An Introduction to Japanese Society*, Cambridge: University of Cambridge Press.

Tabata Yasuko (1982) 'Daimyo Ryukoku Kihan to Sonraku Nyobo-za' ('Daimyo's Rules and Wives' Seats in the Villages'), in Joseishi Sogo Kenkyuukai (eds) *Nihon Joseishi* (*The History of Japanese Women*), Vol. 2, Tokyo: Tokyo University Press.

Tabata Yasuko (1987) *Chusei no Josei* (*Women in the Middle Ages*), Tokyo: Yoshikawa Kobunkan.

Takamure Itsue (1966) *Josei no Rekishi* (*History of Women*), Tokyo: Rironsha.

Tanaka Kazuko (1977) *A Short History of the Women's Movement*, Tokyo: Femintern Press.

Thompson, E.P. (1980) *The Making of the English Working Class*, Harmondsworth: Penguin.

Tokyo University (1986) *Tokyo Daigaku Hyakunen-shi (One-Hundred Year History of Tokyo University)*, Tokyo: Tokyo University Press.

Tsurumi Kazuko (1970) *Social Change and the Individual*, Princeton: Princeton University Press.

Tsurumi Kazuko (1975) 'Yanagita Kunio's Work as a Model of Endogenous Development', *Japan Quarterly* XXII, 3, 223–238.

Tsurumi Kazuko (1977) 'Women in Japan', *The Japan Foundation Newsletter* V, 1, 2–7.

Tsurumi, Patricia (1990) *Factory Girls*, Princeton, NJ: Princeton University Press.

Uno, Kathleen (1991) 'Women and Changes in the Household Division of Labour', in Bernstein, Gail Lee (ed.) *Recreating Japanese Women, 1600–1945*, Berkeley: University of California Press.

Uno, Kathleen (1993) 'One Day at a Time', in Hunter, Janet (ed.) *Japanese Women Working*, London: Routledge.

van Wolferen, Harel (1989) *The Enigma of Japanese Power*, London: Macmillan.

Wacquant, Loic (1989) 'Towards a Reflexive Sociology: A Workshop with Pierre Bourdieu', *Sociological Theory* 7, 26–53.

Wacquant, Loic (1993) 'From Ruling Class to Field of Power: An Interview with Pierre Bourdieu on *La Noblesse d'Etat*', *Theory, Culture and Society* 10, 19–44.

Wakita Haruko (1982) 'Chusei ni Okeru Seibetsu Yakuwari Buntan to Josei' ('The Division of Labour between Men and Women and the View of Women in the Middle Ages'), in Joseishi Sogo Kenkyukai (eds) *Nihon Joseishi (The History of Japanese Women)*, Vol. 2, Tokyo: Tokyo University Press.

Walkowitz, Judith (1980) *Prostitution and Victorian Society*, Cambridge: Cambridge University Press.

Walthall, Anne (1991) 'The Life Cycle of Farm Women in Tokugawa Japan', in Bernstein, Gail Lee (ed.) *Recreating Japanese Women, 1600–1945*, Berkeley: University of California Press.

Yamazaki Tomoko (1985) *The Story of Yamada Waka*, Tokyo: Kodansha.

Yuval-Davis, Nira (1997) *Gender and Nation*, London: Sage.

Yuval-Davis, Nira and Anthias, Floya (eds) (1989) *Woman–Nation–State*, London: Macmillan.

Index

Ackroyd, Joyce, 77, 79–80, 82–3
agriculture, 135, 185; agrarian uprisings, 21, 97; collapse, 22; employment, 60; women's labour, 105–6
Akihito, Emperor, 7
All Japan Feminist Association, 10
Allied Far Eastern Commission, 151
Amamiya Silk Mill, strike, 13, 61
AMPO–Japan Asia Quarterly Review, 166
Anglo-Japanese Alliance, 24
Anglo-Japanese Treaty, 51
Anthias, Floya, 31
Asakawa Kanichi, 89, 92–3
Asian Women's Liberation Group, 10
atomic bombing, of Japan, 27

Bacon, Alice, 34, 45
bakufu laws, 101–2
Baron Kikuchi, 53
Beasley, W.G., 106, 151
Bernstein, Gail Lee, 104
birth rate, 55; decline, 173, 317, 318, 326; 'illegitimate', 128
Bismarck, Otto von, 22
Bonney, Norman, 173, 175
Bourdieu, Pierre, 28–31, 75–6, 111, 119, 141, 144, 156, 162, 167–8, 170–71, 173, 183, 188, 199–200, 205–6, 212–13, 223, 227–8, 234, 238, 242, 260, 279–80, 288, 297, 327
Buddhism: morality tales, 87; priests' lands, 86, 97
bureaucracy, colonial, 124–5
Burma, 26
bushido moral code, 104

China, 17; anti-Japanese alliance, 26; 'comfort women', 68; bureaucratic tradition, 78; communist victory, 151; Japan's 21 demands, 24, military defeat, 23, 51; nationalist coup, 25; Sino-Japanese war 1894, 23, 51, 56, 63, 114, 123; Sino-Japanese War 1931, 13, 15, 47; women's work, 173
China Railway Company, 124
churyu, 183
chusan, 183
civil service, 2, 252; careers, 117; women, 268
civil war, Japan, 96
civilisation, Western-defined hierarchy, 33
clan system, 79–80
class, 69–70, 72, 96, 98–9, 118–19; centrality, 165; composition, 186; denial of, 163–4; divisions, 130; education differences, 201–2; feudal, 108–9; gendered identity, 166, 181, 227–30, 232, 254, 281, 309–11; mobility, 188; perspectives, 183; reproduction, 191, 220, 223, 297; reproduction dilution, 326; status, 115; structure, 113, 182, 184–5, 187; struggle, 114
Cold War, 151
'comfort stations', 69
'comfort women', 59, 68
Commoners' Society, 14
Communism, Eastern Europe collapse, 163
concubinage, 33, 35–8, 43, 101, 128
Confucian ideology, 41, 77–8, 85, 87; family, 43, 46
contracts, employment: informal, 174; segregation, 176; status, 181
Coole, Diana, 166
'corporate warrior' discourse, 232, 239–43, 248, 300
corruption, political, 7
Crompton, Rosemary, 166, 183
cultural capital, 30, 130, 156, 199, 203, 205–8, 260, 284–8

337

Cummings, William, 140, 176, 195–6, 199–201, 203, 248

daughter selling, 65, 67, 69
demilitarisation, 150, 153
division of labour, sexual, 283, 297, 313–16
divorce, 43, 90, 217; rate, 216, 218
Doi Takako, 7, 11–12, 320
domestic work, 240; commercialisation, 316
dominant classes, reproduction strategies, 188
dowries, 98
'dumb innocence', 262, 265
Dutch East Indies, 26

earnings: professional women, 221–2; women, 180, 182
earthquake, 1923, 114
economic liberalisation, 163
Edo period, 100
education, 47, 52–3, 138, 162, 169; career, 2, 117, 129, 158, 179; credentialism, 170, 200, 205, 208, 288; development, 196; family/personal investment, 156, 173; 'field of power', 193; gender divisions, 194; girls, 71; higher, 197–9, 201–4, 207, 211–12, 233–4, 246, 248; imperial regulations, 56; post-war reform, 153; professional women, 209; progressive discourse, 140–1; reform, 150; structural change, 167; universities, 195; western influence, 45; women's, 40
elite: education, 169–71, 193, 195; reproduction, 200–8, 211–12; university qualifications, 196
emperor authority, system, 51, 134, 142–8, 151, 160; promotion, 47
employment, structure, 174
equality, sexual, 153
exploitation, women textile workers, 61–4

family: feudal, 79–80; field of power, 215; gendered power relations, 295–6; state surveillance, 216–17; structure, 219–20
family–state system, 40, 51, 55, 71, 118–19, 121, 133, 135, 138, 142, 144, 147–8, 160, 215
femininity, competing discourses, 233
feudalism, 19, 31, 44, 75–7, 108–9, 325; abolition, 40–1, 157; hierarchy, 79, 83
'field of power', 28, 168, 172, 198, 213
'field of struggles', 119
finance capital, Japanese, 21
First World War, 123
foreign trade, Japanese, 22
France, 17, 23–4; –Japanese trade

agreement, 24
'free-trade imperialism', 17, 32
Fujiki, 81
Fujiwara family, 86
Fukuda Hideko, 13–14
Fukuzawa Yukichi, 24, 32–8, 43
fundamentalism, Shinto, 10

gender: hierarchy in, higher education, 198–9; 'mobility', 30
Germany, 23, 26; authoritarian state model, 42; Civil Code influence, 20
Great Depression, 25
Greater East Asia Co-Prosperity Sphere, 20, 55
Greater Japan Associated Women's Societies, 56
Greater Japan Defence Women's Association, 68
Greater Japan National Defence Women's Organisation, 57
Greater Japan Women's Association, 57
Guam, 17

Halliday, Jon, 19, 21, 26, 114
Hara Kei, 114
Hawaii, 17
Heian era, 85
Heisei era, 277
Hendry, Joy, 42, 200, 233, 256
Hibino Yutaka, 46, 71
Hicks, George, 68, 155
Hideyoshi Toyotomi, 98–9
Hirano Takako, 4
Hiratsuka Raicho, 14–15, 115–16, 139
Hirohito, Emperor, 7
Hitotsubashi University, 249
Hojo Masako, 88
Hollway, Wendy, 227–9, 276
Hong Kong, 26
Hosoi Wakizo, 61–2
'housewife feminism', 9–11
Hiroshima University, 195
Hunter, Janet, 43

Ichikawa Fusae, 7, 15, 57, 154
imperialism, Japanese, 123–6, 135
indemnity payments, Chinese, 23
India: textiles, 22, 25; textiles wages, 64; UK rule, 24
Indochina, French control, 24; Japanese invasion, 26
inequality, reproduction, 199, 202–3
Inoue Reiko, 166
Ishida Hiroshi, 164–5, 180, 183–7, 199, 201–4
Ishihara Osamu, 62
Italy, 26
Ito Hirobumi, 19, 68
Ito Noe, 14, 114

Iwakura Tomomi, 22; Europe mission, 45
Iwasaki Keiko, 328

Japan: dual global positioning, 20–39, 308; occupation authorities, 196, 215; post-war Constitution, 151, 153; 'rapid industrialisation period', 172; US military bases, 152; US reforms, 160; western representation, 319–24, 326–7; womanhood construct, 70–1, 118–19, 260; women's work, 173
'Japanism', 12
Japan Socialist Party, 7, 320
Japan Sociological Association's Social Stratification and Mobility National Survey (SSM), 165, 183, 185, 199, 202, 206
Japan Women's College, 195
Jodo sect, 97
Joei code, 78, 86–8
Jomon period, 89
Joseph, Joe, 320

Kabayama Sukenori, 52
Kagoshima Bay, battle, 18
Kagoshima cotton mills, 59
Kaibara Ekken, 102–3, 140
Kaifu Toshiki, 7–8
Kamishima, 143
Kanai Yoshiko, 8–9, 11, 166
Kaneko Kentaro, 48
Kanno Suga, 14–15
Keio University, 33
Kidd, Yasue, 64
Kipling, Rudyard, 323
Kishida Toshiko, 13, 35, 38, 41
Kishimoto Shigenobu, 165
Kondo, Dorinne, 72, 227, 229–30, 232, 234, 264, 277, 279–81, 299, 301, 304, 306–7
Korea: annexation, 24; colonised, 124, 126; 'comfort women', 68; invasion proposal, 23; Japanese colony, 125; Japanese possessions, 25; Korean War, 151–2, 155
koseki system, 216
Kusunose Kita, 12–13
Kyoto University, 114, 195

Lam, Alice, 173, 176
land ownership, 78, 82–3, 85; inheritance, 81, 86–9, 91–2, 94; reform, 150, 152, 157; women's rights, 75–6, 98, 109
League Against the Revision of the Eugenic Protection Law, 10
legitimation, 31
Liaotung Peninisula, 23–4
Liberal Democratic Party, 7–9, 154, 320
Lieh Tzu, 87
Lotus sect, 97

Lovell, Terry, 28–9, 71, 76, 120, 156, 277, 279, 316
Lowell USA, women textile workers, 37

MacArthur, Douglas, 150
Mackie, Vera, 12
Malaya, 26
male primogeniture, 43, 97, 106
management: corporate, 2; women, 178
Manchuria, 23–4, 26, 124–5; Incident, 25
marriage: arranged, 259; class reproduction, 220; 1947 Constitution, 255; government supported centres, 55; market, 157; matrilineal, 89–90, 108; practices, 256; rates, 218, 326; surname system, 216
Marxism: class concepts, 183, 185; intellectuals, 165; student movement, 140
masculinity, competing discourses, 239
Matsuoka Yoko, 124–6, 128, 132, 143, 155
maturity, Japanese concept, 280, 299–300
medicine, career, 2, 179, 210–11, 249, 265, 284
Meiji Restoration, 1, 18, 20, 31, 40–41, 49, 75, 110, 113, 121, 139, 142, 159; Civil Code, 20, 42–4, 46, 50–51, 91; Constitution, 47; new middle class, 69–70; state, 115
Meiji Six Society (Meirokusha), 32–3, 48
middle-class morality, 44
military: class, 75–8, 80–3, 85, 88–91, 95, 97, 100–1, 106, 109, 240, 325; defeat, 23, 121–2, 134; expansionist policy, 123, 132–3; project, 135, 147; women's contribution, 54, 56
Minamoto family, 78, 86–7
Minamoto Yoritomo, 78, 86, 88, 91–2
Miyake Yoshiko, 54–5, 57
Miyamoto Yuriko, 154
'modern girl' (modan gaaru), 115–16
Mori Arinori, 32–3, 36–7, 52
Moriyama Mayumi, 8
Mother and Child Protection Law 1937, 55

Nagahara, 77, 81–3
Nagasaki, atom bombed, 136
Nakamura Masanao, 45–6, 71
Nakane Chie, 163–4
nation building: women's role, 50–54
nation-state, 31
National Eugenics Law, 55
National Institute of Employment and Vocational Research (NIEVR), 172
National Mobilisation Law, 68
Nayar people, Kerala, 89
Netherlands, the, 18
New Japan Women's League, 154
'new woman' (atarashi onna), 115

Nii Itaru, 115
Nitobe Inazo, 103
Nolte, Sharon, 15, 52

Oda Nobunaga, 98
Okuma Nobuyuki, 144
Organisation of Economic Development
  and Co-operation (OECD), 175
orientalism, 319
Osaka: Incident, 13; siege of, 100
Osugi Sakae, 14, 114
overseas brothels, 65

Pacific War, 55, 127, 207
paternalistic benevolence, 138–9
patrilocal family structure, 80
Patriotic Women's Society, 56
patriotism, women's, 57
peace campaigns, 9
Peace Preservation Law, 114
Pearl Harbor, 26
peasant class: liberalism, 104–5; mutual
  aid, 107; owners, 150; property rights,
  85
Peasant Labour Party, 14
People's Journal, 33
People's Rights Movement (PRM),
  12–13, 19, 32, 47
Peru, slave trade, 65
Philippines, 17, 26
political exclusion, 47–8, 52
polygamy, 43
Potsdam Declaration, 27
professional class, 187–8; reproduction,
  190; structure, 189
'professional housewife', discourse, 230,
  232–6, 238, 243, 245, 247–8, 250,
  255, 258–60, 304
professional women, 211, 219, 276;
  childcare, 257, 269–71, 292–5, 297,
  305, 312; economic independence,
  289–90; education, 209; family
  background, 284–8; promotion
  obstacles, 253, 267; strategies, 282–3
professional work, discourse, 306–7
progressive discourse, 137–40
prostitution, 7, 33, 35, 38, 70, 101;
  export, 68; forced, 66–7; licensed, 59,
  62, 65; US occupation, 154–5

Reading, Brian, 319
'red purge', Japan, 151
Red Wave Society, 14
rice riots, 88; 1918, 113; women's role,
  106
Russia, 17, 23; 1905 war, 51, 55–6, 123;
  Bolshevik Revolution, 24; neutrality
  agreement 1941, 26
Ryang, Sonia, 79, 328

Samson, George, 97

Saso, Mary, 173, 176
savings, women's role, 54
sectoral segregation, employment, 176
Seito group, 14–15, 45, 67
Sekiguchi Hiroko, 89
sex scandals, 8
sexual equality, idea, 36–7
Shima Satomi, 176
Shimizu Tomesaburo, 49
Shimonoseki Straits, battle, 18
Shingoro Takaishi, 103
Shiota, Sakiko, 10
Showa period, 7
Sievers, Sharon, 12, 42, 46, 62
Sino-Japanese Treaty, 23
Skeggs, Beverly, 30, 166
Smith, Robert, 57
social capital, 130, 160, 203, 245, 285,
  296
'social spaces', 111, 119–21, 142, 145,
  156, 181
South-East Asia, 'comfort women', 68
South Manchurian Railway, 24
Spencer, Herbert, 46, 48
Steedman, Carolyn, 120, 131
Stephens, Michael, 37
Stockman, Norman, 173–6, 180
strikes, women, 61
strong state model, 20
structural adjustment policies, 163
student–worker organisations, 114
Suematsu Kaiichiro, 48
suffrage, women's, 12–13, 15, 47–8, 152
Sugimoto Yoshio, 183, 215–17, 220
Sumitomo Life Insurance Company, 318
Supreme Commander of the Allied Powers
  (SCAP), 150–51, 154
symbolic capital, 28, 31, 71, 123, 141,
  144, 148, 157, 160, 242, 258, 268,
  279, 290–91, 294, 297, 316, 326–7;
  loss, 147

Taiho legal code, 77, 86
Taira family, 86–8
Taisho period, 114–16, 140, 159;
  'democracy', 113, 121, 124, 234
Taiwan, 23
Takahashi Takuya, 49
Takahara Sumiko, 8
Takamure Itsue, 42, 57, 89–90
Tanaka Kazuko, 15
Taniguchi Kiku, 53
Tanizaki Junichiro, 116
taxation, 106
tea serving, ritual, 267–8
teaching, gendered quality, 247
tenancy disputes, rural, 114
textiles: exploitation, 69; women workers,
  59–62, 64
'The Great Game', 323
Tohoku Imperial University, 195

Tokugawa family, 100
Tokugawa Ieyasu, 88, 98, 100
Tokyo University, 138, 195–7, 201–2, 204, 207, 209, 212, 233, 235, 245, 247–9, 256, 261, 285, 302, 308; women graduates, 210–11
Tokyo Women's College, 195
Tokyo Women's Reform Society (TWRS), 41, 45, 67–8
Tominaga Ken'ichi, 165
Tomioka silk mill, 60
trade: 'open-door' policy, 17; Sino-Japanese, 97
treaty port system: China, 24; imposition, 18
Tripartite Pact 1940, 26
Triple Intervention, 23
Tsuchiya Oki, 48
Tsuda Mamichi, 48, 65
Tsuda Umeko, 34
Tsurumi Kazuko, 44, 131, 143–4
Tsurumi, Patricia, 61–2, 66
tuberculosis (TB), 62, 67, 137

Ueki Emori, 13
unequal treaties, 18, 21–2, 113
United Kingdom (UK), 17, 24, 245; class, 165, 185; Contagious Diseases Acts, 38; employment structure, 172; female employment, 173–4; horizontal job segregation, 175; Oxbridge, 204; Parliament, 320; suffragettes, 49; trade barriers, 25; women's education, 156
United Nations (UN): International Women's Year, 10
Union of Soviet Socialist Republics (USSR), 151
United States of America (USA), 24, 26, 119, 138; atom bomb use, 27, 142; class structure, 165, 185; Constitution, 153; employment structure, 172; Japan occupation, 126, 133, 149–51, 154–5, 235; US–Japan Security Treaty, 152; Japanese bases, 9; MBA degree, 247; Pacific bases, 17; trade barriers, 25; women's work, 173
Uno Sosuke, 7–8, 321

vertical employment segregation, 178
vertical stratification, 164
Vietnam War, 152, 155; opposition, 9
violence, against women, 217

war deaths, Japanese, 26
Waseda, University, 114
Washington Conference 1921–22, 24–5
Weber, Max, concepts, 183
widows, 86–7, 94, 98
'will to die', 118, 131, 142
Wiswell, Ella, 57
Women Who Refuse to Follow the Road to War, 10
Women's Democratic Club, 154
women's liberation, 12; radical roots, 9
Women's Patriotic Association, 57
Women's Voluntary Service Corps, 68
women: artisans, 86, 105; colonial, 124–6, 132; dockers, 113; educational elite, 212–13; employment structure, 174–82; higher education, 234; immobility, 102; marital status, 218; merchants, 108; middle-class work, 117; professional earnings, 221–2; property rights disappearance, 98; reproductive service, 118; rights discourse, 139; sexualisation, 251; suffrage, 12–13, 15, 47–8, 152; violence against, 217; war work, 119; wartime, 127; work opprtunities, 81–2
work, global pressure, 314
World War II, 26, 111

Yajima Kajiko, 48
Yamada Kakichi, 66
Yamada Waka, 66, 115
Yamakawa Kikue, 14–15, 115, 116
Yamakawa Sutematsu, 34
Yamazaki Tomoko, 155
Yamashita Tokuo, 8
Yanagita Kunio, 41, 107
Yayoi period, 89
Yosano Akiko, 14, 57, 115
Yoshie Akiko, 89
Young Women's Christian Association, 154
Yuval-Davis, Nira, 31

About the Authors

Joanna Liddle lectures at the Centre for the Study of Women and Gender at the University of Warwick. She has carried out international collaborative research on the problems encountered by professional women in several countries, and is currently responsible for the British section of the Comparative Leadership Study. This research project, funded by the EU and the Nuffield Foundation, looks at women and men in positions of power in business and politics in over twenty countries. Her publications include *Daughters of Independence: Gender, Caste and Class in India*.

Sachiko Nakajima, now retired, was formerly on the staff of the National Personnel Authority.